AF228240

Arctic Practices

Design for a Changing World

Bert De Jonghe and Elise Misao Hunchuck

Actar Publishers

"Every design project moves 'at the speed of trust.'"
Elaine Falender, quoted by Todd Saunders

"Every design project moves 'at the speed of trust.'"
Elaine Falender, quoted by Todd Saunders

Contents

Acknowledgments

This book emerged out of many conversations over many years. Each of us came to this book through different paths, but each of us has been asking many of the questions you will find between these pages in our own ways. This book owes its existence to so many of our friends, colleagues, and mentors whom we have had the privilege to meet, speak with, learn with, or, in some cases, collaborate with. Many of those voices and their works you'll find in *Arctic Practices*.

> Working together as editors to curate and foreground such a rich set of contributions to an international design audience has been an honor. We would like to acknowledge the early support of historian of science Michael Bravo (University of Cambridge). In his role as an advisor during the formative stages of this project, he was an academic bridge, introducing us to scholars (some of whom became contributors) we had not yet come across in the past. Similarly, we want to thank friends and colleagues at Harvard University's Graduate School of Design and the Arctic University of Norway for their informal input and advice along the way, including Charles Waldheim, Kira Clingen, Eimear Tynan, and Thomas Juel Clemmensen, among others. Knowingly and unknowingly, their feedback was important to us as we framed the book's intentions.

One of us comes to this project having been born, raised, and trained in the colonial-settler nation-state of Canada, a place whose geographic identity and imagination lean heavily on the Arctic. This is also why, in no small part, learning how to unlearn colonial ways of knowing and doing has been built into the ethical framework of this book and the editorial process. To unlearn is no small feat. It is an ongoing project of process. As you will read in this book, the Arctic has been—and continues to be—a place where the violence and harms derived from the legacies of European colonialism are unevenly distributed, and it is up to those of us who are colonial newcomers to put into place practices and methods that recognize and actively work against these legacies. For their inspirational work in this regard, we wish to thank scholars, artists, activists, mentors, many of whom have become dear friends, including Alethea Arnaquq-Baril, AM Kanngieser, Mere Nailatikau, Garcia Frankowski (Cruz García and Nathalie Frankowski), Ozayr Saloojee, Susan Schuppli, and Zoe Todd. We also want to thank Sámi architect Joar Nango for making the time to engage with us as we worked to critically question the scope and direction of the book.

It is worth noting that this book was developed alongside Bert De Jonghe's Doctor of Design dissertation project at Harvard GSD, and although they are two distinctly different projects, they informed each other in many ways. Therefore, we also need to thank Bert's doctoral committee—Charles Waldheim, Peter Rowe, and Matthew Jull—for their four-year-long dedication and support.

A very special thank-you to the team at Studio Folder for their extraordinary dedication and attention to detail when it comes to the book's design and visual research, from discussing the book's layout and framework to developing a set of new maps that highlight the many generations of place names alongside their contemporary colonial counterparts. Finally, the publication would not have been possible without the trust and support of Actar Publishers and their efforts in bringing this book to a larger design audience.

Above all, though, our deepest appreciation must be shared with our friends and family, each of whom supported us in their own ways and to whom we express our gratitude privately every day.

Introduction to a Polyvocal Assembly
Bert De Jonghe and Elise Misao Hunchuck

Arctic Practices: Design for a Changing World emerges at a critical juncture wherein the very stability of Arctic ecosystems hangs in a precarious balance induced, almost entirely, by humans. This volume assembles forty-six contributors—designers, educators, artists, photographers, filmmakers, some Indigenous, some residents, and some visitors to the Circumpolar North—to create a polyvocal assembly of Arctic practices. This assembly represents an attempt to deliberately depart from traditional academic frameworks that have historically privileged Western voices and epistemologies.

> As a geographical reality, conceptual framework, and region with shared physical characteristics, the Arctic emerges from a complex intersection of Indigenous knowledge systems, colonial histories, and scientific paradigms. From early Greek measurements of Polaris's position to today's satellite monitoring of rapidly retreating ice sheets, understanding of this region has been shaped by successive waves of external observation and internal resistance. This tension between ways of knowing—between Traditional Knowledge holders and (often Western) scientific frameworks—lies at the heart of contemporary Arctic discourse and design practice.

The colonial legacy of Arctic exploration and design cannot be overstated—from Martin Frobisher's 1576 expedition seeking the Northwest Passage to the Franklin Expedition's fatal disregard for Inuit knowledge in 1845, Western approaches to the Arctic have consistently demonstrated what Sheila Watt-Cloutier terms "environmental colonialism." This pattern persisted through the twentieth century, evidenced in the forced relocation of Inuit communities like Inukjuak and Resolute Bay in the 1950s for Canadian sovereignty claims, the displacement of the Sámi people for hydroelectric development in Norway's Alta River project (1979-1981), and the Soviet Union's systematic resettlement of Nenets communities for industrial development in Yamal. The material manifestations of this colonialism remain evident in architectural and planning decisions—from the imposition of southern-style housing unsuited to Arctic conditions in Nunavut communities to the development of extraction infrastructure like the Prudhoe Bay oil complex without meaningful Indigenous consultation. Perhaps nowhere is this more evident than in Soviet and post-Soviet urban development across Siberia, where cities like Norilsk, Vorkuta, and Igarka were constructed according to standardized planning principles that prioritized industrial efficiency over Indigenous land use patterns and traditional ways of life. The massive urbanization program of the USSR's Committee of the North sought to transform the Arctic through microrayon housing blocks and linear city planning—exemplified in Norilsk's strict geometric layout oriented to minimize wind exposure, yet fundamentally disconnected from Nenets and Dolgan peoples' seasonal migration patterns. This historical context demands contemporary engagement with Arctic design: we must first acknowledge its complicity in these colonial structures before attempting to imagine new futures—a process exemplified in recent projects like the Illusuak Cultural Centre in Nain, Labrador, where Inuit knowledge and design principles were centered in the architectural process.

Contemporary Arctic design practice is caught between urgent climatological imperatives and the slower, necessary work of anticolonial reconciliation. The immediacy of environmental change—evidenced in the collapse of Norilsk's infrastructure due to melting permafrost, the seemingly inevitable relocation of Tuktuyaaqtuuq (Tuktoyaktuk in English) from eroding coastlines, and the rapid transformation of traditional hunting grounds in Nunavut—demands immediate technical responses. Yet these responses must be developed alongside and in dialogue with Indigenous knowledge systems and governance structures. Projects like SIKU (Sea Ice Monitoring and Real-Time Information Sharing in the Arctic) and the *Pan Inuit Trails Atlas* demonstrate distinct but complementary approaches to bridging Indigenous and Western ways of knowing. While SIKU combines Indigenous observations with satellite data to understand rapid environmental changes, the *Pan Inuit Trails Atlas* digitally maps Inuit place names and travel routes across Canada's Arctic archipelago using both archival maps and oral histories—effectively preserving traditional spatial knowledge while challenging colonial cartographic assumptions about territory, mobility, and land use. The Atlas reveals complex networks of Inuit mobility and place-making that long predate colonial mapping projects, demonstrating how digital tools can amplify rather than supplant Indigenous knowledge systems. Similar initiatives, such as the Greenland Ice Sheet Project's integration of Kalaallit hunting knowledge with glaciological data and the Snowchange Cooperative's documentation of Sámi ecological knowledge in Finland, showcase how traditional knowledge can inform and enhance scientific understanding of Arctic systems. These projects reveal the deep temporal and spatial understanding embedded in Indigenous place names and travel routes—knowledge that extends far beyond the limited temporal scope of satellite data and scientific monitoring. Yet such bridging must be undertaken with careful attention to power dynamics and knowledge sovereignty—as demonstrated by the Indigenous-led guidelines for research in the North, developed by the Inuit Circumpolar Council, and the establishment of Indigenous-controlled research centers like the Árbediehtu Center for Sámi Traditional Knowledge. These initiatives represent critical steps toward what scholars like Julie Cruikshank term "intellectual sovereignty"—the right of Indigenous peoples to maintain, protect, and develop their own knowledge systems while engaging with Western scientific frameworks on their own terms.

The gaps in current literature—particularly regarding Indigenous design voices and knowledge exchange within global design disciplines—point to the ongoing work needed in this field. By addressing these gaps while acknowledging our own limitations, we hope to contribute to a broader conversation about the future of Arctic design practice in an age of unprecedented change. We hope that this volume's content and organization reflect these complex realities.

> Rather than impose a rigid linear structure, we have allowed chapters and the stories within them to layer and blur across multiple temporal scales—much like the Arctic's own seasonal rhythms and cycles of change. This approach enables readers to trace connections between historical processes of colonization, the contemporary climate crisis, and speculative futures for Arctic design practice.

Our positionality as editors—one Belgian, one raised as a colonial settler in Canada—has required constant negotiation between our academic training and our commitment to anticolonial practices. This tension manifests in our editorial choices, from the selection of contributors to the language we use to frame their (and our) work. We continue to work to unlearn colonial patterns of knowledge production while remaining mindful of our own limitations and ongoing complicity in colonial structures. This has repercussions in many directions, including how we teach, how we conduct research, and, of course, how we edit and how we come into conversation with the texts of others. This is also heavily reflected in our language and curational efforts. Our voice is, at times, in the background and, in some cases, more prominent, such as in interviews. It is an ongoing process, and we are the first to admit that we may not always get it right.

> This edited volume covers a broad range of contributions. The book's structure—deliberately non-linear and layered—invites readers to trace their paths through assembled voices and perspectives. In doing so, it mirrors the complexity of Arctic landscapes, where multiple temporalities and ways of knowing have always coexisted. This approach allows for what we might call a polyvocal assembly—a gathering of voices that speaks to historical injustices, contemporary responses, and future possibilities.

In short, and following the sequence of the book, each contribution can be summarized as follows. *Peter Hemmersam* examines how Nuuk's urban development across three key moments—from Råvad's 1911 colonial vision through modernist transformation to contemporary Arctic aspirations—reflects the evolving dynamics between Danish colonial power and Greenlandic sovereignty. *Olga Petri* examines how Soviet children's literature reflected Arctic urban development through fabulous urbanism, where narratives of Indigenous life and Soviet ideals shaped architectural design and social control in the Far North. *Caitlin Blanchfield* examines how the Mackenzie Institute's appropriation of the Inuvik Research Laboratory in 1971 challenged settler colonial planning and knowledge production while creating openings for anticolonial research methods and Indigenous environmental activism in the Canadian Arctic. *Lasse Rau* examines how the Alaska Native Claims Settlement Act (ANCSA) of 1971 transformed Indigenous land into corporate property while highlighting how some groups, like the Neets'ąįį Gwich'in, practiced urbanisms of refusal by rejecting imposed colonial frameworks of land ownership.

In a generous interview with the editors, *Claudio Aporta* discusses how the *Pan Inuit Trails Atlas* project evolved from mapping place names in Igloolik to documenting a vast network of Inuit mobility across the Arctic, demonstrating how trails function not just as routes but as social spaces that connect communities and carry intergenerational knowledge of the land.

Aniella Sophie Goldinger draws out how sea ice drift challenges conventional marine spatial planning approaches in the Arctic Ocean, arguing for new frameworks that recognize ice as a vibrant material actor and embrace more dynamic, three-dimensional understandings of oceanic space.   *Nicole Luke* reflects on her experiences as an Indigenous architect in Inuit Nunangat, examining the tensions between southern construction timelines and Inuit community needs while highlighting both progress in Indigenous architectural leadership and persistent challenges in achieving true Inuit autonomy in northern development.

Todd Saunders reflects on his architectural practice through an extensive interview that explores his "curious listening" design approach, the influence of his Canadian background and Norwegian experience, and his vision for more community-informed, place-based architecture in the Arctic that moves beyond corporate standardization.   *Dorte Mandrup* describes how her firm's Ilulissat Icefjord Centre in Greenland responds to Arctic conditions through careful site analysis, aerodynamic form, and sustainable construction methods while creating a gateway between town and icefjord that serves as both a climate change education center and community gathering space.   Tromsø-based architects *Gisle Løkken* and *Magdalena Haggärde* eloquently discuss how their architecture studio's participatory design process in Maniitsoq, Greenland, helped residents to define their own reality, developing alternatives to official industrial narratives of so-called progress and prosperity, ultimately leading to a reimagining of the town's identity through whale-watching rather than aluminum production.   *Susan Schuppli* examines how Inuit observations of the sun's changing position in the Arctic reveal tensions between scientific expertise and local knowledge while exploring how climate change has transformed the Arctic landscape—and nature itself—into an unreliable witness distorting traditional ways of seeing and knowing.   *Inuuteq Storch* highlights two of his recent photography projects, sharing intimate portraits of his hometown of Sisimiut, Greenland.   *Nadezhda Filimonova* examines how place attachment and identity formation in Russian Arctic cities influence migration patterns, revealing complex relationships between urban infrastructure quality, social networks, and cultural factors that affect residents' decisions to stay or leave the Russian Arctic Zone.   *Jakob Exner* and *Helena Lennert* unpack their design for a child-centered daycare facility in Tasiilaq, East Greenland, which responds to site-specific conditions while incorporating local color traditions, creating warm, intimate spaces that promote children's well-being.   In an extended conversation between Elise Misao Hunchuck, *Maaretta Jaukkuri*, and *AK Dolven*, the curator and the artist discuss how their decades-long friendship led to the creation of the Maaretta Jaukkuri Foundation and The Place—a residence and library in Lofoten that emerged from an exchange of land for seven bottles of wine—while reflecting on their earlier collaboration on Artscape Nordland, a pioneering public art project across Norway's northern municipalities.

Sophy Roberts and *Michael Turek* document their intimate three-year journey through Siberia, capturing the region's landscapes, complex history, and resilient human stories through photography and personal observations.

Svetlana Romanova offers an intimate portrayal of contemporary Siberian life through *Managa Bar / Rustam's Habitat*, exploring Indigenous experiences, cultural nuances, and everyday realities in Yakutsk and surrounding regions.

Nicholas Gulick and *Elena Krapivina* document the intricate "Road of Life" ice crossing between Arkhangelsk and Kegostrov, revealing the complex human adaptations and daily resilience required to navigate the challenging winter landscape of Russia's Northern Dvina River delta.   *Bertine Tønseth* chronicles the poignant story of Teriberka, a declining Russian coastal village, through the transformative "New Chapter" art project that seeks to preserve cultural memory and highlight the broader challenges facing remote northern communities.   *Thomas Juel Clemmensen* introduces the workings of landscape architectural education above the Arctic Circle, specifically in Tromsø, Norway.

Akie Kono captures the dynamic and transient nature of snow deposits in Tromsø, revealing how these urban snow mounds reshape the city's landscape, movement, and visual experience during the Arctic winter.

Andrey N. Petrov and *Marya Rozanova-Smith* explore the complex process of Indigenous urbanization in Naryan-Mar, revealing how Nenets people negotiate their cultural identity, resilience, and adaptation within the landscape of a Russian Arctic city.   *Arlyn Charlie*'s photographs document his family's intimate relationship with the landscapes of Teetł'it Zheh (Fort McPherson, Northwest Territories, Canada). It is a close view of Gwich'in culture and how they live with the land, sharing ongoing fishing, hunting, gathering, and survival traditions through seasonal activities that connect them deeply to their ancestral territories.   *Konstantin Ikonomidis* chronicles the creation of Qaammat, a unique glass pavilion in Sarfannguit, Greenland, exploring the intersection of architectural design, cultural heritage, and community collaboration in an Arctic landscape.   *Jessica MacMillan* illustrates an act of art at the cosmic scale materialized in the form of a single 10-watt green laser situated in Longyearbyen, Svalbard.   *Anastasia Savinova* makes collages of the towns, villages, and landscapes of Norrbotten County, the northernmost county in Sweden, as a keeper of the memories and spirit of these places.   Inuvialuk artist *Maureen Gruben* and collaborator *Kyra Kordoski* unpack one of Gruben's iconic works based on found photographic aerial survey prints and her father's fox stretchers and traps.   *Morgan Ip* explores the collective urban imagination of Kirkenes and Nikel, revealing how the Arctic borderlands between Norway and Russia are envisioned through local perspectives, historical legacies, and the potential for future urban development that balances cultural preservation, economic sustainability, and environmental harmony. *Mari A. Aston Bergset* discusses the innovative landscape architectural practice of Lo:Le in Tromsø, Northern Norway, highlighting their place-specific approach to design that integrates local cultural contexts, environmental challenges, and sustainable practices across four distinctive projects. *Eimear Tynan* and *Bert De Jonghe* explore the pedagogical approach of teaching landscape architecture in Svalbard, discussing their methods and findings of *Territorial Practices* (a Master of Landscape Architecture studio-based course at the Arctic University of Norway [UiT] taught in the Fall of 2023), focusing on how students can design with dynamic, changing Arctic delta environments by emphasizing iterative design methods, temporal perspectives, and collaborative engagement with complex ecological and human systems. *Lola Sheppard* and *Mason White* discuss the elastic scales of Arctic inhabitation, between home and territory in the Arctic, revealing how domestic spaces and landscapes are shaped by intersecting forces of Indigenous sovereignty, colonial extraction, climate change, and local adaptation across eight circumpolar nations. *Caitlin Jakusz Paridy* proposes a palliative landscape design approach for a decommissioning coal mine in Svalbard that embraces the entropy of changing Arctic landscapes by choreographing natural processes and allowing the community to witness and adapt to the site's transformation. *Sofia Singler* challenges the prevailing narrative that Sámi architecture is solely tethered to the past by arguing for a more nuanced understanding that recognizes how Indigenous architectural practices can simultaneously embrace and resist historical and contemporary influences, thereby liberating Sámi architecture from colonial interpretative frameworks. With a view to the future and the past, *Brandon Bergem* and *Jeffrey Garcia* investigate the intricate visual storytelling of the Museum of Natural History, using digital rendering and diorama techniques to construct speculative narratives that blur the boundaries between scientific documentation and imaginative projection of Svalbard's potential environmental and architectural futures.

> The contributions collected here address critical gaps in published Arctic design literature, particularly regarding Indigenous design voices and perspectives beyond well-documented sites like Norilsk and Resolute Bay. They also represent attempts to imagine new forms of design practice that might respond to the urgency of climate change and the necessity of reconciliation.

This collection emerges at a moment when traditional scientific monitoring struggles to keep pace with environmental change—when Qausuittuq (Resolute Bay) residents observe shore ice forming later each year, when Greenlandic hunters report altered seal migration patterns, and when Sámi reindeer herders note shifting vegetation patterns affecting traditional grazing grounds. These changes demand new frameworks for understanding and action, which this volume attempts to assemble.

Arctic Practices thus stands as both documentation and provocation—an attempt to record current practices while simultaneously imagining new possibilities for Arctic design in an age of crisis. By bringing diverse voices and perspectives together, we hope to contribute to an emerging discourse that recognizes the urgency of climate action and the necessity of anticolonial practice in Arctic contexts. This volume thus represents not an endpoint but rather a series of moments in an ongoing process of learning and unlearning. This process must continue as we collectively face the challenges of climate change and anticolonial reconciliation in Arctic contexts. Through this polyvocal assembly, we hope to open new possibilities for meaningful design interventions across northern lands, seas, skies, and ice, always mindful of both the urgency of our present moment and the weight of historical injustices that have shaped these landscapes and the lives lived with them.

Index of Places

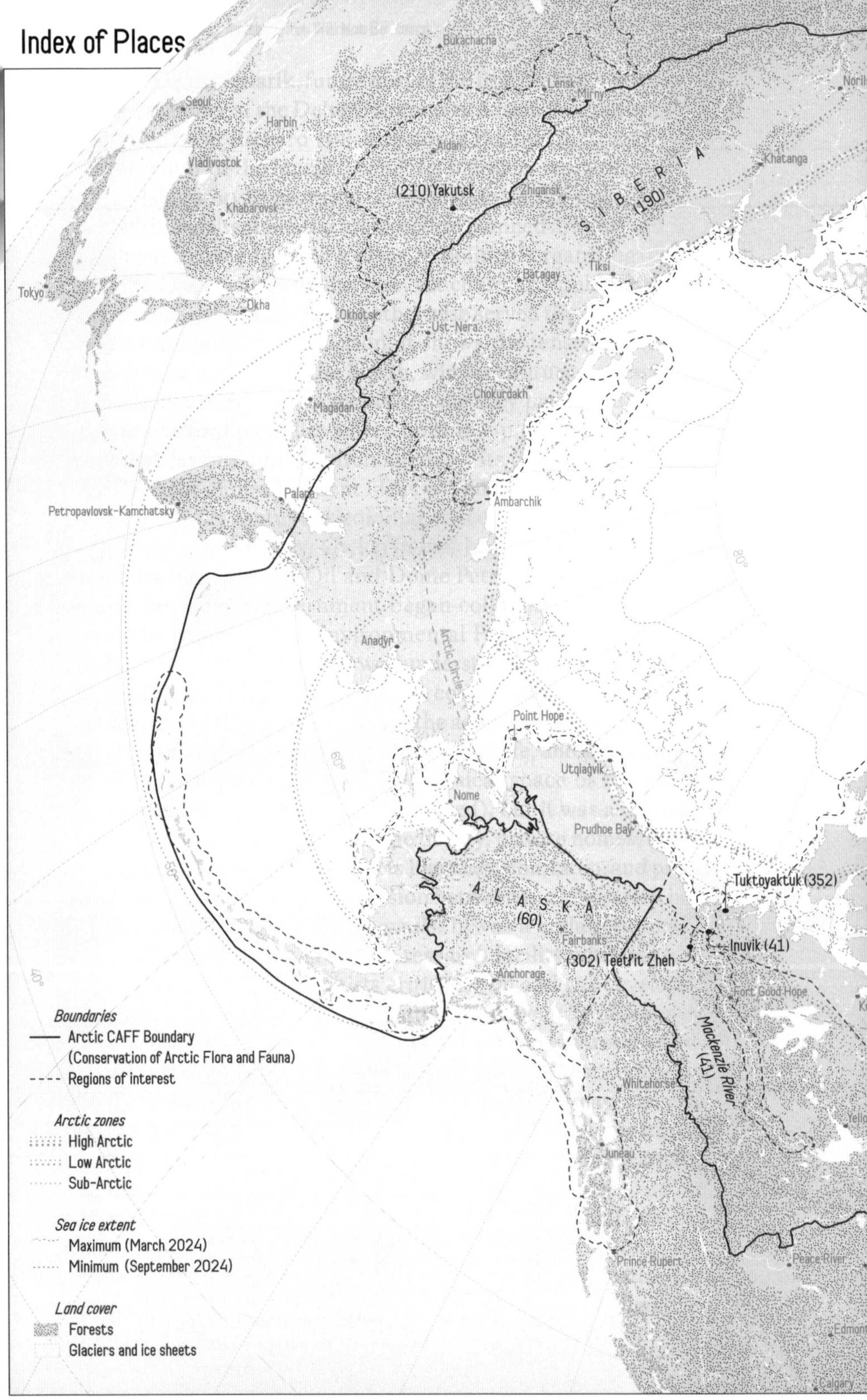

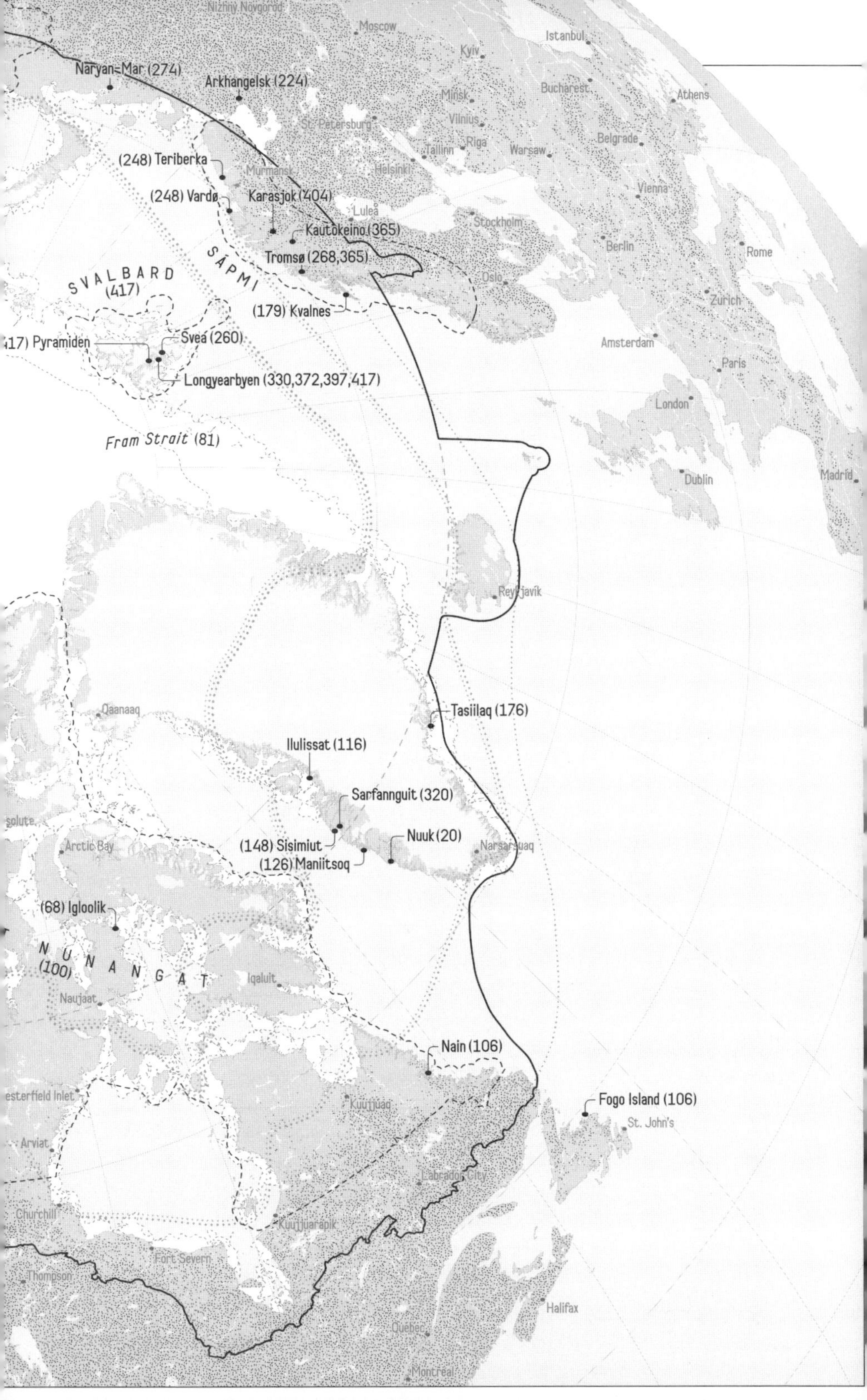

Nizhny Novgorod
Moscow
Kyiv
Istanbul
Naryan-Mar (274)
Arkhangelsk (224)
Minsk
Bucharest
Athens
St. Petersburg
Vilnius
Belgrade
(248) Teriberka
Murmansk
Tallinn
Riga
Warsaw
Vienna
Rome
Helsinki
Karasjok (404)
Luleå
(248) Vardø
Stockholm
Kautokeino (365)
Berlin
Tromsø (268,365)
Oslo
Zurich
SVALBARD
(417)
(179) Kvalnes
S Á P M I
Amsterdam
(417) Pyramiden
Svea (260)
Paris
Longyearbyen (330,372,397,417)
London
Fram Strait (81)
Dublin
Madrid
Reykjavík
Qaanaaq
Tasiilaq (176)
Ilulissat (116)
solute
Sarfannguit (320)
Arctic Bay
Nuuk (20)
(148) Sisimiut
Narsarsuaq
(126) Maniitsoq
(68) Igloolik
N U N A N G A T
(100)
Iqaluit
Naujaat
Nain (106)
esterfield Inlet
Kuujjuaq
Fogo Island (106)
St. John's
Arviat
Labrador City
Churchill
Kuujjuarapik
Fort Severn
Thompson
Halifax
Québec
Montréal

Peter Hemmersam is Professor in Urban Design at the Oslo School of Architecture and Design. In 2021, he published *Making the Arctic City: The History and Future of Urbanism in the Circumpolar North* (Bloomsbury).

Making and Remaking the Capital of Greenland
Peter Hemmersam

Greenland has a fascinating urban planning history. In 1721, Hans Egede established a mission that marked the start of Danish colonization. This mission moved to present-day Nuuk in 1728, but the settlement remained a small administrative and trade post for centuries without formal urban planning. However, in the twentieth century, Danish colonial policies underwent significant changes, and modernization and economic development became intimately tied to urban development. Architects and planners proposed and planned the modern towns and settlements that frame the everyday life of Greenlanders today. The evolving urbanism of the past century reflects the unfolding power dynamics between planners, the Danish state, and the people of Greenland. At the same time, urban planning history reveals evolving ideas and understandings of the role of cities and the built environment in terms of culture, economy, the environment, and the ideal future society of Greenland.

This chapter presents three moments during which urban planning in Greenland was intensely modern. All three instances deal with the construction of a capital city. Political and economic changes influenced the conceptualization, planning, and construction of each capital. Each plan for a capital represented a discontinuity with the previous situation and the creation of a new vision for the country. These three moments also represent instances of urban planning comparison, where cities in Greenland are compared to the exploding North American metropolises of the late nineteenth and early twentieth centuries, to the modernist cities of postwar Europe, and finally, in recent years, to other cities within the Arctic.

In the twentieth century, urban modernity expanded to the entire world. As Marshall Berman argues in his book *All That Is Solid Melts into Air*, modernity is central to the experience of urbanity and urbanization.[1] Modernity dominates everyday life everywhere. It is exhilarating and promises golden futures—but it is also terrifying in destroying all we thought we knew and appreciated. As in many colonial and postcolonial territories, modernization in Greenland was often pursued through the lens of development. Development framed social, economic, and urban policies, replacing established and traditional ways of life. The development framework entailed the diffusion of Western culture and economic growth to Arctic territories and served to perpetuate a structural exploitative dependency on southern capitals.

THE QUEEN OF THE ARCTIC

The first proposal for a capital in Greenland was by the Danish architect and urban planner Alfred J. Råvad in 1911.[2] This was the first published plan for a modern city in the Arctic. Råvad's concern was the cultural and political expansion of the Danish realm to Greenland, and the city was a thoroughbred colonial construct that would play a civilizational role beyond the existing religious and trade colonies. While not directly reflecting official Danish colonial policies at the time, his proposal and broader authorship echoed the 'New Imperialism' at the turn of the twentieth century, fueled by trade rivalries and a belief in new technologies and capitalism.[3] This form of colonialism was also based on a belief in the superiority of European culture and the desire for the prestige of empire.

The city, called Erikshavn, was located near present-day Nanortalik and was intended to be a natural bunker port for an emerging global trade route across the North Atlantic. This route extended from the Pacific across Canada by train and to Europe by steamboat—passing right south of Greenland. Danish architects would design the city, and artists would live here to cultivate the Greenlandic landscape in the same way late-nineteenth-century impressionist painters had inserted the peripheral fishing village of Skagen into the collective

1   Marshall Berman, *All That Is Solid Melts into Air: The Experience of Modernity* (Simon and Schuster, 1982).

2   "Architekten Som Sociolog: K. Store Bølger Og Små [The Architect as Sociologist: K. Large Waves and Small]," *Architekten*, 1911; See also Alfred J. Råvad, "Grønlands Hovedstad: I. Indledning [The Capital of Greenland: I: Introduction]," *Architekten*, 1914; "Grønlands Hovedstad: II. Beliggenheden [The Capital of Greenland: II: The Location]," *Architekten*, 1914; "Grønlands Hovedstad: III. Stedet [The Capital of Greenland: III: The Place]," *Architekten*, 1914; "Grønlands Hovedstad: IV. Den Æstetiske Og Videnskabelige Side [The Capital of Greenland: IV: The Aesthetic and Scientific Aspect]," *Architekten*, 1914; "Grønlands Hovedstad: V. 'All Sorts and Conditions of Men' [The Capital of Greenland: V: 'All Sorts and Conditions of Men']," *Architekten*, 1914; "Grønlands Hovedstad: VI. Turist-Værdien [The Capital of Greenland: VI: The Turist Value]," *Architekten*, 1914; "Grønlands Hovedstad: VII. Eskimo Problemet [The Capital of Greenland: VII: The Eskimo Problem]," *Architekten*, 1914.

3   Mary Gilmartin, "Colonialism/Imperialism," in *Key Concepts in Political Geography*, ed. Carolyn Gallaher et al. (Sage, 2009), 115–23.

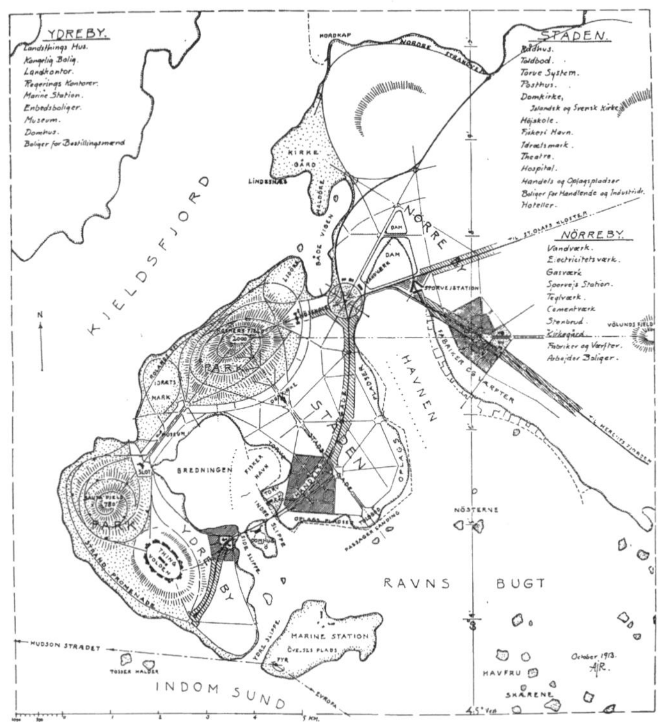

1   In 1914, Råvad wrote: "The proposed city is divided into three parts: one, the outermost, for the government and metropolitan element, the middle one, for trade and the future business district and a third, the innermost, for the industry—for factories and yards."

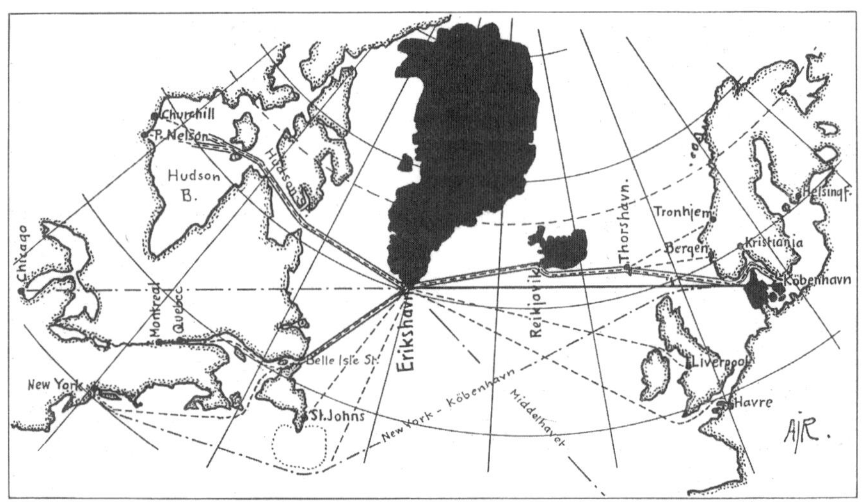

2   Erikshavn was located at the southern tip of Greenland and was to act as a stopover port between Europe and Canada.

national cultural imagination. Danish and Icelandic families would initially populate this new European city.[4] Over time, Råvad envisioned the expansion of Greenland's population to 50,000 and eventually 100,000 and claimed that Greenland would eventually become "Polarlandenes droning" (The Queen of the Polar Lands).[5]

Råvad had lived in Chicago in the 1890s and was influenced by trends in the emerging field of urbanism and modern metropolitan urban planning in the United States.[6] He worked for the famous architect and urbanist Daniel Burnham on the 1893 World's Columbian Exposition, which became celebrated as the inception of the City Beautiful movement. This neo-monumental, Beaux-Arts-inspired urban planning style sought to promote a sense of civic pride and, thus, social harmony in the exploding metropolises of the nineteenth century. It was part of a broader reformist movement aimed at alleviating the squalid living conditions of the industrial labor class. The neo-baroque monumental grandeur of the movement became central to the planning of modern capitals worldwide, such as Washington, DC, Canberra in Australia, and Moscow. City Beautiful was also closely associated with early forms of modern metropolitan planning. Råvad later proposed the so-called Finger Plan for the Copenhagen region.[7] This widely celebrated plan from 1947 still governs the city's regional growth strategy.

Rather than basing the design for Erikshavn on Danish urban planning precedent, Råvad's City Beautiful-inspired plan had boulevards, landmarks and landscaped parks, a palace, and a monumental government district. An electric railway connected the urban center to the hinterland. A technological optimist, Råvad even anticipated a solution to the threat that sea ice posed to shipping. This would enable Erikshavn to become an international tourist destination. Råvad's urban proposal for Greenland was a resolute grab for the driver of economic globalization: the global shipping routes. It was a colonial projection of Western modernity onto a not-yet-modern territory.

Råvad's unsolicited plan did not correspond to the colonial isolation policy of the Danish government, which had no plans for new settlement construction and never built the city. According to professor in architecture Hans Erling Langkilde, Råvad's project nevertheless became important to later urban planners as it presented a unified idea of an urban realm, "a comprehensive picture of Greenland's future and dreams of molding it into a new form whose ideas are derived from a Western, technologically highly developed civilization."[8] No new cities were planned in Greenland during the peak period of Western

---

4   Iceland was, at the time, part of the Danish realm.

5   "Polarlandenes droning" from Råvad, 'Grønlands Hovedstad: IV', 276.

6   Hans Helge Madsen, *Chicago - København, Alfred Råvads univers* (Gyldendal, 1990).

7   "Alfred Råvad," in *Wikipedia*, June 28, 2018.

8   Hans Erling Langkilde, "Grønland under Forvandling [Changing Greenland]," *Arkitektur,* 1968, 21.

colonialism in the late nineteenth and early twentieth century. The same is true for the rest of the North American Arctic. In northern Scandinavia, mining communities like Kiruna were planned and constructed according to German Städtebau principles. Still, the first significant wave of city construction in the Arctic was the many neo-monumental and City Beautiful-inspired industrial cities planned and built across the Soviet Far North in the 1930s and 1940s. According to environmental historian Andy Bruno, these cities were integral to the "deliberate effort ... to transform a periphery into a center of socialist modernity".[9]

A TECHNOCRATIC URBAN VISION

A massive program for modernization accompanied the formal abolishment of Greenland's colonial status in 1953. World War II had altered Greenland's exposure to Western society. Public awareness of the social conditions in Greenland spread in Denmark during the postwar years, and the international movement for decolonization expressed by the United Nations contributed to this change in policy. This new government development program (outlined in the 1950 Greenland Commission's report) led to the rapid construction of towns, housing, and institutions following Danish technical, health, and education standards.[10] In preparation for this endeavor, the Urban Planning Expedition to Greenland's west coast in 1950 outlined the urban and industrial system that came to structure Greenland's economy and cities in the following decades.[11] The Danish planners of the expedition were familiar with Råvad's plan, and like him, they subjected the landscape to modernist tabulae rasa planning. The planners primarily considered the pre-urban territory to offer challenges of a technical nature. At the same time, they assumed that the desires and concerns of the Greenlandic population corresponded to the narratives of social progress inherent in modernist urban planning.

While Råvad had employed the neo-baroque and monumental urban design language of the City Beautiful movement, postwar planners used the abstract geometric design language of high modernism. The expeditions' plans for cities in East Greenland followed the latest ideals for designing and engineering new urban communities, inspired by the postwar reconstruction of war-ravaged European cities. According to Berman, the highly rational planning of international modernism articulated "a spatially and socially segmented world—people here, traffic there; work here, homes there; rich here; poor there."[12] The language of science dominated the evolution of a new aesthetic and the formulation of a contemporary urban society in Greenland. Modernist city planning functioned as a laboratory of modernity. As Serhat Karakayali explains, urban modernism continuously framed the colonial city as deficient compared to Western models. At the same time, the colonial "state of exception" provided an opening for "testing modern social techniques."[13] In Greenland, the prospect of local resistance to such dramatic plans for a new society was remote, and planners could proceed largely unimpeded. Starting in 1956, the Greenland Technical Organization (GTO) undertook the comprehensive planning and construction of a new urban society. Like similar high modernist state colonial planning organizations in the Arctic regions of the USSR, Canada, and Norway, GTO was inspired by American New Deal policies. In particular, they looked to the regional industrialization plans and policies of the Tennessee Valley Authority regional economic development agency that had started in 1933.[14] With an undefined budget, GTO operated as the government arm responsible for constructing infrastructure, ships, industry, and institutions while managing technical and communications infrastructure. Over a couple of decades, GTO created the entire urban environment of Greenland and replaced virtually all housing in the country. Greenland's municipalities did not have their own planning departments, and local Greenlandic politicians relied on GTO's counseling, giving the organization almost total control of urban development.

The plan for Nuuk was the most comprehensive plan for a modern city. After the war, the former colonial administrative and trading post of Godthåb was designated the island's administrative center after experts found its harbor and water supply expandable.[15]In addition, a large, flat, and nearly empty terrain adjacent to the colonial harbor (Narsarsuaq/Store Slette) was suitable for constructing a new city of multi-story residential buildings and public institutions. The expedition's development plan projected that the town's population would reach 9,000 after thirty years, a target surpassed when the city started expanding beyond the city center in the 1970s. The urban plan included political and administrative institutions, industry, and housing for both Greenlanders who relocated to the new city and the Danes who occupied central positions in the administration and central services of the Greenlandic society. Beyond Nuuk, these short-term residents also provided know-how

9   Andy Richard Bruno, "Making Nature Modern: Economic Transformation and the Environment in the Soviet North" (PhD diss., University of Illinois at Urbana-Champaign, 2011), 122.

10   Grønlandskommisionen, "Grønlandskommissionens betænkning [Report from the Greenland Commission]" (Grønlandskommisionen, 1950).

11   Hugo Lund Andersen et al., *Byplanforslag i Vestgrønland, Narssaq, Sukkertoppen, Egedesminde, Godthaab [Proposed Urban Plans in Western Greenland, Narssaq, Sukkertoppen, Egedesminde, Godthaab]* (Grønlandsdepartementet, 1951).

12   *All That Is Solid Melts into Air: The Experience of Modernity*, 168.

13   Serhat Karakayali, "Colonialism and the Critique of Modernity," in *Colonial Modern: Aesthetics of the Past - Rebellions for the Future*, eds. Tom Avermaete, Serhat Karakayali, and Marion von Osten (Black Dog Publishing, 2010), 39–47.

14   James C. Scott, *Seeing Like a State: How Certain Schemes to Improve the Human Condition Have Failed*, Yale University Press, 1998).

15   Andersen et al., *Byplanforslag i Vestgrønland.*

3   Gunnar Rosendahl, director of GTO, surveys a plan for Godthåb (Nuuk).

and a workforce to construct towns and settlements across the island. At the time, Greenland was formally a county of Denmark, and the public buildings of the first city-building were relatively modest modernist structures that echoed the design of the corresponding generation of regional government offices in various parts of Denmark. These mid-century government buildings were deliberately anti-monumental, and their architectural expression was far removed from Copenhagen's baroque and neo-classical national government architecture.

The housing projects that GTO built for the Danish workers and the local population in the 1960s and 1970s dominated, until very recently, the urban landscape of Greenland. Multi-story precast concrete buildings—the height of building technology at the time—allowed for the rapid construction of large numbers of dwellings. The 1960s high modernist vision of social engineering through design was emblematic of twentieth-century colonialism.[16] While controversial and associated with the colonial project, modernist architecture and planning remained central to the mid-century construction of capitals in newly decolonized countries—particularly in the Global South. Modernism's ahistorical ethos thus applied to both the colonial planning of pre-urban societies and newly independent nations' efforts to break with a colonial past. At the same time, aspiring to become contemporary modern urban societies reflects these emerging nations' attachment to Western cultural norms.

THE POSTCOLONIAL CAPITAL OF THE ARCTIC

A century after Råvad published his plans for Erikshavn, the modernist apartment building Blok P in Nuuk was demolished. For decades, this building was the single largest residential structure in the country, with 320 apartments. Following a political decision in 2010, the government bulldozed the dilapidated concrete structure in 2012. In addition to making space for new development, the demolition was a symbolic rejection of the social engineering of modernist architecture and the colonial modernization and assimilation policies. The destruction of the building represented a discontinuity with a technocratic planning tradition and the emergence of a new agenda for Greenland's cities.

Nuuk, now a city with more than 19,000 inhabitants, has transitioned from a colonial capital to the seat of the government of a semi-independent country. The self-rule government now resides in the country's most iconic tower block atop the Nuuk Center complex. It is the tallest building in the country, boasting the first underground parking garage and the first indoor public realm in the form of a shopping center with a central multistorey plaza. In contrast to other major public institutions, such as the Ilimmarfik University campus and the Katuaq Cultural Center, whose wood cladding and nature-inspired architectural iconography attempt to capture and represent an essential Greenlandic character, the government tower block conforms to a contemporary international neo-modernist architectural language. Its glass curtain walls provide transparent views of the offices inside, transforming the tower into an illuminated landmark at night. The building functions as a contemporary International Style statement of the independent politics of Greenland, signaling the construction of a national postcolonial capital with a strong desire to project modernity to the outside world. Echoing such ambitions, the local government of Nuuk considers the city's role to expand beyond the nation. With international ambitions, Semersooq municipality suggests that the city is well positioned to become a meeting place for the polar world's business, politics, and science to become a 'Capital of the Arctic.'[17]

A NEW COMPARISON

Over a century, decision-makers, planners, and architects constructed the capital of Greenland three times: first, as a Danish colonial capital at the start of the twentieth century, to introduce European urban culture to a pre-modern landscape and population. Second, as a Danish regional seat of

16   For example, Mark Crinson, *Modern Architecture and the End of Empire* (Ashgate Pub Ltd, 2003).

17   Kommuneqarfik Sermersooq, "Nuuk — Arktisk Hovedstad: Hovedstadsstrategi for Nuuk" (Kommuneqarfik Sermersooq, 2016).

4   The Nuuk Center, the tallest building in Greenland, was built in 2012. The abstract formal expression
        of the government headquarters echoes the discredited modernism of the postwar era. It had the first
        underground parking garage and combines government offices and shopping around an indoor multi-level
        public plaza. Combining governance with public space and the spectacle of modern retail, the center
        represents modernity in Nuuk.

5   Block P was the largest residential block in Greenland and contained 320 apartments. It was built in
        1965-1966 as part of the Danish government's program to modernize and urbanize the Greenlandic
        population and demolished in 2012.

administration, planned when Greenland began its rapid modernization and industrialization in the 1950s. Third, as a national capital for an Arctic nation, moving towards complete independence as autonomy takes form. Analyzing Nuuk's urban planning and development history clarifies that the modern Greenlandic capital city is a palimpsest of modernities, including colonialism, modernism, and the contemporary neoliberal globalized urban discourse.

The contemporary planning and architecture of Nuuk follow international approaches, and the modernist residential heritage of the city gradually gives way to a city of towers. However, contemporary Nuuk is not only becoming more metropolitan—it is also steadily becoming more Greenlandic, evident in the increasing dominance of the national Greenlandic language in public settings and the dwindling ranks of Danish administrators working and living in the capital. Local political assertiveness is evident in Nuuk's urban development. Still, at the same time, postcolonial tensions become evident when local politics is increasingly exposed to the pressures of international capital that, for instance, looks to invest in the city's hotel industry.

In contrast to the landscape imagery dominating representations of the Arctic, Danish anthropologist Frank Sejersen claims that Greenlandic society—and, by extension, other northern communities—is urbanized and modern.[18] He references Henri Lefebvre, who argues that the urban phenomenon is omnipresent, global, and not confined to the morphological city.[19] Being modern implies—at least to some extent—a comparison to ideals or a utopia elsewhere, and as Colin McFarlane explains, urbanism has always been comparative.[20] For most of Greenland's city-building history, comparisons to southern metropolises were fundamental to formulating plans and directing futures. Integral to the development narrative that dominated the development of Greenlandic urban society was the notion that Greenlandic cities are somehow deficient compared to cities in the developed West and should strive to become like them. Such comparative thinking legitimized the colonial actions that dominated urban planning and development in the country for decades.

Alfred Råvad based his theoretical proposition for a strategic port city on American urban design models. In the heads of mid-century Danish planners, Godthåb was insufficiently modern compared to European standards and ideals. While Nuuk is still relatively small, the city is no longer framed by local decision-makers, planners, and

18   Frank Sejersen, "Urbanization, Landscape Appropriation and Climate Change in Greenland,"
       Acta Borealia 27, no. 2 (2010): 167–88.

19   Henri Lefebvre, "The Urban Revolution [1968]," in *The Global Towns Reader*, eds. Neil Brenner
       and Roger Keil (Routledge, 2005), 407–13.

20   Colin McFarlane, "Crossing Borders: Development, Learning and the North: South Divide,"
       Third World Quarterly 27, no. 8 (2006): 1413–37.

architects as deficient compared to Western paradigmatic models of urbanism. Echoing Råvad, recent thinking about the role of the Greenlandic capital has expanded from being the country's capital to becoming central in the wider Arctic region. Attempts at promoting Nuuk as the Capital of the Arctic indicate that this new urban agenda is also based on comparison. But instead of comparing Nuuk to Danish or other Western cities, the comparison is now to other cities in the Arctic. Several cities now engage in the production of Arctic capitals, and Nuuk forms a league of comparison with cities like Anchorage, Tromsø, Iqaluit, Longyearbyen, Murmansk, and Reykjavik.

The comparison implied in Nuuk's Arctic capital strategy suggests a new form of regional inter-urban policy transfer. However, Eugene McCann and Kevin Ward, who explore inter-urban policy mobility, warn that there is always a reductive deterritorialization and reterritorialization in such transfers.[21] This warning echoes planning theorist Patsy Healey's double concern about over-localizing planning theory as well as over-generalization that leads to the uncritical import of global urban models to particular local contexts.[22] Jennifer Robinson suggests that 'imitative urbanism' results from the hegemony of Western urban theory.[23] However, in recent years, she suggests, a postcolonial 'Comparative Urbanism' has emerged from research on 'ordinary cities' in regions beyond the West. This research agenda opens a two-way exchange between the West and the rest and allows transversal comparisons between cities in various global regions.

Urban plans and architectural designs for Greenland's capital have transformed radically over the last century, reflecting changes in the country's politics and colonial status. Greenland's cities have continuously been formed through urban planning, comparing them with southern towns and settlements to become modern. Twentieth-century planning of cities across the Arctic was dominated by colonialism and the development discourse. They were considered pre-modern and lacked history; thus, they needed a transfer of Southern urbanism. Today, Arctic cities learn from one another in ways that are not restricted to the reductive and climate-centric exceptionalism that dominated the international discourse on the architecture and urbanism of the Arctic. This learning includes experiences with modern Indigenous urban living. Arctic cities like Nuuk also have varied urban planning histories, and residents and local decision-makers have the agency to remake their city as the capital of the Arctic.

21   Eugene McCann and Kevin Ward, "Relationality/Territoriality: Toward a Conceptualization of Cities in the World," *Geoforum* 41 (March 1, 2010).

22   Patsy Healey, "The Universal and the Contingent: Some Reflections on the Transnational Flow of Planning Ideas and Practices," *Planning Theory* 11, no. 2 (May 1, 2012): 188–207.

23   Jennifer Robinson, *Ordinary Cities: Between Modernity and Development* (Routledge, 2006).

Olga Petri is a human geographer whose work bridges urban studies, queer geographies, and more-than-human worlds.

Fabulous Urbanism: Reading Soviet Arctic Cities through Children's Literature
Olga Petri

When my little daughter flipped open the aged pages of *Kruglyi Dom (The Round House)* by Semen Danilov and illustrated by Anatolyi Borodin, her eyes lit up with wonder: "I want to live in such a house!" she exclaimed. I understood her excitement all too well. On the cover, a yurt—a house typically associated with the North—stood at the center of a bustling scene, surrounded by people, several oleni (reindeer), sledges, and dogs, all engaged in communal activities (↔ 1). The smoke rising from the yurt's peak hinted at the warmth within, inviting one to enter and share a meal or a story. Stories and scenes like these about northern urban life are at the heart of this brief text. Stories—or rather, fables—inform our understanding of how children's imaginative geographies and urban policies intertwine in peculiar ways. This is the essence of 'fabulous urbanism,' where the urban reality is 'fabulous,' not in the sense of mere fantasy, but in its ability to blend the real and the ideal, the moral and the amusing, thereby fostering a unique understanding of urbanism among young Soviet citizens and their elders alike.

This essay poses a challenging question: How do urban narratives found on the pages of Soviet children's literature reflect and influence the urban development and communal life of Soviet cities? Recognizing the scope's ambition, I admit upfront that I cannot fully unpack it within the limits of this essay. Nevertheless, I aim to navigate this question through a specific case study of *The Round House* sparked by my daughter's imagination. This exploration into

1   The cover page of *The Round House* by Semen Danilov, translated from Yakut language by V. Berestov
and illustrated by A. Borodin (Izdetel'stvo Malysh, 1970).

a picture book is a gateway to a broader investigation into the imaginative geographies of the Russian Urban Arctic, where children's tales intersect with a unique, almost moon-like urban reality.

Danilov's *The Round House*, a picture book aimed at young children,[1] is inspired by an indigenous Yakut tale. The narrative was translated into poetic form by Danilov and brought to life through A. Borodin's vivid illustrations. The book was published in 1970 in an impressive run of 100,000 copies—one of which was acquired by my parents.[2] The story is straightforward, following daily activities in the taiga and tundra, where Yakuts live well beyond the Arctic Circle, engaged in hunting reindeer, preparing traditional dishes in yurts, and taking care of and playing with their dogs. This story serves as a poignant illustration of colonial knowledge appropriation, repurposing indigenous Yakut culture to both entertain and indoctrinate Soviet youth.

In a contrasting yet related vein, I discuss the establishment of the Sektor Gradostroitel'stva na Krainem Severe (Department for Urban Planning in the North) in 1956 by the Gosstroi (Soviet State Committee for Construction) within the Lenfilial (Academy of Construction and Architecture of the USSR, Leningrad branch). This initiative signified the commencement of a centralized research effort into construction in the Far North, elevating Lenfilial as a key institution in Soviet architecture, explicitly focusing on urban planning in Arctic territories.[3] I argue that the narratives and imagery in children's books like *The Round House* offer a unique lens through which to view Lenfilial's endeavors. Their work was a creative extension of state ideology, promoting a vision of the Arctic not as a distant, frozen hinterland but as a vibrant, lived space teeming with potential. In doing so, they weaved a narrative that reflects and influences the urban planning strategies of the time. Curiously, these stories, like *The Round House*, help us to see the institute's pioneering work in the Arctic from a new perspective, weaving a narrative that both mirrored and supported their efforts in a distinctive way.

1   Children below seven years old (referred to in Russian as doshkol'nogo vozrasta).

2   Danilov Semen, *The Round House.* Translated from Yakut language by V. Berestov. Illustrated by Anatolyi Borodin. Izdetel'stvo Malysh, 1970.

3   Ekaterina Kalemeneva, "From new socialist cities to thaw experimentation in Arctic townscapes: leningrad architects attempt to modernise the Soviet North," in *Europe-Asia Studies* 71, no. 3 (2019): 426–449.

4   See, for example, the most famous: Kevin Lynch's *The Image of the City* (MIT Press, 1964). Some other important contributions include Matthew Gandy's "Cyborg urbanization: complexity and monstrosity in the contemporary city," in *International Journal of Urban and Regional Research* 29, no. 1 (2005): 26–49; Paramita Atmodiwirjo, Mikhael Johanes, and Yandi Andri Yatmo, "Mapping stories: Representing urban everyday narratives and operations," *Urban Design International* 24 (2019): 225–240; and Ruth Finnegan's *Tales of the City: A Study of narrative and urban life* (Cambridge University Press, 1998).

NARRATING RUSSIAN NORTHERN CITIES

Urban studies have long been preoccupied with narratives' role in producing urban spaces.[4] These narratives help us to analyze historical events and social actions, forging new interpretations of causality and re-examining the roles of theory and explanation. Urban storytelling can serve as a conduit between the city's form and the inhabitants' emotional responses, rendering the complexities of urban life—such as cultural clashes, heritage whispers, and development roars—intelligible and poignant.

What narratives of northern urbanism are woven into Soviet children's literature? One prominent theme, identified by McCannon as 'the Arctic myth,' captures the imagination of young readers with thrilling exploits and vibrant drama—a perfect match for the adventurous spirits of children and adolescents. These narratives, glorifying Arctic explorers and pilots, saturated Soviet media from 1932 to 1939, and they shaped many youths' dreams and aspirations. Linked closely to this was the narrative of the Arctic as a conquerable frontier, suggesting that it was a mysterious puzzle the Soviet people were destined to solve. It positioned the Arctic as a canvas for Soviet achievement, implying that the collective will and ingenuity of the new Soviet generation could tame the region's harshness.[5]

The narrative of mystery and the conquest of the Arctic cast a spell of magic and possibility over real cityscapes, transforming children's perception of their urban environment. This enchantment, which I term 'fabulous Arctic urbanism,' does not skew reality but rather augments it, allowing children to view everyday urban life as part of a more extraordinary, animated tapestry. Fabulous Arctic urbanism unfolds beyond the imagination into a nuanced political dialogue with nature. Within the historical context of urban development in the Russian Arctic, this narrative diverges from the dominant ethos of conquest. Architects and urban planners from Leningrad championed a different approach to coexist with the formidable Arctic climate. Their designs were not about subduing the elements but respecting and integrating them, crafting living spaces that were extensions of the natural landscape. This philosophy was a subtle but profound rebellion against the prevailing narrative, reflecting a progressive shift in the Soviet Union's strategy towards the Arctic: from domination to dialogue, from confrontation to collaboration. It was a political statement, advocating for an architecture that aligned with the environment, celebrating the Arctic's character rather than reshaping it, and, in doing so, proposing a blueprint for living in one of the planet's most extreme environments.[6]

THE ROUND HOUSE OF THE RUSSIAN ARCTIC

What most enchanted my daughter about *The Round House* was the depiction of the yurt, with its embracing wall and fire, which underscored a connection between architecture and the environment—or even nature itself, organized in a khorovod (round dance) and movement. These yurts, nestled within northern landscapes, are portrayed as seamlessly integrated with nature, where the omnipresent cold is not seen as an adversary (↔ 2): "The door is always open, inviting guests in," the story tells us, emphasizing a philosophy of openness and hospitality.[7] The illustrations vividly capture reindeer and other animals gathering around this magical house, all participating in a khorovod around the house. These images demonstrate a community united by the yurt's warmth, even as the wind and snow continue their own dance outside. The house, too, "performs a round dance" in the landscape where everything is in motion, uniting people and all living and non-living things. This setting acts as a bastion of life in the North, showcasing how architecture can harmonize with, rather than confront, natural elements (↔ 3).

The Round House vividly showcases a communal lifestyle where distinctions between private and public realms, children and animals, and nature and culture all seamlessly blend. Echoing Donna Haraway's concept of *natureculture*, where humans and non-humans, nature and culture, co-evolve through mutual interactions, this narrative situates itself within a symbiotic dance of life.[8] Here, the khorovod central to the story symbolizes this interconnectedness, with illustrations depicting the yurt's—both human and non-human—inhabitants engaged in their daily activities within a circular motif, reinforcing the idea of cyclical movements akin to the encompassing wind and snow. (↔ 4) Illustrates a scene where women of various ages partake in domestic chores, a small child and a resting dog by their side, highlighting the communal and integrated existence. Subsequent images show children interacting with deer and dogs, blurring roles and lines of care, emphasizing lives where all living and non-living elements contribute to a harmonious whole deeply rooted in the northern landscape (↔ 5).

5   John McCannon, *Red Arctic: Polar Exploration and the Myth of the North in the Soviet Union, 1932–1939* (Oxford University Press, 1998), 135. See also Paul R. Josephson, *The Conquest of the Russian Arctic* (Harvard University Press, 2014); and Lilya Kaganovsky's "The negative space in the national imagination: Russia and the Arctic," in *Arctic Environmental Modernities: From the Age of Polar Exploration to the Era of the Anthropocene* (2017): 169–182; Tintti Klapuri's "Arctic Norway in the Russian fin-de-siècle imagination: Evgeni Lvov-Kochetov's travelogue out in the Arctic Sea (1895)," in *Nordiques* 37 (2019): 25–36. John McCannon, "To storm the Arctic: Soviet polar exploration and public visions of nature in the USSR, 1932-1939," in *Ecumene 2.1* (1995): 15–31; and Elena Penskaya, "Investigating the Laboratory of Popular Arctic Narrative in Russian Literature from the 1930s to the 1950s," in *Arctic Archives: Ice, Memory and Entropy* 194 (2019), 253.

6   On Arctic architecture in the Soviet Union, see: Ekaterina Kalemeneva, *From New Socialist Cities*; Andy Bruno, *The Nature of Soviet Power: An Arctic Environmental History* (Cambridge University Press, 2016); Fiona Hill and Clifford G. Gaddy, *The Siberian Curse: How Communist Planners Left Russia Out in the Cold*, (Brookings Institution Press, 2003); Julia Lajusia, "In search for Instructive Models: The Russian State at a crossroads to conquering the North," in *Northscapes: History, Technology, and the Making of Northern Environments* (2013): 110–136.

7   Danilov, *The Round House*, 4.

8   Donna J. Haraway, *When Species Meet* (University of Minnesota Press, 2008).

Смолкли песни, стихли пляски,
Дом рассказывает сказки.

В нём всего одна стена,
Очень круглая она.
До того она кругла—
Ни единого угла!

2–5   The Yurt; Children performing a khorovod (round dance); A scene in the yurt; Children with a reindeer and birds. Drawn by A. Borodin in *The Round House* by Semen Danilov (1970).

In the spirit of Haraway's call for making kin,[9] *The Round House* invites us to envision a world beyond an anthropocentric lens, where living together extends to all forms of life. This narrative blurs the lines between categories we often consider distinct and serves as a poignant reminder of our entangled existences. Haraway encourages us to think with the world, not merely within it, fostering a kinship that respects and nurtures all relationships. In this tale, the khorovod, emblematic of life's cyclical and interconnected nature, becomes a metaphor for creating (and sustaining) more inclusive and sustainable ways of cohabiting our shared world, challenging us to reimagine our roles within webs of life.

> *The Round House* does more than tell a story. It is also a microcosm of Arctic life, where communal living is necessary. The narrative's khorovod is a powerful emblem of continuity and kinship, inviting us to dissolve the barriers we often erect between ourselves and the 'other' or hostile nature. As we end the book, we carry with us a renewed understanding of kinship—not about mere connections between humans but as deep bonds that encompass all inhabitants of the Earth. *The Round House* is a narrative that challenges us, regardless of age, to reconsider our place in the vast dance of existence that is life in the Arctic—and, by extension, the world.

FABULOUS URBANISM OF THE SOVIET ARCTIC

The Round House, while not urban in its direct theme, entwines indigenous Arctic living with the structured values of urban Soviet life. It layers themes of cooperation and harmony with those of governance and oversight, reflecting the complex ethos of Soviet society, including its urban aspects. The narrative celebrates the joys of communal life and imparts lessons of collective environmental stewardship and the beauty of shared experiences. Concurrently, the house is personified as a guardian and regulator, a nod to Yi-Fu Tuan's concept of "domination as affection."[10] This idea suggests that acts of shaping, guiding, or controlling an environment or being can sometimes be rooted in caring affection. In *The Round House,* this concept can be seen in how the house itself takes on a protective role, organizing and overseeing its lives, akin to a nurturing yet authoritative figure. The house is "leading a round dance, [...] putting logs into the fire, [...] telling stories, [...] and [...] arranging guests around the table."[11] These phrases are not only expressions of care but also subtle assertions of control, reflecting a duality where guidance is an expression of affection. This embodiment of control, masked as nurturing, mirrors the Soviet sentiment of a benevolent yet authoritative presence in every aspect of communal life, echoing the state's role in the personal spaces of its citizens.

9   Donna J. Haraway, *Staying with the Trouble: Making Kin in the Chthulucene* (Duke University Press, 2016).
10   Yi-Fu Tuan, *Dominance and Affection: The Making of Pets* (Yale University Press, 1984).
11   Danilov, *The Round House.*

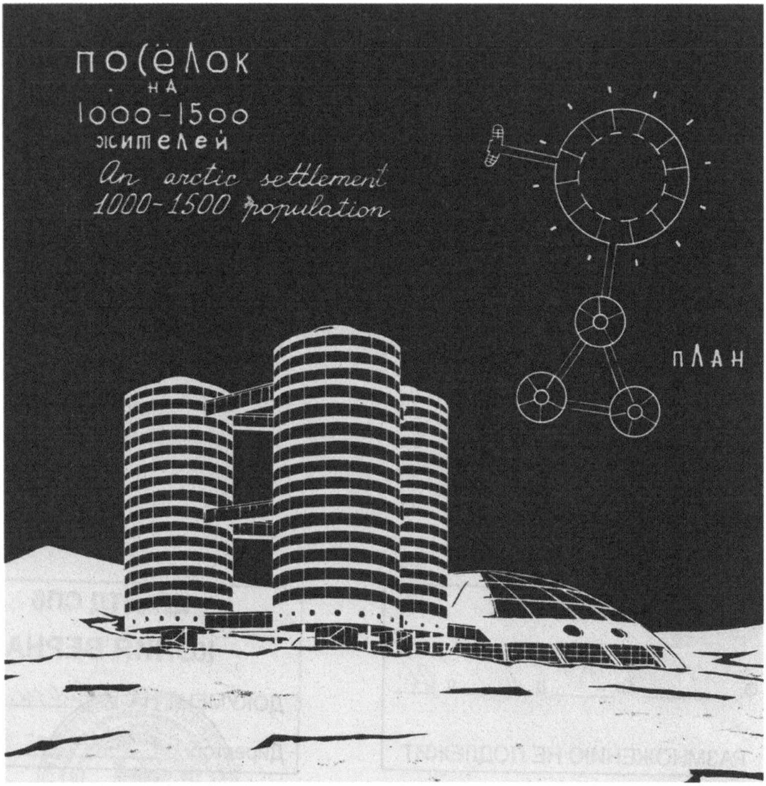

6   The design proposal for the arctic town Amderma by architect Konstantin Agafonov (1960).

7   Arctic town with artificial micro-climate by architect Konstantin Agafonov (1960).

The colonization and industrialization of the Soviet Arctic, from the 1930s through the 1960s, saw the transposition of modernist urban planning into the Arctic's unique context. The motifs of roundness and communal spaces from narratives like *The Round House* found echoes in the urban designs of the period. The transition from wooden houses to multi-story apartment buildings with circular designs to prevent snow accumulation directly responded to the harsh Arctic conditions. The implementation of raised floors to protect permafrost and the creation of roofed galleries as covered streets drew from the narrative's portrayal of a unified and protective community, mirroring the Indigenous philosophy of living harmoniously with nature (↦ 6,7). These designs were functional, aiming to encapsulate the values of warmth, hospitality, and the communal spirit—values also ingrained in Soviet pedagogy and reflected throughout children's literature.[12] The transformation of these values into tangible urban design elements represented the Soviet Union's ideological commitment to forge "normal living conditions" for inhabitants of the Far North. The literature of the time, celebrating Indigenous ways of living and the communal joy of Arctic existence, influenced architects to envision and create urban spaces that facilitated a similar sense of community and interaction despite the formidable climate. This blend of Indigenous wisdom and modernist design in literature helped shape a new urban identity for the Soviet North, one that valued efficiency, communal well-being, and a profound respect for the natural environment.[13]

However, this urban planning also has another side to it. The proposed micro-districts of the Soviet Far North could be seen as a physical manifestation of Bentham's Panopticon.[14] Just as in the Panopticon, where the observer remains unseen, these urban designs suggested a form of omnipresent oversight in alignment with the broader Soviet emphasis on control. The design intended to foster communal living and enable constant vigilance, maintaining the collective ethos. In this sense, the 'openness' of communal spaces was a double-edged sword, offering warmth and connection while also serving as a subtle instrument of surveillance, where 'Big Brother' could theoretically observe all, aligning with the pervasive state presence in individual lives.

12   On Soviet children's literature, see Catriona Kelly's "'Thank-You for the Wonderful Book': Soviet Child Readers and the Management of Children's Reading, 1950–1975," in *Kritika: Explorations in Russian and Eurasian History* 6, no. 4 (2005): 717–53; "Riding the magic carpet: Children and leader cult in the Stalin era," in *The Slavic and East European Journal* 49, no. 2 (2005): 199–224; Jacqueline Marie Olich's *Competing ideologies and children's books: The making of a Soviet children's literature, 1918–1935* (The University of North Carolina at Chapel Hill, 2000); Shirley Petrich, "A Note on Three Contemporary Soviet Children's Stories," in *Children's Literature* 2.1 (1973): 221–23.

13   Kalemeneva, *From New Socialist Cities*, 443.

14   Jeremy Bentham's *Panopticon; or, The Inspection-House* (Thomas Byrne, 1791).

The urban planning of the Soviet Far North remains a narrative as compelling as the story of *The Round House*—a mix of fantasy and pragmatism, communal ideals, and the omnipresent eye of control. It reflects the essence of Fabulous Urbanism, where grand visions of harmony and modernity were crafted yet often remained unrealized due to economic and administrative constraints. These urban plans, much like the tales spun for Soviet children, were meant to inspire and shape perceptions of life in the Arctic. They encapsulate a time when urban spaces were imagined as both a communal embrace and a stage for state surveillance, embodying the complex dance between the individual's aspirations and the collective's oversight. This 'fabulous' urban story, while never fully materialized, lingers as a reminder of a time when urbanism aspired to be as round and encompassing as the narrative dance of the yurt, holding within it the promise of warmth, community, and a watchful eye that guides and protects.

A CONCLUSION

In this text, we navigated the symbolic threshold of the yurt, delving into the fabric of Soviet Arctic Urbanism. *The Round House* emerges not just as a children's tale but as a door to the wider narrative of communal urban Soviet life in the Arctic. It represents 'fabulous urbanism'—an intertwining of imagination and the stark realities of urban planning. Yet, despite the dreams fueled by such narratives, the grandeur of Soviet architectural ambition collided with insurmountable economic and political barriers. This fabulous urbanism—akin to Haraway's call for *staying with the trouble*—remained an unattainable ideal, reflecting the enduring potency of narrative to stir the collective imagination and the enduring difficulty of manifesting such dreams in the face of pragmatic challenges. The tragedy of fabulous urbanism remains a poignant reflection on the narrative of power—to inspire, govern, dream, control, and dominate—even when those dreams prove as ephemeral as the Arctic's fleeting summer.

Caitlin Blanchfield is a historian of architecture and landscape whose work examines the infrastructures of settler colonialism and material practices of resistance.

"If You Do Not Say Anything, You Will Not Be Heard": The Mackenzie Research Institute and Anticolonial Environmental Activism in Inuvik
Caitlin Blanchfield

INUVIK

In June 1956, as the Mackenzie River ice was beginning to break up after the winter freeze, residents of Aklavik—a hamlet home to Inuvialuit, Gwich'in, Métis, and Canadian settlers in a landscape of caribou, cranberries, white fish, and fir—noticed new guests in town. According to the local newspaper, a "wave" of scientists was "inundating" the community.[1] Entomologists sent by the Department of Agriculture and Department of Defense conducted an insect survey and studied biting flies. Anthropologists came up to dig, and the Federal Department of Topographic Surveyors came to map. Many were there to gather knowledge on permafrost. Southern scientists were part of a recent research rush to latitudes that the Canadian government considered under-administered and unproductive—an effort to "redefine the region as *their* territory"[2] through data collection. This was just one of many changes the government agencies were imposing on the town and the lands around it.

As scientists packed up for a summer in the north, many Aklavik residents were in the midst of organizing to move their homes (in some cases literally). The Department of Northern Affairs and National Resources had decided to relocate the village fifty-five miles east to a site it called E-3 (later named Inuvik), which would be a new administrative center for the northern Northwest Territories. Dick Hill, the former mayor of Inuvik and former Director of the Inuvik Research Laboratory, recalled the concerns of then-Canadian Prime Minister

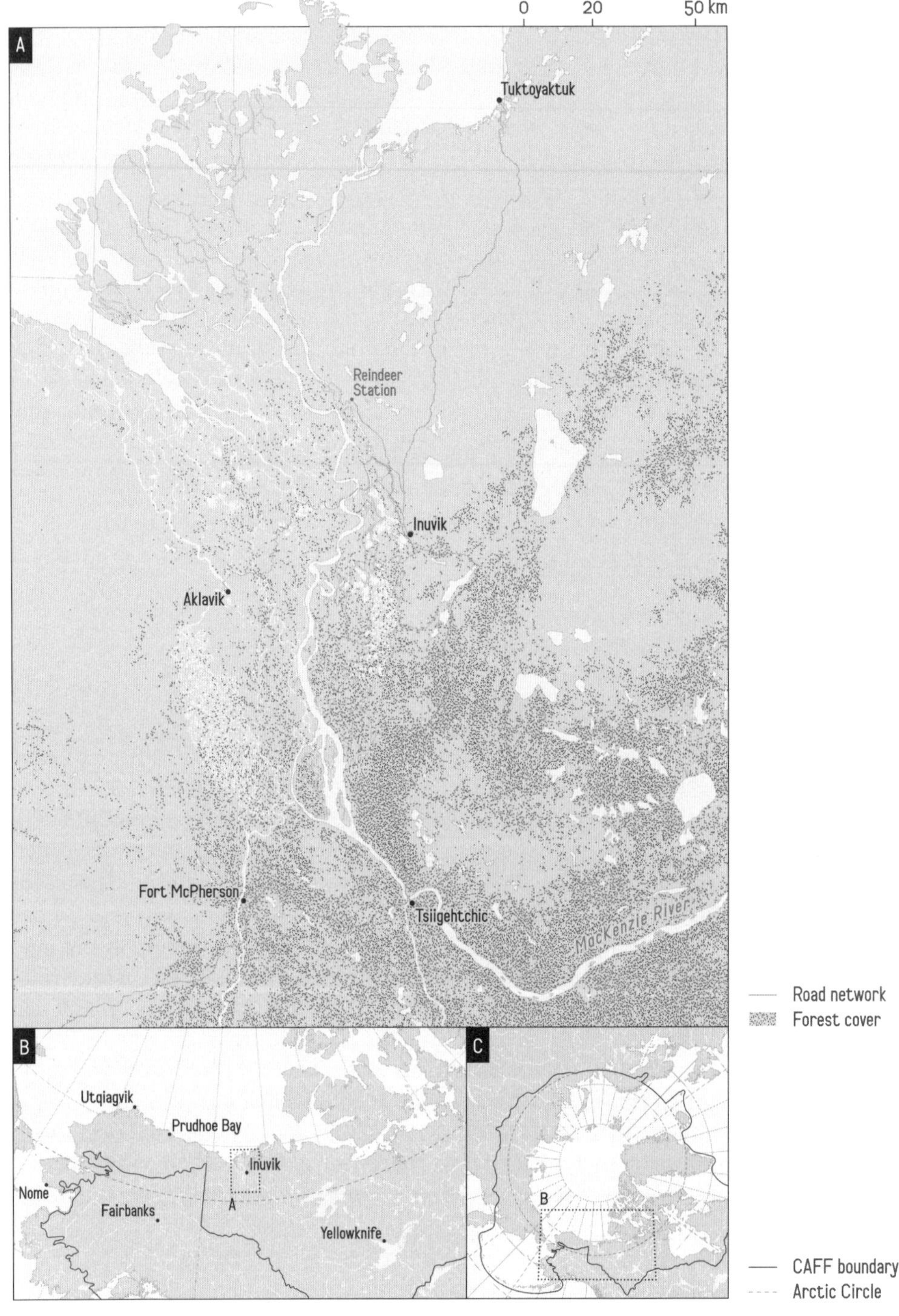

1   Situating the Mackenzie River and the towns of Inuvik and Aklavik (scale 1 : 2,000,000).

Louis St. Laurent: "We have administered these vast territories of the north in an almost continuing state of absence of mind" and the "Security of the North American Continent" was at stake."[3] Aklavik was deemed too muddy to support expansion and too hemmed in by the snaking channels of the Mackenzie River. There was no plumbing because pipes would freeze. Roads were impassable in the summer because the airstrip was too often muddy. E-3 offered a template for new northern development that would be modern, efficient, and suitable for the functions of territorial administration. As a news report put it: "A 20th century community has started to rise from Arctic wastes some 1500 miles north-west of Edmonton."[4] The quotation suggests a kind of civilizing mission in line with nineteenth-century colonial projects. But in the eyes of the engineers who planned it, Inuvik offered more than just the provisions of, as Prime Minister John Diefenbaker said, a "normal Canadian town." It extended modern infrastructure to the Arctic, aiding military systems, such as the Distant Early Warning line station at Tuktoyaktuk, an Inuvialuit settlement on the Arctic coast one hundred and fifty kilometers north of the E3 site.[5]

In its capacity as a modern planned town, Inuvik is symptomatic of the modernization of nineteenth-century settler colonial techniques: here, settlement, segregation, and population management serviced Cold War geopolitics and the extractive industries of postwar consumer culture. Inuvik was an outpost in a geopolitical and scientific frontier, and as geographer Matthew Farish and historian P. Whitney Lackenbauer have written, it was seen as a research laboratory and terrain for "military modernization."[6] Military modernization had to be built. Construction crews would drive pilings twenty feet into the ground to secure foundations while raising utilities above ground in "utilidors" to prevent freezing. These methods reflected the latest in construction on the permafrost, which was a practical consideration for town planners and a terrain of study for Canadian defense research. Town planning was a joint effort of the Defense Research Board and the Department of Northern Affairs and Natural Resources, led by engineer Curtis Merrill.[7] Indeed, Inuvik was

---

1   "Scientists Coming to Aklavik," *Aklavik Journal*, June 1956, 6, in *The Aklavik Journal: A Reprint of the Community Newspaper of Aklavik North West Territories, 1955–57*, ed. Bern Will Brown (Our Lady of the Snows Mission, 1996).

2   Stephen Bocking and Daniel Heidt, "Introduction," in *Cold Science: Environmental Knowledge in the North American Arctic during the Cold War* (Routledge, 2019), 4. Bocking and Heidt note that strategic interest in the Arctic during the Cold War prompted an intensive effort to gather knowledge of the region on the part of the state, even when that knowledge did not seem directly applicable to defense interests.

3   In Dick Hill, *Inuvik: A History* (Trafford, 2005).

4   An article in the *Aklavik Journal* covered the reporting on the "new Aklavik" in an Ottawa-based newspaper. "The New Aklavik," *Aklavik Journal*, February 1956, 6.

5   "Community Profile," Town of Inuvik website.

6   Matthew Farish and P. Whitney Lackenbauer, "High Modernism in the Arctic: Planning Frobisher Bay and Inuvik," *Journal of Historical Geography* 35, no. 3 (July 1, 2009): 517–44.

7   "Biographical History," Northwest Territories Archives, Curtis Merrill Fonds.

2   Inuvik Research Laboratory, Canadian Department of Defense Research and Poole Construction (1968).

an object of much research—both as a testing ground for social and physical planning in northern environments and as a field laboratory for investigations into Arctic climate and geology. Scientific research, colonial development, and geopolitical strategy shaped an urban planning and land use policy that aimed to relocate Indigenous populations while making their territories knowable and controllable. The infrastructures and architectures of urban outposts provided a material substrate for scientific research into northern environments.

Within this context, Inuvik Research Laboratory opened in 1964 to "facilitate northern research by government, university, and industry scientists" and support "technical programs in the Western Canadian Arctic."[8] It was operated by the Northern Co-ordination and Research Centre of the Department of Indian Affairs and Northern Development and featured lab rooms, cold rooms, a workshop, a dark room, a library, offices, storage space, as well as accommodations for researchers, field equipment, camping gear, boats, and snowmobiles.[9] Included in the original plans for Inuvik and built by the Edmonton-based Poole Construction, the lab's architecture followed stylistic and material conventions of the government buildings in town: a two-story timber frame structure built on a foundation of pilings buried ten feet into the permafrost. The lab was one of the first non-residential buildings completed in Inuvik; it was the first permanent scientific research station north of the

Arctic Circle and a prototype for future ones.[10] It was also a node in a campaign to reorganize the North American Arctic through defense and extractive industry research.[11] The facility's design aligned with the modernist ambitions of Inuvik's engineers; its relationship to the surrounding territory facilitated development. Dick Hill, the first director of the research lab—and, later, Inuvik mayor—described the project of modernist progress that his research center was integral to: "Inuvik does incorporate original ideas in design and methods of construction which have proven quite satisfactory. Its modern buildings, planned layout, and complete utility system are all new to Arctic living."[12] "Modern" was a buzzword among northern administrators like Hill, a kind of shorthand for resource extraction and the narratives of social progress that settler agencies like the Department of Northern Affairs used to legitimate their occupation of Indigenous lands. It was imprinted on the land through "planned layouts" and imprinted on residents through their movement in and out of these regulated spaces. The town was, in the words of local historian and native language education coordinator Mike Yip, "conceived by Ottawa bureaucrats and delivered by southern technology and contractors."[13] In this chapter, I examine the Mackenzie Institute as an intervention into the Inuvik Research Laboratory, specifically during the 1971 Man in the North Conference hosted there. By appropriating an architecture of state and industry research for an altogether different kind of institute, the Mackenzie organizers challenged the settler colonial planning of Inuvik and its organization of territory and resources. The institute, I argue, was an opening to anticolonial research methods and agendas, ones that resisted the incorporation of Indigenous ecological knowledge into settler structures. In the Northwest Territories, where land was now valued for resource extraction, the government mobilized use as a means to lay claim to terri-

8   Joy Gareis and Ashely Mercer, "Celebrating the 50th Anniversary of Inuvik Research Laboratory," *InfoNorth* vol. 58, no. 1 (March, 2015): 132; "Inuvik Research Laboratory," *Polar Record* 11, no. 73 (May, 1967): 419.

9   "Inuvik Research Laboratory," 419. Northern Affairs and National Resources was succeeded by Indian Affairs and Northern Development in 1966. "Northern Affairs and National Resources (1953-12-16-196609-30), Parliament of Canada.

10   Gareis and Mercer, "Celebrating the 50th Anniversary of the Inuvik Research Laboratory," 132.

11   There is a robust literature on scientific research and Cold War geopolitical strategy in the Arctic. For more on Cold War Arctic science, see Stephen Bocking and Daniel Heidt (eds), *Cold Science: Environmental Knowledge in the North American Arctic during the Cold War* (Routledge, 2019). On Inuvik specifically, see Matthew Farish and P. Whitney Lackenbauer, "High Modernism in the Arctic: Planning Frobisher Bay and Inuvik," *Journal of Historical Geography* 35, no. 3 (July 1, 2009): 517–44 and Stuhl, *Unfreezing the Arctic.*

12   Richard Hill, "Inuvik: Canadian development in modern arctic living," 1965. NWT Archives/John H. Parker, Ephemera Collection/N-1988-509: 1–3.

13   Mike Yip, *Inuvik* (self-published, 1976), 1.

tory—"modernization" was one visible and quantifiable way to demonstrate use. Yet colonial modernity was tenuous and often undermined by Indigenous politics and knowledge. Modern architecture marked public property in two senses—as property and as that of the state. By thinking with Indigenous counter-mapping and the inscriptions of Gwich'in land use—etched through trails and traplines and articulated in meeting rooms and on the land—I aim to see modern architecture and urban planning differently. This means charting new understandings of the land and its relationship to the built environment, technologies of information and representation, and forms of politics. By looking at histories of contestation over use and of spatial knowledge typically not considered within architectural history, I present an alternative history of modern architecture that antagonizes the authority of the settler state and its operation through the built environment, speaking to both the pluralities and instabilities of modernism in the Arctic.

"Modern," I argue, served in some cases as cover for colonial ineptitudes and run-of-the-mill design solutions; modernization, a reflection of anxious unknowing. This form of modernization extended, quite literally, into the land. What local boosters like Hill, bureaucrats like Gordon Pritchard, and even Prime Minister John Diefenbaker celebrated as particularly modern in Inuvik's Arctic living was the permafrost construction techniques at the town's foundation. Pritchard, who ran the northern construction division in the Department of Public Works, reported in a *Polar Record* article that during the initial years of construction, over 16,500 pilings (mostly timber) were steam jetted and driven, all at a depth of about ten feet.[14] At the time of Pritchard's article, Inuvik was still incomplete. Researchers from the National Research Council were at work addressing permafrost problems—problems caused by the steaming crew's ignorance of subsoil conditions and behavior at varying seasonal temperatures.[15] The Inuvik Research Laboratory was built on top of and for permafrost research. Some of the first journal articles published out of the lab reported on the Research Council's experiments in the town— including stripping moss to provide more drainage (this ended in "more mud") and temperature recordings where pilings had failed.[16] Geographer Mia Bennett has recently argued that the land column and land coverage are crucial in understanding land struggles in the North.[17] The federal government would deploy land categorizations and stratigraphic classifications like surface and subsurface in land claims negotiations in the decades to come, negotiations to which this chapter will soon turn. But even in the 1950s, Inuvik's construction registered colonial attempts to know, control, and operate vertically across land strata. It reveals the racialization of what Indigenous Studies scholar Eve Tuck calls the "false logics of settler colonialism" embedded in surface and subsurface divisions.[18] These false logics, Tuck argues, bend understandings of land to meet the needs of settlers.

And, particularly relevant to construction in Inuvik and the language of modernization that surrounded it, the invention of the subsurface remakes the idea of *terra nullius* a few inches beneath the ground. Building on this idea, I argue that driving foundations into the permafrost was then a way to use architecture to claim the subsurface through technological expertise. The designation of crown land was intended to bring the territory under colonial frameworks of property, the permafrost pilings a means to settle the subsurface and enable extraction from it. What the reports on permafrost construction ignored was Indigenous uses of permafrost for construction and food preservation and the reliance on Indigenous knowledge to build on frozen soil.[19] This is evidenced by reliance on Gwich'in and Inuvialuit knowledge of landscape during the siting of E-3 and Gwich'in and Inuvialuit labor to build the town. It also shows how architecture, at the scale of the building, is put to work in the ordering of territory.[20]

512S

"512s"—512-foot square cabins—were the first structures built on the Inuvik site. They were also called "Eskimo housing," a term that appears informally in articles in the *Aklavik Journal* as well as in the official correspondence of the Department of Northern Affairs and National Resources and the Department of Public Works.[21] Foundation of Canada Engineering Corporation

14   Gordon B. Pritchard, "Inuvik, Canada's New Arctic Town," *Polar Record 11*, no. 71 (May 1962): 145–54.

15   "It became evident, as the work progressed, that permafrost at Inuvik was completely unpredictable, and that subsoil conditions varied at any given point. No set rules could be followed and the pile driving crew had to develop a sixth sense to determine proper steaming time. They soon learned that piles driven in the early spring became frozen-in much more quickly than those placed in October, at the time of maximum thaw." From Gordon B. Pritchard, "Inuvik, Canada's New Arctic Town," 149.

16   G. H. Johnston and R. J. E. Brown, "Stratigraphy of the Mackenzie River Delta, Northwest Territories, Canada," *GSA Bulletin* 76, no. 1 (January 1, 1965): 103–12.

17   Mia M. Bennett, "Gravel Grabs: The Rocky Foundations of Indigenous Geologic Power in the Arctic," *Ambio* 52, no. 7 (July 2023): 1184–97.

18   Eve Tuck, "ANCSA as X-Mark," in *Transforming the University: Alaska Native Studies in the 21st Century*, eds. Beth Ginondidoy Leonard, Jeane Ta'aw xíwaa Breinig, Lenora Ac'aralek Carpluk, Sharon Chilux Lind, and Maria Shaa Tláa Williams (Two Harbors Press, 2014), 252.

19   On the uses of permafrost historically by Gwich'in and Inuvialuit communities see *Gwich'in Traditional Knowledge: Rat River Dolly Varden Char* (Gwich'in Renewable Resources Board, 2010). Karen Gardner, "An Arctic Village is Reclaiming Its Indigenous Architecture," *Sierra*, August 30, 2022.

20   While the analysis of residential schools is not within the scope of this chapter, I want to point to the important work of Crystal Gail Fraser on this topic. In her dissertation, Fraser discusses how Grollier and Stringer Halls, the two residential schools in Inuvik, were designed to be architecturally and educationally "modern." This so-called modernity had two intentions: to provide cover for the residential school system after much scrutiny over the abuse that occurred within it, and to make Inuvik a regional administrative hub. See Crystal Gail Fraser, *T'aih k'ìighe' tth'aih zhit diidich'üh (By Strength, We Are Still Here): Indigenous Northerners Confronting Hierarchies of Power at Day and Residential Schools in Nanhkak Thak (the Inuvik Region, Northwest Territories), 1959 to 1982* (PhD diss., University of Alberta, 2019).

21   *Aklavik Journal*. Letter from R.G. Robertson, Deputy Minister, Department of Northern Affairs and Natural Resources to Major General H.A. Young, Deputy Minister, Department of Public Works, November 21, 1955. Gordon Robertson Fonds, National Library and Archives Canada.

3   The five-hundred-twelve-square-foot cabins, aka 512's, pictured here in Inuvik, were built in 1956.

(FENCO), the company contracted by Canada's Department of Public Works, devised and planned three residential groups for the Inuvik site: Group A, the majority of which was government housing, would have water, sewers, and electricity, as well as central heating. Group B was provided with water, sewers, electricity, and plumbing fixtures to install at least one tap and toilet. Group C had electricity only.[22]

The 512s, initially used as temporary workers' housing, were to become permanent homes for Inuvialuit, Gwich'in, and Métis residents who had been relocated from Aklavik. "With the closing down of the various construction camps," Pritchard described, "the small cabins that had been the first buildings erected were hauled on their skids to their final locations amid the spruce and birch trees on a high shelf overlooking Twin Lakes and the East Channel of the Mackenzie River. Most of them have now been permanently located in this area. They have been cleaned up, painted, and with partitions and kitchens added, have become the permanent homes of the Eskimos who helped to build Inuvik."[23] These became Group C, located on the west side of town. Residents' recollections were not so euphemistic. Tom Wright, who had come to Inuvik in 1955 with his father and brothers to work, described how the town was divided along Reliance Street: "From that side on it was Natives and from this side it was white people."[24] During Inuvik's early years, Wright recalled, houses on the Native side weren't hooked up to the water and sewage line;

it was only later that these utilities reached them. Mike Yip's local history also critiqued the town planning as systematically racist: "When Inuvik was built there was no provision for adequate native housing and the west end of town became an instant slum with substandard crowded houses and no running water or sewers."[25] The 512 typology and grouping of houses around access to infrastructure enacted a colonial form of modernism. Standardized measurements provided what was considered the minimum requirements to house a family. Delaying utility hookups meant that the government did not have to pay for what was an expensive plumbing system and reinforced the colonial idea that Native people needed time to develop into modern living. Yet oral histories describe the urbanization of Inuvik and the processes for bringing housing there in ways that completely bypass the government plan for the 512s. Prior to the 512s, during the initial construction of Inuvik, many residents lived in tents. Oral history from Annie Benoit describes the construction of these tents in relation to the landscape, offering a language of architecture that foregrounds the land. She also recalls how her home was transported from Aklavik to Inuvik, circumventing the government's desire to control how the town was ordered and built: "Lots of willow and they got their chainsaw and started cutting. That time there were lots of blueberries around there. Not now, no berries there now…. Around where the hospital is now, I pick cranberries there. I come back with a big sack of cranberries. Now it's not very clean there with oil and dirt and stuff… We stayed there for three years, we lived in a tent frame. Lots of people live in the tent frame at that time. Then Fred Norris pulled a house over from Aklavik for us."[26] Knowledge of the land, the plants, and the forms of life they supported was also at the heart of debates over the environment and the role of town planning in it, which took place at the Mackenzie Institute at the Inuvik Research Lab in the late 1960s and early 1970s.

THE MACKENZIE INSTITUTE

The Mackenzie Institute had a short run. Operating from 1968 to 1972 out of the Inuvik Research Laboratory, it began as an adult education program, a kind of community college with courses relevant to residents of the Mackenzie Delta. The institute was initiated by Agnes Semmler and Victor Allen, both of whom would go on to help found the Committee for Original People's Entitle-

22   "Description of 1956 Re-siting of Aklavik," Record Number R216, RG85-D-1-A, National Library and Archives Canada.

23   Gordon Pritchard, "Inuvik, Canada's New Arctic Town," *Polar Record* 11, no. 71 (May 1962): 145–154.

24   From an interview with Tom Wright, Inuvik, Northwest Territories, April 27, 2023.

25   Yip, *Inuvik*. See also "COPE: An Original Voice for Inuvialuit Rights," Inuvialuit Regional Corporation, irc.

26   In McCartney and Gwich'in Tribal Council, *Our Whole Gwich'in Way of Life Has Changed*, 134.

ment (COPE); Elijah Menarik, future host of the first Inuktitut television show; John Pascal, member of the Delta Community Action Program and Gwich'in language radio host; Richard Hill, director of the Inuvik Research Lab; and Ian Butters, editor of the *Inuvik Drum*.[27] Its founders reoriented the colonial space of the laboratory by inserting themselves in the lab and changing how it was used, opening a regimented architecture planned around and for expertise and siloed knowledge into a place of political organizing, negotiation, and daily life (uses included a daycare, vet clinic, and public library). As an institute nested within a space that otherwise served the extractive industry and military knowledge production, it shows the tensions and instability in the modernist project for the North, where institutions whose mandate was to modernize were not as monolithic as they presented themselves to be in reports or to the public; where bottom-up projects could challenge spatial classifications and research agendas. Its dissolution in 1972 marks the entrenchment of development ideas within the lab on the one hand and the creation of purposeful anticolonial spaces of political organizing for land rights and protection by Gwich'in and Inuvialuit groups on the other. As companies like Imperial Oil and Dome Petroleum began exploring the region and the federal government began collecting lease payments, the Mackenzie Institute's Delta Environmental Project started to lay out the stakes of the environment, how it was understood, and by whom. Launched in 1970, the Environmental Project was a communications campaign by the institute to inform Delta residents about the actions of the petroleum industry in the region and their impacts on the land, wildlife, and people.

> The institute operated in the physical space of the research lab (where lab operations also continued), but it was a diffuse organization—meeting in schools, the library, private homes, and through various communication outlets like television, radio, and print media. Thus, it undermined the division between the laboratory inside and the community beyond its walls. It was a collaboration between Indigenous activist groups, a research facility with ties to military and industry, and scientists critical of oil and gas development. As such, it became a space of contestation over the Mackenzie Delta environment itself: what knowledge of the environment was and what it would be used for. In its four years, the institute hosted conflicting and ultimately diverging visions of landscape, research, and the politics of knowledge. Ideas of use and impact were crucial in how the environment was represented for those in the institute and the political organizations they would go on to form.

Rose Mary Thrasher, project lead, solicited local input in the *Delta Newsletter*. "The main emphasis of this project," she wrote, "is the petroleum projects and how it affects the land, wildlife, and Delta residents." Information and ideas were gathered through interviews with local residents, petroleum workers, government officials, and researchers to create what she called an overall picture of the Mackenzie Delta environment, while findings were presented in group discussions, radio reports, tapes, and on TV. She closed her letter with a call for involvement: "IF YOU DO NOT SAY ANYTHING, YOU WILL NOT BE HEARD!!!!"[28] Thrasher's pitch represents several aspects of the institute: its focus on bringing the voices of those who lived on the land to conversations about development in the delta and the ambivalent positions of its members on that development. Delta residents, frustrated by how oil companies and government agencies failed to consult with them, saw research as a means of access to information, economic resources, and power.[29] The environmental project was a means to control decisions over what would happen on Indigenous land in the North. Bureaucrats and social scientists, however, had a different vision of the institute and its potential.

> Lab director Dick Hill summarized the Mackenzie Institute more instrumentally. It would, he said, provide a "local balance for regional developments associated with the future production of oil and gas in the area. [...] Operating under the frontier concept of satisfying today's needs with available resources the Mackenzie Institute contributes to total education so that more Northerners may take their rightful place in social, cultural, and economic developments as full citizens of the North, of Canada, and of the World."[30] Hill's description aligns with a frontier mentality that viewed resource extraction as inevitable and social development necessary for Indigenous northerners to assimilate as citizens of Canada. Thrasher's newsletter, however, suggests a more critical ambition, one that would intensify as oil and gas exploration increased in the coming years. Already in 1968, the environment project responded to the "real concerns" hunters and trappers had about prospecting on their lands.

This was not simply a desire to bring local balance to its inevitable production. Tensions between development-oriented ideas about the environment implicit in Hill's language of "local balance" and the real concerns Thrasher alludes to came to a head at the "Man in the North: Conference on Community Development" co-organized in 1970 by the Mackenzie Institute and the Arctic Institute of North America (AINA). AINA was chartered at McGill University in 1945 to "advance the objective study of Arctic conditions and problems." Arctic problems have a long colonial history. At the Inuvik Research Lab, permafrost was one of them. As scholars like Jen Rose Smith have argued, during the eighteenth and nineteenth centuries, the Arctic's ice geographies

27   Amanda Graham, "The University That Wasn't: University of Canada North, 1970–1985," MA thesis, Lakehead University, 1994, 23.

28   Rose Mary Thrasher's call gives this chapter its title. From Thrasher's text, "Mackenzie Delta Environmental Project," *Delta Newsletter* no. 1, August 1970. From the personal collection of Dick Hill.

29   Stuhl, *Unfreezing the Arctic.*

30   Dick Hill, "Concepts Proposal for a Beaufort Institute," July 28, 1969. From the personal collection of Dick Hill.

DELTA NEWSLETTER

No.1 August 1970   **MACKENZIE DELTA ENVIRONMENTAL PROJECT**

PETROLEUM ACTIVITIES IN THE DELTA

The MacKenzie Delta Environmental Project is a communication program to keep in touch with the residents of the MacKenzie Delta about present government and petroleum activities so that they can be more involved in the 'action'. The main emphasis of the project is on the petroleum programs and how it affects the land, wildlife, and the Delta residents.

The MacKenzie Delta region includes Arctic Red River, Fort McPherson, Aklavik, Inuvik and Tuktoyaktuk. Information and ideas are being gathered from local residents, government officials and researchers, and patroleum people so that an overall picture can be made on the MacKenzie Delta environment. We will present these ideas to you through the forms of personal interviews, group discussions, radio reports, tapes and T.V. recordings. With this program it is hoped that everyone will better understand what is happening in their area and how they might have a share in what is happening.

During the past few years oil exploration programs have closed in on the North. We have here, a project underway called 'MacKenzie Delta Environmental Project.' Our aim is that we can bring you up-to-date information on what is going on in oil explorations, government, and thoughts and ideas of the local people in Inuvik and the surrounding area.

The oil companies seem to be co-operative and interested in the location of traplines so that they can do less harm and not disturb the traplines. Several of the local residents are employed on seismic and drilling and seem to be thankful that there are jobs available for them.

Activities of well drilling going on in the MacKenzie Delta area; Blow River, by Imperial Oil, at the depth of 8,000 feet plus; Shell Oil, approximately 6 miles north of Aklavik, at the dppth of 3,000 feet plus; Banff Oil, 15 miles southwest of Aklavik, which is just being set up; also in the area are thirteen summer seismic programs.

If there is real concern, and I know there is, I am willing, with the MacKenzie Institute, which is independent of government and oil companies, to help you bring your messages across to them, and also to bring you up-to-date news on what is happening. So we urge you to get involved. Ideas can be valuable. IF YOU DO NOT SAY ANYTHING, YOU WILL NOT BE HEARD!!!!

Till I hear from you, I remain.

Sincerely yours

Rose Mary Thrasher

MACKENZIE INSTITUTE BOX 1430 INUVIK, N.W.T. ROSEMARY THRASHER
PROJECT LEADER
PRO?

4   The Mackenzie Environmental Project in the Delta Newsletter (1970).

confounded Western natural historians and settler-colonists, who saw the materiality of the land and the people as problems to be overcome in pursuit of resources and territory.[31] This antagonistic understanding was succeeded by biophysical permafrost problems and social problems that conferences like MIN were meant to address. Both brought the military-industrial-academic complex north.

> For its first few decades, AINA's financial grants came from the Canadian War Technical Committee, federal, state, and provincial governments, the petroleum industry, and the US Office of Naval Research.[32] Oil and gas companies and the US and Canadian military funded the Arctic Institute in the hopes that they would benefit from its research. The conference on community development can be understood in this light as part of an effort to bring about "the orderly development of the North" and advance natural and social knowledge towards that end.[33] It also reflects an interest among social scientists in studying the profound and devastating impacts of colonization on Native communities in the North. Of course, not every social scientist affiliated with AINA promoted the developmental theories at the institution's foundations. And those who partnered and participated with them definitely did not. AINA organizers who had conceived of the Man in the Arctic program had only reached out to Northern residents and the Mackenzie Institute afterward. The institute, Gwich'in, and Inuvialuit participants involved, however, intervened in the conference to bring up a conversation omitted from the program: land.

After a closed meeting on Friday, the Saturday session was turned over from civic administration and employment to a series of topics the delegates—all Gwich'in and Inuvialuit—had determined were of utmost importance. The first was "who owns the land." Charlie Abel, Gwich'in chief from Old Crow, opened the Saturday meeting, stating his opposition to the pipeline proposed through the Yukon Territory. Development, if it happened at all, must wait until the people's right to the land had been affirmed. COPE closed the meeting by proposing a petition in support of Chief Abel and in opposition to the pipeline, which was to be sent to the federal government.[34] These were the urgencies that Thrasher had been hearing from trappers in Inuvik and surrounding communities. Mackenzie Institute delegates continued to reorient the conference format by holding workshops at the close of each day on the

31   See Smith, "Exceeding Beringia," Stuhl, *Unfreezing the Arctic*, and Rafico Ruiz, *Slow Disturbance: Infrastructural Mediation on the Settler Colonial Resource Frontier* (Duke University Press, 2021).

32   Robert MacDonald, "Challenges and Accomplishments: A Celebration of the Arctic Institute of North America," *Arctic* 58, no. 4 (December 2005): 443.

33   Lize-Marié van der Watt, Peder Roberts, and Julia Lajus, "Institutions and the changing nature of Arctic research during the early Cold War," in Bocking and Heidt, *Cold Science*, 197.

34   Ibid.

conference itself, conducted in Gwich'in and Inuvialuit.[35] COPE's membership overlapped with the Mackenzie Institute; the Inuvik Research Lab was one site—among several in town—it had used, but COPE was decidedly more political: it was founded in response to the government's permitting of test wells behind the backs of the Gwich'in and Inuvialuit, and it was organized with the aim of giving a voice to Native northerners and realizing Native rights.[36] Environment for COPE was a relationship to land, the health of the land, and the ability to use it; it was a political category inseparable from life and livelihood. Delegates saw oil and gas prospecting as a threat to both self-determination and to their environment.

> Urban development in Inuvik was also out of step with the northern environment and the rights of Native northerners that COPE sought to establish and protect. Speaking to the segregation of Inuvik housing and services, the conference report summarized, "It was stated in the workshops that proper housing should be a right," and a person's position in the community should not decide this quality of housing. It went on to say that people should be consulted about the kind of houses that would suit both their needs and the environment.[37] Further, delegates suggested that a minimum standard of housing should be established, expressing that 512s and prefabricated houses were too cold and small and were designed for utilities such as plumbing and electricity that were not available to residents. By raising the right to housing suited to the northern environment, delegates advanced the idea of an environment not altogether separate from the urban landscape. They did so within a political framework that reflected the well-being of the people and calibrated the relationship between planning and building a town like Inuvik and land dispossession. To talk of rights to land was also to talk of the material realities of how delegates lived on it.

Political theorist Glen Coulthard critiques the developmentalism of an institution like AINA within a critical Marxist analysis of colonial dispossession. He shows that, when understood as a product of colonialism and primitive accumulation, developmentalism is simply a brutal onslaught onto non-capitalist, non-Western, Indigenous modes of life.[38] Against this history, he poses a tradition of Indigenous anticolonial, anticapitalist thought. "The theory and practice of Indigenous anticolonialism," he argues, "is best understood as a struggle primarily inspired by and oriented around the *question of land*."[39] It is a politics that comes from and aims to protect a sense of place and understanding of land as a "field of relations" of things to one another. Coulthard's theorization comes out of his critical history of the land claims process between the Dene Nation and the Canadian government—a process in which both his community, the Yellowknives Dene, and the Gwich'in participated. Dene land claim struggle, of which Gwich'in Mackenzie Institute members played a key part, is one site of anticolonial Indigenous politics.

Abel's speech, the COPE petition, and the reorientation of the Man in the North Conference should be read through an anticolonial framework. Indeed, these events were part of the groundwork for land claim struggles that would come a few years later.

A memorandum just following the conference shows that AINA organizers knew about the importance of land rights to the communities they were seeking to develop but still had not included it on the agenda—nor did they support it.[40] Executive Director Kenneth de la Barre called the demands for Native land ownership and the cessation of oil and mineral exploration and development "unreasonable,"[41] reflecting the agenda of the AINA conference organizers, which was to create a conducive environment for the government to operate in the North. Since the 1950s, Canadian government officials have used technical assistance programs and modernization as a means to assimilate Indigenous northerners and open their lands to capitalist production. This was an extension of the country's long history of colonization and attendant racist ideology, as well as its own involvement in postwar foreign aid, particularly to other nations in the British Commonwealth.[42] De la Barre's hostile response to calls for Indigenous land rights was aligned with the Canadian government's hostility toward the growing political presence of Global South countries on the world stage, expressed in Prime Minister John Diefenbaker's dismay at the inclusion of "Third World" nations at the UN Habitat conference in Vancouver in 1976.[43]

35   Ibid.

36   Nellie Cournoyea described the group's origins and aims: "We functioned as a group of activists, with links to the eastern Arctic, the southern Mackenzie and the central Arctic. It was unusual in those days, and disconcerting to the newly formed GNWT. The Commissioner appointed most of his officials. He had his plan, to set up hamlet councils and institutions, to set direction for the programs and services that would be brought in. And we had questions about whether his institutions had the right to make these decisions. We established COPE because government only seemed to want to deal with institutions that were incorporated or legal bodies." During the first two years of its operation, COPE was a joint organization of Inuit and Dene in the Arctic. By around 1972, the Inuit Tapirisat represented the Inuit of the Eastern Arctic, the IB-NWT the Dene and Métis of the Northwest Territories, and COPE the Inuvialuit. See Inuvialuit Regional Corporation, *COPE: An Original Voice for Inuvialuit Rights*, IRC.

37   Elizabeth Bell, Doug Brown, Eric Gourdeau, and Addy Tobac, *The Man in the North Conference on Community Development Report* (The Arctic Institute of North America, 1971), 12.

38   Glen Sean Coulthard, *Red Skins, White Masks: Rejecting the Colonial Politics of Recognition* (Minneapolis: University of Minnesota Press, 2014), 90.

39   Ibid.

40   Kenneth de la Barre, "Memorandum of Record from Executive Director," December 2, 1970, Library and Archives Canada, MG28-179, vol. 131.

41   Ibid.

42   For more on the intersection of Canadian developmentalism in the North and international foreign aid see David Meren, "'Commend me the Yak': The Colombo Plan, the Inuit of Ungava, and 'Developing Canada's North,'" *Histoire Sociale* 50, no. 102.

43   Felicity Scott, *Outlaw Territories: Environments of Insecurity/Architectures of Counterinsurgency* (Zone Books, 2016), 228.

The Mackenzie Institute delegates challenged this agenda over the coming decade. Gwich'in participants in the Mackenzie Institute contested colonial definitions of land use and environment in their approaches to negotiating a land claim agreement with the Canadian government. They did so under intense pressure from the federal government to domesticate political claims to nationhood and self-determination.[44]

> The Dene Declaration, issued in 1976, called for dismantling colonialism and imperialism, the right to self-determination, and solidarity with the anticolonial struggles of the Third World. The declaration was an Agreement-in-Principle that called for Dene political and economic autonomy and renegotiated terms for their relationship with the state through a legal claim to the land of Denendeh (Dene homelands) from Canada. The political structure of the Dene government was the subject of research undertaken by the Indian Brotherhood, as was Dene land use, which would back its land claim through the Dene Mapping Project—a cartographic project to demonstrate land occupancy for the legal claim with the Canadian government.[45] This kind of research for self-determination, I argue, was cultivated by the work of the Mackenzie Environmental Project, as were the ways it was simultaneously confined by, yet exceeded, settler colonial institutions.

Phoebe Nahanni, the Dene geographer from Fort Good Hope who had led the research for the Dene Mapping Project, attended the MIN conference as a community development specialist. She was there alongside Gwich'in community members who would go on to play a role in the Dene and Gwich'in claims, such as William Macdonald, Hyacinthe Andre, Mary Kendi, and Edward Nazon. In 1977, writing on the land use and occupancy research she had directed, Nahanni critiqued social science research practices. Theorizing a Dene research methodology, she centered the land use of trappers as an anticolonial politics of land, much like Abel had and like Coulthard discusses: "We know from our past experiences that government research by white researchers has never improved our lives. Usually white researchers spy on us, the things we do, how we do them, when we do them, and so on. After all these things are written in their jargon they go away and neither they nor their reports are ever seen again."[46] The mapping project was different. Research initiated by the IB-NWT was conducted by Dene fieldworkers with the specific aim of providing evidence for self-determination and control over territory. The project also documented the true costs of development on the land, animals, plants, and people.

> Land use and occupancy studies were imposed on land claimants by the federal government—an exercise in having to prove that Native lands were Native lands in terms set out by the colonial government. They required time and money and, because they were addressed to the federal government or courts, the use of colonial

structures in how land was discussed, represented, and understood. Tom Andrews, an anthropologist who worked on the mapping project, recalled, "It was a hoop that the other government forced Indigenous people to jump through, spending years and hundreds of thousands of dollars collecting all of this information and just to be able to sit at one meeting with a white negotiator and have him point at a map and say, show me the land use for that particular [place]."[47] However, in spite of these constraints, land use studies affirmed aboriginal land rights, enacted Indigenous research methodologies, and had meaning outside of their legal role. They also undermined colonial standards of representation and language. "Land use"—a way of classifying land within modern land management regimes that has roots in colonial notions of private property and "improvement" through agricultural use—is not only a colonial category. Use is also part of how Dene and Gwich'in land relations are understood. In an interview with Nahanni, Willie Macdonald of Fort McPherson explained: "We know that long before us this country been used lots and long time before that. People still using it. I mean the people that were brought up to the life of hunting and trapping. We belong to it. We belong to the land and we look at it like that land is our mother."[48] This kind of land use constitutes the field of relations of things to each other that Coulthard theorizes and situates that relation in an intellectual tradition of belonging rather than of ownership. Use was a way of talking about history, belonging, and way of life that translated into the cartographic methodology and concepts of environment. Nahanni explained how the mapping project showed not just the use that the government required for the land claim but also how use, its impression on the land, and its entanglement with the environment were already under threat by development: "That the proposed oil and gas pipeline routes and construction sites conflict with our land-based activities is obvious in the cartographic representation of those activities. These routes show no sign of regard for our trails, travel routes, trap lines and our camps. The implications of such intrusions not only affect the trails, travel routes, and traplines; they also indiscriminately and without discretion affect the animals, fish lakes, and the environment and our way of life."[49]

44   Coulthard, 67.

45   Ibid.

46   Phoebe Nahanni, "The Mapping Project," *Dene Nation: The Colony Within* (University of Toronto Press, 1977), 27.

47   Interview with Tom Andrews, via Zoom, April 3, 2023. This was when the Dene Nation's geographic information system was put to use.

48   Ibid., 21.

49   Ibid., 27.

Trails, travel routes, and trap lines were forms of use that produced knowledge of the land and defined what the land itself was. These lines of movement were part of the environment—along with the animals and the fish lakes—that the pipeline would impact. Mapping, while a constraint imposed by the federal government, was also a means to represent the environment in Dene terms, as established in the literature on counter cartography. And, as discussed in the opening to this chapter, the demands of representing the intensity of Dene land use pushed forward cartographic science in Canada. Andrews again recalls how the mapping project's geographic information system was used during the land claim negotiations: "When the federal negotiator asked this question of the Dene [regarding a specific place], I would run downstairs and run the computer and plot a map and bring it back upstairs to be able to prove that the Dene had, in fact, used that spot."[50]

Maps show a web of overlapping, intersecting lines around Fort McPherson, a Gwich'in community south of Inuvik on the Peel River. They vary in length, some straight and some winding, all branching off the Mackenzie and Peel Rivers. Instead of property ownership, which would divide land into discrete boundaries, this land use was imbricated and environmental, with movement layered in time and over space. The cartographic process included annotating 1:250,000 scale maps that were then taped together into a "map mosaic."

Colored lines with directional arrows marked trap lines and trails of different families; symbols stood in for fish camps, cabins, burial areas, hunting grounds, and species harvested. Accompanying the map mosaic was a map biography detailing the movements of the trapper being interviewed across their life and the land. It also included a "comment on land settlement." Christopher Colin of Fort McPherson, eighty-eight years old at the time of the interview and present during the 1921 signing of Treaty 11, opposed the pipeline being rushed through before the land claim process. He also reflected on the relationship between the pipeline and government use of the land, contrasting it to Gwich'in land use. "We don't make use of this land from the ground," he said, "taking out different minerals. Now, only now, the government and different kinds of oil companies are making use of it. And then they're living good from them, but we don't get nothing out of it, no money."[51] Colin's statement reveals the government's strategy of holding crown land in reserve until a productive use could be found for it, and it differentiates Gwich'in land use from the extractive use of government and industry that divided the land from the ground. The government would mobilize this distinction in a strategy to keep a hold on land title during the land claim negotiation.

Through methods of research and cartography, land claims research and mapping subverted norms around land use and its representation common to colonial planning processes. Land use would have zoned surface and subsurface for extraction, as well as infrastructure like roads, pipelines, and radar stations under the mantle of crown lands. The Inuvik Research Laboratory (and its position within the administrative hub of Inuvik) was created as part of the organizational and informational system that made such a vision of land use possible. Gwich'in land use offered an understanding of land and mobility that foregrounded knowledge through oral history and interdependence with environmental cycles, plants, and animals, as well as a non-extractive, non-militarized future orientation.

In addition, it can be read through the research lab itself. Today, the Inuvik Research Lab (now the Western Arctic Research Centre), but also environmental research more broadly, is incorporating things like traditional ecological knowledge into its work—bringing this knowledge into the laboratory walls and its structures of funding, acquiring, and disseminating information. The Mackenzie Institute and the movements that came out of it offer a history of how power relations might be reconfigured through the spaces and places of environmental research. Instead of fitting Indigenous knowledge into colonial architectures, the intervention of the Mackenzie Institute into the Man in the North conference and its afterlives shows how environmental knowing can unsettle and exceed the structures of settler colonialism, which will be necessary as these communities address the climate crisis.

50   Interview with Andrews. See also Mark P. Stoller and Thomas D. Andrews, "Mapping Denendeh: The Dene Mapping Project and the Enduring Legacy of Indigenous Cartographies," in *Just Relations: Anthropology and Law in Canada*, ed. Joshua Smith and Robert P. Wishart (University of Alberta Press, forthcoming). In this article Andrews and Stoller describe how the GIS system worked: "Two teams undertook the data entry: One team working at night at the University's computing department digitized the trails, breaking them into numbered segments. These were plotted on paper and sent with the original map to the Department of Anthropology the next morning, where another team verified that the trails had been digitized correctly. The team then entered the corresponding land use information including basic biographical information of the informant, years that the trail segments were used, mode of travel, species sought, and other data, on 80-column coding sheets to be transferred later to punch cards and entered into the GIS system. The teams spent more than two years digitizing and coding the trails and land use data. The result of this effort was a digital data set of four megabytes of trails and land use information... at the time it stretched the limits of the mainframe computing facility at the University of Alberta."

51   Christopher Colin in *Repatriating Gwich'in Traditional Knowledge from the Dene Mapping Project*, prepared by Randy Freeman, Down North Consulting for the Gwich'in Social and Cultural Institute, 2006.

Lasse Rau is a PhD student in architectural history and theory at the Columbia University Graduate School of Architecture, Planning and Preservation (GSAPP).

Urbanisms of Refusal: Indigeneity and Land in Alaska
Lasse Rau

Empire is the constant failure to dispossess the other. During the second half of the twentieth century, the national governments of the United States and Canada actively incorporated definitions of indigenous identity into regional development projects by tethering them to Native land ownership.[1] The systems of property and ownership of land in North America are colonial and were fashioned precisely to remove land from the use value of indigenous peoples. By making land measurable, transferable, and improvable, the parcel remains an integral tool through which indigenous lives are governed and dispossessed of land and its resources.[2]

In Alaska, the push for statehood in the 1950s and the petrochemical development launched in 1968 emphasized the lack of a formalized land tenure system for broad swaths of the state claimed by more than two hundred tribes. Although the ethnonym 'Alaska Natives'— a heterogeneous group with competing values and goals and different levels of attachment to people, places, and things—was commonly used since the purchase of the region by the United States in 1867, it was only with the extinguishing of indigenous land claims in 1971 that its identity became legally homogenized and made synonymous with land entitlement.[3] In contrast to the historical legal contracts that other American indigenous land movements were forced to navigate, tribal land in Alaska remained untreatied. Previous settler-colonial endeavors in Alaska had, for the most part, circumvented the issue of land claims.[4] Albeit colonized, the territory of Alaska had not ceased to be primarily organized through precolonial relations to land in which traplines and fishing practices acted as temporary claims to land use, never to land itself. In legal terms, this signified that Alaska Natives could not base their claims on historical contracts that defined their historical land use and protected their current land titles. Instead, indigenous land in Alaska was considered public domain.[5]

Conventional accounts of the indigenous land claims struggle in Alaska, initiated in the late 1960s in response to the discovery of oil in the North Slope and concluded in 1971 with the Alaska Native Claims Settlement Act (ANCSA), describe the legal process of land settlement as a constitutional negotiation between a homogenous Native constituency, state and federal policymakers, and oil corporations.[6] Its outcome constituted a legal framework that redefined land ownership for broad swaths of the state, parceled 44 million acres of indigenous land into private property held by regional and local Native corporations and, through it, abolished cultural claims based on Native land use and constructed a private Native sector. This seemed to represent a success for both oil firms and Alaska Natives in that it allowed for the development of 'underutilized' lands while at the same time empowering indigenous groups. The claim borrowed from a discourse of land improvement through parceling, extraction, and development that reduced the use value of land to monetizable practices of cultivation and real estate.[7] Cultural, educational, and environmental values of Native land were nullified. Ultimately, the land settlement enabled the operation of an oil field at Prudhoe Bay in the North Slope and the construction of an 800-mile-long pipeline transporting oil to the southern Alaska coast owned by the Alyeska Pipeline Service Company—a consortium of oil companies with drilling rigs in Prudhoe Bay.

ANCSA prompted economic prosperity, cultural production, and political emancipation by expanding investment in Native-led museums, artistic venues, and businesses such as hotels and casinos.

1 Duane Champagne, Karen Jo Torjesen, and Susan Steiner, eds., *Indigenous Peoples and the Modern State,* Contemporary Native American Communities 14 (AltaMira Press, 2005). The anthropologist played a key role in the reification of indigenous identity as economic, monetizable culture. The reliance of this article on anthropological studies and concepts does not in any way unburden the discipline from its imbrication in colonial practices of dispossession.

2 See Brenna Bhandar, *Colonial Lives of Property: Law, Land, and Racial Regimes of Ownership*, Global and Insurgent Legalities (Duke University Press, 2018).

3 On nineteenth and early twentieth century Alaska indigenous identity, see Terrence M. Cole, "Jim Crow in Alaska: The Passage of the Alaska Equal Rights Act of 1945," *The Western Historical Quarterly* 23, no. 4 (1992): 429–49.

4 David S. Case, David Avraham Voluck, and David A. Voluck, *Alaska Natives and American Laws*, Third edition (University of Alaska Press, 2012), 24–25.

5 Robert D. Arnold, *Alaska Native Land Claims* (Alaska Native Foundation, 1978).

6 See, for example, Mary Clay Berry, *The Alaska Pipeline: The Politics of Oil and Native Land Claims* (Indiana University Press, 1975).

7 On improvement and underutilized land, see Bhandar, *Colonial Lives of Property*.

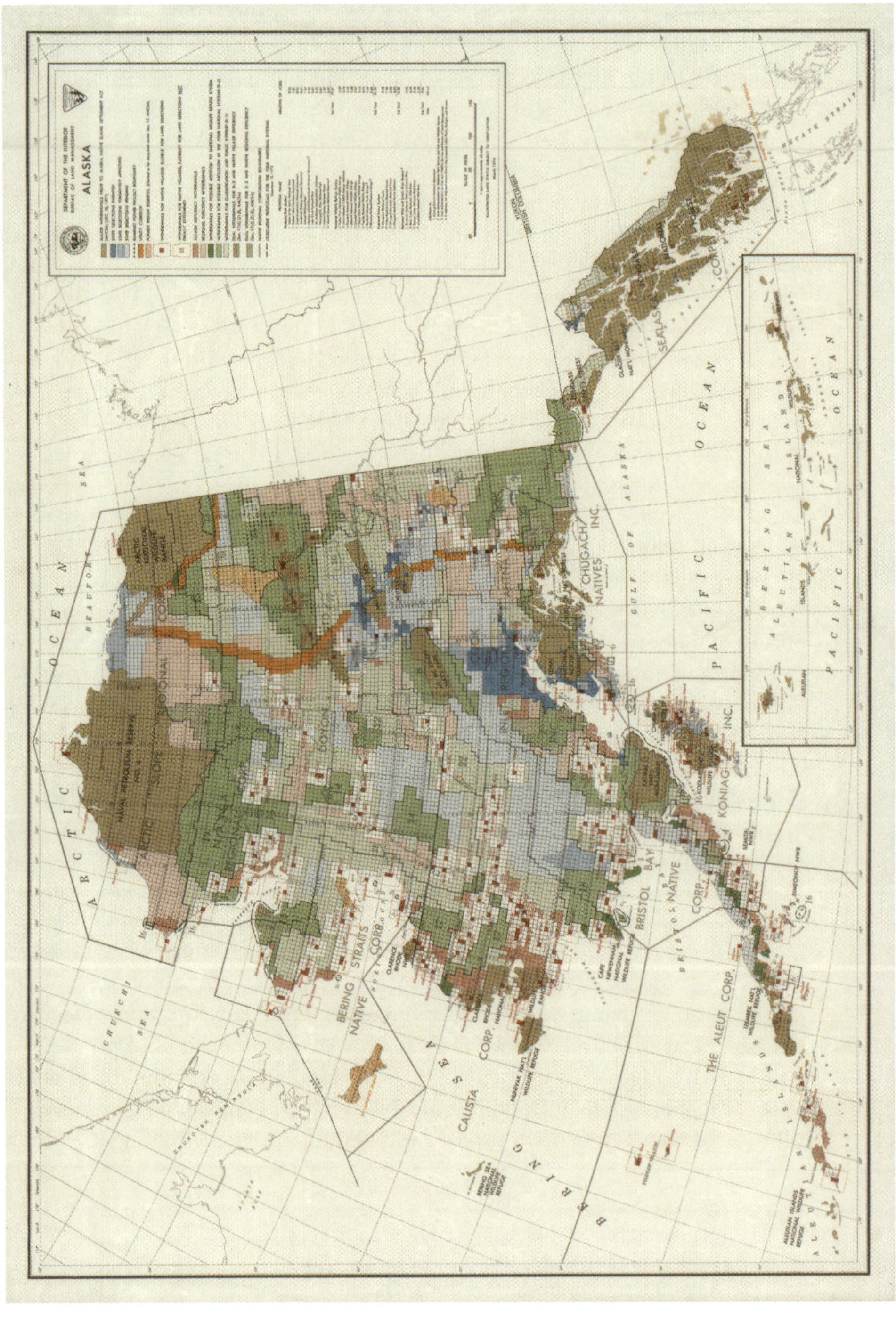

1   *Alaska* [Map], Scale ca. 1 : 2,500,000. Department of the Interior, Bureau of Land Management (March 1974).

However, such a linear narrative fails to comprise the variegated actors, discourses, and impacts that a redefinition of Native land involves. If, instead of focusing on the outcome, one looks at the object of its transformation—property rights and their relation to indigenous culture—a different picture emerges. A 1974 cadastral map produced by the US Bureau of Land Management showcases the systematical nature of the resulting property regime. A grid of 6-by-6-mile townships is projected onto the territory. The extents of regional and village corporations are rigidly placed within it and compete with state, federal, military, infrastructural, and private land selections (↪ 1). Previously foreign to most areas of Alaska as they were seen as lacking value, the Public Land Survey System imposed by the 1974 map was initially implemented in mainland US by Thomas Jefferson in 1785 to promote westward expansion through the private acquisition of land and by thwarting any prior claims to Native land. Referencing the previous colonial project of turning Native land into agricultural parcels, the inscribed property regime of the Alaska map made indigenous land claims across the state spatially and legally fungible with commercial and governmental land uses.

Alaska land claims were not defined by a clear opposition of stakes. Oil companies and state and federal politicians collaborated on land reform with a politically active, acculturated, and middle-class indigenous constituency whose attachment to the Native rural experience was largely marginal.[8] The resulting settlement of 1971 supported Native leadership to foster petroleum development on their newly acquired land by differentiating below and above-ground ownership. Instead of basing land selection on cultural and hunting use, villages with a majority of indigenous inhabitants selected four townships—or 92,160 acres—from a predefined area of 25 townships around their perimeters. Property income from the sale, development, and lease of regionally held parcels would be shared with the local corporations.[9] In practice, ANCSA converted the land struggle into a tax negotiation and diverted local indigenous sovereignty to corporations.[10] The colonial dominance of dispossession by treaty was replaced by settler-colonial governance of extinguishment by property regime.[11]

Although ANCSA provided Alaska Natives with economic and political leverage, it depoliticized Native land through its commercialization. Further, it uprooted indigenous activism, making it difficult

8   Alexander M. Ervin, "Styles and Strategies of Leadership during the Alaskan Native Land Claims Movement: 1959-71," *Anthropologica* 29, no. 1 (1987): 21–38.

9   Arnold, *Alaska Native Land Claims.*

10   Eben Hopson, "Testimony before the Berger Inquiry on the Experience of the Arctic Slope Inupiat with Oil and Gas Development in the Arctic" (Eben Hopson Archives, 1976).

11   On the history and legal theory of dispossession, see Robert Nichols, *Theft Is Property! Dispossession & Critical Theory*, Radical Américas (Duke University Press, 2020).

for dissenting positions and radical approaches to take shape in its aftermath. At stake for Native leaders was also the creation of a shared experience and legal and economic definition of indigenous identity in Alaska that could bridge tribal affiliations and political differences. Forms of activism that circumvented the money-value on land imposed by ANCSA, such as a refusal to engage in negotiations over land that Native inhabitants already considered their own or the sabotage of invasive infrastructure, were frowned on by state legislators and oil lobbyists and in some cases federally criminalized. Some activist groups, such as the American Indian Movement, were categorically left out of conversations and classified as extremist.[12] In 1977, Dene social worker Phillip Blake from Fort McPherson addressed the Canadian government's plan to route an additional pipeline through the Yukon and the Northwest Territories, stating: "If your nation becomes so violent that it would tear up our land, destroy our society and our future, and occupy our homeland, by trying to impose the pipeline against our will, then of course we will have no choice but to react with violence." Local and federal US lawmakers used Native testimony such as Blake's to legislate an apparatus of national security around the pipeline tract. In a hearing on the threat of sabotage, Alaska Commissioner of Public Safety Richard L. Burton concluded that "attacks on the [private] pipeline are not an attack on the State of Alaska; they are attacks on the people of the United States."[13] This transposition from protest to terrorism mirrored a constructed national security threat in the wake of the 1973 oil embargo that Alaska oil was supposed to resolve.

The fears of paralegal engagement felt by lawmakers and oil corporations propped up Native corporations as the sole entities allowed to participate in negotiations around indigenous land. As some of the largest land-holding agents in Alaska, Native corporations set up by ANCSA continue to play a key role in the urbanization of the Arctic. The profit-driven aspect of the Native land endowment sanctioned urbanization and corporate architectures of regional offices and hotels to thrive on Native property in Alaska. These projects were tethered to depoliticized claims to an indigenous culture devoid of the relation of Native people to land.

Instead of building an economy from local practices, ANCSA reversed the classical economic assimilation theory and ordered Native groups to organize as corporate entities that formalized economic opportunities.[14] Native corporations were required, by law, to run nonprofit arms, producing varied results. Despite the colonial spatial framework of property in which they were set up, ANCSA non-profits have pushed for equal housing opportunities, the safeguarding of Native land, and the support for alternative cultures. For example, the Taġiuġmiullu Nunamiullu Housing Authority of the Arctic Slope

Regional Corporation operates as the regional housing authority for tribal villages in the North Slope to provide homeowner loans and develop rental housing. While the property regime of the Alaska Native Claims Settlement Act has proved to be a hurdle for shedding colonial bonds, it has still provided an opportunity to rethink the relation of land to people from the North outwards, negating the linear timelines (pre-/post-) and geographies (South/North) of Arctic colonialism.

Various indigenous groups in Alaska have sought to claim partial sovereignty by rejecting the federal practices of taxation and housing imposed by ANCSA. In 1973, the inhabitants of the former Viihtąįį Indian Reserve, the Neets'ąįį Gwich'in group of central Alaska—spread primarily between the tribal villages of Viihtąįį and Vashrąįį K'ǫǫ, located both on the Chandalar River—voted to reject enrollment in the regional and village corporations set up by ANCSA. The group forwent the payments of the claims settlement to retain the titles to their former reservation lands. As a result, the villages gained federally sanctioned rights to the 1.8 million acres they inhabited, holding the land in common through a tribal government structure. This approach reappropriated their legal claim of "Indian Country"—categorical Native sovereignty over tribal land—not only to preserve Native rights to the land but to prevent it from being instrumentalized as a tool for capitalization.[15]

Ownership of land remained with the municipal councils of Viihtąįį and Vashrąįį K'ǫǫ and use of individual sites was decided communally. Instead of becoming alienable tracts of land, lots were bound to land use claims by their occupants. Sale and inheritance of land was defined not by a federal property regime but by local tribal practices and values.[16] Viihtąįį and Vashrąįį K'ǫǫ councils used their ownership of the land to steer the development of public infrastructures, housing, and cultural spaces. Both village councils operate their own tribal housing authorities that direct tribal and federal funds toward home construction.[17] A 1991 memo by the municipal government titled *Nakai' t'in'in: "Do it yourself!"* clearly expressed this stance: "We will

12

12   See "Investigative Information on the Activities of the American Indian Movement (AIM), Formed in 1968 as a Civil Rights Organization, but Comprised of Many Militant Chapters with Extremist Beliefs" (United States: Federal Bureau of Investigation, 1974).

13   Trans-Alaska Pipeline, Problems Posed by the Threat of Sabotage and the Impact on Internal Security: Hearing before the United States Senate, Committee on the Judiciary, Subcommittee to Investigate the Administration of the Internal Security Act and Other Internal Security Laws, 2nd Session, 94th Court at p. 149 (1977). Phillip Blake's statement is attached as exhibit No. 4, p. 187–90. Anthropologist Glen Coulthard contextualizes Blake's statements and the power it held in indigenous protests in Canada. Glen Sean Coulthard, *Red Skin, White Masks: Rejecting the Colonial Politics of Recognition, Indigenous Americas* (University of Minnesota Press, 2014).

14   Ernest S. Burch, "Native Claims in Alaska: An Overview," *Études/Inuit/Studies* 3, no. 1 (1979): 7–30.

15   Maximilien Zahnd, "An Alaska Tax Story: Tribal Sovereignty, Settler Colonialism, and the Indigenous Tax Space," *Environment and Planning D: Society and Space* 41, no. 5 (October 2023): 784–804.

16   Case, Voluck, and Voluck, *Alaska Natives and American Laws*, chap. 4.

2   *Arctic Village on East Fork Chandala.* Aerial view (June 17, 1972).

not let money change our special status or consider any economic development project which could negatively affect our tribal lands."[18] The rights of the Neets'ąįį Gwich'in were quickly contested by oil companies and the Alaska government as encroaching on private and state rights. In 1989, Viịhtąįį fought to solidify its claim to land by instating tax sovereignty over Native and non-Native subjects. This tribal tax space sought to invert the dominance over colonial subjects as taxpayers by making outside investors pay for their use of tribal land. This sovereignty extended beyond the structures of local administration and clashed with the boundaries of the settler-colonial state. Accordingly, a 1996 Supreme Court ruling in favor of the State of Alaska prohibited the Viịhtąįį council from levying taxes on non-Native entities, limiting, if not canceling, indigenous sovereignty over tribal land.[19] Two years prior, a similar court ruling restrained Kluti-Kaah, a tribal village located in the south of the state, from taxing the owners of the pipeline for traversing Native land.[20] Notwithstanding these defeats, tribal activists have used indigenous claims to sovereignty as structuring ideals for local governance.

The Neets'ąįį Gwich'in's urban approach embedded the legal and political frameworks of "indigenous space" and "Indian Country," often understood more closely with mainland tribal structures, into the localized practices of caribou hunting and communal structures of Arctic indigenous groups. By protecting the communal management of tribal lands, inhabitants actively claimed that their powers of self-governance had never been extinguished.[21] Beyond opposition to ANCSA-imposed corporate structures, the Neets'ąįį Gwich'in enforced their sovereignty by taking recourse in the Alaska Native Allotment Act of 1906 which allowed indigenous inhabitants to apply for up 160 acres of unclaimed land. Beginning in the 1970s, the inhabitants of Vįįhtąįį and Vashrąįį K'ǫǫ subverted the policy to lay claims to key areas lying outside of the tribal boundaries. Individually, they amassed ownership of hunting ranges, fishing spots, and culturally significant areas of value to the larger community.[22]

These approaches echo what Dene scholar Glen Coulthard has termed a "rejection" of state recognition through which indigenous groups seek distance from the settler state in constructing and maintaining their identities. Through the schism of rejection, cultures are not badges of homogenous group identity but lived experiences that are fluid, contested, and resist definition.[23] Mohawk anthropologist Audra Simpson expands on Coulthard's concept to argue that indigenous groups continuously engage in practices of "refusal" of colonial structures.[24] Simpson traces contemporary and historical cases in which Mohawks have refused to pay taxes, adhere to ethnographic definitions of indigeneity, or legitimize extractive projects. Their attitude amounts to a refusal to cooperate in the multiculturalism of "postcolonial" states such as the United States and Canada. Refusal in the post-ANCSA villages of Vįįhtąįį and Vashrąįį K'ǫǫ entailed the detachment of tribal land from speculation and a reconstruction of the relation of land use to land.

Speaking of an urbanism of refusal in the Arctic acknowledges the difficulty of defining terms such as indigenous, postcolonial, and sovereignty. It allows for heterogeneity of indigenous constituencies and their respective value systems to narrate urban practices and critiques colonialism's linear temporality in lieu of a more muddied understanding of the ongoing effects of colonizing legal and economic structures. Neither tribal structures nor communal practices are categorically exempt from hegemonic power relations. Refusing colonial urbanism is not a single-step process. It requires continuous dedication to disruption.

17   Charlene Barbara Stern, "From Camps to Communities: Neets'ąįį Gwich'in Planning and Development in a Pre- and Post-Settlement Context" (Dissertation, University of Alaska Fairbanks, 2018).

18   Cited in Stern, 119.

19   Erin Chrisbens, "Indian Country after ANCSA: Divesting Tribal Sovereignty by Interpretation in Alaska v. Native Village of Venetie Tribal Government," *Denver Law Review* 76, no. 1 (January 1, 1998): 307.

20   Zahnd, "An Alaska Tax Story."

21   Zahnd.

22   Stern, "From Camps to Communities: Neets'ąįį Gwich'in Planning and Development in a Pre- and Post-Settlement Context," 100–101.

23   Coulthard, *Red Skin, White Masks*. The Dene are a cross-national cultural and linguistic constituency of Natives living between the Canadian Northwest Territories, Nunavut, and eastern Alaska. The Dene Nation is a Canadian political organization that represents the Dene of the Northwest Territories.

24   Audra Simpson, *Mohawk Interruptus: Political Life across the Borders of Settler States* (Duke University Press, 2014).

Claudio Aporta is a cultural anthropologist specializing in Indigenous knowledge of marine and coastal environments.

The Trail as Home: Claudio Aporta in Conversation with Bert De Jonghe and Elise Misao Hunchuck

Each of us came to Claudio's work at different times and for different reasons. Bert first learned about his work from other scholars, including political geographer Mia Bennett and historian of science Michael Bravo. I first encountered the red lines of the *Pan Inuit Trails Atlas* upon its release in 2014[1] and was moved to rethink my and my profession's complicity[2] in what was, until then, an abject lack of consideration for the long histories of displacement, occupation, and erasure of cultures and histories. At just over ten years since its publication, the *Pan Inuit Trails Atlas* continues to be a standard in demonstrating that collaborative mapping projects are not only possible but can be generative when they are formulated as a series of coordinated acts of care, from which communities and histories and futures can be represented and even made anew. It is for this reason, among others, that we reached out to one of the project's co-directors, Claudio Aporta,[3] to learn more about the project and methods that gave form to the atlas we—and so many others—still look to, today. *EMH*

Bert De Jonghe and Elise Misao Hunchuck When we speak about mapping in a settler-colonial context such as Canada, it is easy to start the conversation from a position of mistrusting maps, as they were the tool of choice for colonialism and continue to be for surveillance and control. (We can't help but think of Mark Monmonier's *How to Lie with Maps*.) Maps, their data, and related visualizations have historically been deployed as tools for the extraction of knowledge or resources, whichever are deemed to be more valuable. But when we speak about your work, Claudio, and in particular, the *Pan Inuit Trails* project, we can see how mapping can be a generative project, a series of acts of care in which community and history can be represented and rebuilt. Can you tell us about how the project came to be, who your collaborators were, and how you sought to ensure that you held yourselves accountable to the people, territory, and history being represented?

Claudio Aporta The overarching project of documenting Inuit trails and mobility started organically. I was doing my doctoral research in Igloolik,[4] in the eastern Canadian Arctic, between the autumn of 2000 and the end of spring 2001. At the time, I discovered an old document that was an interview with an elder done in the 1980s. In this document, the Inuit interviewer asked the Inuit elder to remember the place names that were familiar to him. He started listing names, and then the interviewer asked him about the location of the names and meanings, and in the process, they included geographic coordinates. I am not a geographer or a GIS expert, but I found that I could map the Inuit place names using simple GPS companion software. Suddenly, these place names were on the map on my screen.

I realized there was a sense of emotion among the Inuit who saw the map. People got emotional when they saw their place names on maps because the maps they had seen before had Canadian or British place names given to the places in the process of exploration and colonization of Canada. So it was the first time Inuit in Igloolik saw the Inuktitut names on the map. I found that fascinating. Then, I also started mapping how the Inuit used the sea ice. I realized people recognized a topography on the sea ice, consisting of features that recurred every year. So, I also put all those features on the map. Then, when I started traveling with hunters, I started using a GPS, recording some of the trips and uploading them to my computer. I realized that people were talking about those GPS tracks on the screen as if they were well-known trails, which was surprising because, coming from the south, I wasn't aware that these routes were followed year after year. The trails were linked to historic events and personal and community stories (memories) along those trails. The stories were linked to events that had happened while they were children, their parents

1   First seen in a news story featured on CBC (Canadian Broadcasting Corporation, the public broadcasting network of the Canadian government): The Canadian Press, "New atlas documents traditional Inuit trail network," *CBC*, June 12, 2014.

2   Personally, as a settler-colonial subject of Canada from my birth in Toronto on what were for thousands of years the traditional lands of the Huron-Wendat, the Seneca, and the Mississaugas of the Credit, and professionally, as someone trained in both landscape architecture and geography at the University of Toronto.

3   At the time of the project, Claudio was affiliated with the Marine Affairs Program at Dalhousie University, Halifax, Nova Scotia, Canada.

4   In Igloolik (now they may use a different spelling, Iglulik). I still write Igloolik to refer to the settlement, as there is a place name on the south of the island called Iglulik.

and grandparents, and other community members. Gradually, I realized there was a network of trails that people would use regularly and organically—that information and knowledge I was documenting became a part of the maps that I was making. People wanted hard copies, so I printed those maps out, which were shared in the community and often taped on the walls of people's homes or in their places of work. That was the beginning of my systematic mapping of Inuit trails.

My research partners were mostly the hunters I met in Igloolik. I met most of them through the Igloolik Research Center. The coordinator of the center, John MacDonald, was also fascinated by the maps, and we had a conversation about what we do with this information and knowledge. Through dialogue with the community, we came up with the idea of printing large-size maps and making a multimedia CD-ROM that could be used in schools. At the time, it was a CD-ROM, but now it is online: it is called Anijaarniq.[5] A few years later, with my colleagues at Cambridge University, Michael Bravo, and Fraser Taylor at Carleton University, we put together a proposal for an atlas of Inuit trails. We came up with the idea of mapping Inuit geographic knowledge through digitizing historical material. That atlas was an attempt to trace the historical roots of the trails and some of the place names through digitizing and geo-referencing 'Inuit' maps produced during encounters between Inuit and explorers in the nineteenth century and twentieth centuries. The atlas is a very small (but intriguing) snapshot of Inuit use of their environment. It is one way of showing the historical depth of place names and trails.

BDJ, EMH   In your article in *Human Ecology*, you refer to "the trail as home."[6] In another article, you suggest that for Inuit, wayfinding and traveling through the landscape is more than just moving from point A to B: it is a way of being.[7] Can you expand on these two claims? And, based on this, how much of the knowledge transmitted across generations about trails and place names includes a focus on the domestic, the interior, or the home?

CA   Inuit have historically been a semi-nomadic people. In that context, traveling is not just about the destination; it is about the journey and about your experience and encounters on that journey. Especially before settlements were established in the 50s and 60s, Inuit would have seasonal camps and seasonal residential patterns. So traveling was connected to seasonal variations (whether the sea ice was solid enough, the conditions of the snow, where the animals were, etc.). People would eventually have a destination, but there was not necessarily the sense of "oh, we are taking a trip" in the way we think today of a city trip to Berlin, for example. It was more about moving on "the land" (both marine and terrestrial areas) in a way that was connected to the seasonal availability of animals. Inuit would travel similar trails for obvious reasons: the seasonal availability of resources. Therefore, the Inuit Arctic is really a social space where people meet seasonally. Before permanent settlements, there was usually no urgency to arrive at a destination. It depended on the conditions of the land, the weather, etc. In terms of how the trails connected to the domestic space, I think trails are another dimension of the home in terms of how they connect to the domestic space (which today is permanent, but that was seasonal in the past). If you think about it, the trails always start and finish in the domestic space. You will find, even today, that people's houses are filled with traveling items and activities (preparations for the trip, the outcome of the hunt/fishing, sleds outside of the houses, people fixing tools or sleds, or snowmobiles, etc.). If you look at some of the trails I've documented by GPS, unsurprisingly, the trails start and finish in people's homes. So there is a connection between the domestic space and the land. At the same time, there is a sense of separation nowadays between the domestic space and the land in the settlement. However, the domestic space is a part of the journey. This distinction was blurred before permanent settlements (where residences were, in a sense, part of the trail), and it is more distinctive today, but the connections between the journey and the domestic space have not disappeared.

BDJ, EMH The Atlas describes itself as unique in that one can start to get a sense of "the bigger picture," which is a "territorial coherence of the Inuit people over Arctic waters." To us, this is fascinating because it points towards how an Inuit understanding of a trail or a path, one that traverses land and sea and ice and water, can be a way to unlearn some of the historically colonial mappings and understandings of the Arctic itself. Can you tell us more about what you understand "territorial coherence" to be?

CA First of all, I would bring nuance to calling it unique. I would not use that word anymore today. But to the point of territorial coherence. I think there are two parts to it. One is related to the interconnection between marine spaces and land. In a place such as Igloolik, you have many months (approximately eight) of the year when some of the sea ice is part of the landscape. When you look at the trails in detail, you'll see that the movement between land and ocean is clearly prevalent.

5   ᐊᓂᔿᕐᓂᖅ (ANIJAARNIQ) can be seen here: anijaarniq.com
6   "The Trail as Home: Inuit and Their Pan-Arctic Network of Routes," *Human Ecology* 37 (April 2009): 131–146.
7   "Routes, trails and tracks: trail-breaking among the Inuit of Igloolik," *Études Inuit Studies* 28, 2 (December 2004): 9–38.

1   A stop along the trail to Naujaat from Igloolik (March 2006).
2   Snowmobile and sled tracks make a well-known trail visible, northeast of Naujaat (2006).
3   Community members work on a map of trails in Qamani'tuuq (Baker Lake, 2008).
4   A participant of a mapping session in Pond Inlet explores a composite of maps of the region (2011).
5   Participants of mapping session in Puvirnituq (2018) draw sled trails (red), summer boat routes (blue) and the floe edge (dashed).
6   A mapping session in Puvirnituq (2018).

There is also the structure and topography of the sea ice that is in itself unique and dynamic. Then, there is also open water within the sea ice or a floe edge. The floe edge, when you think about it in terms of a cartographic line, becomes a more important line than the shoreline. The territoriality manifests itself also in the sea ice dynamic. But the floe edge is not really a line; it is a moving, dynamic space that breaks and forms. It also, of course, changes seasonally. So, that is one part of the answer. The second important part of territorial coherence is the interconnections between communities. That is one of the things that came up very quickly in my research documenting trails. It was evident that the trails of one community interacted with the trails of another community. If you want to move from, let's say, Igloolik to Arctic Bay (Baffin Island), then you would have the trails of those communities connected, resulting in a network of trails. That doesn't necessarily mean that people from the western Canadian Arctic are knowledgeable of the trails of the eastern Canadian Arctic, but at the same time, there is a different sense of home that is not based on the boundaries of the settlement but that actually exists within a network of movement. There is a connection across the Inuit homelands. Of course, this is not a new idea (e.g., the Fifth Thule Expedition in the 1920s). One of the main points of Rasmussen's expedition was to establish that there was an Inuit culture that basically connected all the way from Greenland to Siberia. However, the trails are a very clear visualization of that territoriality that goes beyond a community as we understand it, maybe wrongly, as a bounded place.

BDJ, EMH The ability to communicate an in-depth knowledge of routes and place names carries high social value and represents a source of personal pride. What is the significance of Inuit trails and place names for today and in a post-Arctic context? By post-Arctic, we mean to suggest the rapidly changing contexts, including climatic, political, and so on.

CA I was not familiar with the term "post-Arctic," and it sounds like a charged term. But I will try to answer your question. The trails show a social landscape that is historically embedded. The trails and the place names connect, again, to historical events and stories. The environment may be different, but they also connect to experiences or performances today. When people travel, they still connect to those places and their historical dimensions. And, if those places have changed to a dramatic extent, there is still that historical knowledge that is building those places. One example is that of Qikiqtaarjuk, a former island northwest of Igloolik that became a peninsula with receding sea levels over a long period of time. But, still, the name that people use today to refer to this place is "small island," even though it is a peninsula.[8]

So, I think that is a fascinating example because people know that it is not an island, but the place name brings back the historical connection, the indication of change, and the adaptation to those changes. Changes are not necessarily anomalies, but they are just a part of life, and there are many ways to adapt to them. Of course, if changes become more dramatic, then the adaptation becomes more dramatic, too—and difficult. They could bring this issue to a post-Arctic context. In a way, the changes that people observe are understood in an unfolding context.

BDJ, EMH These trails give us but a glimpse of Inuit mobility and occupancy of the Arctic—spatial, historical narratives that were once all but ignored by the Government of Canada. Today, however, it is no secret that as perennial and seasonal sea ice gives way to easier movement through the Arctic, the Government of Canada is eager to fortify its claims to the North; in particular, the cynics in us would point to the fish stock, the oil, gas, and rare earth minerals in the seabed. How do you see your work playing into Canadian claims to sovereignty and territory?

CA First of all, I've approached my work mostly as *documenting* and not providing a lot of meaning to what is being documented. I experienced a sense of urgency from the local communities to document historical and oral knowledge that was, perhaps, not going to survive or that was going to get lost (or at least some of it) as a result of the changes in the education system, etc. So, up to a point, I do not want to exercise control over what I produced. Having said that, I'm in the process of transferring all my data to the Inuit Circumpolar Council Canada (ICC) with the hope that they will make the decisions that are best for them. But another side of the question that is interesting and adds a layer of complexity is whether recognizing Inuit occupancy (and you know, my work is only a tiny drop in the ocean) through documents or oral knowledge is also a potential way of providing agency to Inuit. What is the alternative, an empty space that has no Inuit traces? So it is a question about providing meaning to maps. In a sense, it shows that Inuit are actively and systematically using the space. I stop there. After that, it is up to the Canadian government to decide if some of this information has an impact in terms of claiming, historic use, and sovereignty. That is a different story. It is not a straightforward answer.

BDJ, EMH Following that, how do you see Inuit maintaining control—or at least authorship—of documented "Inuit spatial narratives" in the coming years? Are you a part of this conversation? Is this something you think or speculate about?

CA In terms of authorship, in Canada, there are better regulations now about what to do with oral knowledge in connection to Indigenous peoples, as researchers must recognize the authorship of the data and the outcome of projects that involve Indigenous communities, etc. There is one issue with maps, and that is the issue of scale. In my experience, Inuit communities are worried about the scale of maps in terms of how much detail they show or will show (about potentially sensitive areas, culturally significant areas, spiritually significant areas, harvesting sites, etc.). By controlling the scale of the output map, they can control the information they want to share. The scale of the map is also methodologically interesting because it filters the answers and the knowledge that you are documenting. My hope is that, for example, by transferring my databases to the ICC, they can influence or control future narratives and interpretations of the maps and knowledge.

In this, it is fair to ask what controlling really means (in terms of controlling interpretations). I think that there is a point where, once something is in the public domain, you have a risk-benefit conundrum or balance in terms of why you want to share it or why you want to protect it. If sharing means that your rights and your identity will be recognized and that you as a people will have more chances of making sovereignty claims, etc., I think it is potentially a good thing. It's an empowering thing. Once something is in the public domain, however, it is open to other interpretations and uses. I think that we sometimes think too much about the fragility of oral knowledge, and we compare it to written knowledge as something that is frozen. But things that are materially preserved can also be interpreted. Whenever we see a painting, read a book, or play a song, we incorporate different layers of meaning. Once the object becomes a text, it is not only about the object but also about how you interpret the object, which is something that Barthes beautifully pointed out in his 1973 book *Le Plaisir du Texte*. So a map of trails and place names would have a very different meaning to an Inuit community, a mining company, or a non-governmental organization (NGO). Authorship can be maintained according to the type of arrangements that are made when oral knowledge is made public. However, in

8   I refer to this in my chapter "Markers in Space and Time": "Qikiqtaarjuk, for instance, means little island, but the feature with that name on Igloolik Island is actually a peninsula. The name is made sensible only in the context of Iglulingmiut history and cosmology. According to local tradition, the legend of Uinigumasuittuq (a woman who married a dog and bore offspring that turned out to be white people) took place here long ago when Qikiqtaarjuk was still an island. Receding sea levels eventually turned the island into a peninsula, but the name and stories were retained through time." For more, see "Markers in space and time: Reflections on the nature of place names as events in the Inuit approach to the territory," in Robert Whallon and William Lovis, eds., *Marking the Land: Hunter-Gatherer Creation of Meaning within their Surroundings* (Routledge, 2019), 67–88.

7   A composite map of Inuit trails. Over the course of several projects, several communities of Nunavut (green lines), Nunavik (yellow lines) and Nunatsiavut (red lines) are drawn out.

terms of the interpretations of the oral knowledge (including on the maps), that is a different story. Regarding my work, I hope that the narratives and interpretations are influenced by Inuit through ICC.

BDJ, EMH How do you see the impact of climate change on mobility and reliability on the trails or knowledge contained within your maps? We're thinking specifically about drastically changing ice seasons and freezing and thawing patterns, but we wonder what other impacts there are. How is that danger or concern communicated? How could it be?

CA Some of the trails are changing, and these changes are mostly connected to changes in the conditions of the ice. Changes are sometimes permanent and sometimes seasonal, and they result in situations such as where people used to travel across an inlet and now they have to go around the inlet so that travel distances may be longer. Even with faster snowmobiles, it still comes down to more time and more expense. Generally speaking, the maps I created are not meant to be navigational tools. In fact, I made a conscious decision not to make the GPS versions of the trails available. It was clear that there were seasonal changes. The GPS version would tell you something about space but not necessarily about time or seasonality. So the mapped trails are not navigational tools. The main goal is for communities to keep records of social memories in a time of change and as oral histories may be dwindling. Even if the trail on the map is not usable anymore, if the documentation process is clear enough, people could still find the trail useful because it recreates a memory of the place as it used to be.

It was never in my research goals to make an up-to-date description of what the trails are like, even if the trails on the map are up to a certain point still accurate today. There are even trails that were mapped by Inuit in the 1820s, the result of encounters with the explorers Lyon and Parry.[9] Those trails can still be retraced. So, people would look at the trail and say, yes, we still use that trail. But things have changed a lot, of course. They may not use it a lot, or it may no longer be the main trail since the old ones were more connected to the use of dogsleds, the weather has changed, etc. But people still recognize them as part of the social memory of the place. That makes the Inuit Arctic so fascinating as com-

9   For more, see G. F. Lyon's *The private journal of Captain G.F. Lyon, of H.M.S. Hecla, during the recent voyage of discovery under Captain Parry: with a map and plates* (John Murray and Thomas Davison, 1824) as well as William Edward Perry's *Journal of a second voyage for the discovery of a north-west passage from the Atlantic to the Pacific: performed in the years 1821-22-23, in His Majesty's ships Fury and Hecla, under the orders of Captain William Edward Parry: illustrated by numerous plates* (John Murray, 1824).

pared to other regions where you may have permanent transportation infrastructures. For Inuit, those infrastructures are almost invisible; they are imprinted on people's memories. Sometimes they are visible, like piles of rock or the remains of a tent ring. But it is mostly imprinted in people's memories. That is what the map of trails and place names does, visualizing what those memories are like. Mark Nuttall wrote *Arctic Homeland: Kinship, Community, and Development in Northwest Greenland*, where he introduced the *memoryscapes* in Greenland. This term influenced how I thought about these topics.

BDJ, EMH How is the methodology of the Pan-Inuit trails project (and your work more broadly) and its generated knowledge relevant for other Arctic regions (for example, regions that are not yet incorporated in the project or regions in other Arctic regions of the world)?

CA Most of my trails data has not been published. I have covered most of the Canadian Arctic, but only parts of the network have been published. I've been trying to expand the project toward Alaska and Greenland, which has been difficult due to time and funding constraints. In a way, there is a political purpose to map trails and place names: to reclaim a vision of the Arctic as an Inuit homeland. It is about making visible the history of dwellings and the use of the land. A lot of people still think of the Arctic as an empty space, and this way of conceptualizing the Arctic has consequences and impacts on decisions related to shipping, mining, etc. We tend to think of Inuit communities as isolated from each other, while the mapped trails materialize networks of mobility across the Arctic and among communities.

Maps have become a way of visualizing and representing space cross-culturally. I think place names are very significant, also in other cultural settings (e.g., Iceland). In other geographies, trails may not be as significant. However, for Indigenous peoples, mapping or counter-mapping can become a political instrument to reformulate colonial ideas of the territory. Most people understand maps. The Inuit would not really use maps before they met European explorers, but they immediately understood what maps were and learned the principles of cartography, resulting in some beautiful "Inuit" maps from the eighteenth and nineteenth centuries. Mapping Inuit oral knowledge can be thought of as a counter-mapping exercise that has multiple purposes: one is for a community to document and preserve their stories and narratives for younger generations in a changing social and linguistic context, and another one is as a political statement from the Inuit to the outside world: "We are using and have used these marine and terrestrial areas for a very long time."

BDJ Was there, at any point in the project, a discussion about going beyond a 2D map toward more tactile versions?

> *CA* I fantasized about that. However, there is something about a traditional map that makes it more transferable and understandable across cultures. The digital versions of the map also become very relevant. But I never explored alternative ways of mapping in a systematic way. I realized early on that large paper maps are conducive to more engaging participatory mapping sessions. I started pasting topo maps together on the floor, and later, using large printers. The big dimensions create a different relationship; the map becomes walkable, and people can sit, have tea, and walk around the map. People can have conversations on top of the maps. That creates an engaging experience in documenting and observing or interacting with the map after it is all documented.

BDJ, EMH How can we bring the pan-Inuit trails in relation to (historic, contemporary, and future) settlement development in a changing Arctic?

> *CA* After looking at the network of mobility and how the settlements are situated, I realized I needed to stop thinking of settlements as something enclosed, as residential areas bounded and separated from the land. We need to start thinking of settlements *as part of* the network of movement—as well as rethinking the concept of settlement itself. When you start conceptualizing settlements as a part of a network of routes, the physical town may also become more connected to the rhythms of life in the Arctic in the context of Inuit historically rooted residential patterns.

BDJ, EMH A common thread that has come up in conversations with different practitioners and community organizers and designers in northerly regions is that there is an extant lack of northerly precedents and issues instructed in design schools, in part because there are so few design school in northerly geographies. Do you think the "Pan-Inuit Trails" project could function as a kind of support for design education or practitioners as they look to teach or practice northerly concerns (or creatives more broadly) up North? If so, how?

> *CA* When you look at the Arctic settlements today, you cannot help but think that Canadian Arctic policies failed to conceptualize domestic and public spaces in the Arctic. Of course, housing structures and public buildings must be adapted to Arctic climate and conditions, but there are also Inuit social and cultural realities that were probably never considered. It would be interesting to see a systematic survey of the Canadian Arctic designs regarding private

and public spaces and to explore why they are not working. And also, what are some of the buildings/designs that work? I am thinking about two examples of public buildings that seem to have worked. The first is Piqqusilirivvik, an Inuit cultural learning facility in Clyde River. My understanding is that the architects consulted quite a bit with the local community. I was there a long time ago, but my impression at the time was that it was a social space that worked because there were a lot of open spaces, and there were conscious decisions about design that were relevant. The second is the Igloolik Research Center, which looks like a white UFO from a movie. I spent a lot of time there during my doctoral research. It is a very fascinating building. It is weird, and people make fun of it. But there is a big open circular space inside, probably one of the biggest indoor rooms in Igloolik outside the schools and arena. It is round. I don't want to read too much into it, but igloos are also circular. It is a wonderful space for people to interact, or it used to be. The offices are on the sides by the windows. The building has a 360-degree view. It is a remarkable social space, even if it's unusual. It looks out of place, but it seems to work. Please note that my examples here are not made from my architectural knowledge (which I don't have). They are simply observations.

BDJ, EMH Can you share with us some of the most striking findings from the project? How do you imagine moving this project forward, if at all?

CA Doing this research in Igloolik was a life-changing experience. The most remarkable aspect was gradually realizing and learning about the social spaces and historical narratives connected to the trails. It takes a long time to understand that there is a social dimension to the Arctic. It takes time, interaction, and learning. I was extremely fortunate to meet hunters and other Inuit community members who became interested in what I was doing and made me a part of their experiences. I learned about their narratives, the meaning of snowdrifts, what the wind was telling them about directions, the structure of the ice, etc. The Inuit-inhabited Arctic is a very complex social landscape. This sociability was what I found most fascinating. For example, we would be traveling in one direction, and someone else would come from the other direction, and we would stop for coffee and talk, and there was a sense of community on the trail; it was not random that people met! It was part of a seasonally tuned network of people along the trails, harvesting sites, camps, etc. There was a sense of community along the trails. It is not only about your experience as an individual but also and mainly about your experience as part of a community.

Aniella Sophie Goldinger is a transdisciplinary spatial researcher with a focus on critical mapping of polar oceanscapes.

Drifting as Agency: Between Ice, Space, and Territory in the Arctic Ocean
Aniella Sophie Goldinger

"The sea—a material, spatial, ecological, and recreational resource—is undoubtedly the site of one of this century's greatest planning challenges."[1]

Climate change models predict a nearly ice-free summer Arctic Ocean as early as 2030.[2] With the drastic decrease in multiyear sea ice, an increase in resource extraction,[3] marine traffic, and military activity is expected[4] to impose unprecedented risks onto the fragile ecologies and the communities— and the attendant livelihoods and cultures—of the oceans of the Arctic. As an increasingly saturated space of disruptive activities, movement, and fluxes, the ocean, difficult to restrict and make fit into a terrestrial planning logic, emerges as a complicated but necessary subject for more-than-human-based planning solutions. Within the Arctic, the oceanscape is further complicated by the presence of sea ice and its viscosity gradient, neither land nor open water. This complex materiality calls for a new, interdisciplinary approach to fully understand this changing cryoscape's impact on its surrounding socioenvironmental systems. Across disciplines, multiple scholars call for a paradigm shift[5] and a need for transdisciplinary research and planning strategies to conceptualize these complex spaces of drastically changing oceanscapes.[6] An oceanic planning approach challenges predominantly Western land-based spatial perceptions. It demands new ways of thinking about and representing the ocean as an increasingly urbanized and instrumentalized space of constant movement and flux, difficult to restrict into bounded spaces.

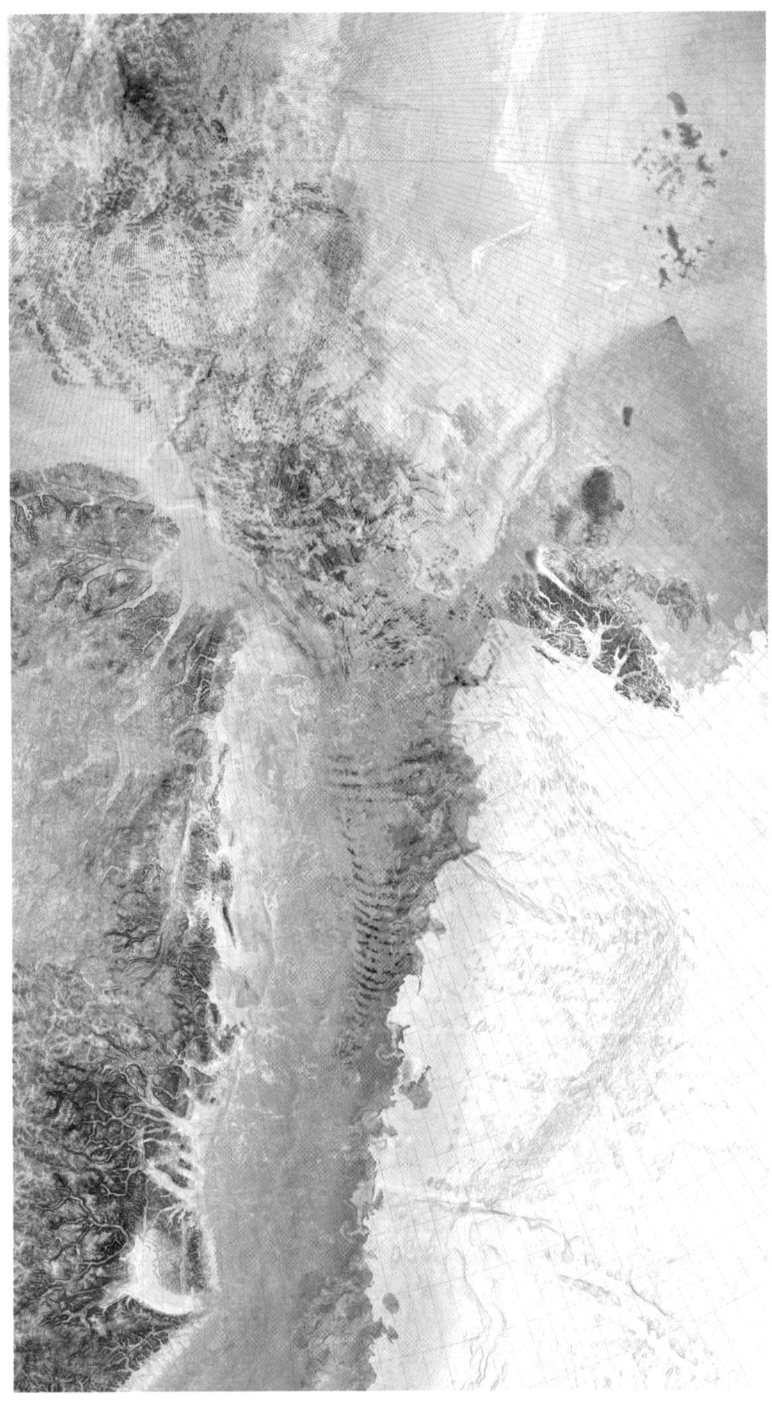

1   Sea ice extent in the Fram Strait, April 2023. Mapping the movement of drifting sea ice and the shifting character of the ocean as both surface and bathymetry.

This chapter explores sea ice as a vibrant material actor[7] within the Arctic, rendering visible some of the myriad ways in which drift ice—unruly, filled with sediments, and surprisingly gritty—emerges simultaneously as a more-than-human ecological infrastructure and actor within the Arctic Ocean.

SEA ICE

The drifting sea ice impacts the marine ecosystem's physical, chemical, and biological systems on a micro and macro scale: sea ice influences heat transfer between the atmosphere and the ocean and plays a critical role in reflecting solar energy.[8] Sea ice affects global circulation patterns by its impact on ocean salinity and density gradients, hosting microbial communities, and, although rarer and rarer, large ice algae forests. The formation of sea ice in itself constructs a fascinatingly poetic and intricate system of distinct formation phases as shifting, drifting agents of landscape becomings. The structural development of sea ice does not follow a linear process but is marked and named within scientific discourse: the shallow Russian marginal seas, home to the large systems of Siberian polynyas where a majority of Arctic sea ice is formed, is often referred to as "sea ice nurseries."[9] These specific conditions,

1   Nancy Couling, "Imagining the Invisible: Spatial Design for the North Sea," *Planning Practice and Research* 37, no. 3 (2022): 278.

2   Yeon-Hee Kim, Seung-Ki Min, Nathan P. Gillett, Dirk Notz and Elizaveta Malinina, "Observationally-constrained projections of an ice-free Arctic even under a low emission scenario," *Nat Commun* 14 (2023): 3139; Alexandra, Jahn, Marika M. Holland, and Jennifer E. Kay, "Projections of an ice-free Arctic Ocean," *Nat Rev Earth Environ* 5 (2024): 164–76.

3   Besides the country's oil and gas explorations, Norway has, as per 06.07.2024, not yet joined the international moratorium on seafloor mining. See Miranda Bryant, "Norway votes for deepsea mining despite environmental concerns," *The Guardian* (January 9, 2024).

4   Mia M. Bennett, Scott R. Stephenson, Kang Yang, Michael T. Bravo, and Bert de Jonghe, "The opening of the Transpolar Sea Route: Logistical, geopolitical, environmental, and socioeconomic impacts," *Marine Policy* 121 (2020): 104178; PAME, *Arctic Shipping Status Report - The Increase in Arctic Shipping 2013-2019 (ASSR #1)* (2019); PAME, *Arctic Shipping Status Report - Heavy Fuel Oil (HFO) Use by Ships in the Arctic 2019 (ASSR #2)* (2019).

5   A shift towards a sea-to-land perspective within planning disciplines, as opposed to inflicting land-based logics onto the oceanscape.

6   Nancy Couling and Carola Hein, eds., *The Urbanisation of the Sea; From Concepts and Analysis to Design* (nai010, 2020); Philip Steinberg, Greta Ferloni, Claudio Aporta, Gavin Bridge, Aldo Chircop, Kate Coddington, Stuart Elden, Stephanie C. Kane, Timo Koivurova, Jessica Shadian, and Anna Stammler-Gossmann, "Navigating the Structural Coherence of Sea Ice," in *Laws of the Sea: Interdisciplinary Currents*, ed. Irus Braverman (Routledge, 2022): 165–183; Kimberley Peters and Philip Steinberg, "The ocean in excess: Towards a more-than-wet ontology," *Dialogues in Human Geography* 9, no. 3 (2019): 293–307.

7   Jane Bennett, *Vibrant Matter: A Political Ecology of Things* (Duke University Press, 2010). This text is a further reflection on the author's graduate landscape architecture thesis project (Oslo School of Architecture).

8   As sea ice melt and reveals the darker melt ponds or ocean water in its place, the ice-albedo-feedback causes the sea ice to melt even further.

9   Thomas Krumpen, H. Jakob Belter, Antje Boetius, Ellen Damm, Christian Haas, Stefan Hendricks, Marcel Nicolaus, Eva-Maria Nöthig, Stephan Paul, Ilka Peeken, Robert Ricker, and Rüdiger Stein, "Arctic warming interrupts the Transpolar Drift and affects long-range transport of sea ice and ice-rafted matter," *Scientific Reports* 9 (2019): 1–9.

2   Sea ice prognosis of an ice-free Fram Strait in September 2100, encroached by the Norwegian sea floor mining area south of Svalbard.

where open water meets cold inland winds and strong coastal circulation, create the formation of young sea ice filled with essential sediments. Transporting the sea ice into the central Arctic Ocean is the Transpolar Drift, also described as an underwater "river,"[10] which plays a critical role in transporting these sediments to the nutrient-poor Central Ocean. Finally, both the Fram Strait (situated between Kalaallit Nunaat and the Norwegian archipelago of Svalbard) and the Gyre Drift are known as "sea ice graveyards," where the sea ice ultimately drifts through or gets stuck and melts away in the meeting with warmer currents and globally increasing temperatures. While having a clear and tangible impact on the cryospheric ecosystems, sea ice directly impacts the laws and politics of the region as well, where historically, differing material understandings and the definition of its extent have had direct implications on the establishment of the Western colonial nation-borders, extractive regulations and attempts to compartmentalize the Arctic Ocean.[11] While this essay specifically focuses on sea ice perceptions and practices around the Svalbard Archipelago, across the Arctic and sub-Arctic Oceans, Indigenous sea ice practices and local knowledge exhibit a far richer, more complex, and comprehensive understanding and relation to the shifting dynamics of the frozen ocean—crucially important counterapproaches to the failing conceptions rooted in Western dualities—too rich and diverse to do full justice within the scope of this text.[12]

A STATIC COMPARTMENTALIZATION OF OCEANSPACE

Up until the formulation of the United Nations Convention on the Law of the Sea (UNCLOS)[13] in 1982, the ocean was largely seen as a common and devoid of large-scale territorial claims. Prompted by the increase in human seabound activities and the geopolitical insecurities of the end of the century, the fixed Exclusive Economic Zones (EEZs)[14] were established as part of the UNCLOS, compartmentalizing the ocean into what was supposed to be clearly

10   Melissa Chierici, Agneta Fransson, and Mats Granskog "The Transpolar Drift current — the largest Arctic river — transports materials into the central Arctic Ocean from Siberian Shelf across the North Pole," *The Nansen Legacy* (2021).

11   Shake et al., *(Un)frozen Spaces*; Jeppe Strandsbjerg, "Cartopolitics, Geopolitics and Boundaries in the Arctic," *Geopolitics* 17, no. 4 (2012): 818–42; Philip Steinberg and Kate Coddington, "From Ice Law to ICE LAW: Constructing an Interdisciplinary Research Project on the Political-Legal Challenges of Polar Environments," [Briefing note] (2014); Philip Steinberg, and Berit Kristoffersen, "'The Ice edge is lost... nature moved it': mapping ice as state practice in the Canadian and Norwegian North," *Transactions of the Institute of British Geographers* 42 (2017): 625–41.

12   See "SIKU," The Indigenous Knowledge Social Network; the SmartIce project within the homelands and unceded territory of the Inuit, Métis, and First Nations people, "SmartICE," SmartICE; the Pan Inuit Trails project within Eastern and Central so-called Canadian Arctic, and co-production projects of knowledge such as in Jonathan Ryan, Parnuna Dahl, and Brigt Dale, "Co-production of sea ice knowledge in Uummannaq Bay, Greenland," *Oceanography* 35, 3–4 (2022): 196–97.

13   United Nations, *United Nations Convention on the Law of the Sea* (1986).

14   Defining a sovereign state's exclusive right to exploration of maritime resources within the 200 nautical miles beyond the limit of the territorial water (12 nautical miles).

defined national and territorial waters, but which quickly revealed the multiple conflicting ways of interpreting oceanspace extent and territoriality.[15] The EEZ is one example of a land-based logic put upon the oceanspace, a type of zoning based solely on distance and a flattened understanding of the ocean as merely a surface. To some extent, similar to Marine Protected Areas (MPA), which also operate after an enclosing and static logic, these attempts compartmentalize the ocean space, rendering it static and predictable, and become exemplary of the discrepancy between the drifting, moving ocean space and governance attempts to restrict it into bounded spaces. Oceanic spaces demand a departure from strictly two-dimensional perspectives; the oceanscape is volumetric and spatial, and more than a flat surface as it is often portrayed within spatial planning documents, where the fluid, three-dimensional nature of the ocean complicates and poses challenges for planners accustomed to terrestrial perspectives.

The complex materiality of sea ice within this oceanic context calls for a new, interdisciplinary approach to fully understand the impact that the melting cryoscape has on its surrounding material and socioenvironmental systems, human as well as more-than-human. However, within the Law of the Sea, the frozen state of the ocean is only mentioned in one of the 320 articles.[16] Throughout history, examples clearly show how dominating cartographic sea ice perceptions often result in overly simplified and highly politized conflicts.[17] In 2015, the Norwegian state presented a new map in which the Arctic sea ice edge had been mapped 70 km further northward than previously depicted; the dynamic and constantly changing nature of sea ice being simplified into a clearly defined frontier line, continuously being pushed further and further northward. The map, based on a seemingly scientific declaration of the minimum sea ice extent, however, extraordinarily coincided with a roll-out of newly opened Barents Sea oil exploration fields within this newly declared ice-free buffer zone.[18] This becomes exemplary of how resource extractivist governance plans appear based on static, two-dimensional representations and understandings of an oceanic surface and clearly show the discrepancy in nation-states' attempts to stabilize the highly dynamic oceanic cryoscape. As commercial activity within the Arctic oceanscape is drastically increasing, the question arises to what extent urbanization of the space is happening, allowing for an "urban" theoretical framework to be tested upon this space, so often falsely depicted as "pristine" and "untouched."

THE URBAN OCEAN

Closely related to the field of planetary urbanization and its definitions of "operational landscapes,"[19] the notion of oceanic hinterlands explores how the scales of capitalist processes, operationalized oceanspace, and the urban are intertwined and interconnected. As a continuation within the field of planetary urbanization,[20] Nancy Couling and Carola Hein propose an oceanic spatial analysis that draws attention to the extended urbanization of logistical, infrastructural, and legislative systems transforming the oceanspace outside of what is conventionally conceived as the urban environment.[21] They argue that the ocean, although often neglected in urban studies, functions as an operationalized hinterland in which the dominant narrative of its so-called natural-ness has prevented the ocean from being perceived as an urban issue.[22] Oceanic urbanization can thus be understood first and foremost as materialized through energy and communication infrastructure,[23] as a space saturated by not only the material manifestations such as internet cables, vessels, and oil platforms but as a specifically "envirotechnical"[24] space of scientific and legal infrastructures.[25]

OPERATIONALIZATION OF THE OCEAN SPACE

As the ocean becomes an exponentially more instrumentalized, inhabited, and extracted space, saturated with an amplified presence of marine and petro-capitalistic infrastructures, frameworks for how to plan for, design with, and approach the drifting ice as a more-than-human community need to be developed for future spatial planning and policy making. While contemporary urban theory primarily focuses on land-based urbanities, oceanic spatial scholars are researching the myriad ways in which the ocean functions as a designed space.[26] Studying the oceanscape from an interdisciplinary, spatial perspective calls for the fluid seascapes to be included in the disciplines of architecture and spatial planning, with Couling defining the ocean, for a long time excluded from the planning disciplines, as "one of this century's greatest

15   Strandsbjerg, "Cartopolitics, Geopolitics and Boundaries in the Arctic."

16   United Nations, "Article 234. Ice-covered areas," in *United Nations Convention on the Law of the Sea* (1986): 115.

17   See Kristen L. Shake, Karen E. Frey, Deborah G. Martin, and Philip E. Steinberg, "(Un)frozen Spaces: Exploring the Role of Sea Ice in the Marine Socio-legal Spaces of the Bering and Beaufort Seas," *Journal of Borderlands Studies* 33, no. 2 (2018): 239–53; Steinberg et al., "The ice edge is lost."

18   Steinberg et al., "The ice edge is lost," 625.

19   Neil Brenner and Nikos Katsikis, "Operational Landscapes: Hinterlands of the Capitalocene," *Architectural Design* 90, no. 1 (2020): 22–31.

20   Neil Brenner and Christian Schmid, "Planetary Urbanization," in *Urban Constellations*, ed. Matthew Gandy (Jovis, 2012), 10–13.

21   Couling et al., *The Urbanisation of the Sea.*

22   Ibid., 8–9.

23   Ibid., 11; Nancy Couling, "Formats of extended urbanisation in ocean space," in *Emerging Urban Spaces: A Planetary Perspective (Urban Book Series)*, eds., Philipp Horn, Paola Alfaro d'Alencon and Ana Claudia Cardoso (Springer, 2018), 149–76.

24   Caitlin Blanchfield, "Envirotechnical Lands: Science Reserves and Settler Astronomy," in *Technical Lands: A Critical Primer*, eds. Jeffrey S. Nesbit and Charles Waldheim (Jovis Verlag, 2022), 188–203.

25   See also Keller Easterling, *Extrastatecraft: The Power of Infrastructure Space* (Verso, 2014).

26   See also the work of Charity Edwards; Giulia Foscari, and UNLESS, eds., *Antarctic Resolution* (Lars Müller Publishers, 2021).

planning challenges."[27] The urban can thus no longer be understood as a bounded space, restricted to what is normally perceived as "the city," but as a phenomenon that spreads out extensively and dramatically restructures its terrestrial as well as oceanic hinterlands.[28] Understanding the spatial development of the more accessible and centrally located oceanic spaces becomes imperative for recognizing the patterns of increased activity within the Arctic Ocean, where, up until recently, the sea ice has acted as a physical barrier for further resource extractivist explorations and other urbanization efforts.[29]

This calls for the ocean to be addressed spatially and volumetrically. Aligned with the recent turn towards volumetric geographies,[30] the work of Kimberley Peters and Philip Steinberg explores the notion of a "more-than-wet"[31] oceanic ontology and the myriad ways in which the oceanspace exceeds both its own materiality and the bounded space through which it is often cartographically portrayed.[32] Peters and Steinberg position the more-than-wet oceanspace as an arena for reconceptualizing understandings of space, time, and movement, offering new perspectives beyond "the static simplicity of landed place."[33] In the polar oceanspace, where the unruly drifting of sea ice is defying these common binaries of solid and fluid, a more-than-wet ontological approach becomes crucial in order to engage with these territories and to fully understand their connectedness to global environmental, geopolitical, and capitalist systems.

DRIFTING AS AGENCY

Drifting constitutes a very specific type of global oceanic mobility[34] but has also continually played an active role in both acts of territorialization and knowledge production of the Arctic Ocean, and thus becomes an essential concept to address the inherent mobility and fluidity that challenges oceanic spatial understandings and representations. Historically, the drifting of sea ice has been attempted to be utilized for both the gain of territorial claim and military and scientific power within the Arctic. One of the first known examples of the Western nations' attempts hereof was the drifting expedition of Fridtjof Nansen, who, in 1893, intentionally stuck the ship *Fram* into an ice floe to let the Transpolar Drift carry it in an attempt to become the first to reach the geographical North Pole.[35] During the Cold War, drifting ice islands were occupied by both US and Soviet forces, on which they established floating science labs and military bases – here, the ice islands came to act as territorial prosthetics within a tense geopolitical context.[36] In 2019, the German research icebreaker Polarstern embarked on the yearlong MOSAIC research expedition, stuck, as Nansen, within the ice, drifting along the Transpolar Drift.[37]

The mentioned examples highlight the historical relationship between the taming of drifting as a territorializing tool and the Arctic as a frontier landscape. The notion of drifting thus emerges as a crucial tool for navigating the complexities of the Arctic environment, planning with the unruliness of sea ice, and engaging in less binary approaches to the frozen ocean space. It challenges traditional notions of speed and progress and offers an alternative perspective on engagement with the cryoscape and the Arctic oceanscape, where the changing viscosity of the ocean space[38] challenges Western oceanic spatial representation, marine spatial planning, and conventional mapmaking.

THICK OCEANIC MAPPINGS

The difficulties with mapping sea ice—drifting, melting, and ever-changing—have resulted in either diagrammatically simplifying daily overviews from ice databases or boiled-down lines on a map depicting a static border. This reveals itself as a sort of "cartographic silencing,"[39] which inadequately captures the dynamic inherent within an oceanic space, with the result of the drifting vibrancy of sea ice and complex materiality being frozen in inadequately spatially fixed cartographic representations within marine spatial planning documents and governance practices. Drawing documents based on this kind of "thick representation"[40] hints at a strategy to overcome these representational limitations of traditional marine spatial planning, introducing

27   Nancy Couling, "Imagining the Invisible: Spatial Design for the North Sea," *Planning Practice and Research* 37, no. 3 (2022): 278.

28   Ibid., 20.

29   Klaus Dodds, "A Polar Mediterranean? Accessibility, Resources and Sovereignty in the Arctic Ocean," *Global Policy* 1, no. 3 (2010): 303–11.

30   See Stuart Elden, "Secure the Volume: Vertical Geopolitics and the Depth of Power," *Political Geography* 32, no. 2 (2013): 35–51; Stuart Elden, "The Instability of Terrain," in A *Moving Border: Alpine Cartographies of Climate Change*, eds. Marco Ferrari, Elisa Pasqual and Andrea Bagnato (Columbia Books on Architecture and the City/ZKM, 2019): 51–61; Kimberley Peters, Philip Steinberg, and Elaine Stratford, eds., *Territory Beyond Terra* (Rowman & Littlefield International, 2018).

31   Peters et al., "The ocean in excess."

32   Ibid.; Philip Steinberg and Kimberley Peters, "Wet Ontologies, fluid spaces: giving depth to volume through oceanic thinking," *Environment and Planning D: Society and Space* 33 (2015): 247–64.

33   Peters et al., "The ocean in excess," 305.

34   Kimberley Peters, "Drifting: Towards mobilities at sea," *Transactions of the Institute of British Geographers* 40, no. 2 (2015): 262–72.

35   Fridtjof Nansen, *Farthest North: Being the Record of Exploration of the Ship Fram, 1893-96, and of a Fifteen Months' Sleigh Journey* (Cambridge Library Collection, 1897/2011).

36   Johanne Bruun, and Philip Steinberg, "Placing Territory on Ice: Militarisation, Measurement and Murder in the High Arctic," in *Territory beyond Terra*, eds. Kimberley Peters, Philip Steinberg and Elaine Stratford (Rowman & Littlefield International, 2018); L. S. Koenig, K R Greenaway, Moira Dunbar, and G Hattersley-Smith, "Arctic Ice Islands," *Arctic* 5, no. 2 (1952): 66–103; Donat Pharand, "The Legal Status of Ice Shelves and Ice Islands in the Arctic," *Les Cahiers de droit* 10, no. 3 (1969): 461–75.

37   "*MOSAiC expedition*," Alfred Wegener Institute, Helmholtz Centre for Polar and Marine Research (AWI), accessed June 7, 2024. mosaic-expedition.org

38   Nancy Couling and Carola Hein, "Viscosity," in *The Urbanisation of the Sea: From concepts and analysis to design*, eds. Nancy Couling and Carola Hein (nai010 publishers, 2020), 55–60.

39   Claudia Bode and Lizzie Yarina, "Thick representations for oceanic space," in *The Urbanisation of the Sea: From concepts and analysis to design*, eds. Nancy Couling and Carola Hein (nai010 publishers, 2020), 71–92.

40   Bode et al., "Thick representations."

density as an understanding of the ocean's materiality and its needed representational tools. Equating a design methodology to a narrative, a thick or dense representation calls for cartographies that delve into the depth, movement, and temporal aspects of oceanic space. This shift from fixed and bounded conceptions of space to deeper, richer, multifaceted, and dynamic representations emerges as an important step to provide a more comprehensive understanding of the dynamic unpredictableness of the ocean realm. A more complex way of drawing and softer, more adaptive marine spatial planning strategies centered on ecological concerns and hydrographic areas rather than rigid boundaries—flows, connectivity, and non-human actors—could bridge the current gap between policymakers and oceanic spaces and emerge as a viable alternative to traditional land-based views of space and territory.[41]

> The materiality of sea ice resides at the center of this complexity, making it, as this text argues, a spatial and landscape architectural matter in which sea ice is to be taken into account as a material actor, existing between both "biophysical forces and social interactions."[42] This dynamic materiality of both solidity and fluidity, as well as constant movement, challenges dominant Western discourse of land and sea and complicates territorial disputes in the region: "Despite operating on a different temporal scale, sea ice should not be perceived merely as a disappearing entity but rather as a continuous, ever-present substance challenging stationary conceptions of law and spatial boundaries."[43] Considering the difficulties in mapping the ocean and sea ice, the concept of drifting emerges as a conceptual framework for thinking with such a viscous, more-than-wet[44] oceanscape.

DESIGNING WITH THE OCEAN AS A THREE-DIMENSIONAL SPACE

Proposing drifting as an analytical framework for design, planning, and management operations, the project accompanying this text calls for a recentering of more-than-human stakeholders in Arctic marine spatial planning scenarios and a shift toward a more dynamic, fluid understanding of the agency of sea ice. While this has been explored extensively within geopolitical and scientific studies, a spatial perspective can unfold a more embodied, material understanding of sea ice and render visible its territorial network of social and meteorological entanglements. Thinking through the agency of drifting allows for exploring the linkage between dominating Western perceptions of sea ice and capitalist projects of extractivism and boundary-making in the Arctic Ocean, calling for a re-understanding of mobility and fluxes.

> The prospect of increased marine activity within an increasingly warming Arctic Ocean necessitates a sharpened focus on the planning issues of these melting regions, a reconfiguration of the drifting sea ice, and a recognition of the Transpolar Drift as a piece of environmental infrastructure within more-than-human marine spatial planning negotiations. As new transpolar futures emerge within the

warming Arctic, drifting sea ice plays a crucial role in the increased operationalization of the oceanscape, demanding novel approaches to marine spatial planning questions. Within this context, the material state of sea ice and the dominant perception hereof directly affect Arctic nation-states' political and economic projects and their increased interest in developing this once hard-to-reach territory. Thinking with sea ice, as simultaneously matter and drifting movement, however, allows us to navigate along a gradient of viscosity as a way of questioning the rigidness of such state-induced boundaries in fluid territories and allows for speculations into a re-materialization of this unruly material actor.

Learning from, thinking about, and designing with the ocean signifies a meaningful engagement with the watery spaces of our globe but is also a spatial exercise toward understanding territories in terms of volumetric and spatial aspects. The Arctic oceanscape becomes especially relevant in this regard, as a space in which the clear distinction between land and sea, between floating and grounded territory, is blurred, and where sea ice as "a materialization of time"[45] holds a material agency, far exceeding these dichotomies. Drifting ice proposes a much-needed story of spatial agency by spatializing what is often portrayed by two-dimensional mappings or in the flattened imagery of so-called pristine and frozen landscapes.

41   Ibid.
42   Shake et al., "(Un)frozen Spaces."
43   Ibid., 249.
44   Peters et al., "The ocean in excess."
45   Bruun et al., "Placing Territory on Ice," 156.

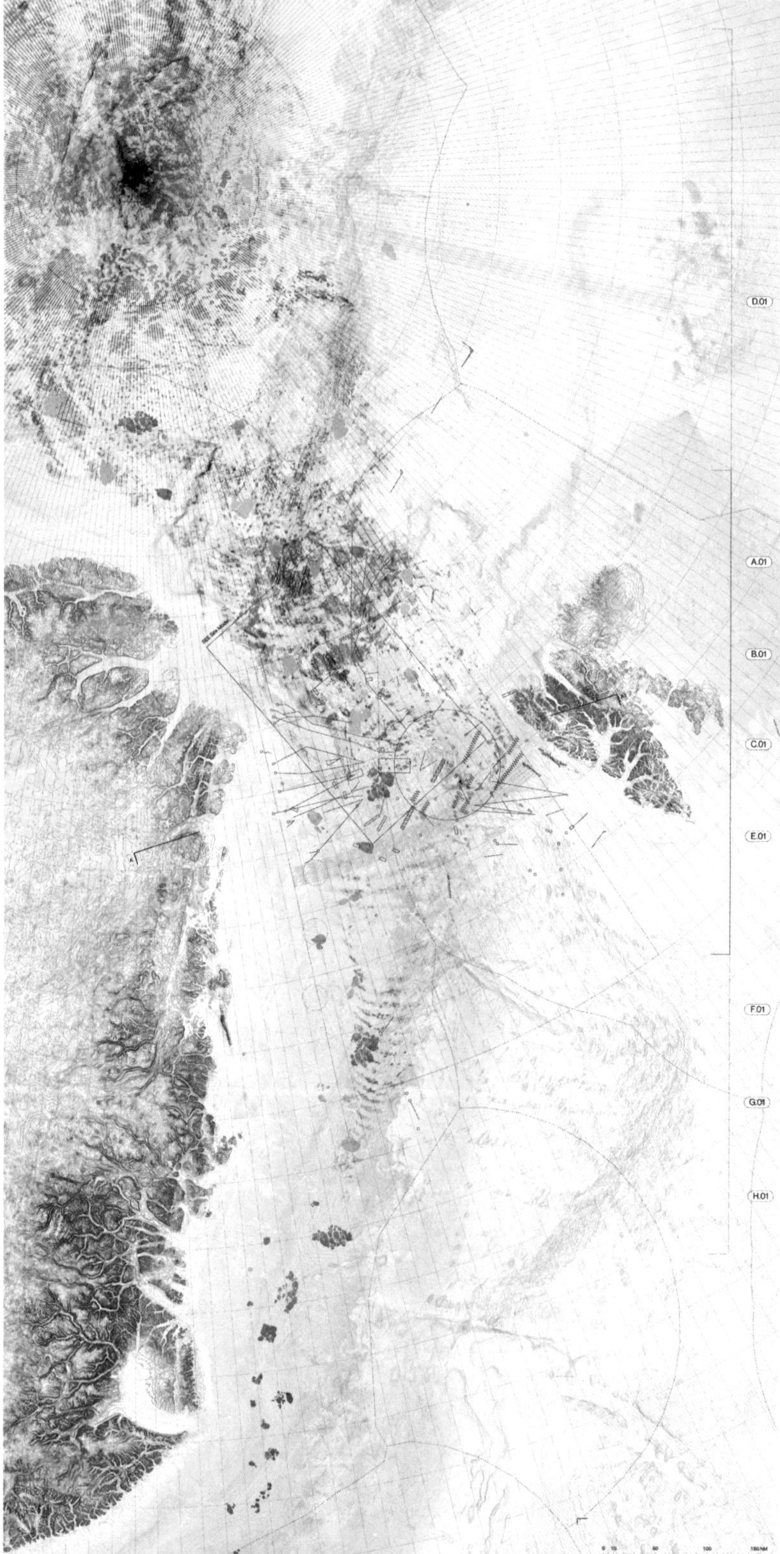

D.01
A.01
B.01
C.01
E.01
F.01
G.01
H.01
1 : 4,000,000
0   10   50   100   150 NM
0   50   100   200 KM

A drifting planning document proposes a dynamically fluctuating marine spatial strategy for the Fram Strait and a spatially responsive system integrating various factors such as ice export levels, spawning periods, migration routes, fuel emission control, noise pollution, and ship hull criteria. By considering each passing actor, whether human or non-human, as a drift passenger, this project challenges the dominant Western anthropocentric approach to marine spatial planning, advocating for designs based on unruly viscosities and recognizing the complex and fluid interactions within marine environments.

Ice Edge Community
Polynya Community
Ice Lead Community
Meltwater Pond Community
Ice Ridge Community
Sub-Ice Community
Sea Ice Community
Benthic Residents

A section perspective depicting the Arctic ecosystem's current spatial conditions and characteristics, emphasizing the interplay between sea ice, marine life, and the environment. The marginal ice edge is a vital habitat for numerous key species within the Arctic ecosystem, where the pelagic community is concentrated near the upper part of the water column, relying on and feeding off the drifting sea ice, leaving the deeper water column less active. However, the sedimentation of dead organic matter is essential for the benthic community. Serving as a feeding ground for bird species such as the ivory gull and thick-billed murre, the various ice features of the ice edge (polynyas, leads, meltwater ponds, and ice ridges) facilitate exchange between the atmosphere and sea surface, enhancing conditions for microbiotic species inhabiting the ice surface and brine channels. During the spawning season (December to March), Arctic cod eggs, with their thin membranes, are protected by the thick and stable multiyear ice cover, which acts as both a feeding ground and protection for mature fish.

Note   The labels in these drawings have been revised from their original format to improve clarity and legibility for this publication.

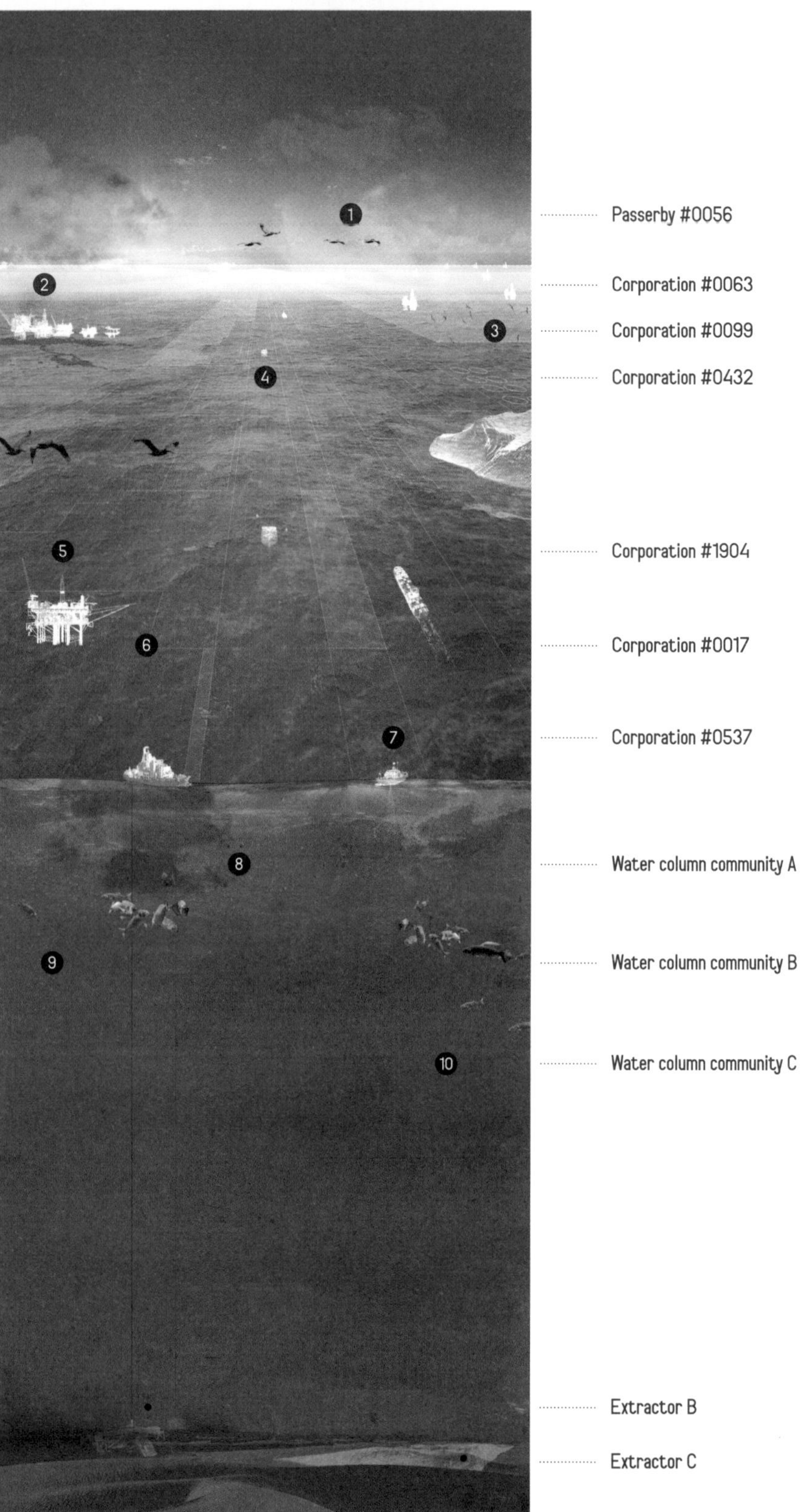

Passerby #0056
Corporation #0063
Corporation #0099
Corporation #0432
Corporation #1904
Corporation #0017
Corporation #0537
Water column community A
Water column community B
Water column community C
Extractor B
Extractor C

A dystopian speculative section perspective, anno 2100, in which the ocean is densely urbanized, compartmentalized, and drawn out in rigid fields of ownership and nationality, the transpolar route a major new maritime shipping highway. The decrease in sea ice and the rich resources of the Arctic underground became a battlefield for a twenty-second-century frontier resource hunt. The slowing of the Transpolar Drift and sea ice loss has depleted the inner Arctic Ocean of nutrient distribution, and the once-rich benthic ecosystem is now gone.

1 *Passerby #0056*
A flock of ivory gulls migrate across the Arctic. Bird migration patterns have been pushed by the lack of sea ice and feeding grounds, forcing birds to have longer and more unstable migration patterns.

2 *Corporation #0063*
A newly opened oil field platform experiences a massive oil leak, resulting in multiyear pollution.

3 *Corporation #0099*
A newly established fish farm was set up to test commercial aquaculture's possibilities in the warming Arctic Ocean.

4 *Corporation #0432*
A cargo vessel en route from Hamburg to Shanghai.

5 *Corporation #1904*
Equinor's first opened oil field above 79°N.

6 *Corporation #0017*
As the Norwegian Oil and Energy Department declined to join the international moratorium on seafloor mining, the rich mineral ground of the volcanic ridges surrounding the Fram Strait is being mined (Extractor B). Excess plumes of drawn-up material are discharged within the epipelagic zone.

7 *Corporation #0537*
A survey ship scans the sea floor using a multibeam sonar scan (Extractor C) to locate potential oil and gas reserves. Cooperating and sharing its data with Arctic research institutions gives Corporation #0535 future goodwill.

8 *Water column community A*
The increased shipping traffic and the lack of regulation in terms of Heavy Fuel oil (HFO) use results in constant leaks of crude oil particles, which, even in small amounts, drastically affect drifting fish eggs and phytoplankton.

9 *Water column community B*
The absence of sea ice drastically changes the light conditions of the ocean, and what was once a concentrated spike in bio productivity during a narrow window in the summer months is now an increasing algae bloom. As the Transpolar Drift becomes more and more stagnant, the Arctic Ocean, like the Mediterranean Sea, with little inflow and outflow, begins to resemble a thick, stagnant soup.

10 *Water column community C*
Atlantic fish species like the Atlantic cod have pushed out Arctic species as the water warms up. Globally distributed invasive species have been brought up through ship hulls.

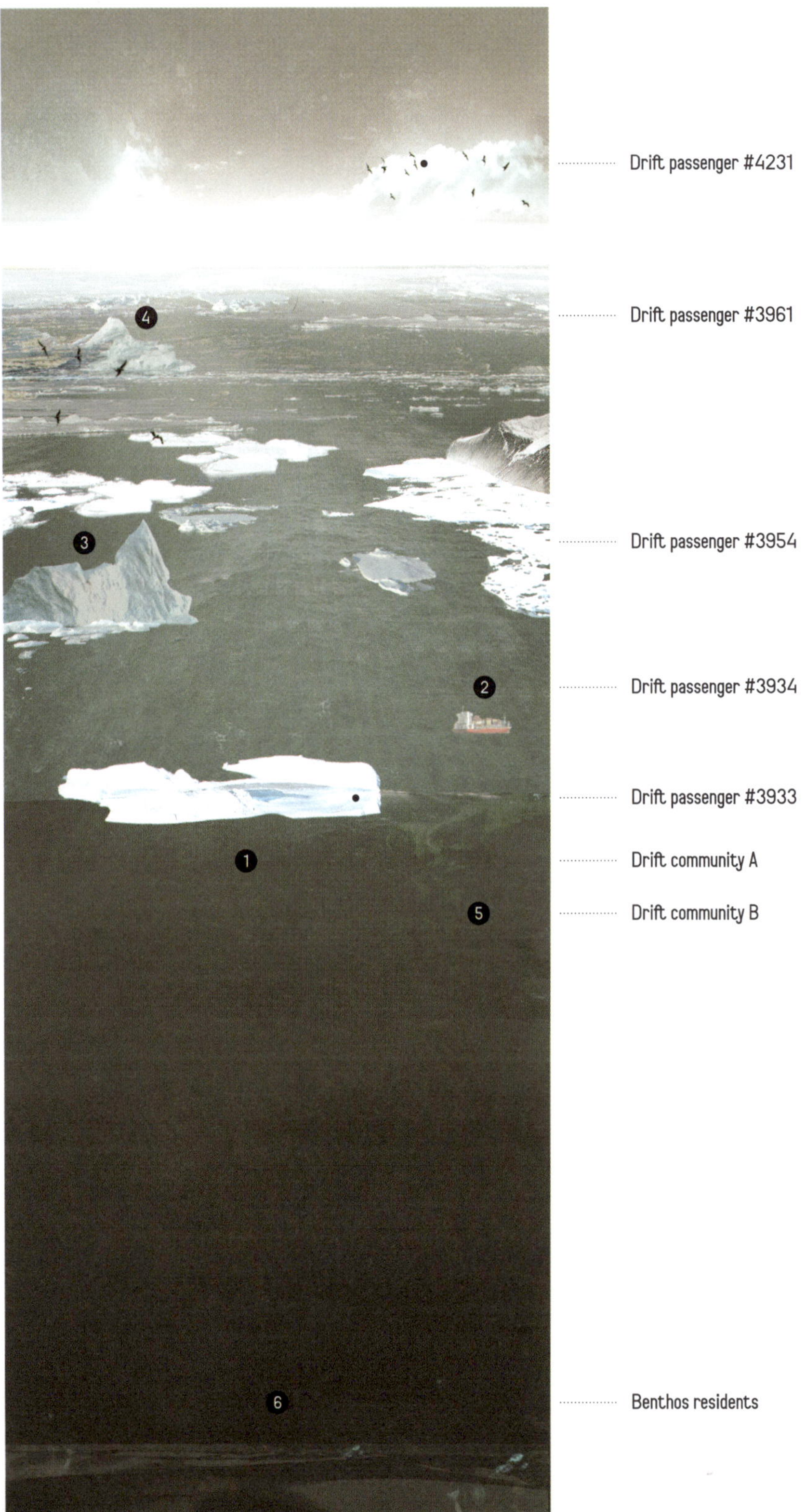

Drift passenger #4231
Drift passenger #3961
Drift passenger #3954
Drift passenger #3934
Drift passenger #3933
Drift community A
Drift community B
Benthos residents

A section perspective of the Fram Strait, anno 2050, in which a future planning scenario has been implemented. Thinking with other-than-human actors through movement and viscosity became instrumental to further de-categorize the affected stakeholders: the notion of drifting becoming a crucial tool for navigating the complexities and engaging in less binary approaches to the frozen ocean space.

1 *Drift Community A*
A drifting sea ice floe, a remainder of the quickly diminishing multiyear ice, having survived its long journey from the Great Siberian Polynya Ice Nursery, passed 3 years in the periphery of the Beaufort Gyre before traveling further south along the Transpolar Drift, to finally pass through the Fram Strait.

2 *Drift passenger #3934*
A cargo vessel headed towards the Behring Strait is called to dock due to the high activity of the Spitsbergen bowhead whale population within the Fram Strait TSS. The vessel docks at the Longyearbyen Harbor. The vessel type adheres to regulation E.01 re. Ship hull design: There is a low probability of importing invasive species.

3 *Drift passenger #3954*
Drifting fast ice in the form of an iceberg calved from the so-called Ellesmere Island set to melt in the warm Atlantic water as it drifts along the Transpolar Drift. As it melts: freshwater discharge.

4 *Drift passenger #3961*
Drifting fast ice in the form of an iceberg calved from the so-called Peterman Glacier in Northern Kalaallit Nunaat. It will take ten days to grind along the eastern coast, leaving significant scour marks on the sea floor and damaging a traversing oil pipe. As it melts: freshwater discharges.

5 *Drift community B*
Ice edge algae bloom.

6 *Benthos residents*
Nourished by the downfall of organic matter from the active layer of the water column, the Fram Strait seafloor ridges and canyons become inhabited by rich benthic communities. The passing melting ice entities ensure the circulation of sediments and nutrients crucial for the benthic scavenger ecosystem.

Nicole Luke (BEnvD, MArch) is an emerging Indigenous designer born on the territories with family residing in the Kivalliq region of Nunavut. She is one of the first Inuk architectural graduates in Canada and the first Inuk to receive her Bachelor's and Master's degrees from the Faculty of Architecture at the University of Manitoba.

My Notes on Architecture within Inuit Nunangat
Nicole Luke

The territory of Nunavut is the most recent territory of Canada. It was created from the Northwest Territories on April 1, 1999, by way of two legal tools: the Nunavut Act and the Nunavut Land Claims Agreement Act. There are fifty-three communities within Nunavut, all created within the last century. Each of these communities has a distinct history in how and why they were created. Some are related to the existence of Hudson Bay Posts, and some are related to the location of residential schools and mines. Some are the result of forced relocation by the government, and some are near traditional hunting grounds. There are many other possible and related factors. But whatever the reason each community has come to be where they are, each settlement is rich with distinct Inuit culture. These communities face unique challenges as they become increasingly involved with southern and international developments while building capacity for their community members.

In the context of architectural development in the Arctic, Inuit and remote Indigenous communities have created a perplexing mismatch of timelines, as there are different perceptions of how development is seen and understood. Construction deadlines and Inuit culture and community timelines vary: companies and the government plan the completion of a project to certain dates or times of the year and then move on to the next job. Conversely, communities plan beyond the completion date, incorporating the building into their community life. There exists a kind of synergy between those designing and

1   *The Architecture of Inuksuit* (2024). The comparison of inuksuit (plural for Inuksuk) and today's methods of stacking.

2   *Energy and Activity* (2024). Inuit games, utility poles, the land, and the sea can.

constructing and the users who inherit something ongoing, which companies and the government would instead consider an end result. Despite knowing this, the processes of architectural development and construction differ from project to project, continuing the misalignment of timelines and the friction between ideas of completion and care. These are my current observations as I navigate the architectural and construction realm early in my career. I look forward to comparing my observations again in the coming years.

In the past few decades, Indigenous architects and designers have become powerhouses in designing and advocating within the architecture realm, with and for Indigenous communities, an opportunity that wasn't as common or even available in previous decades. I am pleased to say there has been a lot of movement with Indigenous architects in practice and academia, which inspires me to continue within the industry. Inversely, however, there has been a struggle to retain Inuit within the construction industry and on the job site. The Nunavummi Nangminiqaqtunik Ikajuuti (NNI) is a preferential procurement policy wherein the Government of Nunavut requires a certain percentage of Inuit or local workers, as this helps workers gain skills so that they then might continue to apply them within the community. NNI is meant to assist in local labor and generating local economy rather than solely relying on southern business. Unfortunately, a flaw in this policy emerges when the community experiences so much development that the demand for local labor outstrips the projections or quota conveyed to the local community. Depending on the population of the community and the type of work available related to construction, the percentage of applicable local labor can struggle to meet the minimum NNI percentage (which may vary from project to project); therefore, having southern workers becomes an important factor in the development of construction projects in these Arctic communities. In addition, there are also existing competing priorities that come in the form of seasonal pressures as hunting flourishes at only certain times of the year. Inuit—perhaps most Indigenous people—are faced with the need to balance working a day-to-day job to practice a modern lifestyle to support themselves within capitalistic systems with being on the land, freely practicing and maintaining their cultural skills, including obtaining sustenance through hunting, fishing, berry picking, etc.

It is something beyond irony when people need to work to provide for themselves and their families by purchasing groceries at super-inflated prices when the land and all that it contains is at their doorsteps. The mark-up on standard food items in Nunavut has long been known to be unfair due to the monopoly of grocery stores (in addition to the lengthy travel required for these items). We need to challenge this monopoly. If one had to choose between the working conditions of construction labor and being on the land, most of us agree that spending our days outdoors provides both much-needed therapeutic value and autonomy.

It is also worth noting that educational opportunities in the North are few; it is important to understand that the number of educators present is limited, and this is but one of many factors contributing to the need for specific careers and training. This is why we commonly see southern workers sent up for weeks or months at a time. Although this may be business as usual, this, too, adds to the need for more planning, increasing the demand and cost for flights, food, and accommodations in already housing-short and overinflated communities. To even ship the needed construction materials on the limited number of ships that are able to travel before the ice sheets form is already an extreme cost factor to be considered in all northern construction. Each community relies on these same ships to deliver the diesel fuel that heats their buildings during the long, dark winters; every drop of fuel and second of warmth counts. It is a constant push and pull between resource and restraint.

> In most cases, there are very limited spaces for Indigenous leadership and practice of autonomy related to culture and identity for roles within architecture, construction, and development. From my observations, and even though much work has been done, Inuit continue to be used to fill labor-intensive construction jobs with a very limited percentage of Inuit in management (i.e., running job sites). The lack of Indigenous autonomy continues to be glaringly obvious, even if we know better. In time, I hope to see this evolve into a range of roles readily available for Inuit in their communities to contribute to development at a variety of levels in planning. Representation matters.

Inuit have experienced unique introductions to the southern and global realms. It's something I'm still learning. But what makes it special for me is that I am observing these young communities changing slowly in a way that works *with* them as they gain retention within the industry. This does not mean the process is perfect, but forward development is progressive. This is not to disregard the hardships of Inuit due to colonization—this should be a fundamental requirement for all architects and construction companies working in the Arctic to learn about—but this is an example of Inuit developing sovereignty for Inuit.

> I used to perceive teaching and tradition as something of the past, but I now understand it is up to us—Inuit and Indigenous—to listen and apply our cultures respectfully, which inherently makes them modern. Not only am I continuously learning about my own Indigeneity, but I'm also learning what it means to be an architect and what it means to develop these identities to coexist.

3   *The Land Provides* (2024). Food for the Inuk soul.

Todd Saunders is a Norway-based Canadian architect known to infuse his contemporary buildings with an artistic sensibility that is deeply in tune with the uniqueness of northern terrains.

A Most Curious Listener: Todd Saunders in Conversation with Bert De Jonghe and Elise Misao Hunchuck

It is said that it was the earliest Portuguese fishing boats who bestowed the name of 'Fogo'—their word for fire—onto an island that was but a "sliver of the North American continent" protruding above the surface of the waters where the Labrador Sea meets the North Atlantic Ocean. In the not-so-distant memory of Canadians, Fogo Island and Newfoundland and Labrador, the province of which it is a part, was synonymous with the collapse of the (near-shore) cod-fishing in the 1990s due to hundreds of years of overfishing a once plentiful cod population that was said to have filled the waters of the Atlantic itself. But in just over ten years, a new, highly localized economic model—community tourism—emerged, and with it, the much-lauded (and even more photographed) Fogo Island Inn, designed by Canadian architect Todd Saunders. The undeniable success of the inn and its iconography is due in no small part to the remarkable care taken during the design, build, and early days of its opening, when everything from the flora and fauna that live in and around the building's footprint was considered by building platforms to protect them, to the use of local materials and craftspeople, to the warmed, low lighting above the shared dining room tables in its early, opening days.

A practice of attenuation and listening is one that Todd Saunders has developed over the long arch of his illustrious career, which we contend began when he was a young teenager, building a cabin with his father and his uncle in his home province of Newfoundland.

We met with Todd twice, on October 2 and 12, 2023, to speak about Fogo Island and his recent Tekαkαpimǝk project in Maine, USA. In this conversation, he speaks about how his approach has changed and developed over the years and what he hopes will be the future of his practice. *BDJ, EMH*

Bert De Jonghe and Elise Misao Hunchuck Can you tell us about your curious listening design approach and what makes one a curious listener?

Todd Saunders It is something I learned later in life. I call it curious listening / active listening, where I pick up on things by asking questions. I learned this technique—asking *for* questions—from Ray Brown, an older Scottish man. This was not just asking one question and moving on to the next but asking a series of questions that were designed to go deeper and deeper. He said that by the fourth or fifth question, you would usually get to the core of the answer. I've been trying it out on myself and in conversations, and I think you can get to the essence of things this way.

For example, when we design houses in Norway, the first question is usually, "What do you want?" Every Norwegian then answers relatively the same. But by asking a second and third question, you will likely find out they may all want the same thing, but each for different reasons. It is a matter of *making and holding space* to try to get to the core of the issue at hand. The way we do it, we aim first to establish the *needs:* what does the client need, and what does the site need? After we have that nailed down, we move on to the *wants.* The wants are extras, but the needs are non-negotiable.

In one book publication I did, *Share*, we interviewed thirty architects in Scandinavian countries, and the above-mentioned approach was productive, too.[1] Also, Jonathan Bell, with whom I did my first book,[2] was listening to the interviews and taught me some listening techniques. For example, leave five to ten seconds of quietness after your answer—this way, the other person can feel encouraged to fill the space. So curious listening is not just part of the design approach. It is more of a life approach. I have always been curious, but I can still work on being a better listener. It is a process, a practice.

BDJ, EMH Have you used this practice or technique in any of your projects in the Circumpolar North?

1   Todd Saunders and Jonathan Bell, *Share: Conversations about Contemporary Architecture* (Artifice Press, 2022).

2   Todd Saunders, Jonathan Bell, and Ellie Stathaki, *Architecture in Northern Landscapes* (Birkhäuser, 2016).

TS I've used this technique with the consultants of the Illusuak project in Labrador[3] and with some community members. The project where I used it the most was Fogo Island Inn. In this project, it was not me alone but Zita Cobb and me.[4] Zita and her brothers (Alan and Anthony Cobb) were also there. And we were able to share the effort: we'd have three-hour meetings, but we wouldn't get exhausted. It is like peeling a piece of fruit. But you also have to know when to stop asking. I probably ask too much sometimes. But it goes both ways. They can also ask me questions. It is more about developing a kind of openness and trust.[5]

When we were working on the Katahdin project in Maine,[6] Elaine Falender,[7] who has since passed away, used a great expression. She said *we move at the speed of trust.* And the speed of trust is different in different situations. For me, in northern Labrador, it did not go so fast. It went very quickly in Fogo because I was one of them: I speak the language and understand the accent. In some cases, I don't think I belong in some climates and communities; there is probably a better person there for the job. I also think that the process of choosing an architect in the North should not be done on paper; it should be done in person. It should be done over a series of meetings. I'm tired of the RFP/RFQ process. The larger companies have more labor and effort to put into these requests. The problem is that when they get hired, there are often different architects who get switched in and out of the project during the process.

What we like to do is to meet the client and build a rapport and a relationship with them over time. By the third or fourth meeting, they can then make an informed decision on whether or not to move ahead with us. It all starts from there. I think the better projects are usually with companies owned by people and not by corporations. I recommend that small communities be very, very careful of going the route of trying to check off all the boxes they think they need and instead finding a group of people that they think they can work well with and will look out for their needs. It can work better.

BDJ, EMH Who are some of the interdisciplinary team members you include in your contemporary projects—who you may not have included in your earlier work? And why?

TS We have a very small team, and they are always involved. But there are some people from outside of the firm who I've worked with over the years. Kato Hiroshi is a Japanese architect with whom I have some week-long and in-person working sessions in Bergen, Norway. Hannes Wingate is a survival expert and an artist who has done a couple of my interiors. We've also worked with some furniture designers like Ineke Hans and we also worked with Eirik Glambek Bøe, an architect and musician. There are always different combinations of people involved, depending on the project. I think it is important to have a small core team and then to invite others.

BDJ, EMH Have you found that your Canadian background influenced your Norwegian projects? How has living in Norway affected or influenced your (Canadian or other) projects? How does the experience of living in Norway influence your Canadian projects?

TS It goes both ways. I realized the other day that it has been thirty years since I did my Master of Architecture at McGill (in Montréal) and twenty-eight years since I moved to Norway. That's more than half of my life! I'm probably more Norwegian. I've spent more time in Norway than in Canada. I've lived in Germany (Berlin), Russia (thirty minutes from Volkov), Austria (Vienna), and the States (Providence in Rhode Island). So my professional architecture life—the technical side—is mostly influenced by Norway.

But I learned everything about architecture growing up in Newfoundland by building a cabin with my dad and uncle. Everything.

3   Located in the northernmost community of Labrador, Canada, Illusuak is a new cultural center and administrative hub for the region that makes an important statement of autonomy for this Indigenous community. The 1,200 square-meter building was commissioned by the Nunatsiavut Government and acts as a living room for the community, with an auditorium for language classes, café, a craft shop, studio space, and seventy-five-seat theater. The building also provides offices to the Nunatsiavut Government as well as Parks Canada. Designed by Saunders Architecture, Illusuak makes a bold architectural statement using forms and materials derived from the region's tradition and heritage.

4   Zita Cobb is co-founder (alongside her brothers Alan and Anthony) of the Shorefast Foundation, a social enterprise based in Canada that is focused on building economic and cultural resilience on Fogo Island, Newfoundland.

5   Saunders explains: Today, we do the same with office meetings; we usually have two or three people from the office in meetings and we throw out questions.

6   In the present and traditional homeland of the Penobscot Nation, Tekakapimək Contact Station is a stunning 734-square-meter interpretive environment welcoming the global public to Katahdin Woods and Waters National Monument in northern Maine. In consultation with the US National Park Service, Tekakapimək (Dah-gaga-bee-mok), Penobscot for "as far as one can see," is imbued with Indigenous knowledges from the Wabanaki Nations: Houlton Band of Maliseet Indians, Mi'kmaq Nation, Passamaquoddy Tribe — Sipayik and Motahkomikuk, and Penobscot Nation. It intentionally incorporates cultural narratives, languages, images, kinship relations, ancestral representations, contemporary practices, and native materials of these lands and waters. The project was conceived as a gift by Maine-based Roxanne Quimby and Elliotsville Foundations, who selected Norway-based Saunders Architecture.

7   From project inception, Elaine Falender worked with Todd as a Project Manager. She masterfully coordinated complex permitting and was instrumental in facilitating a relationship with Wabanaki Tribes, who ultimately contributed in a way that transformed the design. Elaine also helped create underlying contract templates for the myriad of partners and subcontractors. Sadly, Elaine passed away on April 21, 2022. Elaine Susan Falender dedicated her life to law, community service, and strategic planning, impacting the development of Tekakapimək, Katahdin Woods and Waters National Monument Visitor Contact Station.

1–4   A small hands-on project supported by sketching on top of iPad photos made on the spot, resulting in a flexible and iterative design process (2020).

The whole process is still there. It was three people, like a three-legged stool. We all respected each other; we worked together. One designs and presents (my uncle), and my dad and I would help and discuss.

Three years ago, I had a workshop and built this little project inside, and it was the exact same process; I went down there, took a picture with my iPad, and changed it as we went (↔ 1–4). That process of building a cabin with my dad and uncle is still part of every good project that I've done. It is very hands-on. *It is not about the drawings, but it's about discussion.* And I think that changed all my Norwegian projects.

When we did the Aurland Lookout,[8] for example, I could draw construction details, but the conversations were so slow and technical. We built a two-meter section of it and had it in my office. And we used that as the conversation piece. And when we did the tower studio on Fogo, we built three different models—nobody looked at the drawings—we looked at the models. My way of making architecture was very influenced by being that fourteen, fifteen-year-old kid who built a cabin. That's my Canadian background, which infiltrated everything. No matter if I went to Indonesia or Japan or anywhere else.

Norway has a lot of rituals and a lot of respect for nature. And a very formal relation to nature. Certain times of the year, they do this or they do that. For example, I'm thinking of the huge bonfires at Sankthansaften (St Hans Eve) or eating oranges and chocolate outside during Easter. The way they use architecture is related to the seasons, too—at Easter and during summer, they go to their cabins. It is very clear. That influenced my Canadian way of working and brought rituals based on Norwegian culture and architecture to the houses I make. Another thing worth noting is that the Norwegians (not all, of course) are very proud of simplicity, whereas Canadians (not all either, of course) are a bit ashamed of simplicity.

BDJ, EMH In what capacity, if at all, does the discipline and practice of landscape architecture influence your work?

TS It's all landscape architecture. I don't really believe there is an interior architect, a landscape architect, or an industrial designer or architect. It is all a process of creating a place or relating to a place. We did the Aurland Lookout, which was a bit too much for the Norwegians. There is a really nice article in *Morgen Blad*[9] about how good that project was, but the author, Gaute Brochmann, said it was very 'non-Norwegian'. Brochmann gave the architecture a ski-jumping score of 20/20. The lookout asks the question: is it architecture or landscape architecture? I believe there is a field between the three professions; that's where I am. It is an intersection where they all meet, and you can't really put a finger on it. But I also think it is more about placemaking. *I would rather have a company about placemaking.*

Right now, we are designing and building the Fedje Hotel (Norway), and it is very much on the landscape and wanting to be seen, whereas further up the coast, we are doing another one where we don't want to see the building. They are both Norwegian projects, and both are on the coast, but the sites and the communities need very different things. So one becomes more of an architecture project placed *on* the landscape, and the other becomes an architecture project (a building) placed *in* the landscape. Some might say the first is architecture; the other is landscape architecture. But for me, *each is both.* It's also why I am very happy to work with such good landscape architects like Maria Auböck, Jane Durante, and Hans Loidl. I met Cornelia Hahn Oberlander[10] after I gave a lecture

8   Aurland Lookout was designed by Todd Saunders and Tommie Wilhelmsen. The project won first prize in an invited competition in 2002. This project is part of a national program on tourist routes commissioned by the Norwegian Highway Department.

9   *Morgen Blad* is Norway's oldest daily newspaper.

5   The Fogo Island Inn surrounded by rugged shorelines.

some years ago, and she came to me and said, *you are not an architect; you are an artist.* I think my architecture influences the landscape, and the landscape influences my architecture. It goes both ways, but there is no immediate answer to which one goes first. I'm very comfortable getting a project and turning it into landscape architecture, not architecture. For example, the Solberg Tower project was more landscape.[11] In the Fogo Island Inn and the Illusuak projects, there was no landscape architecture. In the Katahdin project, we didn't want to see landscape architecture in the traditional sense. Instead, the landscape architects (Reed Hilderbrand) did paths that looked like they had always been there.

I would like to erase the words from all these professions, eventually. We could argue that this already started happening with West 8 and Günther Vogt, landscape architecture firms that do much better architecture than most architects. While Arthur Erickson worked with Cornelia Oberlander to design the Law Courts building (in Vancouver), you can ask, who did the landscape there? The point is that architects can inform landscape, and landscape architects can inform architecture. The idea is to make the best possible project and not to have a line or delineation between professions, as it leads to insular thinking and unresolved projects.

BDJ   What is a big challenge for you in design today?

TS I think that a lot of the projects in the North are now going to larger companies. The really good designers are not getting a chance to even get into the ring. The really good architects out there who can do hyper-specific community-based architecture are not allowed to get this work. I call it franchise architecture: you get the same processed food and products and architecture in all of the communities. The biggest challenge for us is not design, per se, but being able to design! The people who care about these communities do not even get a chance to design with them. I find it much harder with governmental and group clients. It's probably a better process because you include more voices, but it's harder. The decision-making process is longer. Maybe when I get older, I can deal with more people in the project. I enjoyed Fogo the most because it was a private client.

In Fogo, Newfoundland, we built a wooden platform around the construction site so that we did not touch the land—or we touched it as little as possible. If you destroy something in this landscape, it doesn't come back right away—it takes a very long time to grow back if it comes back at all. In northern Norway, there are a lot of scars on the landscape, which is kind of sad. They use a lot of dynamite there. Sometimes, they use it in a good way, and sometimes it is quite heavy-handed. The further north you go, the less forgiving the landscape is once you've touched it. The further north you go, the softer you have to step on the landscape. You have to understand the microbiology of these areas—the flora and fauna are extremely fragile.

Another challenge at Fogo: I sensed during the design phase that the dining room was going to be too small. When it opened, people wanted to sit down and have long conversations and dinners—but there wasn't enough room for all the guests to be seated at once. People want quietness, low or limited lighting, and to sit together at one big table. Fortunately, in the end, the problem of the dining room being too small was fixed. I had so many meals and conversations there. It was your choice if you were going to sit next to someone you didn't know. It is a really enjoyable spot when the sun goes down. That building was informed by what guests needed to get away from their phones, and so on.

BDJ How does research feature in your work?

10   Cornelia Hahn Oberlander CC OBC LL.D. (20 June 1921–22 May 2021) was a German-born Canadian landscape architect.

11   Saunders explains: We were commissioned to design a park at the entrance of Norway (in Sarpsborg) coming from Sweden. Completed in 2010, it is one of the first places travelers stop when entering Norway. The park is surrounded by a long wall composed of Cor-Ten steel on the outside and wood on the inside surface. The wall encompasses a two-thousand-square-meter space, making it into a quiet park. The wall continues to surround the park and then rises thirty meters in the air to form a tower.

6   The Aurland Lookout is a stunning piece of contemporary architecture jutting out high above the small community of Aurland, Norway (2006).

TS What I like to get involved in is research projects that go from design-built work to research. Not just research, design, and build. The best information is when you can get a pulse on how the building is functioning in real time after it is built. This information feeds into the research. Everything can be analyzed. The bookends of each project should be research, and I tend to do that on my own time. My goal for the future is to work with communities over a longer time span. Instead of coming in and doing just one project, I would like it if we could come in, do one project, learn from that, and do another, and so on. I would like to engage with a community over a twenty-year period, for example, instead of just one or two years.

BDJ What does it mean to fail, or what does failure mean in Arctic design?

TS Thinking that you know it all. That you have the solution. It is a failure not to visit buildings after they've been finished. It is a failure not to understand a community fully before you start. At a more practical level, can your building last one hundred years? If it can't, maybe that's a failure. (Maybe it's a success.) Maybe that can be a criteria? A failure is when a community doesn't love your architecture. You created something in their community that they don't like.

   Also, a community in the North doesn't necessarily need a chair or desk from Toronto, but instead, it should come from that specific area.

This is how a hyper-specific design culture will come. It's there in the arts and crafts, but it's not yet been translated into architecture. This is due in large part to the corporate companies that maintain a separation between a design system for specific architecture and the existing arts and crafts cultures.

Also, it is true that there is a lack of design schools in the Arctic. Why do so many of the Canadian architecture and landscape architecture programs take their students to Rome? All the schools in Canada could develop a joint program where students spend a whole semester—not just a few days—up north. It takes time to learn a place. You have to have lived the seasons to understand the people of the place and design for them. In the Bergen School of Architecture, for example, students live outside for the first month of their studies. Maybe this should be a requisite for being a Canadian architect: spend at least one month outside.

The conclusion for this book is that we need more people (local and Indigenous, together) from communities informing the architecture. We need less people like me. By no means am I an Indigenous expert. I would like to see more architects and designers doing work in places they have come to know, either because they are from there, they have spent time there, or they have cared enough to learn and know the people and place they are working with. This, I think, could be the answer to this book.

Dorte Mandrup is the founder and creative director of the Danish architecture studio Dorte Mandrup, internationally recognized for forming architecture in synergy with the context.

Kangiata Illorsua — Ilulissat Icefjord Centre
Dorte Mandrup

In Greenland, severe cold, relentless wind speeds, snow, and ice are normal features of everyday life. Almost 80 percent of the country is covered in ice. Distances are immense, and measuring any human scale in vast landscapes is almost impossible. Kangiata Illorsua – Ilulissat Icefjord Centre is located on the west coast between the small town of Ilulissat and the UNESCO-protected Kangia Icefjord, 250 kilometers north of the Arctic Circle. The project was initiated through an international competition to establish a visitor center as a natural connection between Ilulissat and the Icefjord, functioning as a meeting-, knowledge-, and learning space for locals and visitors alike.

Ilulissat is Greenland's third-biggest city, with approximately 5,000 people. About twenty-five kilometers from Ilulissat lies the world's most active glacier, Sermeq Kujalleq (also known in English as Jakobshavn Glacier). Every year, more than forty-six cubic kilometers of ice calves from the icecap of the rapidly retracting glacier, floating as massive icebergs out to Qeqertarsuup tunua (Disko Bay in English), making Kangia Icefjord one of the world's most important places for monitoring climate change. In 2004, Kangia Icefjord was deemed a UNESCO World Heritage site, and with this status came an obligation to tell the story of its unique natural heritage and to communicate the importance of ice and the consequences of climate change both locally and globally. This is the purpose of Kangiata Illorsua – Ilulissat Icefjord Centre.[1]

The architecture derives from a thorough analysis of the local context—the geology, culture, climate, wind, ice, snow, and Inuit knowledge of survival and subsistence in an environment with scarce resources and extreme weather conditions. A thorough analysis of these aspects of the place in close dialogue with renowned geologist Minik Rosing[2] created the foundation for deep contextual understanding throughout the design phase, shaping an architecture defined by the conditions of nature—an architecture closely related to the Greenlandic landscape. Like the wing of a snowy owl gently touching the bedrock, the building sits lightly, seemingly levitating over the terrain. In a poetic sense, the lightness also emphasizes the idea that the building represents time by creating a contrast between the wooden structure's perishability and the ancient bedrock's permanence. A dynamic movement is created with its boomerang form, allowing visitors to discover the icefjord while moving through or over the building. The aerodynamic shape of Kangiata Illorsua has both a practical function and poetic purpose—it sculpturally anchors the building in the landscape and prevents snow from building up against the façade; analyzed in a wind tunnel, using potato flour to simulate the movement of the snow, it was ensured that the curvature would allow the wind to naturally clear snow from the façade.

1   This project is explored at length in Bert De Jonghe, *Inventing Greenland: Designing an Arctic Nation* (Actar Publishers, 2022), 125.

2   Dr Minik Rosin is currently the Greenlandic Professor of Geology at the GLOBE Institute of the University of Copenhagen. In the late 1990s he discovered traces of microorganisms dating back at least 37,000 million years in rock material found in Isua on the west coast of Greenland, thus revealing that life is much older than we previously thought. Minik has since been the curator of the Danish Pavilion *Possible Greenland* at the Mostra di Architettura di Venezia (Venice Biennale of Architecture) in 2012, and in 2023, he won the Frederik Paulsen Arctic Academic Action Award for his initiative that proposes to use glacial rock flour to reduce atmospheric CO_2 concentrations and improve global food security.

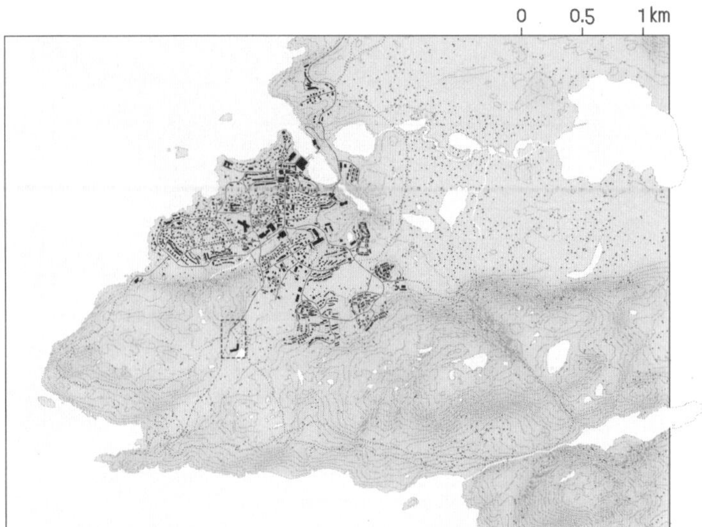

1–2   Above: Map of Ilulissat. Opposite page: Site and floor plan of Ilulissat Icefjord Centre: Entry terrace (1), Entry (2), Shop (3), Café (4), Cinema (5), Exhibition (6), Ice Lab (7), Office (8), Exit terrace (9).

Designing a building in the Arctic is a challenging task. You have to comprehend the extreme cold, freezing winds, and the seemingly infinite scale of the landscape. To ensure a durable and lightweight building, the load-bearing structure is steel-enforced, consisting of fifty-two prefabricated frames from which 80 percent of the steel is recycled. Continuously moving in a soft curve from triangle to rectangular and back to triangle again on the opposite side, each frame has a unique geometric shape. Due to thawing permafrost, the steel warrants less maintenance, fewer replacements, and generally a longer lifespan in an increasingly volatile climate. The resilient European oak is chosen for most of the construction, interior cladding, and flooring.

The knowledge and experience of local contractors and builders with buildings in harsh climates were crucial in making sure the building was completed on time. The remoteness of the site, combined with the lack of naturally sourced building materials in Greenland, underlines the importance of meticulously planning, calculating, designing, and testing in advance: when winter sets in, pack ice sometimes forces the harbor to close, and with temperatures dropping far below zero, the construction process is made increasingly challenging. The building was shipped and mounted in four months, before the ice moved in.

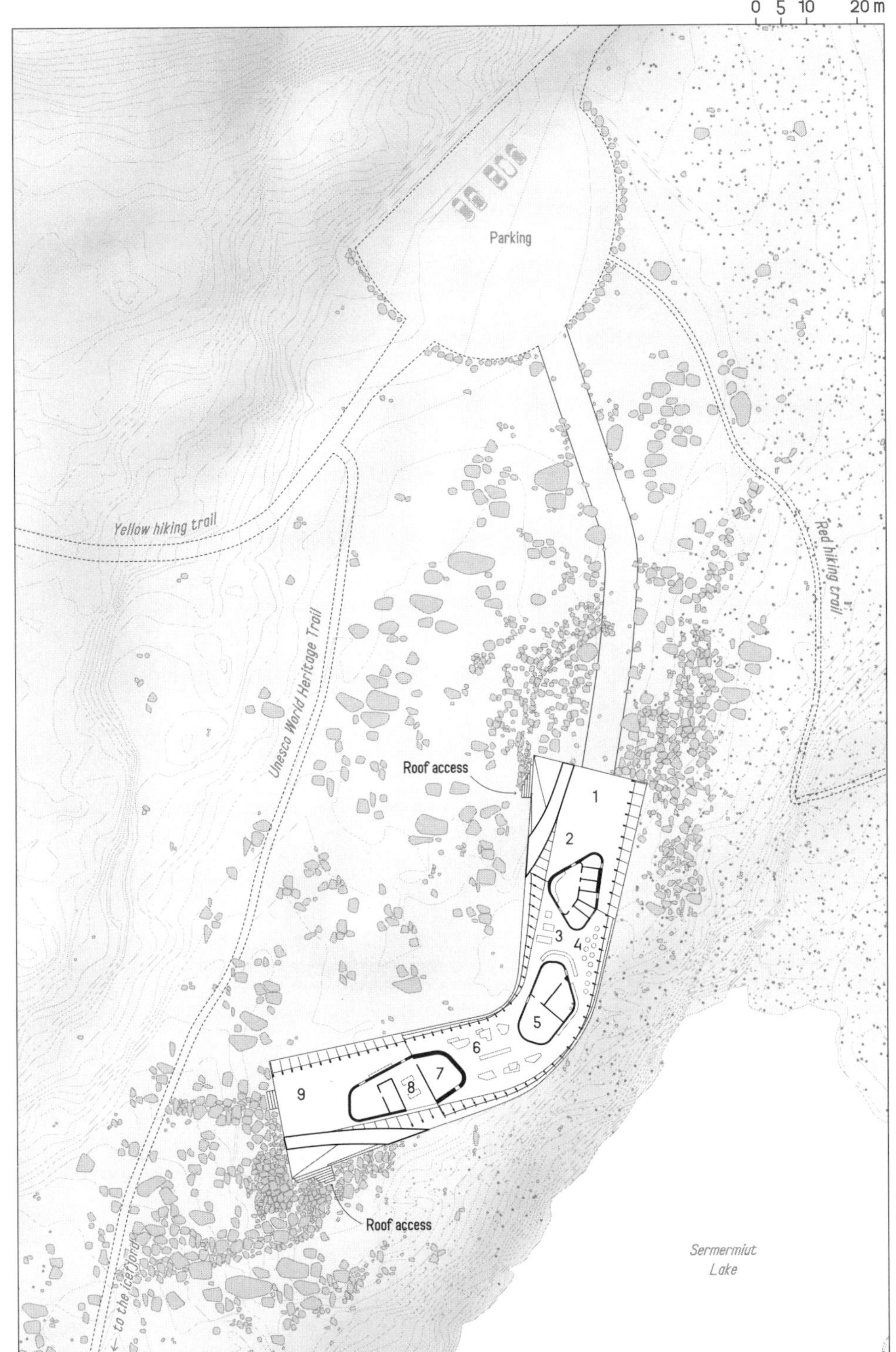
0 5 10   20 m
Parking
Yellow hiking trail
Red hiking trail
Unesco World Heritage Trail
Roof access
1
2
3
4
5
6
7
8
9
Roof access
to the icefjord
Sermermiut
Lake

The roof provides a natural extension to existing hiking routes, creating an accessible gathering place overlooking the landscape. Without having to pay for entry to the exhibition, you can freely move up and over the roof, discovering the Kangia Icefjord in the distance as you move across to the other side. Allowing this movement above and through the building makes the building act as a kind of gateway (or shelter) between the town of Ilulissat and the Arctic landscapes beyond.

The idea of creating something that could serve as a refuge in the Arctic landscape and a departure point from where you can proceed into nature was an important aspect of the design. Covered spaces at each end of the building allow someone to seek shelter before venturing into the landscape. Today, the new public spaces are widely used by locals for social and celebratory gatherings, events, and informal meetings.

The Greenlandic bedrock is one of the oldest exposed rocks in the world, and the flora and fauna that can grow here can be extremely fragile. The building was constructed as carefully as possible to avoid destroying the marshes and the small plants; the terrain was disturbed only when absolutely necessary. By lifting the building on small stilts, the spring and summer meltwaters—that need to be drained from the ground—can follow their desired path from underneath the building down into the Sermermiut Lake in front. The only new elements in the landscape, apart from the building itself, are a reflecting pool that collects meltwater flowing from the rock and running off the roof, a gravel parking area, and a wooden boardwalk that leads down to the icefjord and Sermermiut, the four-thousand-year-old archaeological remains of an early Inuit settlement.

The exhibition space is defined by three 'floating' cores containing the service and research functions and a small cinema. The exhibition space is between the two largest cores in the open interior landscape. Here, visitors are taken on a journey through time in *Sermeq pillugu Oqaluttuaq – The Story of Ice*. Designed by JAC Studio, the exhibition responds to the environmental concerns of climate change by communicating past, current, and future conditions. It tells the story of ice through multi-layered storytelling, conveying the remarkable scales at which ice can be considered, from the birth of the ice crystal to the enormity of Sermersuaq (the Inland Ice) and its impact on the world.

A main feature of the exhibition is the authentic ice cores from the Niels Bohr Institute, which are placed in the center of the interior landscape. Originally drilled from the Inland Ice and analyzed, they are housed in large display cases under precise temperature control. Changes in climate are logged in the ice. Through the cores, you can find traces of time back to 124,000 BCE. They can tell changes in the atmosphere, a day's exact snowfall, a volcanic eruption, and the precise appearance of industrialization.

Gisle Løkken is an architect and theorist working with architecture and planning in an Arctic context.
Magdalena Haggärde is an architect and university lecturer in landscape architecture working with architectural
and artistic means in Arctic territories.

The Case of Maniitsoq–Alcoa:
The Re-emergence of a Conscious Subjectivity
Gisle Løkken and Magdalena Haggärde

"A hunter from the Yup'ik culture in Alaska has said that what they most
fear from the West is their ability to change the landscape. [...] He calls
the people of the West 'those who change nature.'"[1]

"Greenland is not for sale."[2]

The response by Kim Kielsen, then Prime Minister of Kalaallit Nunaat's
(Greenland), was clear to all when he, in August 2019, reacted to then President Donald Trump's claim to be interested in buying Greenland for the
United States.[3] Even if the US president's claim caused disbelief and elicited
sarcastic comments from the world's press, it was meant seriously and initiated months of diplomatic activity between the US and Denmark. However
tactless the statement, it brought a larger reality to the surface, where Greenland has, in recent decades, been increasingly dragged into the globalized
rush for minerals and energy, often between multinational companies and
nation-state superpowers like China and the US.

Although Frederiksen used the occasion to emphasize the official
narrative of close relations between Greenland and Denmark, Kielsen
nevertheless stated that "Greenland is not Danish. Greenland is
Greenlandic."[4] The Trump incident revealed the complex situation
of contemporary Greenland, caught between the competing desires
of globalized economies and geopolitics—at the same time pushing

for independence but still being held economically dependent by Denmark in the wake of the colonial era.[5] Not least, Greenland, in the context of global environmental crises, has become an "icon of climate change,"[6] as the inland ice sheet's ablation zone is decreasing by half a meter every year due to global warming.[7]

THE INTRODUCTION OF ALCOA

The mining history of Greenland is not a recent one. However, it can still be considered a paradigmatic shift when, in 2006, the world's largest aluminum producer, Alcoa, wished to locate a new aluminum smelter in Greenland run by hydroelectrical power derived from the melting Sermersuaq, the Greenland Ice Sheet. Hence, anthropologist Klaus Georg Hansen at Ilisimatusarfik Kalaallit Nunaat (University of Greenland) claims it to be "the ultimate introduction of the era of global industrialisation to the Greenlandic society."[8] The localization process included every aspect of social, environmental, and political issues. When Maniitsoq was chosen to host the factory in its vicinities, it triggered a number of different, more targeted processes, including a program initiated by the municipality for citizen involvement to motivate and engage the citizens "in the development of the town and stimulating them to take ownership over the projects."[9] The possibility that the smelter would be built was also a preparation to "develop competence for being engaged in the expansion of the town."[10]

At first, the plan for introducing aluminum production in Maniitsoq was almost unambiguously received as good news for the town and its residents. The presented prefiguration of the project was that it would bring new activity and labor, new residents, and new public investments in schools, sports facilities, culture, roads, and other forms of infrastructure. However, a report released in 2007 from NIRAS,[11] the construction engineering company responsible,[12] stated that although the new plant was expected to employ some 4,000 new workers in the

1 Arne Christian Stryken, *Grønland* (Topografisk forlag, 2005), 150.

2 Matthew Lee and Jan Olsen, "US to boost aid to Greenland in bid to counter Russia, China," *Associated Press*, April 22, 2020.

3 First reported by *The Wall Street Journal*, August 16, 2019.

4 Lee and Olsen, "US to boost aid to Greenland in bid to counter Russia, China."

5 Even if Greenland's colonial status ended in 1953, it is still incorporated into the Danish realm as an amt (county), holding two parliamentary seats of representation. Through a referendum in 1979, Greenland gained Namminersornerullutik Oqartussat (home-rule) with formation of the Inatsisartut (the Parliament of Greenland), extended in 2009 to greater autonomy with the Namminersorlutik Oqartussat (self-rule). Roger Pihl et al., "Grønland," Store norske leksikon.

6 Steve Gillman, "Most ice on Earth is very close to melting conditions." Interview with Professor Andreas Kääb. *Horizon, The EU Research Magazine*, January 6, 2020.

7 Jason E. Box et al.,"Greenland ice sheet climate disequilibrium and committed sea-level rise," *Nature Climate Change*, August 29, 2022.

8 Klaus Georg Hansen, "The aluminium smelter project in Greenland — New aspects of an industrialization process?" in *Urbanization and the role of housing in the present development process in the Arctic*, eds. K. G. Hansen, S. Bitsch, L. Zalkind (Nordregio Report, 2013:3), 85–101.

9 Frank Sejersen, *Rethinking Greenland and the Arctic in the Era of Climate Change: New Northern Horizons* (Routledge, 2015), 153.

10 Ibid., 153.

construction period and approximately 800 in the operation phase, approximately two-thirds would have to be trained specialists.[13] At the time, the population of Maniitsoq was nearing 2,800 residents, declining to 2,516 in 2022, of which only 13 percent held some form of higher education.[14] The report estimated that the maximum contribution of the local workforce from Maniitsoq could be expected to be equivalent only to twenty-five man-years.[15] The numbers demonstrated clearly that a significantly large portion of the new labor force would have to be imported or commute from other places, meaning that the town would experience a significant influx of people from other places in Greenland, but mostly from abroad. With the likelihood of a sudden and significantly unbalanced shift in population, it became evident that there was a high probability that challenging social sustainability issues would occur. When it slowly but surely became clear to the local population and politicians that Alcoa did not plan to contribute to the building of a 'bright new society' in Maniitsoq to the anticipated extent, expectations cooled, evoking a new comprehension of the place and a more realistic basis for the subsequent citizen processes.

EXTENDING CITIZEN PROCESSES

Greenland Development A/S drove the formal processes for promoting the smelter in Maniitsoq on behalf of Alcoa and the government, where they commissioned reports that "took the plans in a direction where close causalities were upheld and uncertainties were controlled for different purposes."[16] On the other hand, the local processes were different and triggered reflection and awareness of the changes on a different local, social, and individual level of lived experience, where "expectations, dreams, stories, and myth were spun together in endless webs of narratives linking people and place, intimately."[17] In general terms, Mark Nuttall claims this to be a dichotomy between "traditional knowledge" and "scientific knowledge,"[18] as an exploration of what 'a good life' in Maniitsoq could be. Where Greenland Development A/S worked with "a discourse of positive but radical national transformation, which can be understood as a shift in paradigm," on the contrary, Maniitsormiut (people from Maniitsoq) worked with "the possibilities of changing in an analogue sense"[19] where all kinds of everyday matters, historical references, and future expectations were laid on the table for discussion.

In 2009, as a part of these extended citizen processes, the authors' architecture studio, 70°N arkitektur, was invited by the Qeqqata kommunia (Qeqqata municipality) to conduct a study of the physical and social impacts of Alcoa's plans in Maniitsoq. The municipality wished to anticipate the potential of Alcoa's plans as well as the physical and social consequences for the town in order to prepare and formulate an informed 'counter-proposal' based on their own perceptions and needs. Accordingly, the aim was to publish the results and make them available for use among people, politicians, and administration in the municipality. The published report was highly visual, and the topics discussed and elaborated were based on a comprehensive participation process.[20] The report was reprinted in a new edition, and according to Frank Sejersen, it became familiar to "everyone in Maniitsoq," and as the topics and illustrations came directly from the inhabitants' concrete interests and needs, it "often functioned as a point of reference and a tool for communicating ideas. During meetings and conversations, the publication would typically be brought forth and opened up in order to explicate what 'a good view' or 'a large building' might look like."[21] In other words, the publication was entirely made out of people's conceptions of the place—in the local historical and contemporary context, and equally their collective position in a 'larger world'—with ideas, dreams, narratives, and concrete anticipations about the future of the place and people living there. The impressions were gathered, analyzed, translated, and visualized in a format where people could recognize their interests, issues, and inputs and use them to gain confidence in their own notions and beliefs, but without pre-assessments of anything being more relevant or more important than anything else.

AIMING FOR A SMOOTH SPACE

The process was, from our (70°N arkitektur) side, intended to be anti-hierarchical and anti-colonial, in the sense that we wanted to evoke the particular social, environmental, cultural, and material conditions of Maniitsoq—by stimulating people to define their own reality without being framed by the official industrial narrative of so-called progress and prosperity. The process was meant to create a Deleuzoguattarian 'smooth, fluid space,' as "an open

11   NIRAS Greenland, *Økonomiske konsekvenser af etablering af aluminiumsindustri i Grønland. Analyse af kapasiteten [Economic consequences of establishing an aluminum industry in Greenland. Analysis of the capacity]* (Greenland Development A/S, 2007), 4.

12   NIRAS is a major consulting engineering firm in Scandinavia founded in 1956 with Greenland as the primary focus area at that time.

13   Ibid., 6.

14   *Greenland in Figures 2022*, ed. Naduk Kleemann (Statistics Greenland, May 2022).

15   NIRAS Greenland, *Økonomiske konsekvenser af etablering af aluminiumsindustri i Grønland. Analyse af kapasiteten* (Greenland Development A/S, 2007), 10.

16   Frank Sejersen, *Rethinking Greenland and the Arctic in the Era of Climate Change: New Northern Horizons* (Routledge, 2015), 154.

17   Ibid.

18   Mark Nuttall, "Living in a World of Movement: Human Resilience to Environmental Instability in Greenland," in *Anthropology and Climate Change — From Encounters to Actions*, ed. Susan A. Crate and Mark Nuttall (Left Coast Press, 2009), 292.

19   Sejersen, *Rethinking Greenland and the Arctic in the Era of Climate Change: New Northern Horizons*, 154.

20   70°N arkitektur, *Takorluukkanut nalunaarusiaq // Visjonsrapport // Maniitsoq // 70°N arkitektur.* (70°N arkitektur, 2010).

21   Sejersen, *Rethinking Greenland and the Arctic in the Era of Climate Change: New Northern Horizons*, 154.

space throughout which things-flows are distributed, rather than plotting out a closed space for linear and solid things."[22] Deleuze and Guattari distinguish between smooth and striated space. The two spaces are not of the same nature and communicate with each other in different ways, but still "exist only in mixture: smooth space is constantly being translated, transversed into striated space; striated space is constantly being reversed, returned to a smooth space."[23] The smooth space is heterogenous and curved and resembles a river with a measurable "cadenced rhythm, relating to the coursing of a river between its banks" and also to the unmeasurable rhythm of the "upswell of a flow,"[24] whereas the striated space is homogenous and straight and resembles the riverbanks.[25] Where a smooth space is "occupied without being counted," the striated space is "counted in order to be occupied."[26]

The Alcoa case in Maniitsoq exposed how the state, or institutions acting on its behalf, tried to "striate the space over which it reigns"[27] with means and methods of "abstract plans, theories, and calculations"[28] that did not correspond to or communicate well with the needs and expectations of the population. Instead of stimulating and strengthening residents' means to take responsibility and ownership of their own place and future, it worked "to utilize smooth spaces as a means of communication in the service of striated space."[29] This means that the partly parallel processes conducted by the State and by the inhabitants—even though aware of each other—were of a different nature and followed different trajectories, creating very different images of the current reality and the space for unfolding the future. Consequently, the citizen processes, with public meetings, debates, workshops, and city walks, created an open free space and an unlimited field for experimentation and association of any theme or subject. In the workshops, according to Sejersen, "people created storylines in order to set the local place-evaluation in motion," an approach that helped people to reassemble the official process and information "in order to animate (the) place, making it tangible—but at the same time making it fluid and negotiable."[30] It was a process with the distinct awareness of the social and material reality of Maniitsoq, and it included the realistic possibility that the smelter might not be built, where the Maniitsormiut—the people of Maniitsoq—had to envision different futures regardless of the industrial alternative.

THE WORK AND METHOD OF 70°N

The invitation from the Qeqqata kommunia to 70°N arkitektur came from the then-head of the municipal planning office, Finn Ellehave Petterson. He explained there was a strong wish for a non-Danish architect since Greenland, throughout colonial times, had been strongly influenced by Danish urban planning ideas, architecture, and ways of thinking about society that still resonate with difficult conflictual connotations.[31] In addition, our first-hand practical and theoretical experience with various concepts of Arctic urbanity and the realities of inhabiting and working in Arctic territories—also concerning climate issues, historical and contemporary colonialism, and Indigenous people and culture—were of particular importance.

In its simplest form, our approach is to listen to and engage with people living in the topical landscape in order to gain what Donna Haraway describes as "situated knowledge" as "partial perspectives" where "the possibility of sustained, rational, objective inquiry rests."[32] The aspiration is to provide a sense of "grounded normativity"[33] as an "ethical framework" generated by "place-based practices and associated knowledges" of "process-centered modes of living" coming "through the practice" and "modes of intelligence."[34]

By different means, like meetings, workshops, focus groups, city walks, and interviews, we wished to explore the town's particular social, cultural, and environmental state, stimulating a deeper understanding of what was going on at the time and the potentiality in different lines of becoming. It is an intersection of artistic, architectural, and ethnographic methods that are not framed to give predefined answers, but instead, is a method meant to stimulate creativity within an open dialogue through free associations and Deleuzoguattarian "lines of flight"[35] and imagination, which become "the openings that allow thought to escape from the constraints that seek to define and enclose creativity."[36] Keywords and enunciations from the inhabitants, like *melting ice, energy, food trees, light, Alcoa, laughter, infrastructure, self-government, a nice view, exercise, CO_2-emission 90 percent higher, dependence on Denmark, bigger windows, the last wilderness, without Alcoa, empty villages, mountain top, benches, industrial country* and many more were noted and became a consistent plane for the work with new concepts and proposals.[37]

22   Gilles Deleuze and Félix Guattari, *A Thousand Plateaus. Capitalism and Schizophrenia*, trans. Brian Massumi (University of Minnesota Press, 1987), 361.

23   Ibid., 474.

24   Ibid., 364.

25   Ibid.

26   Ibid., 361-362.

27   Ibid., 385.

28   Sejersen, *Rethinking Greenland and the Arctic in the Era of Climate Change: New Northern Horizons*, 154.

29   Deleuze and Guattari, *A Thousand Plateaus. Capitalism and Schizophrenia*, 385.

30   Sejersen, *Rethinking Greenland and the Arctic in the Era of Climate Change: New Northern Horizons*, 154.

31   Finn Ellehave Petterson, oral transmission to the author, 2009.

32   Donna Haraway, "Situated Knowledge: The Science Question in Feminism and the Privilege of Partial Perspective," *Feminist Studies* 14, No 3 (Autumn 1988): 584.

33   Glen Sean Coulthard, *Red Skin, White Masks. Rejecting the Colonial Politics of Recognition* (University of Minnesota Press, 2014).

34   Leanne Betasamosake Simpson, *As We Have Always Done: Indigenous Freedom through Radical Resistance* (University of Minnesota Press, 2017), 22.

35   Deleuze and Guattari, *A Thousand Plateaus. Capitalism and Schizophrenia*.

36   Hugh Tomlinson and Graham Burchell, Translators' Introduction, in *What Is Philosophy?* by Gilles Deleuze and Félix Guattari (Columbia University Press, 1994), viii.

37   70°N arkitektur, *Takorluukkanut nalunaarusiaq // Visjonsrapport // Maniitsoq // 70°N arkitektur*, 6.

1   Citizen processes, involvement, workshops, and city walks were organized by 70°N arkitektur and Qeqqata Komunia.

2   A mosaic of different housing types and urban infrastructures in Maniitsoq, presenting a general overview of the city.

3   Point of Departure: Whale Watching Platform and Path
     Nasiffik at Tunoqqusaaq, Maniitsoq.

Tunoqqusaaq – c+7 – rest area and viewpoint
built as a *premature gratification* in August 2010
as a gift from the municipality to the citizens of Maniitsoq

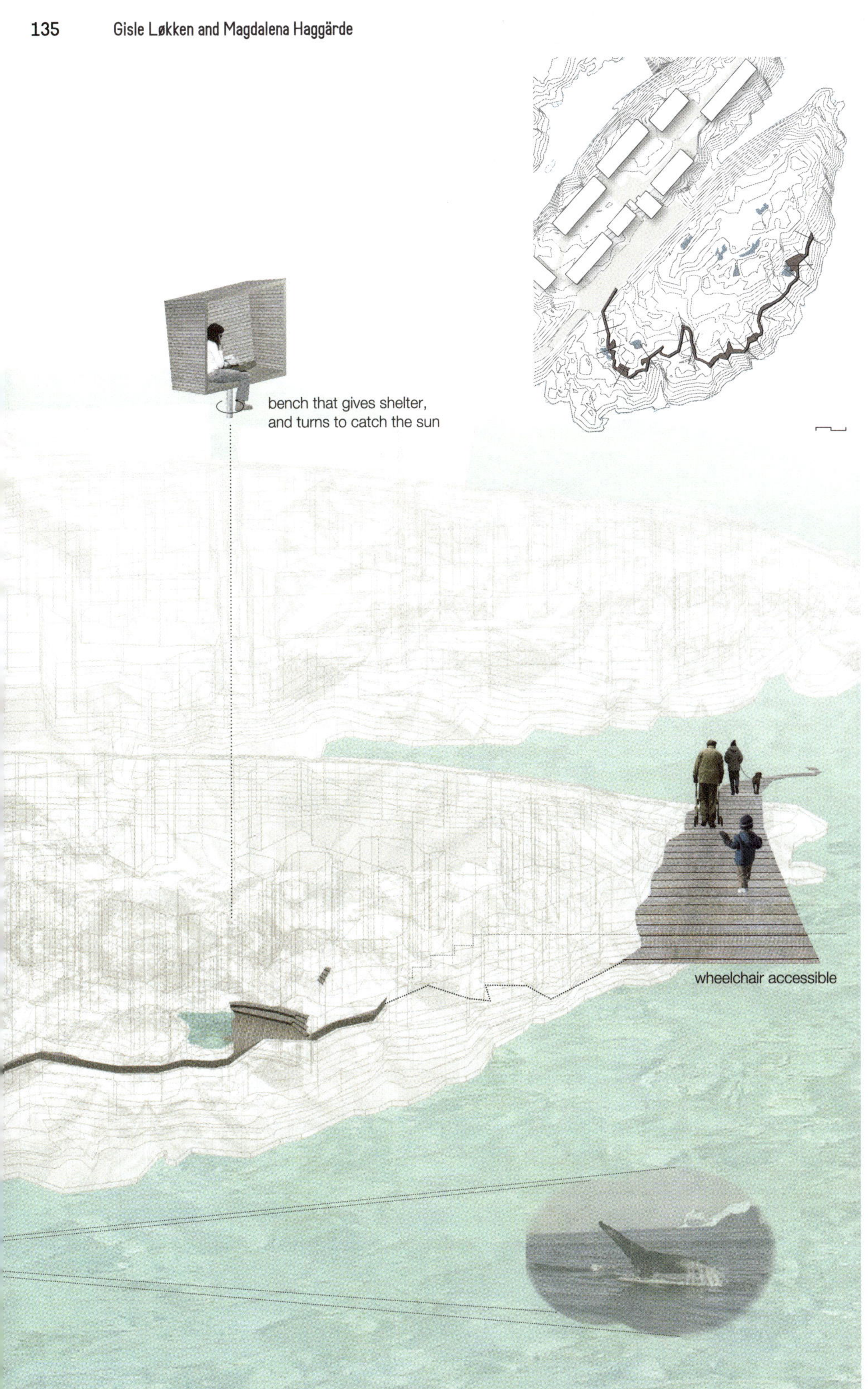
bench that gives shelter,
and turns to catch the sun
wheelchair accessible

In retrospect, Sejersen states:

> Issues, scales and causalities are laid out in a floating and levelled-out
> structure. In the report [...] the keywords make their appearance—not in
> the form of an ordered list but rather as spread out all over the page, with
> no apparent system among the words. This serves to prompt the activities of
> making more free associations, of exploring new aspects in the complex field
> of issues and of assembling the keywords in new and meaningful ways.[38]

Even if the page of free associations is considered seemingly difficult to read, it also marks an important position closer to the reality and experience of people in Maniitsoq—as an "imaginative reinvention of Maniitsoq as a place" where a multitude of scales, issues, and causalities are assembled into new agendas and narratives:

> Abstract plans, theories and calculations—as are often presented in
> the reports prepared by Greenland Development A/S—were, so to speak,
> reassembled here, in order to animate (the) place, making it livable
> and tangible—but at the same time making it fluid and negotiable.[39]

As such, it became a manifestation of citizen power and a counter-act to the instrumentally aimed process of Greenland Development A/S, where the concept of 'free association' of any expectation, dream, story or myth, narratives through which "people help each other explore how ideas of 'the good life' can be made meaningful in a living town."[40] In itself, it became a strategy for defining and interconnecting people, place, and territory.

RE-INVENTION OF PLACE IDENTITY

In the process of sharing local and situated knowledge and histories, the history and significance of Maniitsoq as a whaling town emerged prominently from several participants.[41] The intensive whaling and fishing of mostly cod and halibut by European and American fleets resulted in the near extinction of the Greenland whale (in the eighteenth century) and the large halibut (in the twentieth century).[42] Where the town of Maniitsoq used to play a significant role in the whaling industry—it is today merely a memory, and it was the immanent notion of being a whaling town sparked the idea of a possible new industry of spotting and experiencing whales—not killing them. It is a notion that also re-connects with the pre-industrial and pre-colonial culture and traditions linked to the whales. This realization triggered the need for a better and more accessible place for whale spotting, and an ideal location was pointed out on the nearby cliffs of Tunoqqusaaq.

> In a process with unclear time frames and great expectations of a
> new becoming, there exist varying needs for things to happen and for
> different elements to evolve at different speeds in order to keep the
> process alive. Consequently, we made a proposal for a whale spot-
> ting platform at the place that was pointed at, and the municipality

was activated to build it. The place was given the name Nasiffik, meaning "the place to spot whales."

In the aftermath of the process, the platform has become an important place for the residents of Maniitsoq and for the imagination of the town as something other than a potential industrial transformation.[43] In 2019, filmmakers and visual anthropologists Sidse Torstholm Larsen and Sturla Pilskog made *Winter's Yearning*, a documentary film in which they followed the inhabitants of Maniitsoq during a period when it had become likely that the Alcoa plans would not be implemented:

> The film zooms in on Maniitsoq as the years pass and the local inhabitants are put on hold, waiting for the American Dream. Through dark and cold winters, the film explores human existentialism and the relation between personal self-reliance and a nation's independence. When we finally arrive at the summer light, a promising revelation arises from deep beneath the ocean's surface. It is a visually ambitious film about dreams, hopes, and lives on hold and the human capacity to rise again.[44]

In the film, the whale identity is prominent, and the platform for whale spotting is a point of departure for the process of creating a new storyline about Maniitsoq's reinvented identity as a whale town. Nevertheless, the most iconic moment in the film is when it is clearly stated by Peter S. Olsen, the municipal manager and one of the film's main subjects, as he stands at the platform overlooking the sea: "We have started to realize that we can use them [the whales] for other than food" and "we have to be first with the idea [of utilizing the whales in the tourist industry...] we already got the whale spotting platform."[45]

The other decisive moment in the film, constituting a line of becoming different from the one framed by state and industry, is when the above-mentioned Peter S. Olsen, who at the beginning of the film is presented as the municipality's aluminum coordinator, makes the transition to become, instead, the new sustainability coordinator. It is an example of self-management and locally driven entrepreneurship where natural phenomena contribute to the reinvention of a place, changing "the meaning and the imaging of the place."[46]

38   Sejersen, *Rethinking Greenland and the Arctic in the Era of Climate Change: New Northern Horizons*, 154.

39   Ibid.

40   Ibid.

41   70°N arkitektur, *Takorluukkanut nalunaarusiaq // Visjonsrapport // Maniitsoq // 70°N arkitektur.* (70°N arkitektur, 2010).

42   Erik Lyberth, "Tiden omkring anlæggelsen af 'Kolonien Manîtsok,'" in *Manîtsok' – Sukkertoppen* 1782-1982, ed. H. C. Petersen (Manîtsup kommunia, 1982), 43. Peter Egede, "Erhvervsliv," in *Manîtsok' – Sukkertoppen* 1782-1982, ed. H. C. Petersen (Manîtsup kommunia, 1982), 88.

43   An example of the Nasiffik being considered an important and significant place is that it is used for public gatherings and celebrations like festivals and the marking of Greenland's National Day. "Program for nasjonaldag 2022 – Maniitsoq og Sisimiut," Qeqqata kommunia, accessed March 13, 2024.

44   NIF, Norwegian Film Institute, "Winter's Yearning" [introduction].

45   Sidse Torstholm Larsen and Sturla Pilskog, *Winter's Yearning* [Documentary film], Blåst Film AS, 2019.

They mentioned ALCOA and London Mining in the news this morning.

There are many whales outside Maniitsoq.

Therefore, we are developing a new idea.

4–9   Film stills from *Winter's Yearning* (2019). All captions in italics are quotes from Peter S. Olsen while in his office or standing at the whale spotting platform.

Whale watching platform at Tunoqqusaaq.

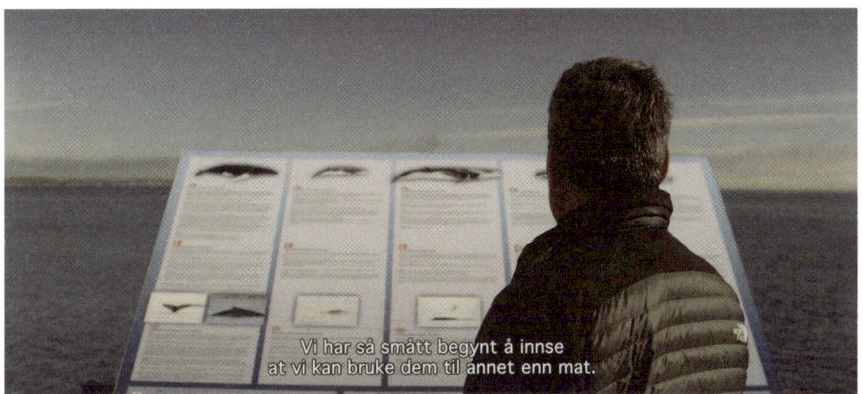

We have slowly begun to realize that we can use them for more than just food.

We have to be the first to come up with ideas, while we already have the whale watching post.

In this case, the place is no longer identified as becoming one of industry but, instead, "increasingly complex and contested," where "the meaning of the place is being renegotiated" as socio-political as well as "socio-cultural constructs."[47]

CONCLUSION

The incidents in Maniitsoq since early 2000 tell us stories that are familiar yet unique to this place. They recount how places that have historically been considered marginal can become places of great global interest because of strategic positioning or natural resources. Due to changing geopolitical circumstances, they are suddenly moved to the environmental, economic, or political center of attention. It is also a story about habitation and that all inhabited places exist within a historical narrative that holds situated knowledge that can gain importance when confronted with the forces of globalized capital. It is also a story and a reminder about the need to produce counter-narratives and knowledges that are strong enough to critically confront prevailing narratives, to produce smooth spaces that are dynamic, agile, and diverse against those striated spaces that are linear, fixed, and homogenous.

In the case of Maniitsoq, comprehensive citizen processes prepared the ground for real counteraction and the re-invention of place identity. The making of the whale spotting platform became symbolic yet fundamentally important for the subsequent commitment to whale identity, linking traditional nature-based knowledge and traditions (in the film represented by the oil painting in the office of Peter S. Olsen) with contemporary ideas and urgent insights about sustainability, serving as a catalyst to new perceptions about the future. Perhaps most important is the awakening of a collective consciousness about diversity and self-management, which is no longer dependent on a form of 'neo-colonial' industrialization but working to enable a new becoming connected to history, nature, and existing society.

In the ever-increasing demand for minerals and energy, the proposed smelter from Alcoa will not be the last multinational industry initiative to try to exploit the country's resources, and at the time of writing, Maniitsoq has been designated as a highly relevant site for hydrogen production.[48] However, there are now reasons to believe that the residents of Maniitsoq have established a strong enough narrative about their own existence that the population as a collective can use to set their own terms of engagement.

---

46   Torill Nyseth, "Towards an understanding of place reinvention," in *Place Reinvention in the North. Dynamics and Governance Perspectives*, edited by Torill Nyseth and Brynhild Granås (Nordregio, 2007), 155.

47   Ibid.

48   "Greenland Hydropower Resources," Naalakkersuisut (Government of Greenland).

Susan Schuppli is a researcher and artist based in the UK. Her fieldwork and documentary film practice is situated at the intersections between environmental struggles, climate science, and affected communities with a contemporary focus on the cryosphere and the politics of cold. She is Professor and Director of the Centre for Research Architecture, Goldsmiths University of London, where she is also a Research Fellow and Board Chair of Forensic Architecture.

Solar Sensing
Susan Schuppli

In the nineteenth century, German physicist and optical lens-maker Joseph von Fraunhofer embarked upon a series of experiments to explore the optical spectrum of the sun. His work would eventually come to be used by scientists to determine the chemical composition of a remote object—our sun, some 149.6 million kilometers away—not through direct testing but by treating it as an image, one whose chromatic variance could be translated into the complex language of chemistry. Fraunhofer's absorption and emission lines enabled scientists to conduct spectral analyses of different gases suffused by sunlight as they passed through the Earth's atmosphere over the course of a day's rotation, thus changing the ways in which sunlight would come to be studied and known today. His assertion that the essence of objects could be determined by virtue of the aesthetic judgment of chemistry would prevail, setting the course for the primacy of the visual in deliberating truth claims.

Another solar proposition was advanced by a US judge in 1886, when he asked the rhetorical question "Can the sun lie?" during deliberations over the probative value of photographs as testimonial agents.[1] In pondering the sun's aesthetic capacity and animistic potential for deception, the judge implied that nonhuman entities and technical processes would come to play a crucial role in the production of evidence. In suggesting that the mode of appearance of the media object, the photograph put before a jury, was equal in consideration to the epistemic claims that could be made on behalf of its representational stance,

1   US courtroom interior, nineteenth century.

2   Film still from *Can the Sun Lie?* (2014) by Susan Schuppli. HD video, color with sound, 13 minutes.

he gestured toward key attributes of the "material witness," a concept I developed in my book project (and from which this short essay is adapted) to account for the emergence of a forensic imagination in which nonhuman entities would come to play a decisive evidential role as witnesses to historic events. But when the judge was faced with the improbable prospect of cross-examining the sun directly—after all, the sun obeys only the laws of nature, not those of anthropos, as once believed by the geocentrics of the ancient world—he also opened the proceedings of the court to the influence of scientific norms and, with it, new forms of expert knowledge that would progressively be called upon to ventriloquize the object world. The judge continued: "Perhaps we may say that though the sun does not lie, the liar may use the sun as a tool. Let us, then, beware of the liar who lies in the name of the sun."[2]

The legally sanctified gaze of the human had a rival in this new technical witness, which deeply troubled the courts. Photographs taken in the aftermath of a crime or for the purposes of legal explication were not only presented as aids to memory to assist with testimony but also positioned as demonstrative evidence in their own right. If evidence could be deliberately manufactured after the fact, then the self-evident facts of the case could themselves be thrown into doubt. The introduction of these photographic materials into legal trials came to inaugurate a significant transformation in evidence law as the sovereignty of the human eyewitness was called into question by new modes of machinic witnessing, contributing to what has been referred to as an episteme of mechanical objectivity.[3] While objects in the form of models and diagrams had already entered into legal proceedings in cases of patent law, or to assist with clarifying property disputes, the arrival of photographic materials must be understood as singularly unique because of sunlight's persuasive power of analogisation.[4] Chemically provoked by the radiological emissions of the sun, the resulting photograph produced such a convincing picture of the "real" that the subjective processes of human recollection and memory could, it seemed, be set aside in favor of a new regime of scientifically produced truth. Indeed, proponents of the legal aid provided by sunlight were swift to dismiss any doubts as to its fidelity, and countered such reservations with statements such as the following:

1   "Can the sun lie? asked the Virginia Law Journal in 1886. Perhaps we may say that though the sun does not lie, the liar may use the sun as a tool. Let us, then, beware of the liar who lies in the name of the sun." From Thomas Thurston's "Hearsay of the Sun: Photography, Identity, and the Law of Evidence" in *American Quarterly in collaboration with the American Studies Crossroads Project at Georgetown University and the Center for History and New Media at George Mason University. 1996–2009.*

2   Ibid.

3   See Lorraine Daston and Peter Galison, *Objectivity*. Zone Books, 2007.

4   See Alain Pottage, "Law Machines: Scale Models, Forensic Materiality and the Making of Modern Patent Law." *Social Studies of Science* 41, 5 (2011): 621–43.

3   A glass negative of a sunset on the Labrador Coast.

4   A film still from Zacharias Kunuk and Ian Mauro's *Inuit Knowledge and Climate Change* (2010).

> We cannot conceive of a more impartial and truthful witness than the sun, as its light stamps and seals the similitude of the wound on the photograph put before the jury; it would be more accurate than the memory of witnesses, and as the object of all is to show truth, why should not this dumb witness show it?[5]

This historical controversy around the objectivity of manufactured proofs, the testimony of nonhuman agents, and the opposition between lay and scientific knowledge has only been exacerbated with the advent of an ever-increasing range of technologies for measuring, monitoring, and recording data. Indeed, the very lack of agreed-upon protocols governing the use of many new technologies—satellite imagery is a case in point—and the absence of consensus as to the interpretation of their datasets have, if anything, reanimated such debates. This is particularly evident within the context of climate change disputes, and especially so with regard to the interaction between the different regimes of witnessing, notably those represented by scientific expertise and local knowledge practices. Yet Indigenous observations are crucial for extending and enriching the epistemic frameworks that are required for understanding long-term environmental transformations, enabling a reordering of expertise based on relational understandings that are at the heart of Indigenous life worlds.

The vicissitudes of material witnessing are perhaps best exemplified by the range of stakeholders, knowledge claims, moral values, and risk strategies that gather around issues of global warming. For example, in Zacharias Kunuk and Ian Mauro's film *Inuit Knowledge and Climate Change*, several Inuit elders make the repeated observation that the setting sun has slowly been moving further west, and that the location of the stars has also altered. Has the earth shifted on its axis, they ask, causing the position of the sun and stars to change?[6] When their documentary was pre-screened at the Copenhagen Climate Change Conference (COP15) in December 2009, the filmmakers were admonished by the scientific community for presenting such a spurious hypothesis on the part of the Inuit, despite the fact that they had clearly looked to Western physics in attempting to explain this extraordinary transgression on the part of the sun. "We had a litany of scientists come back to us, responding after seeing this news, saying, this was great to be speaking to indigenous people about their views, but if you continue to perpetuate this fallacy that the Earth had tilted on its axis, [the Inuit] ... would lose all credibility."[7] The Inuits' deep ancestral knowledge of the environment in which they lived and the events that they had witnessed was insufficient for conferring a contingent legitimacy on their observations and

---

5   *Franklin v. The State of Georgia*, 69 Ga. 36 (1882).

6   Zacharias Kunuk and Ian Mauro's *Inuit Knowledge and Climate Change* for Isuma TV, 2010. 54 minutes.

7   Guy Dixon, "New Documentary Recounts Bizarre Climate Changes Seen by Inuit Elders," *Globe and Mail*, 19 October 2010.

speech acts if their testimonials ran counter to widely accepted scientific truths and their rationale seemed specious. Yet how else should they have explained the dramatic migration of the setting sun? The epistemic virtue of objectivity turned, not upon a distinction between Western rationality and native cosmology, as might have been expected by their critics at COP15, but on who has the authority, and thus the expertise, to speak on behalf of science itself?[8] Linguist Paul Goodwin diagnoses this condition as the "professional vision" of trained judgment: "Different professions—medicine, law, the police, specific sciences such as archaeology—have the power to legitimately see, constitute and articulate alternative kinds of events. Professional vision is perspectival, lodged within specific social entities, and unevenly allocated."[9] Although the Inuit may have come to the wrong scientific conclusion in speculating that a physical realignment of the earth's axis had caused the locational drift of the sun rather than the cumulative effects of industrialization resulting in the production of greenhouse gases, their observations were not in and of themselves flawed—their eyes had not deceived them.

> Indeed, the rapid and extreme environmental changes that have overturned established perceptions of the natural world throughout the North suggest that only an equally radical proposition might begin to explain the hallucinogenic dynamics of matter—now evident—in these transformative geographies. Not only is Arctic sunlight bending and deceiving the eyes that have tracked the position of the sun for generations, but as black carbon deposits accrue throughout the region, and rising temperatures diminish sea ice, melt glaciers, liquefy snow packs, and thaw permafrost, the natural indexicality of such northern topographies has also become increasingly unreliable.[10] Ecological registration systems that formerly directed Inuit hunters home with cartographic certainty are distorting as the contours of snow-encrusted landscapes are resurfaced by climatic changes. No longer can the wind-carved tongues of snowdrifts alone offer up the icy signs that permit confident action. Matter is undergoing dramatic phase transitions throughout the cryosphere, and nature has itself become a hostile witness, troubling the veracity of testimonials once offered up by the constancy of its frozen landscapes.

The nineteenth-century suspicion once directed toward the sun's capacity to mislead, to turn stable realities into distorted versions of the real, is refracted in this twenty-first-century corollary as climate change transforms the surfaces of the earth into a vast proto-photographic array which is recording the atmospheric chemistry of terrestrial processes. For the Inuit, the world that they once knew finds no analogy, no mirror image, in the world that they now see. In the Circumpolar North, this process has accelerated at between two and four times the global average and intensified as tropospheric warming and temperature inversions trap ever-greater concentrations of atmospheric pollutants within particles of ice and snow, whereas previously they would have been diffused at higher altitudes. Snow and ice produce different spectral variations. The visible spectrum of light is better refracted by snow, whereas the optical properties of ice have superior absorption capacities toward the spectrum of the near-infrared.[11] This is why, in part, Indigenous observations of the changing pathway of the sun are made in regions covered by continuous snow. The material registration of light by silver halide particles that came to define the photographic process is warped in a landscape where matter is out of place, and sunlight lies. Not only do granular snow particles absorb and capture light, converting billions and billions of grains into a vibrating plate of solar-charged particles, but they also act as vast networks of finely ground crystal lenses focusing and refracting light across the Polar region. Yet as chemical impurities saturate the snowpack and temperature increases modify the crystalline structure of ice, the land itself becomes a disputed image—overexposing and distorting rays of sunlight as they are redirected back up into the atmosphere—giving rise to new forms of perceptual proof that may even come to challenge established truths.

8   "There once was a time, a time that includes the present, when scientific observation was equated with objectivity, when perception was thought to be a transparent and neutral act, and when the identification of mind and reason as incorporeal and transcendent over nature was pre-requisite to the determination of truth. Although a plethora of research in the sciences actually contests such ill-informed assertions, this cartoon representation of science fundamentals is widely held. Many science practitioners continue to explain their goals and achievements in such terms, and perhaps ironically, even cultural and social analysts who reject them may require this caricature as their interventionary departure point." From Vicki Kirby, "Matter out of Place: 'New Materialism' in Review," in *What if Culture Was Nature All Along?*, ed. Vicki Kirby (Edinburgh University Press, 2017).

9   Kelly Gates, "The Cultural Labor of Surveillance: Video Forensics, Computational Objectivity, and the Production of Visual Evidence." *Social Semiotics* 23, 2 (2013): 242–60.

10   During the 1950s the Soviet Union actually experimented with accelerating glacial melt (climate forcing) by deliberately blackening snow surfaces with coal dust to boost their capacity to absorb solar radiation and thus aid in irrigation and supplement water supplies to areas affected by drought. Today vast swaths of the Arctic are wholly saturated by airborne contaminants including black-carbon deposits from industrialization that combine to "fast-track" the global melting of ice as the surface albedo of snow is reduced. "While climate forcing resulting from black-carbon contamination of snow is considered minor when averaged across the entire globe, regional forcing over the snow-covered regions of the Arctic and the Himalayas is devastating, comparable to the degree of carbon dioxide accumulation in the atmosphere since pre-industrial times." Climate models have demonstrated that the reduction of surface albedo in dark snow is itself a contributing factor to global warming and a source of the decline of ice sheets and glacial melt. Arctic snow has become an unwitting accomplice in bringing about the very changes that were directly responsible for generating its own damaged and dirty condition. From Odelle L. Hadley and Thomas W. Kirchstetter. "Black-carbon Reduction of Snow Albedo." *Nature Climate Change* 2, 6 (2012): 437–40.

11   Stephen G. Warren, "Optical Properties of Snow." *Reviews of Geophysics and Space Physics* 20, 1 (1982): 67–89.

Note   This chapter is based on an excerpt from "Closing Arguments" in *Material Witness* (MIT Press, 2020).

Inuuteq Storch is a photographer who lives and works in Greenland.

Keepers of the Ocean: At Home We Belong
Inuuteq Storch

This visual essay highlights two of my recent documentary projects.

At Home We Belong is my first published photographic series (2010–2015) and it is an expression of needing to be accepted at different levels—as a person, as an artist, and as part of a society. I come from a small society. My hometown, Sisimiut, is the second-largest town in Greenland. We are about 5,000 people. The whole country has around 55,000 people. Even though nature has given us so much, we cannot entirely sustain ourselves from what—and who—is already here: the need and cost of importing goods is very high. Wood and other building materials, music, art, cars, clothing; almost everything is imported. Because of the high level of importing, we have a very open view of the rest of the world. Because of the low amount of exporting, the world has very narrow knowledge about us. This has led to the prioritization of foreign acceptance: as an artist, I need to first be accepted in other countries in order to get the acceptance of my people. Still, we are fighting against stereotypes that were created when we were a colony. This series of images is part of the fight we are in: the fight to remain, to know who we are, to keep our identity.

Keepers of the Ocean[1] is part of my place project and is an intimate portrait of my hometown, Sisimiut, and the life we have there over the past three years (2019–2022). The weather controls everything and nature gives us everything we need. The intimacy we have is created with the nature we are surrounded by, which is rough and honest. The more I spend time away, the more I understand that what we have at home is special.

---

1   *Keepers of the Ocean* was published as a photobook by Disko Bay in 2022, while works featured in *At Home We Belong* (2010–2015) have been widely exhibited.

From Inuuteq Storch's first photographic series, *At Home We Belong* (2010–2015).

Olsenip Aqq.
Orlaap Aqq.

A portrait of Inuuteq Storch's hometown, Sisimiut, from his photobook *Keepers of the Ocean* (Disko Bay, 2022).

Nadezhda Filimonova is a political scientist specializing in urban environmental governance.[3]

Place Bonding and Migration
Nadezhda Filimonova

What motivates a person to remain in a remote urban settlement often subject to severe weather conditions? Igor Popov reflected on this question as he described a small Russian settlement on Wrangel Island in the Arctic Ocean, where a sharp population decline in the 1990s led to its closure in 1997,[1] and according to media reports, one resident remained until 2011. Perhaps surprisingly, this case is not unique. Another instance was the Old Varandey village in the Nenets Autonomous Region of Russia, which was declared a zone of emergency due to the threat of flooding. Subsequently, a regional law was enacted mandating the closure of the village. In 2000, all residents of Varandey were resettled to larger urban settlements such as Naryan-Mar, Nenets Autonomous Region, and Usinsk, Komi Republic.[2] However, not everyone could adapt to their new living arrangements; some eventually returned. As of 2015, some ten to fifteen people reside year-round in the village, embracing a traditional way of living focused on fishing and hunting.[3] Popov contrasts the dedication of these few residents to the Arctic lifestyle with the prevailing reluctance of most individuals to reside in the region for extended periods.[4]

Popov's writing primarily focuses on individuals who migrated to northern areas for socio-economic purposes during the Soviet period. It's worth contextualizing Popov's work: scholars broadly categorize urbanization processes in Arctic regions, including Russia, into three waves. The first wave relates to the period from the sixteenth century to the early twentieth century (sometimes referred to as the "colonial wave"); the second one lasted from the 1920s to the 1980s (the "Soviet wave"), and the third wave that started in the 1960s and 1970s continues today (the "globalized wave").[5] The colonial wave in Russia traces its origins to as early as the twelfth century when Novgorod and Moscow principalities, spurred by interests in the fur trade, dispatched merchants to the northern territories.[6] The early permanent towns were built in the sixteenth century on land previously inhabited by Indigenous populations.[7] These settlements were fortified and served as outposts for further exploration and expansion into the North and Siberia. However, most cities found their origins in the twentieth century, often in conjunction with the Soviet Union's policies aimed at industrializing the Arctic.

Initially, industrialization was done through forced labor, but later, it transitioned to providing economic incentives to encourage people to relocate to northern areas.[8] Still, the dissolution of the Soviet Union led to significant demographic shifts, resulting in the depopulation of cities and towns throughout the Russian Arctic. For three decades, from 1989 to 2020, the population of the Russian Arctic Zone decreased from 3,537,400 to 2,431,500 people.[9] The primary reason for out-migration was deteriorating socioeconomic conditions in urban areas, worsened by the cessation of funding from the Russian government and industries. These funding sources were essential for covering the high maintenance costs of social infrastructure in the face of shrinking municipal budgets.[10] Additionally, numerous cities and towns in the Russian Arctic were monotowns with economies specialized in resource production. This made them vulnerable to industry closure due to the lack of demand for specific resources in the global markets. In such cases,

1   Igor Popov, "Prospects of Development for Urban Areas in the Russian Arctic," *Sibirica* 21, 1 (2022).

2   Timofei Zhukov, "Из Оленеводов в Нефтяники [From Reindeer Herders to Oil Workers]," *Няръяна Вындер* [Naryana Vyder], (2015): 20244.

3   Irina Hazerova, "Без Света На Краю Света [Without Lights at the Edge of the World]," *Красный Тундровик* [Krasniy Tundrovik] 92, no. 20294 (2015).

4   Popov, "Prospects of Development for Urban Areas in the Russian Arctic."

5   Marlene Laruelle, "The Three Waves of Arctic Urbanisation. Drivers, Evolutions, Prospects," *Polar Record* 55 (2019): 1–12; Sofya Prokopova, Svetlana Kravchuk, and Nikolai Garin, "ГородскаяСреда Арктики: Оптимизация и Цифровизация [Arctic Urban Realm: Optimisation and Digitalisation]," *Akademicheskij Vestnik Uralniiproekt* RAASN 3, 50 (2021): 40–44.

6   Laruelle, "The Three Waves of Arctic Urbanisation. Drivers, Evolutions, Prospects."

7   Ekaterina Kalemeneva, "From New Socialist Cities to Thaw Experimentation in Arctic Townscapes: Leningrad Architects Attempt to Modernise the Soviet North," *Europe - Asia Studies* 71, 3 (2019); Popov, "Prospects of Development for Urban Areas in the Russian Arctic." In the Russian Arctic such representatives of Indigenous small-numbered peoples live as Nenets, Chukchi, Khanty, Evens, Evenks, Selkups, Sami, Eskimos, Dolgans, Chuvans, Kets, Nganasans, Yukaghirs, Enets, Mansi, Vepsians, Koryaks, Itelmens, Kereks.

8   Laruelle, "The Three Waves of Arctic Urbanisation. Drivers, Evolutions, Prospects."

9   Viktor Vilgelmovich Fauzer et al., "Вызовы и Противоречия в Развитии Севера и Арктики: Демографическое Измерение [Challenges and Contradictions in the Development of the North and the Arctic: Demographic Dimension]," *Arktika: Ekologia i Ekonomika* 12, 1 (2022): 111–22.

10   Maria Gunko, Elena Batunova, and Andrey Medvedev, "Rethinking Urban Form in a Shrinking Arctic City," *Espace-Populations-Societes,* 2020/3-2021/1 (2021): 1–16.

these urban settlements today face the challenges of restructuring their economies and seeking alternative funding to fulfill their welfare functions.

The socio-economic challenges were compounded by the weak sense of place attachment among newcomers to the Arctic, which is often coupled with the fact that newcomers to the Arctic had frequently considered northern cities as temporary places of living. Terence Armstrong provides an example of shift workers who move to northern areas for work temporarily while their families and homes remain established in southern regions.[11] As a result, they lack incentives to develop a sense of attachment to the northern areas. After the Soviet Union collapsed, those individuals with the least attachment to the Arctic often left the region. In contrast, residents who were either born or had resided for a long time in Arctic and sub-Arctic urban areas resisted migration,[12] ultimately either settling in northern settlements permanently or revisiting these sites after leaving the region.[13] In different ways, they formed bonds with northern urban spaces.

To attract people to the Arctic regions, including the Russian Arctic Zone, there has been a longstanding tradition of building cities to appeal to outsiders.[14] Initially, urban planners and architects sought to replicate southern cities' urban landscapes and architecture.[15] Architecture was also a crucial instrument for the symbolic colonization of the North, as Soviet authorities saw Soviet towns as symbols of and tools for establishing socialist culture.[16] The former mining settlement Pyramiden on Spitsbergen, which the Soviet Union bought from Sweden in 1927, was utilized to demonstrate the benefits of Soviet living.

The earliest studies of northern urbanism, dating back to the Soviet period, represent the scientific and urban planning communities' efforts to address the challenges of northern engineering and the psychological aspects of residing in urban areas.[17] Full-scale research on northern architecture started in 1956, coinciding with the establishment of the Urban Planning Division focused on the Far North, housed within the Leningrad Branch of the Academy of Architecture of Construction and Architecture.[18] In 1963, the Leningrad Zone Scientific Research Institute for Standard and Experimental Design of Residence and Communal Buildings was established, with a mandate to organize construction and engineering projects in the North. Over the years, architects proposed various experimental projects to address housing construction in extreme weather conditions.[19]

Contemporary research on urban livability in the Russian Arctic Zone extends beyond construction and engineering to encompass a broader range of topics. One key research area is conceptualizing and measuring urban sustainability in the northern areas.[20] Additionally, scholarly literature scrutinizes institutional challenges and the impacts of the Soviet legacy on the formulation of climate change adaptation and resilience policies in cities in the Russian Arctic Zone.[21] Other studies explore socio-economic factors and out-migration trajectories from urban areas in the region.[22]

With rare exceptions, contemporary research seldom explores the development of the sense of place bonding to Russian Arctic cities among various groups of residents.[23] However, as depopulation poses a significant threat to most Russian Arctic cities' future development and functioning, scholars and policymakers must comprehend the factors and processes of place bonding. This knowledge can inform policies aimed at countering out-migration trends and attracting in-migration. Furthermore, a clearer understanding of place bonding dynamics could help urban planners and designers build livable and

11   Terence Armstrong, "The 'Shift Method' in the Arctic," *Polar Record* 18, no. 114 (1976): 279–81.

12   Alla Bolotova and Florian Stammler, "How the North Became Home: Attachment to Place among Industrial Migrants in the Murmansk Region of Russia," in *Migration in the Circumpolar North: New Concepts and Patterns*, edited by T. Southcot and L. Huskey (Canadian Circumpolar Institute Press, University of Alberta, 2009), 193–220; Timothy E. Heleniak, "The Role of Attachment to Place in Migration Decisions of the Population of the Russian North," *Polar Geography* 32, no. 1–2 (2009): 31–60.

13   Bolotova and Stammler, "How the North Became Home: Attachment to Place among Industrial Migrants in the Murmansk Region of Russia."

14   Peter Hemmersam, "Arcticness and the Urbanism of the North," *Arctic Yearbook* 2021 (2021): 1–15.

15   Hemmersam; Prokopova, Kravchuk, and Garin, "Городская Среда Арктики: Оптимизация и Цифровизация [Arctic Urban Realm: Optimisation and Digitalisation]."

16   Kalemeneva, "From New Socialist Cities to Thaw Experimentation in Arctic Townscapes: Leningrad Architects Attempt to Modernise the Soviet North."

17   Hemmersam, "Arcticness and the Urbanism of the North."

18   Prokopova, Kravchuk, and Garin, "ГородскаяСредаАрктики: ОптимизацияиЦифровизация [Arctic Urban Realm: Optimisation and Digitalisation]."

19   Hemmersam, "Arcticness and the Urbanism of the North"; Kalemeneva, "From New Socialist Cities to Thaw Experimentation in Arctic Townscapes: Leningrad Architects Attempt to Modernise the Soviet North."

20   Robert W. Orttung and Colin Reisser, "Urban Sustainability in Russia's Arctic: Lessons from a Recent Conference and Areas for Further Investigations," *Polar Geography* 37, no. 4 (2014): 37–41; Benjamin DiNapoli and Matthew Jull, "Urban Planning Sustainability Metrics for Arctic Cities," *Environmental Research Letters* 15 (2020): 124023; Alexander Sergunin, "Russian Arctic Cities' Sustainable Development Strategies," in *Handbook of Research on International Collaboration, Economic Development, and Sustainability in the Arctic*, ed. Vasilii Erokhin, Tianming Gao, and Xiuhua Zhang (IGI Global, 2019), 495–513.

21   Harley Johansen and Yelizaveta Skryzhevska, "Adaptation Priorities on Russia's Kola Peninsula: Climate Change vs. Post-Soviet Transition," *Polar Geography* 36, no. 4 (2013): 271–90; Nadezhda Filimonova and Stacy D. VanDeveer, "Multi-Level Governance, Climate Chnage, and Municipal Solid Waste Management: Insights from Murmansk, Russia," *Urban Studies and Practices* 5, no. 1 (2021): 80–101; Nikolai Bobylev et al., "Building Urban Climate Change Adaptation Strategies: The Case of Russian Arctic Cities," *Weather, Climate, and Society* (2021): 875–84.

22   Nadezhda Zamyatina, "Migration Destination Choice as a Criterion of Self-Identification: The Case of Young People Leaving Noril'sk and Dudinka," *Sibirica* 16, no. 3 (2017): 57–76; Genevieve Parente, Nikolay Shiklomanov, and Dmitry Streletskiy, "Living in the New North: Migration to and from Russian Arctic Cities," *Focus on Geography* 55, no. 3 (2012): 77–89; O. N. Popova and I. V. Vicentiy, "Migration Situation in the Russian Arctic (on the Example of the Murmansk Region)," *IOP Conference Series: Earth and Environmental Science* 302, no. 1 (2019).

23   Heleniak, "The Role of Attachment to Place in Migration Decisions of the Population of the Russian North."

inclusive urban environments in the Russian Arctic, especially in the face of rapid climatic changes, local socio-economic constraints, and demographic shifts. Lastly, this question holds particular significance for Russia, as the Russian Ministry for the Development of the Russian Far East and Arctic, in cooperation with other state agencies, is currently developing comprehensive plans for the long-term socio-economic development of key urban settlements.[24] The development of these settlements is intended to enhance economic growth and improve the quality of life for residents in the Russian Arctic Zone.[25] The contribution of this chapter is twofold. First, this preliminary study sheds light on the state of academic research on migration and place bonding in the Russian Arctic Zone, providing some illustrative examples from the Norwegian, Finnish, and Swedish parts of the Arctic for comparative purposes. In this study, place refers to urban physical forms (the built environment), activities, and meanings constructed by residents in the Russian Arctic Zone. Additionally, this study defines the concept of place bonding in relation to the terms of place identity and attachment, which are discussed in detail in the following section. Second, this chapter examines whether and in which forms the topic of human–place bonding is present in scholarly discussions of migration to and from the urban Arctic. When considering the generalizability of findings from the Russian cases to cities worldwide, it is essential to recognize that the interplay between migration and a sense of place bonding is contingent on individual cases. There are additional factors that might impact migration decisions that fall beyond the scope of this chapter and, therefore, require further research.

ON PLACE IDENTITY AND ATTACHMENT

Scholars have developed different frameworks for comprehending a person's relation and bonding to a specific place, including, but not limited to, the sense of place, identification of a place between past and present, and place dependence.[26] This paper mainly focuses on place identity and place attachment, both widely discussed concepts in the literature. Others, like Lewicka, note that those notions might reveal a person's attitude towards the history of their place of residence.[27] Massey highlights that all places are in a constant state of change, and this rate of change can vary depending on the movement of people.[28] Future research, therefore, might grasp the relationships between other constructs of urban space and migration processes across the Arctic. The following sections delve into academic discussions on place identity and attachment concepts.

The term 'place identity' was introduced in the late 1970s in a study by Proshansky as "those dimensions of self that define the individual's personal identity in relation to the physical environment..."[29] In this way, place identity can refer to how a place's physical and symbolic features define a person's identity and sense of self, and it can be considered a part of self-identity that represents a sub-categorization of social identity similar to gender or nationality.[30] Place identity comprises various personal interpretations and meanings that might be grouped into values, thoughts, memories, and relationships at different dimensions (e.g., neighborhood and home).[31] In such operationalization, place identity mainly deals with a person's individual aspects.[32] However, the relationship between place and identity is temporal and socially constructed based on one's changing meanings and perceptions over time. Finally, place identity can also refer to characteristics that distinguish one place from another (e.g., politics, culture, nature).[33] This chapter uses Proshansky's definition of the term, referring to place identity as self-identification and categorization with a city located in the Russian Arctic and northern urban areas.

Along with place identity, in its broader sense, place attachment refers to a person's bonds or links with a specific place.[34] Although scholarly approaches lack consensus on the definition, Low and Altman state that most notions encompass the following three components: affect, cognition, and practice.[35,36]

24   The list of key settlements includes: Murmansk agglomeration (comprising Murmansk, Kola district, and Closed Administrative-Territorial Unit Severomorsk), Kirov-Apatitskaya and Monchegorsk agglomerations in the Murmansk Region, Kemsko-Belomorskaya agglomeration in the Republic of Karelia, Arkhangelsk agglomeration (including Arkhangelsk and Severodvinsk) in the Arkhangelsk Region, Naryan-Mar in the Nenets Autonomous Area, Salekhard-Labytnangi agglomeration and the cities of Novy Urengoy and Noyabrsk in the Yamal-Nenets Autonomous Area, Vorkuta agglomeration in the Komi Republic, Norilsk-Dudinka agglomeration, Dikson and Igarka and Tiksi with its surrounding territories in the Republic of Sakha (Yakutia), as well as Anadyr and Pevek in the Chukotka Autonomous Area.

25   n.d., "Определен Перечень Опорных Населенных Пунктов Российской Арктики [A List of Key Settlements in the Russian Arctic Has Been Determined]," Far East and Arctic Development Corporation, 2023.

26   Jianchao Peng, Dirk Strijker, and Qun Wu, "Place Identity: How Far Have We Come in Exploring Its Meanings?," *Frontiers in Psychology 11* (2020); Doreen Massey, "Places and Their Pasts," *History Workshop Journal* 39 (1995): 182–92.

27   Maria Lewicka, "Place Attachment, Place Identity, and Place Memory: Restoring the Forgotten City Past," *Journal of Environmental Psychology* 28 (2008): 209–31.

28   Doreen Massey, *For Space* (SAGE Publications, 2005).

29   Harold M. Proshansky, "The City and Self-Identity," *Environment and Behavior* 10 (1978): 155.

30   Proshansky; Harold M. Proshansky, Abbe K. Fabian, and Robert Kaminoff, "Place-Identity: Physical World Socialization of the Self," *Journal of Environmental Psychology*, 1983, 57–83; Åshild Lappegard Hauge, "Identity and Place: A Critical Comparison of Three Identity Theories," *Architectural Science Review* 50, no. 1 (2007): 44–51; Peng, Strijker, and Wu, "Place Identity: How Far Have We Come in Exploring Its Meanings?"

31   Hauge, "Identity and Place: A Critical Comparison of Three Identity Theories"; Gavin Parker and Joe Doak, "Place and Sense of Place," *Key Concepts in Planning* 9563 (2014): 156–70.

32   Lewicka, "Place Attachment, Place Identity, and Place Memory: Restoring the Forgotten City Past."

33   Lewicka; Peng, Strijker, and Wu, "Place Identity: How Far Have We Come in Exploring Its Meanings?"

34   Gerard T. Kyle, Andrew J. Mowen, and Michael Tarrant, "Linking Place Preferences with Place Meaning: An Examination of the Relationship between Place Motivation and Place Attachment," *Journal of Environmental Psychology* 24 (2004): 439–54; M. Carmen Hidalgo and Bernardo Hernández, "Place Attachment: Conceptual and Empirical Questions," *Journal of Environmental Psychology* 21, no. 3 (2001): 273–81.

The affective component most often refers to emotional attachment to a place, which, according to Lewicka, is scientists' most commonly measured component.[37] The cognitive component refers to knowledge and beliefs about a place, and practice deals with activities within a specific space.

In scholarly works, different approaches exist when considering the relationship between place identity and place attachment.[38] For example, Hidalgo and Hernández note that some scholarly works use place attachment as an element of place identity.[39] In contrast, other academic studies use these concepts as synonyms without distinction. This chapter's definitions align with Lewicka's approach, where place identity and place attachment are used as different but (inter)related concepts. That means that individuals might feel emotional bonds and identify with some aspects of an urban space.

FINDINGS

My analysis of the scholarly literature demonstrates that migration and place bonding in the Russian Arctic cities still represent understudied areas of academic research, along with general studies of urban areas in the Arctic regions. With rare exceptions, most articles used case studies as their methodology and qualitative data collection methods (e.g., interviews, ethnographic approaches, focused groups).[40] One explanatory factor for the predominance of qualitative research use in the reviewed papers is that such studies attempt to grasp individual perceptions and experiences related to migration, place attachment formation, and place identity negotiation. Most scholarly articles with a case study belong to cities in the Russian Arctic Zone. Despite rigorous prior research on Indigenous communities, a limited number of studies on cities and towns in the European and North American Arctic tend to focus on questions of Indigenous communities in urban contexts.[41] The following sections explore various ways in which place bonding and migration are connected or disconnected in the Russian Arctic urban settings, with fewer examples from the European Arctic for comparative analysis.

OUT-MIGRATION, PLACE ATTACHMENT, AND URBAN INFRASTRUCTURE

One noteworthy topic that emerged from my analysis is the link between the physical quality of northern urban infrastructure, an individual's sense of place attachment, and the decision to stay or leave. Earlier studies conducted outside of the Arctic region indicate that an individual's level of place attachment may be positively influenced by a city's socio-economic conditions and physical environment.[42] Lewicka describes this type of attachment as physical, indicating that it is connected to the physical characteristics of a place, including, for instance, access to recreational spaces.[43] Yang, Shi, and Runeson find that improving the accessibility of urban green areas in Sydney, Australia, can strengthen a sense of place attachment.[44] Similarly, Leviston et al. argue that in Perth, Western Australia, the anticipation of environmental degradation determines whether an individual's sense of place attachment diminishes or strengthens.[45] Well-developed, well-maintained, and easily accessible urban infrastructure can enhance the feeling that a place meets someone's wishes and needs, increasing the sense of place attachment and positively impacting an urban space's vitality and livability.[46] Therefore, an urban built environment's physical features may be crucial in fostering an individual's attachment to an urban space.

However, the relationship between the presence and state of urban social infrastructure and place attachment is not always linear, and additional factors can come into play. As an example, Anand and Sharma demonstrate that within communities in Greater Faridabad, a semi-urbanized part of India's National Capital Region, an individual's sense of place attachment is significantly impacted by their local interpersonal connections. At the same time, both the inaccessibility of infrastructure (e.g., sanitation, power supply, public transport) and its inadequate physical quality primarily cause dissatisfaction.[47] The development and accessibility of urban social infrastructure, therefore, may influence an individual's satisfaction with an urban space

35   Vittoria M. Giuliani and Roberta Feldman, "Place Attachement in a Developmental and Cultural Context," in *Journal of Environmental Psychology* 13 (1993): 267–74.

36   Setha M. Low and Irwin Altman, "Place Attachment: A Conceptual Inquiry," in *Place Attachment*, edited by I. Altman and S. M. Low (Plenum Press, 1992), 1–12.

37   Lewicka, "Place Attachment, Place Identity, and Place Memory: Restoring the Forgotten City Past."

38   Peng, Strijker, and Wu, "Place Identity: How Far Have We Come in Exploring Its Meanings?"

39   M. Carmen Hidalgo and Bernardo Hernández, "Place Attachment: Conceptual and Empirical Questions," *Journal of Environmental Psychology* 21 (2001): 273–81.

40   Nadezhda Zamyatina and Ruslan Goncharov, "'Agglomeration of Flows': Case of Migration Ties between the Arctic and the Southern Regions of Russia," *Regional Science Policy and Practice*, 14.

41   A note of clarification that here I am focusing on the body of work that is focused on the 'urban Arctic'. Torill Nyseth and Paul Pedersen, "Urban Sámi Identities in Scandinavia: Hybridities, Ambivalences and Cultural Innovation," *Acta Borealia* 31, no. 2 (2014): 131–51; Marlene Laruelle, "Indigenous Peoples, Urbanization Processes, and Interactions with Extraction Firms in Russia's Arctic," *Sibirica* 18, no. 3 (2019): 1–8; Marya Rozanova, "Indigenous Urbanization in Russia's Arctic: The Case of Nenets Autonomous Region," *Sibirica* 18, no. 3 (2019): 54–91.

42   W. M. Lestari and J. Sumabrata, "The Influencing Factors on Place Attachment in Neighborhood of Kampung Melayu," *IOP Conference Series: Earth and Environmental Science* 126 (2018): 12190.

43   Maria Lewicka, "Place Attachment: How Far Have We Come in the Last 40 Years?" *Journal of Environmental Psychology* 31 (2011): 207–30.

44   Chunyan Yang, Song Shi, and Goran Runeson, "Towards Sustainable Urban Communities: Investigating the Associations between Community Parks and Place Attachment in Master-Planned Estates in Sydney," *Sustainable Cities and Society* 96 (2023): 104659.

45   Zoe Leviston et al., "Anticipating Environmental Losses: Effects on Place Attachment and Intentions to Move," *Journal of Migration and Health* 7 (2023): 100152.

46   T. R. Alrobaee and A. S. Al-Kinani, "Place Dependence as the Physical Environment Role Function in the Place Attachment," *IOP Conference Series: Materials Science and Engineering* 698 (2019): 33014.

47   Rashmi Rani Anand and Poonam Sharma, "Assessing Inadequate Urban Infrastructure and Place Attachment Perception Among Residents of Gated Societies in Greater Faridabad, India.," *International Journal of Social Science and Economic Research* 6, no. 2 (2021): 605–27.

but may exert a moderating impact on developing an individual's bonds with a city and its neighborhood. These various instances suggest that the relationship between the physical features of the urban built environment and place attachment might also be contingent upon the context.

The relationships between migration, place attachment, and quality of built environment observed in the Arctic cities correspond with previous studies, yet they also illustrate some context nuances. Scholarly literature examines explicitly how social capital and the quality of urban infrastructure influence northern residents' out-migration intentions and patterns. In his work, Istomin studies the difference in migration rates from the Russian cities of Vorkuta and Ukhta in the Komi Republic, which share similarities with crumbling social infrastructure.[48] In both cities, the inadequate quality of urban infrastructure is a source of discontent among their residents. In contrast to Ukhta, where residents view migration not as necessary but as something desirable, residents in Vorkuta frame migration as essential, signaling a lack of attachment to the city's future.[49] Istomin explains the higher rates of out-migration from Vorkuta compared to Ukhta by the presence of many former Vorkuta inhabitants from Ukraine in the southern Russian city of Belgorod.[50] Like the Indian case described by Anand and Sharma,[51] individuals in Belgorod form interpersonal relations and create social networks to support new migrants from Vorkuta. The social networks formed by the prominent group of former Ukrainian inhabitants of Vorkuta facilitate and promote out-migration from the city, making out-migration regarded as a more accessible and appealing option for the remaining inhabitants.[52] This instance not only reinforces the idea that interpersonal relations contribute to place attachment but also indicates that one's sense of place attachment, through social capital, transcends urban boundaries and might be developed outside of its original location.

Similarly, in their work, Bolotova, Karaseva, and Vasilyeva demonstrate the complexity of interconnections between "underdeveloped" social infrastructure and northern residents' out-migration intentions.[53] Despite challenging living conditions in Taimyr villages, their residents have a strong sense of place attachment and less inclination to migrate. This contrasts with the Murmansk and Magadan regions, where the social infrastructure is more developed. However, residents are still either moving out or considering out-migration from Murmansk and Magadan regions.[54] In their study, Nedoseka and Zhigunova arrived at a different conclusion, suggesting that a well-developed social infrastructure is a defining feature of local identity when examining single-industry cities in the Murmansk region.[55] Thus, they indicate that improving socio-economic conditions in the Murmansk region leads to increasing identification with the cities among its residents.[56]

Currently, social infrastructure development falls short of the national average in many villages, towns, and cities in the Russian Arctic. It often fails to meet the minimum social standards the federal government sets.[57] One reason for the current state of affairs is that in the 1990s, after the collapse of the Soviet Union, the Russian government significantly reduced spending on social infrastructure. The maintenance and development of the infrastructure in the northern areas primarily relied on funds from industries that conducted economic activities within those areas.[58] During the 2000s, the federal government increased funding for social infrastructure in the national budget. However, a significant portion of regional and federal funds was allocated toward developing social infrastructure in administrative centers, even though smaller urban settlements and villages have greatly needed such investment.[59] Within the expert community, the approach to addressing the current challenges associated with urban infrastructure is primarily intertwined with tackling the problem of out-migration from the Russian Arctic. Therefore, it is widely suggested that the establishment of advantageous working and living conditions, which includes building modern residential facilities, kindergartens, schools, sports facilities, and hospitals, would contribute towards halting the trend of out-migration.[60]

48   K. V. Istomin, "'Who Would Want to Lay down into the Permafrost?': An Attempt to Explain Differences in Migration Rates, Strategies and Attitudes in Two Russian Northern Cities," *Acta Borealia* 38, no. 2 (2021): 104–30; Zamyatina, "Migration Destination Choice as a Criterion of Self-Identification: The Case of Young People Leaving Noril'sk and Dudinka."

49   Istomin, "'Who Would Want to Lay down into the Permafrost?': An Attempt to Explain Differences in Migration Rates, Strategies and Attitudes in Two Russian Northern Cities."

50   Istomin.

51   Anand and Sharma, "Assessing Inadequate Urban Infrastructure and Place Attachment Perception among Residents of Gated Societies in Greater Faridabad, India."

52   Istomin, "'Who Would Want to Lay down into the Permafrost?': An Attempt to Explain Differences in Migration Rates, Strategies and Attitudes in Two Russian Northern Cities."

53   Alla Bolotova, Anastasia Karaseva, and Valeria Vasilyeva, "Mobility and Sense of Place among Youth in the Russian Arctic," *Sibirica* 16, no. 3 (2017): 77–124.

54   Bolotova, Karaseva, and Vasilyeva.

55   Elena V. Nedoseka and G.V. Zhigunova, "Features of Local Identity of Single-Industry Town Residents (the Case of the Murmansk Oblast)," *Arctic and North* 52, no. 37 (2019): 98–111.

56   Nedoseka and Zhigunova.

57   L.A. Ryabova, "О Неотложных Мерах По Повышению Уровня и Качества Жизни Населения Арктической Зоны РФ [On Urgent Measures to Improve the Level and Quality of Life of the Population of the Arctic Zone of the Russian Federation]," *Sever i Rynok* 1, no. 29 (2012): 67–71.

58   E.E. Toropushina, "Оценка Уровня Развития Социальной Инфраструктуры в Регионах Севера и Арктики России [Assessment of the Level of Development of Social Infrastructure in the Regions of the North and Arctic of Russia]," *Eco* 6 (2016): 99–108.

59   Ryabova, "О Неотложных Мерах По Повышению Уровня и Качества Жизни Населения Арктической Зоны РФ [On Urgent Measures to Improve the Level and Quality of Life of the Population of the Arctic Zone of the Russian Federation]"; Toropushina, "Оценка Уровня Развития Социальной Инфраструктуры в Регионах Севера и Арктики России [Assessment of the Level of Development of Social Infrastructure in the Regions of the North and Arctic of Russia]."

To conclude, human-to-urban relationships in the Russian Arctic are not solely shaped by an individual's attachment to the physical quality of urban infrastructure. The factors shaping an individual's place attachment include interpersonal connections and social networks. The interrelated perceptions and meanings one can possess about a city and oneself also influence an individual's sense of place attachment.[61] At the same time, an individual's perceptions and meanings are not constant but relatively flexible: newcomers' perceptions might be challenged by the city's geographical location, climatic conditions, and everyday urban practices, as discussed in the following section.

IN-MIGRATION, PLACE IDENTITY, AND PLACE ATTACHMENT

Some scholarly works have explored a different angle of place bonding by centering on immigrants' experiences forming a sense of place attachment and place identity. Academic attention has focused on the growing Muslim immigrant population in the Russian and European Arctic caused by forced migration driven by military conflicts and labor migration processes. The primary question explored in these academic papers is how immigrants negotiate place attachment and identity in a new urban setting while maintaining ties with their home country.[62] Immigrant communities' negotiation of their place attachment and their sense of identity is not solely driven by a desire to be included in a new society but also by such factors as climatic conditions and urban remoteness in the Russian and European Arctic, which might influence the traditional way of practicing their religious rituals. The geographic isolation of Russian Arctic cities poses difficulties to everyday halal food consumption practices, as their disconnection from major transportation roads and railway systems hinders halal food delivery to these northern areas.[63] In a creative manner, the lifestyle in Arctic cities is reflected in Muslim communities launching businesses that blend Arctic characteristics, such as offering halal reindeer meat or halal fish.[64]

Although immigrant communities demonstrate varying adaptability to Arctic urban contexts, they also attempt to maintain connections with their homelands. However, these efforts can provoke othering and alienation of the immigrant population by other residents, who perceive them as threats to established social norms and practices.[65] In their article, Laruelle and Hohmann describe how the construction of a mosque in Norilsk, Krasnoyarsk krai, provoked a negative reaction from non-Muslim residents and led to tension between the native-born and immigrant communities.[66] In this way, the immigrants' place attachment to their home country stipulates a change in the place identity of the city where they reside. Laruelle argues that cultural diversity associated with labor migrants might lead to the negotiation of Russian and

European Arctic cities' identity as pluralistic and multicultural urban spaces.[67] In some instances, the negotiation of place attachment and identity by Muslim immigrant communities involves their recognition and acceptance of established social structures and hierarchies, alongside the acknowledgment by local authorities and residents of societal and urban transformations that newcomers introduce into their new living environments.

Such openness and acceptance might be grounded in shared values, perceptions of self-identification, and life experiences among residents and newcomers to the Russian and European Arctic. Paulgaard and Soleim examine how cross-generational collective memory of World War II in Norway's Sør-Varanger County helped residents identify with refugees as individuals pursuing security and shelter while fleeing from military conflicts in their home countries.[68] In her work, Laruelle provides a different perspective, discussing Muslim immigrants' admiration of Indigenous communities' respect for older people and family—a common value for both groups.[69] Such shared features and experiences might lead to the construction of shared place identification between different groups of Arctic residents.

INDIGENOUS PEOPLES AND PLACE IDENTITY

Earlier research on migration and Arctic Indigenous peoples in the urban context depicts cities as sites for the communities' assimilation, adaptation, and integration.[70] Searles provides a historical illustration of northern Canadian communities overseen by Northern Senior Officers who mentored Inuit in acquiring education and employment opportunities with the goal of

60   Anna Aristokesovna Cygankova, Ol'ga Viktorovna Romanchenko, and Ol'ga Leonidovna Shemetkova, "Инфраструктура Арктической Зоны РФ: Состояние, Экономические Инструменты Развития и Приоритетные Проекты [The Infrastructure of the Arctic Zone of the Russian Federation: The State, the Economic Development of the Tools and Priority Projects]," *Regional Economy and Management: Electronic Scientific Journal* 4, no. 48 (2016): 1–14; Nedoseka and Zhigunova, "Features of Local Identity of Single-Industry Town Residents (the Case of the Murmansk Oblast)."

61   Cliff Hague and Paul Jenkins, *Place Identity, Planning and Participation* (Routledge, 2005); Zamyatina, "Migration Destination Choice as a Criterion of Self-Identification: The Case of Young People Leaving Noril'sk and Dudinka"; Nedoseka and Zhigunova, "Features of Local Identity of Single-Industry Town Residents (the Case of the Murmansk Oblast)."

62   Anne Sigfrid Grønseth, "Migrating Rituals: Negotiations of Belonging and Otherness among Tamils in Norway," *Journal of Ethnic and Migration Studies* 44, no. 16 (2018): 2617–33; Gry Paulgaard and Marianne Neerland Soleim, "The Arctic Migration Route: Local Consequences of Global Crises," *Journal of Peace Education*, 2023, 1–21; Marlene Laruelle and Sophie Hohmann, "Polar Islam: Muslim Communities in Russia's Arctic Cities," *Problems of Post-Communism* 67, no. 4–5 (2020): 327–37.

63   Laruelle and Hohmann, "Polar Islam: Muslim Communities in Russia's Arctic Cities."

64   Marlene Laruelle, "Postcolonial Polar Cities? New Indigenous and Cosmopolitan Urbanness in the Arctic," *Acta Borealia* 36, no. 2 (2019): 149–65.

65   Laruelle.

66   Laruelle and Hohmann, "Polar Islam: Muslim Communities in Russia's Arctic Cities."

67   Laruelle, "Postcolonial Polar Cities? New Indigenous and Cosmopolitan Urbanness in the Arctic."

68   Paulgaard and Soleim, "The Arctic Migration Route: Local Consequences of Global Crises."

assimilating them into Canadian society.[71] However, during the 2000s, there was a shift in scholarly literature towards examining cities as sites for the mobilization of indigeneity.[72] Given the accelerated migration of Indigenous people to urban areas in the Russian Arctic, primarily due to the opportunities for education, health treatment, and employment, it is imperative to allocate more scholarly attention to this under-researched topic of Arctic studies.[73]

The outcomes of Indigenous peoples' migration prompts scholarly discussions about the manifestation of Indigenous identity in urban settings.[74] Searles argues that many Inuit in the Canadian Arctic resist extending their identity into urban spaces even though more Inuit are moving into urban settlements.[75] Urban environments and institutions in the Russian Arctic might promote the development of Indigenous cultures within city settings, yet they could also lead to a renegotiation of Indigenous place and attachment.[76] As illustrated by the case of Naryan-Mar, urbanized younger Nenets generations are experiencing a loss of culturally ingrained knowledge and information and a reduction in language proficiency due to their inability to engage in traditional nomadic activities in urban environments.[77] In Yakutsk, the Republic of Sakha (Yakutia), Kuklina, Ignatieva, and Vinokurova highlight that students face limited chances to support their ethnic identity beyond school, mainly because many of their home villages are distant and challenging to reach.[78] Simultaneously, efforts to preserve Indigenous languages and culture in urban environments in Russia might result in the renegotiation of an urban space identity.[79] This change is evident, for instance, in the architectural designs of buildings in Naryan-Mar, where traditional ornaments are incorporated.[80] Indigenous symbols and signs are also displayed on public buildings in some northern cities in Nordic countries, with Tromsø, Norway, serving as a particularly prominent case.[81] Another manifestation of Indigenous cultures across Russian and Nordic urban cases is evident in including public services, educational programs, and cultural events tailored to these communities. For instance, Nyseth and Pedersen illustrate diverse civic Sámi associations, such as sports and student organizations, active in the Norwegian city of Tromsø and Umeå, Sweden.[82] These instances speak to an increasing salience of Indigenous place identity in cities across the Russian and European Arctic.[83] However, the potential outcomes of fostering indigeneity are highly context-specific and rely on various factors, including the historical and current state of Indigenous peoples within a specific Arctic country. Lastly, the extent of Indigenous self-identification with urban space is also shaped by the connection to the place of origin, which, for instance, includes visits to rural areas to reunite with family members.[84] As in the abovementioned cases, the extent of this connection varies from individual to individual.

CONCLUSION

Many cities and towns in the Russian Arctic Zone continue to face population decline, raising important questions about the future of these urban settlements as sites for welfare services providence and their roles in regional and national economic growth. Out-migration problems are also closely intertwined with broader scholarly and political discussions on the importance of maintaining urban settlements in the Russian Arctic.[85] Beyond Arctic studies, scholars suggest that local governments should forge a "strong, independent image" for various community members.[86] The reasoning for such a proposal is that identity formation enables a deep sense of affiliation among long-term residents and newcomers with the (new) place of living in urban areas, thereby

69   Laruelle, "Postcolonial Polar Cities? New Indigenous and Cosmopolitan Urbanness in the Arctic."

70   Laruelle; Nyseth and Pedersen, "Urban Sámi Identities in Scandinavia: Hybridities, Ambivalences and Cultural Innovation"; Peter Schweitzer, "Коренные народы и урбанизация на Аляске и канадском Севере [Indigenous Peoples and Urbanization in Alaska and the Canadian North]," *Etnograficheskoe Obozrenie* 1 (2016): 10–22.

71   Edmund (Ned) Searles, "Placing Identity: Town, Land, and Authenticity in Nunavut, Canada," *Acta Borealia* 27, no. 2 (2010): 151–66.

72   Schweitzer, "Коренные народы и урбанизация на Аляске и канадском Севере [Indigenous Peoples and Urbanization in Alaska and the Canadian North]."

73   Vera Kuklina, Sargylana Ignatieva, and Uliana Vinokurova, "Educational Institutions as a Resource for the Urbanization of Indigenous People: The Case of Yakutsk," *Sibirica* 18, no. 3 (2019): 29–53; Rozanova, "Indigenous Urbanization in Russia's Arctic: The Case of Nenets Autonomous Region."

74   Searles, "Placing Identity: Town, Land, and Authenticity in Nunavut, Canada"; Nyseth and Pedersen, "Urban Sámi Identities in Scandinavia: Hybridities, Ambivalences and Cultural Innovation."

75   Searles, "Placing Identity: Town, Land, and Authenticity in Nunavut, Canada."

76   Kuklina, Ignatieva, and Vinokurova, "Educational Institutions as a Resource for the Urbanization of Indigenous People the Case of Yakutsk"; Rozanova, "Indigenous Urbanization in Russia's Arctic: The Case of Nenets Autonomous Region."

77   Rozanova, "Indigenous Urbanization in Russia's Arctic: The Case of Nenets Autonomous Region."

78   Kuklina, Ignatieva, and Vinokurova, "Educational Institutions as a Resource for the Urbanization of Indigenous People: The Case of Yakutsk."

79   Rozanova, "Indigenous Urbanization in Russia's Arctic the Case of Nenets Autonomous Region"; Marlene Laruelle, "Indigenous Peoples, Urbanization Processes, and Interactions with Extraction Firms in Russia's Arctic," *Sibirica* 18, no. 3 (2019): 1–8; Kuklina, Ignatieva, and Vinokurova, "Educational Institutions as a Resource for the Urbanization of Indigenous People: The Case of Yakutsk."

80   Rozanova, "Indigenous Urbanization in Russia's Arctic: The Case of Nenets Autonomous Region."

81   Nyseth and Pedersen, "Urban Sámi Identities in Scandinavia: Hybridities, Ambivalences and Cultural Innovation."

82   Nyseth and Pedersen.

83   Christine Hudson, Torill Nyseth, and Paul Pedersen, "Dealing with Difference: Contested Place Identities in Two Northern Scandinavian Cities," *City* 23, no. 4–5 (2019): 564–79; Kuklina, Ignatieva, and Vinokurova, "Educational Institutions as a Resource for the Urbanization of Indigenous People: The Case of Yakutsk"; Laruelle, "Indigenous Peoples, Urbanization Processes, and Interactions with Extraction Firms in Russia's Arctic," 2019.

84   Kuklina, Ignatieva, and Vinokurova, "Educational Institutions as a Resource for the Urbanization of Indigenous People: The Case of Yakutsk"; Hudson, Nyseth, and Pedersen, "Dealing with Difference: Contested Place Identities in Two Northern Scandinavian Cities."

85   Kuklina, Ignatieva, and Vinokurova, "Educational Institutions as a Resource for the Urbanization of Indigenous People: The Case of Yakutsk"; Hudson, Nyseth, and Pedersen, "Dealing with Difference: Contested Place Identities in Two Northern Scandinavian Cities."

encouraging them to stay in the locality and deterring migration.[87] As there are multiple ways for building such local strategies, this chapter mainly focused on examining how different groups of individuals construct and exchange place identity and attachment across various cities in the Russian Arctic Zone, with several cases from the northern regions of Finland, Sweden, and Norway. My preliminary research outcomes contribute to comprehending the interplay between place bonding and migration in the two principal ways.

First, the study examines the processes and mechanisms involved in urban place-making among members of Indigenous communities and foreign immigrants moving into Russian Arctic cities. Unlike long-term or native-born residents, newcomers often need to actively develop a sense of attachment to a new place of living.[88] The analysis of Russian city cases mirrored overarching findings from previous studies, discussing challenges immigrants face in navigating between being accepted in the new place of residence by other residents while maintaining social ties with their home country.[89] From a long-term residents' standpoint, my analysis shows common patterns of discussions on the established urban hierarchies and the degree of residents' acceptance and openness to their cities' cultural and demographic changes. This study's outcomes are relevant to broader research questions concerning the trajectories for cities in the Russian Arctic Zone and other parts of the Arctic to evolve into multicultural and inclusive urban communities.[90] Therefore, future research should unpack factors that enhance or weaken feelings of place identity and attachment among Indigenous and non-Indigenous residents and foreign immigrants in different Arctic cities.

Further, the experiences of immigrants in constructing a sense of attachment to a new urban environment shed light on the unique characteristics of living conditions in the Arctic. In this context, the negotiation of newcomers' place identity is impacted by severe weather and climatic conditions relevant to the region. These research findings echo previous scholarly conclusions that personal place identity and place attachment to an urban space might vary from one individual to another.[91] Therefore, local governments and, particularly, urban planners in the Russian Arctic need to consider these diverse perspectives and attitudes in urban planning and development. Local governments and urban planners should build on these divergent perspectives and attitudes as they represent essential knowledge on what constitutes a livable city in the harsh conditions of the Arctic.

Notes on Method

Data sources and search strategy: This literature review is an introductory examination. Further qualitative research in the identified cities is needed to enhance an understanding of the interplay between place bonding and migration. A search strategy was developed to collect data for the review to identify relevant articles that align with the research objectives. The search strategy included a combination of notions of place bonding (OR place attachment OR identity) AND migration (OR mobility) AND city (OR urban OR urbanization) AND Arctic (OR Russia OR polar OR Far North OR Indigenous). The search was conducted from August to September 2023 using Web of Science, Scopus, and Taylor & Francis databases. These databases were selected because of their comprehensive coverage of Arctic-related research. Additional articles were found by reviewing reference lists of included full-text articles. Simultaneously, focusing only on these three databases represents an important limitation of this study; future research should examine databases of articles published in languages other than English.

Identification selection of studies: Studies were considered eligible if they met the following inclusion criteria: (1) research focus on the interplay of the city, place identity, and migration; (2) geographical area of cities' location included Russian Arctic or sub-Arctic; (3) the paper was published in a peer-reviewed journal in English; (4) the study was published between 2012 and 2022 and is available in full text. The study selection encompassed the following three steps: (1) title screening, (2) abstract screening, and (3) screening of the paper's full text. Depending on whether studies met the selection criteria, papers were included in or excluded from further analysis.

Data collection and analysis: Several criteria were used for data collection and thematic analysis: (1) an article's general information (author[s], year of publication, study design, and urban geographical location in the Russian Arctic); (2) whether and how the topic of place attachment and migration to and from Russian Arctic cities is addressed in an article; (3) what types of interplay between migration and place attachment are revealed in an article. For each selected paper, two major themes were assigned: the first theme referred to the paper's primary focus (e.g., out-migration or in-migration), and the second one referred to specified identity (e.g., Indigenous urban identity) and types of place attachment formed with a northern city (e.g., maintenance of personal connections). The findings and discussion are presented in the sections entitled *Findings* and *Conclusion*.

86   Derya Oktay, "The Quest for Urban Identity in the Changing Context of the City," *Cities* 19, no. 4 (2002): 270.

87   Ibid.

88   Brit Lynnebakke and Aadne Aasland, "Striking Roots: Place Attachment of International Migrants, Internal Migrants and Local Natives in Three Norwegian Rural Municipalities," *Journal of Rural Studies* 94 (2022): 488–98.

89   Paolo Boccagni and Carlos Vargas-Silva, "Feeling at Home across Time and Place: A Study of Ecuadorians in Three European Cities," *Population, Space and Place* 27, no. 6 (2021): 1–13; Vanessa Sieng and Ágnes Szabó, "Exploring the Place Attachments of Older Migrants in Aotearoa: A Life Course History Approach," *Advances in Life Course Research* 57 (2023): 100560.

90   Marlene Laruelle, "Postcolonial Polar Cities? New Indigenous and Cosmopolitan Urbanness in the Arctic," *Acta Borealia* 36, no. 2 (2019): 149–65; Torill Nyseth and Paul Pedersen, "Urban Sámi Identities in Scandinavia: Hybridities, Ambivalences and Cultural Innovation," *Acta Borealia* 31, no. 2 (2014): 131–51.

91   Lewicka, "Place Attachment, Place Identity, and Place Memory: Restoring the Forgotten City Past"; Lewicka, "Place Attachment: How Far Have We Come in the Last 40 Years?"

Jakob Exner is an architect, CEO, and partner at the Greenland-based design office TNT Nuuk.
Helena Lennert is an architect, creative director, and partner at the Greenland-based design office TNT Nuuk.

Color and Comfort: An Architectural Tribute to the Children of Tasiilaq, Greenland
Jakob Exner and Helena Lennert

INTRODUCING TASIILAQ

Imagine stepping into a world where warm colors and safety embrace little ones from the moment they first step inside. In the heart of Greenland's rugged and stunning nature, TNT Nuuk A/S had the unique opportunity to shape a small part of Tasiilaq's urban landscape through the design of the local daycare center. Tasiilaq is the largest town in East Greenland, with a growing population of around 2,000 people, mainly due to the migration from smaller settlements in the region. The town's unique climate is characterized by strong winds from the inland ice, known as Piteraq, and heavy winter snowfalls, making design and construction particularly challenging.

DESIGN PHILOSOPHY

Our design philosophy is not driven by radical architectural paradigms but by a user-centered approach that focuses on the unique challenges and opportunities of the Arctic environment. Respecting Tasiilaq's specific conditions, we avoided an overwhelming institutional expression by breaking the building into smaller elements. This creates an intimate and informal atmosphere that supports a key aspect of our design: to create a homely and close relationship between the building and its users, an environment that exudes a kind of homely coziness, ensuring that children feel safe and at home. This warm and welcoming atmosphere is woven into every part of the institution. Additionally, the use of colors in the design is a deliberate interpretation

1 At the edge of Tasiilaq, the largest town in East Greenland, five colorful volumes are seen twisted and turned in response to the rocks, winds, snow, and sun.

2 In the short days of winter, lights from inside Meeqkerivik spill out onto the snow, sharing the warmth and closeness of the carefully designed interior.

of the traditional colors typically found in Greenlandic buildings. Historically, these colors had significant meaning, indicating ownership or function. For example, healthcare buildings were—and often still are—painted yellow, while telecommunication buildings were green. This tradition inspired the color palette used in the daycare, bringing aspects of local and Greenlandic cultural heritage into the modern design.

DESIGN OF THE DAYCARE CENTER

The daycare consists of five buildings that are carefully positioned and rotated in relation to one another, creating a dynamic spatial experience. Inspired by the colorful houses of Tasiilaq and the majestic mountain peaks, the institution is designed to harmonize with the landscape and enhance its beauty. The sloped terrain allowed us to give the building a more intimate scale at the entrance side and a grander scale on two floors facing the side where the mountain is visible in the background. This shift in scale fits harmoniously with the grandeur of the surrounding landscape.

The sloped terrain also provided a practical solution to a significant challenge: creating substantial storage space, which is crucial in an area where sea freight is only possible during the short summer months before the sea freezes over in autumn. Careful logistical planning is required to ensure that building materials and daily necessities are transported during this time, and the project's ample storage facilities will greatly benefit those using it. Developing the project with the municipality as the client helped to ensure that local needs and considerations were integrated into the process from the very beginning.

LEARNINGS AND OPPORTUNITIES

Tasiilaq's extreme weather conditions and logistical challenges offer valuable lessons for future projects in the Arctic. Not only did the design have to account for strong winds and heavy snowfall, but it also had to accommodate logistical limitations of the seasons, where all shipping must be planned within a short summer window. This experience helped us to develop more efficient, sustainable solutions, finding a balance between functionality and comfort.

CONCLUDING NOTES

This project is one of many where TNT Nuuk A/S applied its deep local knowledge and experience to create buildings that shape and support the societal development of modern Greenland. Here, with the daycare center in Tasiilaq, we aimed to create a warm and inviting environment that embraces each child and ensures their well-being and development alongside that of the community—all while respecting the grandeur and challenges of the surrounding environment.

Maaretta Jaukkuri is a Finnish curator and professor of contemporary art who has, throughout her career, influenced students, theorists, artists and the public. She spends her time between Helsinki and Kvalnes, Lofoten, Norway.
A K Dolven is a Norwegian artist. She works across painting, film, sound, sculpture, and interventions in public space.

The Place on the Island by the Sea: Maaretta Jaukkuri and A K Dolven in Conversation with Elise Misao Hunchuck

"At a certain point," Anne Dillard wrote in *Teaching a Stone to Talk*, "you say to the woods, to the sea, to the mountains, the world, Now I am ready. Now I will stop and be wholly attentive. You empty yourself and wait, listening."[1] So there I was in Kvalnes, in the winter months when 2019 became 2020. I was ready, empty, waiting, and listening on Vestvågöy, "an island in Lofoten, on the edge continental shelf. Like other faraway peripheries, the place is sensitive to changes. It is a region of extreme fragility, where we are implicated with changes in nature and the urgent challenges these create."[2] I would be there, at the Place, for just over three months, returning to my home in Berlin and my teaching posts in London just as the world fell into the chaos that was the COVID-19 pandemic. Years later, I'm still moved by the premise of the invitation I received from Maaretta Jaukkuri that brought me to the Place: come to Kvalnes, where you will be given everything you need for two months of "studying, reflecting, writing, meditating and dreaming" in an environment that is a place for "wandering, wondering and experiencing" and where cultural inspiration is found in books, digital connections, and a telescope to look at the stars.[3] On November 15, 2023, I travelled to Helsinki to speak with Maaretta Jaukkuri at her home while Anne Katrine joined us online. What follows has been edited and shortened for clarity. What happened was a meandering conversation wherein Maaretta and Anne Katrine (A K) Dolven generously shared their stories about how they met, about the foundation, the Place, about how they learned about art, themselves, and the

1   At the edge of the Lofoten-Vesterålen continental shelf is an unassuming rectangle of a house (designed by Kimmo Aslak Liimatainen). It's a clean, tidy box with generous openings that let—depending on the time of day or year—light spill out or in. This was the view in 2020, standing at the shore in front of the house. Beyond the horizon are the Spitsbergen Islands, followed by Greenland.

northern landscapes from which one of them came and one of them learned so much she could not quite leave. Ultimately, it's a story about friendship and learning about oneself and each other through learning about a place. *EMH*

Elise Misao Hunchuck Maaretta, Anne-Katrine, maybe we can start with you telling us about the Place and how it came to be.

Maaretta Jaukkuri I can tell you the story of how the Place got its name. I was teaching art and architecture students at the university in Trondheim at the time, the art academy, and we talked about the differences between the concepts of space and place. So it had a very clear meaning for me. My idea was that the name would be the Place. There's life, and then there's an in-between time and place when you can go to the Place, gather yourself, and continue. At the time, I was in conversation with Antony Gormley about this project because his contribution, along with Anne Katrine's, was crucial to realizing it. And he said the Place was the perfect name.

Anne Katrine Dolven We met in Oslo because Maaretta was the artistic director of Kunstnernes Hus [The Artists' House], an interesting and independent artists-run Kunsthalle in Oslo. At the time, I was also a part-time professor at the Art Academy in Oslo. And I told Maaretta that I bought land for a studio in Kvalnes. I had a small house there already. [To Elise: you know the place.] And I had the option to buy land, part of an old farm. The whole idea was kind of unbelievable. Who would come there? But I just felt something at that moment: in life, you can say yes, or you can say no. But I remember thinking: I can't say no to this. So my instinct said yes.

Then sometime later—I think it was 2010—I met with Maaretta, and we had a good meal in a nice place in Oslo. We were talking about the Arctic and the North. Friends meet and talk and celebrate by having some good wine. I felt she should have the piece of extra land that was a little bit away from the place where my future studio would be. I decided to give Maaretta this land, about one kilometer from the studio. We both were very happy and full of expectations about what we could do in Kvalnes. It was fantastic and very inspiring. It became Maaretta's land and then the basis of the foundation when it was registered. But we didn't have a house, and we didn't have money for a house.

1   Anne Dillard, "Teaching a Stone to Talk: Expeditions and Encounters," *The Atlantic*, February 1981.
2   "The Foundation," Maaretta Jaukkuri Foundation, at mjfoundation.no.
3   Maaretta Jaukkuri, email to the author, October 27, 2018.

AKD The initiative for the house and the foundation came from artists. Antony Gormley and his studio arranged an auction at Sotheby's in London featuring both his artwork as well as artworks donated by some of the artists Maaretta had worked with throughout her career. Sotheby's liked the idea so much that they decided not to take any commission. At the time, Maaretta had not been told about this.

The value of the land made it possible to register the foundation and the income from the art sales to build the house. The program Innovation Norway also contributed to the building. That's how this all started; it was all based on friendship. The foundation of all of this is Maaretta because she has done such amazing work. From the beginning, Maaretta wanted to share the Place with people like you and others, locally and globally.

EMH I was in the Place during the winter. Preparing to speak with you today, I looked back at the website, and while reading Maaretta's text, I was held by how you wrote about the Place, about how everything you do has to respond to what's happening outside and around you. And I think there was something really profound about that. Many of us are not used to that kind of attunement and attention. I don't mean this in a nostalgic way, but it was something remarkable to experience.

AKD I also love the wintertime. The moon becomes so important during the blue hours.

EMH I remember you told me before polar night began that people always say polar night is the darkest time of year, but instead, you thought of it as the most colorful.[4] And I couldn't understand what you meant until I saw it. I was curious, so I looked it up more and learned that there are three types of twilight (some argue four, including antitwilight): civil, nautical, and astronomical. And polar night in Lofoten is not actually polar night, but what happens is that daytime is, in effect, replaced by civil twilight. While I was in the Place, the polar night began December 8, 2019, and daylight only reappeared on January 6 for—meteorological records tell me—forty-seven minutes. But every twilight of that polar night, I would obsessively photograph the landscape framed by a window in the second story of the house in an attempt to record the gradients of blue that would present themselves, as if I might miss a color or a shade.

AKD It is true that something always happens when you stay in that place. I also remember, earlier on, my neighbor there, an older woman. I used to phone her when I wasn't there, and she always had something to tell me about what she'd seen. And I would think: Really? And she would always say: "You should have been there.

You should have seen this and that." I think she was ninety then. It would have been different had she been living in a city with lots of people and looking out at some stone wall. As she was living there, she always had something to tell. It didn't matter if it was November or December or January. And now you have been there. You have experienced this.

EMH I have, and I did. And I think of it often. Your work is based on this, too—knowing the place so well, knowing the light so well. The MJF (Maaretta Jaukkuri Foundation) house is like a light in the dark on the edge of the island. Can you tell us a little about the designer?

> *MJ* At a time when there was no idea of how we could finance a building in Kvalnes, I asked the Finnish architect Kimmo Aslak Liimatainen if he might be interested in sketching ideas for a small house in Lofoten. I knew him from my time at Kiasma (the Museum of Contemporary Art in Helsinki), but also because he, together with three other young architects, had won the Golden Lion in Venice just after they graduated. Despite the lack of secured financing for the project, he was inspired by the idea, the land and its proximity to the ocean, and the light of the place. He started working on it without any clear promise that the house would ever be built.

EMH It's true that the house is both a kind of beacon and a lantern. At that time of year, when the lights are on, it compels people driving or walking to slow down to see what is happening. Maaretta, how did you come to know northern Norway so well?

> *MJ* I come from the northern part of Finland, and though I moved to Helsinki when I was very young, the northern area is part of my background.

> *AKD* Yes, but I think of Norway in particular. It all started some years earlier when I wrote you a letter—it was not an email. No one had ever written about my work. At the time, I had a residency in Künstlerhaus Bethanien in Berlin, and a part of the residency was to have an exhibition. They suggested making a catalog—my first catalog ever. Per Hovdenakk, who at the time was the director of the Henie-Onstad Museum, said that if there's someone who could write about these

4   A phenomenon limited to the polar circles, polar night occurs when the sun remains below the horizon for more than twenty-four continuous hours. The darkness—or lightness—of the night is measured along a gradient of different types of twilight, depending on how much of the sun's light can refract over the horizon itself, which depends on one's location by latitude. Polar night can be just twenty-four hours just inside the polar circle to, at the north and south poles, one hundred and seventy-nine days long.

2   Just within the Arctic Circle as it dips down across the Lofoten Islands is Dan Graham's *Untitled*
(1994), a sculpture of a two-way mirror and stainless steel. Set into the rocks and mossy flora
alongside the E10 near an abandoned ferry station at Lyngvær, *Untitled* is one of the 36 sculptures
throughout 32 Nordland municipalities that comprise *Skulpturlandskap Nordland* (2019).

works, it is Maaretta. And I thought, how dare I write to her about that? But then I did. And she said something like, thank you, I will be glad to write about your work. And I was so moved by what she wrote. That was the first connection we had.

And then it was November 9, 1989. We all know what happened that day. I lived in Berlin then, but I was invited to a meeting about the planned Nordland sculpture project in Oslo, so I left Berlin on the evening of November 8. There was a kind of magic energy in the air. The same year, the head of culture of Nordland County called me and asked if I could come to Norway, as they would have a seminar about what they could do to advance the position of contemporary art in this northern county. I was inspired by the Berlin of those days—1987, 1988, when it was still an island in the east part of GDR (German Democratic Republic)—and by the place as an island. The city invested a lot in inviting artists through DAAD (Deutsche Akademischer Austauschdienst, the German Academic Exchange Service). They invited authors, musicians, and artists to Berlin. Inspired by this idea of inviting artists to live and work in a kind of "island" situation and thinking about questions of periphery and center, I gave a talk in November 1988 on Vega, another island where this seminar took place. I proposed that we think of the whole county as a geographic space and each of the county's municipalities as an exhibition space with their different landscapes and seascapes as well as histories. After my talk, the county mayor at the time, Sigbjörn Eriksen, said in a radio interview: "This idea is so crazy that we should take it very seriously."

MJ At the time, I was the chief curator at Kiasma, which had recently opened in Helsinki. Somehow I managed to take a year's leave from the museum to work a year on this project. I had in fact already moved to Bodö before the county made the final decision about launching the project. The political process became quite complicated and took a long time. Basically, it might have been that I had moved there without a project!

But the project was really very important for me. At the time, free interpretation of art was very much discussed, and the role of the spectator was the focus. I was reading Zygmunt Bauman's texts and was very inspired by the openness that spectators might have in their encounters with art. Bauman also attended our seminar on the topic as well as a later seminar on curating arranged by NIFCA (the Nordic Institute of Contemporary Art). I spent the whole year in Bodö, traveling all over the county with the invited artists, discussing their choices of sites for their works and negotiating both the artistic and practical issues emerging from these choices. It was important to be there, to spend time both with the local people and the visiting artists, and to try to be honest about everything, including the finances, because you have to be able to create trust both with the artists and among the local residents to have any chance of succeeding with this kind of a project.

AKD Maaretta now has deep knowledge of the county and the north of Norway. She knows more about every municipality than I do—and I am from there! She knows the people. She knows the social and political structures there. And I think, as a curator who has worked in a big institution, her institution here was the people, and the place was this huge area of Norway.[5] The county is a long strip along the sea. Some inland counties and municipalities know more about hunting moose than fish. In Lofoten, we know more about fish. It's all these different spaces that Maaretta knows so much about, so it felt natural and right that she should have a house here, as she somehow belongs here. And so, as I had an extra piece of land, I gave it to Maaretta.

MJ When preparations for Artscape Nordland started, we were four people making the first selection of artists and placing them in all the municipalities of the county. However, it didn't quite work out exactly as planned. There were municipalities that did not want to participate, and there were artists who did not want to contribute for different reasons. Seven artists were invited afterward because some artists thought, for example, that the fee was too low, they had no time or interest, or they came up with proposals that we couldn't approve of. Some municipalities did not like the idea of what they called "modern art," some thought that instead of these international artists, local artists should have been preferred.

It is a long story, and I learned a lot and found something interesting about how contemporary art is perceived in these areas, which are far away from the centers of art. They had this idea of "modern art," and some people even knew what they were talking about. Others had mainly just prejudices created by the popular press. However, when a project was ready, we invited people to the opening, and they came and enjoyed the ritual. Ultimately, they adopted the works as their own and are, in most cases, proud of their sculpture.

We also invited anyone to interpret what they saw and to write a text. Some of the texts are beautiful, but they tend to view the works as if they were "modern art" or a kind of traditional public art that usually already contains a pre-given message to think about. We did not apply any pedagogical methods in this process; we just briefly informed viewers about what the artist had as their premises to do just this work. And, of course, the artists had total freedom.

MJ I was in Bodö from May 1992 to May 1993. I continued to work on the project from wherever I was throughout the entire project that ended in 2015. While in Bodö, I kept on traveling all the time to different communes on these small airplanes. I think a crucial thing here is that the artists came, met local people, drove around the area, and discussed with the local people where the work should be. This is not how things normally work, of course. Usually, artists are met by institutions, and they are mainly met by the staff of the institution. But this was different. It was direct. The artists were meeting people who would live with the work. And I know that was also very important for most of the artists. I also think that the local people got to know that person from the beginning and developed a feeling of connection very early on to the planned work and the site where it would be.

EMH I was able to travel to a few of the artworks. One day, I drove out to Eggum, a fishing village that lies on the outer (seaward) side of Vestvågøy island, between the ocean and the mountains, to see *Head* by Marcus Raetz. In graduate school, for a brief time, I was obsessed with optical illusions, so I was drawn to this sculpture that is both a head upright and a head turned upside down. It's on a granite pedestal, around which the ground is worn down, many centimeters below the surface.

MJ You know, that has become a project for local sheep as well. They walk around it and scratch themselves against the granite pedestal, causing this dark, fatty ring in the middle. The stone is a local granite. Because there are no trees there, the sheep walk there, around and around. That's why the ground right around the sculpture is the way it is. So some works are not just for people—they're for all the resident animals, birds, and sheep. And not always with the desired consequences.

AKD I had a nice experience two days ago. I have a public work in Oslo that is called *Untuned Bell by the Harbour*. And I was going to Biltema [a shop in Norway that sells all kinds of tools], a huge warehouse. I visit it now and then to buy things I need for my work. And there was a man who asked me why I was buying these things. He presumed I was not a carpenter or builder, but I bought their tools. I said, Yes, I'm an artist. Oh, what do you do? Do you paint? (That's always the first question I get.) Yes, I do, I answered, but I also make sculptures or outdoor projects. And then I mentioned the bell because this was in Oslo. And he said, I know that work because

5   Nordland is a diverse and long county—560 kilometers in length—covering an area of some 40,000 square kilometers.

it has a pedal, and one has to step up on the pedal to sound it. I go there with my children. And just like that, so simple, he recalled a memory that made me so happy.

EMH The Place and its fellowships and activities have been made possible, as you said, first by a significant contribution by Antony Gormley and other artists, and then the residency plan was funded by the Saastamoinen Foundation and the Kone Foundation for a few years. How do you imagine the future of the Maaretta Jaukkuri Foundation?

> *MJ* Saastamoinen Foundation is still supporting us. Kone is no longer a sponsor, so the funding is strained for the time being. We can only take three or four fellows a year. I hope and trust that we will be able to continue to host the fellows. However, if we want support from the Norwegian systems, they will demand that we be more outward-orientated instead of letting the fellows decide how they spend their time. We are thinking of ways to communicate more with people in the Lofoten Islands. We wish to find ways that are inspiring also to the artists. I think it's so important that fellows continue to come from many countries and that the fellows there have no pre-defined obligations.[6]

> *AKD* I'm really happy about Maaretta's library being there now. It's very well organized. That kind of archive is unique. It's not in the cloud, like many archives today; it's there, in the Place, by the sea— just imagine walking down the road and thinking a collection of books is available in the house. The collection is growing, and now it's well organized, so perhaps we can connect more with the local communities or use it to create talks.

EMH For readers who don't know, there is an expansive library on the house's second floor. Every fellow is asked, when they come, to leave a book or two. It seems like people have left more than just a few. And now you have a remarkable library archive containing the thoughts, interests, dreams, and works of people who have found their way to this little house on the edge of an island at the edge of the continental shelf. There's an artist who Anne Katrine introduced me to, Even Bie Larsen, who lives in Lofoten, in Kabelvåg. His flat is small, tiny even, but every surface is filled with books or paper for drawing. He told me: I don't need to travel the world. I travel when I read these books, and I learn about these places when I draw their maps. These two worlds, these two archives, exist so close together—they can come into contact through the fellows, and they [the archives and the fellows] can make their way back out into the world, creating connections and relations we can't yet imagine.

MJ I'm very happy about it, too. And more will come. Yes, more books
will come.

6   An update on the MJF since this interview was conducted: The general situation has improved with
           the development of an agreement with the Suomen Kulttuurirahasto (Finnish Cultural Foundation).
           The MJF is now a part of its international residency programs for artists from or residing in Finland.
           Three months a year are available for artists, curators, and researchers of contemporary art selected
           by the Finnish Cultural Foundation. The MJF is now in conversation with a few other countries about
           similar cooperation.

Note   To learn more about the Maaretta Jaukkuri Foundation, including calls for fellows, visit mjfoundation.no.

Sophy Roberts is a British author and journalist specializing in history, culture, and conservation in remote parts of the world, from Central Africa to the Himalayas. Michael Turek is a British–American photographer focusing on documentary assignments for national and international media.

Travel Notes from Siberia
Sophy Roberts and Michael Turek

February 26, 2016

Over a three-year period, I spent time in Russia researching a book about the country's musical culture and history. It was a huge project, spanning three hundred years between the reign of Catherine the Great and the present day. But what all my research for *The Lost Pianos of Siberia* couldn't prepare me for was the scale of the Arctic landscapes I would find when I ventured into the field, and the extraordinary adaptability of the people who make their home in these often snowbound territories—some who choose this life, and others who don't. For many of my Russian journeys, I was joined by the American photographer Michael Turek. He worked on his own project, a photographic monologue called *Siberia*, published by Damiani. Michael's eye felt important—replacing stereotypical fantasies and nightmares of Arctic Russia with an intimate, contemporary portrayal of everyday lives. He shot everything on film, which felt significant, too; a slowing down that let relationships form organically and open-heartedly.

This image (and the one that follows) shows the shores of Lake Baikal, butting up against the popular local tourist village of Listvyanka. It was winter, and people from far and wide had come to Listvyanka to enjoy the frozen lake, with hovercrafts, ice fishing, and even a seesaw set up for children. We ate smoked omul (a local fish) and set out to join the fun. Baikal is the deepest lake in the world, and its depth can make it seem impenetrable; this scene shows the human element of life along its shores, thriving in a seemingly inhospitable environment.

This image was made in Susuman, a mining community in Russia's remote northeastern Kolyma region, flanking the icy Sea of Okhotsk. Some of the Soviet Union's most brutal forced-labor camps, or Gulags, were located in Kolyma's Arctic territory, which used to be impossible to access except by air or boat. The sea voyage to Kolyma took anything between five and thirteen days, with prisoners stuffed into the holds in four-tiered bunks.

For those who survived the journey, it didn't get any better: from 1929 to 1953, 2,749,163 forced laborers died in the Soviet Gulag. These days, there's a road to and from Kolyma, which branches twelve hundred miles south to Yakutsk, one of the coldest cities on Earth. To me, the region felt like the saddest place in the world. So when Michael pointed out the man wearing a matching stripe as he walked past this strange block with a Soviet-era airplane sticking out, it was a welcome absurdity. It's summer in this image, and the mosquitoes were dreadful—a reminder of the old Siberian legend that they were born from the ashes of a cannibal.

This image is taken inside an Old Believer's house—descended from a community
of religious dissidents who refused to sign up to reforms in the Russian Orthodox
Church in the mid-seventeenth century and fled east of Russia's Ural Mountains
to escape repression. We were driving south towards the Siberian Altai region
and stopped to meet this woman. The snow was knee-deep outside in the thick
of winter, but once indoors, the scene resembled a tropical holiday home.
Michael made this image after the Old Believer had served us tea—made from dried
wildflowers—and snacks of jam and honey-soaked bread. Life in these remote parts
has always been difficult; perhaps that's why strangers are so generous with their
hospitality. In the days of the tsars, when exiles would be banished into Russia's
far-flung regions, people used to leave free bread on windowsills to help the exiles.
As we left, Michael hung back to take this image. When I look at that table, I can
hear the plastic-wrapped candies crinkling in the woman's hand.

This is the town of Ust-Koksa, near the southern edge of the Russian Altai.
We were here to visit a retired Aeroflot navigator called Leonid Kaloshin, who'd
made it his mission to bring culture and education to Siberia's backcountry.
He'd set up a community library and bought pianos for local children to play.
His shelves were filled with novels, poetry, history books, and collectors' editions
of the works of Robert Byron and Oscar Wilde. When I remarked how far-off this
place seemed, Leonid replied: "The world is very remote. We are at the center."
It was in Leonid's house—so cold we kept our coats on the whole time we were
there—that our guide told us about the time he'd seen a yeti. The cold was so intense
that Michael had to be very careful with shooting outside; if the film in his camera
became too brittle with the chill, then the tension when advancing the film might
cause it to rip. He'd take a photo, then bring the camera indoors to warm it up
before winding the film forward again.

Novosibirsk is Siberia's de facto capital. It's home to Russia's largest opera house, founded under Stalin in the 1930s. The so-called Siberian Colosseum was built on dimensions so large that Soviet tractors could be driven from the street to the stage. The stage curtain weighed ninety-nine tons. The Novosibirsk Opera and Ballet Theatre is also where the Soviet Union's cultural treasures were evacuated for safekeeping during the Second World War. Thousands of items from Moscow's Tretyakov Gallery and Leningrad's Pavlovsk Palace and State Hermitage Museum were loaded onto railway wagons bound for the city, together with fifty museum employees and their families. The treasures and their custodians spent over two years in the building. The scale of this enormous, lively city, in the middle of somewhere we'd both considered 'nowhere', which in fact had such deep historical significance, marked a real perspective shift for us both.

The Indigenous Nenets community traditionally lives in and around Russia's Arctic Circle, farming reindeer. The largest population lives in the Yamal Peninsula, where some still migrate up to eight hundred miles a year in pursuit of lichen to graze their reindeer. Pictured here is a family of Nenets who lived in the forests around Lake Numto, to the south of the Yamal Peninsula. The only way for us to reach them was by helicopter and snowmobile. In summer, it would've been even more difficult, with the Arctic tundra turning into a muddy swamp. The Nenets were persecuted under the Soviet regime—especially during the late 1930s. They were forced into state education systems and stripped of their culture. Settled living was imposed around collective reindeer farms. These days, the fragile remnants of Nenets culture are threatened once again, this time by the lucrative oil and gas industry. New roads, gas fields, and well heads interfere with the Nenets' old migration routes, while the melting permafrost presents a new challenge for survival.

March 28, 2017

Surgut is the largest city in Khanty-Mansiysk. Although it was founded in the sixteenth century, its boom years didn't hit until the mid-twentieth century, when huge oil reserves were found in the region. There's a lot of oil and gas money pouring in, and many families have settled in these new build homes. You feel the press of infrastructure here—the clash between big money and new people versus a simpler, Indigenous way of life. Climate change is hitting these northern regions hard. The permafrost is melting, and the landscape is febrile: giant plugs of tundra collapse without warning; bubbles formed of methane explode and then fall in like soufflés. We came here from Lake Numto; our hosts took us as far as they could reach via snowmobile before we hitched a ride with some oil and gas workers south to Surgut. Everyday life continues, even when the playground is buried under several feet of snow.

Taming the Arctic with roads and infrastructure has always been Moscow's biggest
challenge. You will find towering skyscrapers in oil and gas regions such as Surgut.
But look a little harder and go a little deeper, and you'll also discover numerous
white elephants from the Stalinist regime. In 1947, for instance, Josef Stalin ordered
the construction of a new railway connecting Salekhard in the west to Igarka, a
thousand miles further east along the polar circle. It was part of what Stalin called
his Great Plan for the Transformation of Nature. By the summer of 1950, the
workforce included seventy-five thousand convicts conscripted from the Gulag
camps. Most of them were imprisoned for political crimes—teachers, musicians,
engineers, scientists, and Japanese prisoners of war. They were fed starvation
rations and endured unfathomable cold. By 1953, nine miles of track were laid each
month, the work never stopping even when the temperatures dipped to -50 degrees
Celsius. After Stalin died, the project was abandoned, but not before so many
thousands had died. The line was renamed Dead Road.

Sakhalin Island lies five miles off Russia's Pacific Coast and is around twice the size of Belgium. Its proximity to Japan has made its ownership a historical point of contention between the two countries. After the 1905 Russo-Japanese War, the Japanese controlled the southern portion of the island until after the Second World War, when Russia was able to demand the island's return from a defeated Japan. Michael made this image in Yuzhno-Sakhalinsk, the island's capital. We stayed in a hotel for a few days just behind the apartment block you can see in this picture. This little patch of woodland, with a stream running through it, was used as a shortcut by locals to get from one area to another. The verdancy felt almost shocking against the severity of Soviet-era buildings—an 'island of abandonment', per the evocative phrase coined by Scottish writer Cal Flyn. It's summer in this image, but one of the hallmarks of traveling in northern territory is the sense that the default setting is winter. Summer always feels borrowed; an ever-present wind chill takes away any brief illusion of warmth.

Valentin Lekus was a retired fishing captain who lived in a Khrushchev-era apartment block on Sakhalin Island at Russia's Pacific edge. The corridors were lined with posters telling its residents how to survive a nuclear attack. He had spent fifty years operating a fishing trawler in the Sea of Okhotsk, sometimes spending six months at a time at sea. He persuaded his crew to chip in to buy a piano, which entertained them on the long months spent aboard the fishing trawler. They'd travel through the Bering Sea, up and down the Kuril Islands, and all the way up to the Russian Arctic. Valentin taught himself to play the instrument, which brought the crew some entertainment. Sometimes, in winter, the storms were so brutal that the water would freeze the sides of the ship until the whole vessel was listed at a dangerous tilt.

This image, taken in Yuzhno-Sakhalinsk, spoke to Michael's sense of absurdity. The gap between the buildings is so narrow the man walking between them has to turn his shoulders to fit through. Sakhalin Island was home to the most notorious of the Russian penal colonies under tsarist rule—Aleksandrovsk. Some eight thousand prisoners died on their marches through the swamps surrounding it.

For me, Sakhalin Island couldn't have felt further from home—just as it was for the Russian writer Anton Chekhov when he traveled four thousand miles from Moscow to visit the then-penal colony in 1890. He complained of a disintegrating identity this far from Moscow and a loss of Russianness. Michael felt differently; Sakhalin Island was strangely close to home. Here, on Russia's Pacific coast, Michael was the closest he'd been to North America since leaving.

Svetlana Romanova is an artist and filmmaker whose practice gravitates toward critical self-historicization.

Everything Is the Same: Managa Bar / Rustam's Habitat
Svetlana Romanova

Yakutsk is the capital city of the Sakha Republic, the largest in the Russian Federation, and is known to be the coldest inhabited city in the world. Svetlana Romanova's *Managa Bar / Rustam's Habitat* follows the filmmaker's social circle in the city, depicting local artists, punks, and other community members. Divided into two discrete parts, the film operates as vignettes of memories, from open-air recitals of Sherwin Bitsui's poetry to rave parties. It strives to imbue a strong feeling of familiarity and universality to both its subjects and its scenes.

Everything is the same

Rustam delivers a monologue about his experience growing up in Yakutsk against the backdrop of the Stalin statuette and the Almazy Anabara building (Diamonds of Anabar).

Siberia
I bet this word associates with bears to you
With taiga
Oil and diamonds
But people live here as well
And we don't really see these diamonds or oil
We are surrounded by concrete and cars
I think we really wanted to illuminate that
That what we are living in is not much different from your situation
And the world's
Everything is the same

Rustam poses between the pioneer boy statue (a Soviet remnant) and a traditional Sakha Serge: a hitching post, property marker, and ritual pole used among Buryats and Yakuts.

Lana and Rustam are both double-Indigenous. One is of Even/Sakha descent, and the other is of Sakha/Chuvash descent. Although the term has not been coined within the Sakha Republic or the Russian Federation, we felt it was important to highlight our presence by inserting ourselves in mundane daily situations.

Rustam gives Max a buzz cut on the shores of the Lena River.

Lana reads poems from Navajo poet Sherwin Bitsui's *Shapeshift* (2003) by the abandoned factories in the Khangalas region. One poem, entitled "The Sun Rises and I Think of Your Bruised Larynx," goes as follows:

Sister,
blue like the larynx of rushing rainwater,
I think of you when I squeeze static from the river's bent elbow.

I am counting:
ten to zero, zero to nothing
underneath the dawn oak
whose roots resemble your hair
after you've danced counterclockwise
around steel-rimmed America
and returned home
with back spasms and a foaming mouth.

Do you still want to bury your shoes
in the blue mountains west of the Rio Grande,
where white birds shout sunlight
and people don't ask you to repeat your last name?

I tie my feet to the thinning hair of our old ones;
their eyes burn, staring into the headlights of passing cars;
they saw footpaths bloom into black-boned factories,
rivers into pipelines,
and children delivered by IHS doctors
without tongues, without the fifth finger.

I think of your cupped hands tucked into the petals of a mud-caked sun.

the raven browned by the winter moon's breath
releases its wings,
stretches its neck,
resembles for a second
the silhouette of a horse's head
carved from the nugget of coal
found in your grandmother's clenched fist.[1]

---

1   Sherwin Bitsui, "The Sun Rises and I Think of Your Bruised Larynx," in *Shapeshift* (University of Arizona Press, 2003), 26–27.

Constructed out of personal notes—verbal and visual—*Voyage of Jeanette* (2024) poses questions about image production's intersection with the creation of narratives that are embedded now in our perception of contemporaneity and manifest themselves in our performances of ideas like history, heritage, and memory. Positioned in the Yakutian Arctic, this visual essay invites the viewer to ask vital questions concerning peripheral discourse that seems to be inseparable from the etymology of the word Arctic and how Western ontologies in relation to discovery and creation of history fit in immediate Yakutian realities.

A few questions may arise when viewing the images from this film: Did we manage to create a nation outside of the "state"? Who had the right to narrativize "Arctic" into territory? What forms of radical self-historization are present in the Bulun region?

Alina poses in front of the *I Love Kyusyur* sign.

Sakhaya Lazarevna and Nyurguyana show the Arctic greenhouse, where plants like tomatoes, flowers, and cucumbers grow. It was built in Kyusyur, located on the Lena River in the Bulunsky region; it is a national Eveny and Evenki village in the Arctic Circle.

РЕСПУБЛИКА САХА (ЯКУТИЯ)
МО "БУЛУНСКИЙ УЛУС (РАЙОН

Chorik and Slava are returning from a fishing boat in Kumakh Surt, the traditional and industrial fishing grounds of the Lena Delta. We fish year-round. Summer fishing occurs from June until late September, depending on the weather. This particular fishing summer village is located in the waters of Lena. These are our ancestral lands, and most of the people who fish here live in the village. The difficulties we face are obvious and are not exclusive to us but rather shared throughout the circumpolar region: global warming, neighboring military complexes, and hardships in relation to obtaining the rights to fish, especially as individuals.[2]

Semion Semionovich in the central square of Tiksi in the Bulun region.

2   Further details are not shared here in order to ensure the anonymity of those depicted.

Images of Siberia are often limited to exoticized portraits of rural communities living in harsh conditions, with residents often cast as provincial wanderers trapped in a different time. Aiming to describe a more grounded contemporary reality visually, *Тарыҥ* (*The Season of Dying Water*, made with Chelsea Tuggle) argues that life in and around Yakutsk, a region in Siberia, is more complicated. Inspired by Chris Marker's 1957 travelogue film *Lettre de Sibérie* (*Letter from Siberia*), *Тарыҥ* offers an update—a letter back to Marker—sixty-five years later.

We berry-pick. A typical lunch break during berry gathering season.

Three girls pose at their home with their calves in the Megino Kangalasski region.

Nicholas Gulick is an American-Swedish landscape architect based in Stockholm with a broad portfolio of work in the United States, Norway, Sweden, and Russia. Elena Krapivina is an Arkhangelsk area native currently based in Stockholm, pursuing a Master's degree in Landscape Ecology and GIS at Stockholm University.

The Road of Life. An ice road on the Northern Dvina River between the city of Arkhangelsk and the island of Kegostrov in Arkhangelsk Oblast, Russian Federation.
Nicholas Gulick and Elena Krapivina

«Дорога жизни» в Архангельске. Ледовая дорога на реке Северная Двина между городом Архангельск и островом Кегостров в Архангельской области на севере России.
Николас Гулик и Елена Крапивина

The icebreaker *Dikson* on the Northern Dvina River. The icebreaker fleet plays a crucial role in facilitating commercial shipping along the Northern Dvina River during the winter months. By breaking up ice and maintaining open channels in the river delta, these icebreakers ensure that cargo vessels can safely access the ports of Arkhangelsk.

Unfortunately, the same channels that allow for the transportation of much-needed goods and materials present real challenges for individuals who have traditionally depended on the river's solid ice during the winter months. In areas where no road bridges exist and ferries are unable to operate due to the presence of river ice, crossing the river becomes much more difficult and potentially much more dangerous. This disruption to traditional modes of winter travel over the ice can have significant and deleterious impacts on local communities, limiting access to essential services and increasing the isolation of certain areas.

Ледокол «Диксон» на Северной Двине. Флот ледоколов играет решающую роль в обеспечении коммерческого судоходства по Северной Двине в зимние месяцы. Ледоколы поддерживают фарватеры в дельте реки свободными от льда и таким образом обеспечивают безопасный доступ грузовых судов к портам Архангельска.

К сожалению, наличие судоходного фарватера создает проблемы для людей, зависящих от прочного ледового покрова на реке в зимние месяцы. В районах, где отсутствуют мосты, и работа паромов прекращается на зимний период, пересечение реки становится более сложным и потенциально опасным. Это нарушение традиционных способов передвижения по льду может иметь значительное влияние на местные сообщества, ограничивая их доступ к необходимым услугам и увеличивая их изоляцию.

Lighting along the Road of Life disappears into the horizon leading toward Kegostrov Island.

Освещение вдоль «Дороги жизни», ведущей к Кегострову.

A man can be seen crossing the movable wooden walkways that provide a footpath over the floating ice chunks left behind by the icebreaker fleet. After breaking the ice, the icebreakers run their engines in reverse to push the chunks of floating ice into their broad wake. Workers on the ice road disassemble and reassemble these movable walkways when icebreakers and commercial shipping vessels must navigate the shipping lanes on the river.

Мужчина идет по деревянным мосткам с поручнями, которые служат пешеходным переходом над раздробленными ледоколами кусками льда. После того, как ледокол расчистил фарватер, двигатель переводят на обратный ход, чтобы собрать плавающие льдины в то место, где проходит переправа. Работники переправы разбирают эти деревянные мостки перед прохождением ледокола и судов, а затем укладывают их обратно.

The workers' cabin and a parking area for commuters can be seen on the Kegostrov side of the open channel on the Road of Life.

Домик для работников и парковка для тех, кто пользуется переправой, расположенные на «Дороге жизни» со стороны Кегострова.

The workers' cabin and other service structures—like this latrine—are anchored in the frozen river ice near the halfway point on the nearly two-kilometer-long crossing between Arkhangelsk and Kegostrov.

Домик для работников и другие сооружения, такие как этот туалет, закреплены во льду замерзшей реки примерно по середине почти 2-километровой ледовой переправы между Архангельском и Кегостровом.

The churned-up ice displaced by the icebreakers vividly depicts the harsh conditions of the ice roads in the Northern Dvina River delta. Despite the challenges of maintaining and traversing these crossings, the residents of Kegostrov Island depend on this lifeline to survive the winter months.

Разломанные ледоколами куски льда наглядно показывают суровые условия на ледовых переправах в дельте Северной Двины. Несмотря на все трудности, связанные с обслуживанием и использованием этих переходов, ледовые дороги жизненно необходимы жителям Кегострова в зимние месяцы.

As one approaches the Embankment along the waterfront, the elevated boardwalk on the Road of Life near Cape Pur-Navolok in Arkhangelsk aids in the navigation of the river's shifting ice edge.

The Embankment is an important promenade in Arkhangelsk. Naturally, residents are drawn to the riverfront, where numerous public events and daily activities take place. The Road of Life is intrinsically linked, both visually and physically, to this urban infrastructure, involving nearly every individual who steps foot on its stage.

Приподнятые надо льдом деревянные мостки на «Дороге жизни» возле мыса Пур-Наволок в Архангельске помогают преодолеть подвижную кромку льда при приближении к Набережной Северной Двины.

Набережная играет важную роль в жизни местных жителей: это и основная прогулочная зона, и место проведения общественных мероприятий. «Дороге жизни» тесно связана с Набережной как визуально, так и физически, вовлекая практически каждого, кто ступает на ее территорию.

A view from Arkhangelsk toward the protruding headland of Kegostrov Island reveals people moving along the raised, compacted ice path following the Road of Life and its string of pedestrian lights anchored in the frozen river ice. Additionally, small figures can be seen approaching the channel, crossing from various smaller, informal paths on the frozen surface. The workers' cabin, the parking area, and the movable wooden boardwalk lie along the open water channel, a dark line of broken ice visible against the frozen river surface.

Вид на выступающий мыс Кегострова. В далеке можно различить людей, движущихся по приподнятой, уплотненной ледовой тропе, идущей вдоль закрепленной во льду линии пешеходного освещения. Несколько человек идут к ледовому переходу по одной из тропинок, протоптанных на поверхности реки. Домик работников, парковка и подвижная часть переправы расположены рядом с расчищенным от льда фарватером, видимым как темная линия на замерзшей поверхности реки.

The elevated boardwalk on the Road of Life near Cape Pur-Navolok bridges the liminal zone at the edge of the Northern Dvina River and the beachfront of Arkhangelsk. This edge, visible in the photo, is where the ice is most sensitive to warming temperatures and the hydraulic forces exerted by the flowing water. Red signs posted along the liminal zone declare the ice unsafe for passage, while a green sign on the light pole in front of the boardwalk informs pedestrians that the ice road is open and that they may use the boardwalk safely.

Деревянные мостки на «Дороге жизни» возле мыса Пур-Наволок перекрывают зону у края Северной Двины и пляжного берега города Архангельска. Лёд в этом месте наиболее чувствителен к повышению температуры и гидравлическим силам, создаваемым течением воды. Красные знаки, размещенные вдоль берега, предупреждают о том, что движение по льду запрещено, тогда как зеленый знак на столбе освещения перед деревяными мостками информирует пешеходов о том, что ледовая дорога открыта и они могут воспользоваться переходом.

April 05, 2018, 13:58h. Moscow Standard Time (MSK), UTC+3
5 апреля 2018 года, 13:58. Московское время (МСК), UTC+3

The liminal zone at the edge of the Northern Divina River and the beachfront of Arkhangelsk is bridged by an elevated boardwalk on the Road of Life. The red sign on the right side of this image warns pedestrians against crossing the ice at the liminal zone without the help of the boardwalk.

Береговая зона Северной Двины и пляж Архангельска перекрыта приподнятыми деревянными мосткам, являющимися частью ледовой переправы. Красный знак справа на этом изображении предупреждает пешеходов о том, что ходить по льду запрещено.

Here, the green sign on the light pole informs pedestrians that the boardwalk
is open and passage across the ice road to Kegostrov is safe.

Зеленый знак на столбе освещения информирует пешеходов,
что переправа открыта и переход по ледовой дороге на Кегостров
безопасен.

The boardwalk feels securely embedded within the river ice; its warm hues and
the rough textures of the spruce and pine frameworks evoke a sense of familiarity,
connecting visitors to the vernacular of the region. These wood resources, relatively
abundant and accessible, are favored for their practicality and affordability.
Their inherent resilience to moisture and freezing temperatures makes them ideal
for enduring the harsh conditions of these cold climates.

Деревянные мостки ледовой переправы прочно встроенной в лед
реки. Теплые оттенки и грубая текстура ели и сосны, из которых
сделаны мостки, вызывают чувство привычности, демонстрируя
местный колорит. Эти породы дерева, которыми славится
Архангельская область, ценятся за свою практичность и доступность.
Их устойчивость к влаге и низким температурам делает их
идеальными для использования в суровых условиях севера России.

April 05, 2018, 14:08h. Moscow Standard Time (MSK), UTC+3
5 апреля 2018 года, 14:08. Московское время (МСК), UTC+3

A mother and her two children proceed carefully along the thickened ice path as they journey from Kegostrov to Arkhangelsk. The planned route across the frozen river has been reinforced by workers, who add layers of water to strengthen the pathway, mitigating the risk of standing meltwater.

Мать и двое детей направляются из Кегострова в Архангельск, осторожно продвигаясь по ледяной тропе через замерзшую реку. Работники переправы с помощью воды наращивают толщину льда той части, где проходит ледовая дорога, чтобы укрепить лед и снизить риск образования стоячей талой воды.

As spring sets in, the ice begins to break up along the liminal zone at the edge of the Northern Dvina River near Cape Pur-Navolok on the Embankment of Arkhangelsk. Despite the receding ice edge and accumulating meltwater on the surface of the frozen river, the ferry is still unable to operate, and people continue to rely on the ice road crossing.

По мере наступления весны лед начинает раскалываться вдоль берега Северной Двины возле мыса Пур-Наволок на Набережной города Архангельска. Несмотря на то, что лед начинает отступать и уже видна водная поверхность реки, работа парома все еще не может быть возобновлена, и люди продолжают полагаться на переход по ледовой дороге.

Bertine Tønseth is a human geographer and teacher from Bergen, Norway.

Like a Phoenix: A New Chapter [1]
Bertine Tønseth

Located in the north of Russia on the northern part of the Kola Peninsula by the Barents Sea, you will find Teriberka, one of the few northern Russian coastal settlements with seemingly unlimited access to the ocean. There are no fences, guards, or military restrictions. You can smell, touch, and taste the saltwater. This is what attracts Russian—and now Chinese tourists—here year-round.

> Once upon a time, this was a prosperous town. The sea, which attracts people from near and far, once formed the basis of the village's existence. The first written reference to Teriberka dates back to 1000 BC. By the 1960s, five thousand people lived here. The primary industry was fishing, and there were several factories, various shops, bakeries, schools, and kindergartens. There was also a Boy Scout club, a choir, a vibrant social scene, and plenty of accessible fish in the sea.

Almost overnight, things began to change. By the late 1960s, Teriberka had lost its status as a town and its role as an administrative center. Local seafarers' fishing rights became formalized in a quota system where larger quotas were awarded to big trawlers and even bigger private companies. After the fall of the Soviet Union, Teriberka's decline continued. Today, the fishing industry is reduced to small-scale catches of limited species of white fish. Catching species beyond this is punishable by significant fines. Being caught poaching two king crabs can result in three years of prison service.

> In 2007, the local school was shut down. Two years later, the hospital suffered the same fate. The kindergarten finally shut its doors after two more years. Today, the village has a shop, hotel, restaurant, dairy farm, and many empty buildings. The official number of inhabitants has been reduced to a fraction of what it once was. Probably less than two hundred people remain in what today is called Old Teriberka.

YOUR HOME WILL BE MOVED

The sand, once forming the base of the road network in Teriberka, now blows through broken windows. Century-old brown woodwork stands aslant. People stopped crossing the threshold of these doors a long time ago, and it has been some time since smoke rose from the chimneys. This scene is by no means unique but is apt for the empty homes in Teriberka. Common to these many buildings is a shining yellow sign nailed to their walls reading, "Your home will be moved."

---

1   More than just a project, *A New Chapter* is a story about common understandings, relationships, and friendships. The project was intended to have a long life span but has had to change course in a way no one could have predicted. In recent years, the COVID-19 pandemic and the escalation of the Russo-Ukrainian War on February 24, 2022, have turned this world upside down. Today, the borders between Norway and Russia are nearly closed, and Norwegian actors like Komafest are highly restricted in how they can work within Russia—if at all. The Ural is in transit in Nickel, and we may have to wait years before we can cross the border again. When that time comes, we will probably see a different town; extensive tourism has been rolled out, with several hotels and tourism infrastructure actively visible around old Teriberka. Meanwhile, we remain in touch with our friends across the border and try to keep the story of Teriberka alive. This chapter may have been written for us, but we hope, in time, to write the next one. The following text was first published in *Arkitektur N* (7-2017). This version has been adjusted to reflect events since its first publication.

Closed Chapter (2017)
The idea for the project *A New Chapter* was conceived in Teriberka's abandoned school library.

One can even find these signs on buildings still occupied by families. About 85 percent of the state-owned wooden buildings are earmarked for demolition. The authorities say this is due to building code violations. But instead of enriching old Teriberka with new residential housing developments, a newly constructed high-rise apartment block has been built in the neighboring village of Lodeinoe. The residents of old Teriberka can elect to move to Kola town, about ten kilometers from Murmansk. Unlike Vardø, where people chose to leave, the people of Teriberka do not have a choice. Their homes will soon be gone.

ONE CHAPTER CLOSES, ANOTHER CHAPTER OPENS

"We are trying something innovative through this project.
We think that combining art and placemaking in this way
is something innovative. A new and different approach."
Svein Harald Holmen

The *New Chapter* project is the story of a community headed in the wrong direction. For six weeks during the summer of 2017, ninety-four people worked on *New Chapter*. This project was spearheaded by the Norwegian artist Pøbel with placemaker Svein Harald Holmen and landscape architect Brona Keenan, both of whom were working with urban development in Vardø Restored. The vision behind the project came to life when Pøbel surveyed the abandoned and vandalized school library in Teriberka. He was overwhelmed with an array of different emotions: the bookshelves were barely standing, engulfed by a sea of books that stretched out like a dirty, bulging quilt across the floor. For Pøbel, this was an artwork in itself. He painted "CLOSED CHAPTER" on the wall and was inspired to create other works both in and outside the school. At the time, he thought that the school might have reached its intended conclusion, but it still carries the possibility of creating new things.

The result was the slightly more optimistic *New Chapter*, combining art, placemaking, architecture, and cultural heritage into one project. A library and a banya (a traditional Russian sauna) were created utilizing local know-how, craftsmanship, and history. A Ural-4320 military truck and trailer have had their interiors torn out and replaced with books, benches, and a sauna stove. The truck is now a library, and the trailer, a banya. Both are now venues for conversation and exchange of ideas.

The artworks are constructed using materials from a total of thirty-five abandoned buildings (then) scheduled for demolition. These houses have been granted new life. Elements of local cultural heritage, such as the Russian painting style from Arkhangelsk and Teriberka, have also been used, repurposing local materials and using the local color palette and building styles. It might not be obvious why the constantly traveling Pøbel and the Vardø-based Holmen and Keenan have spent two years planning and implementing a project in rural Russia. To find the answer, we have to turn back time and visit Norway.

THE TOWN THAT ONCE WAS

> "The project is not over, and we intend to keep working with it for another year. We want to do something positive. If we fail at that, the whole project is a failure."
> *Pøbel*

A nine-hour drive and one border control check away from Teriberka lies the town of Vardø. Norway's easternmost settlement, Vardø, has also experienced a depopulation of 60 percent since the 1960s. As the fishing industry collapsed along the Varanger Peninsula, fishermen in both Vardø and Teriberka experienced restrictive access to the resources in the Barents Sea. For many, what was a sea of possibilities has now turned into a sea of limitations. Coastal life, once made possible by the ocean, is increasingly hard to sustain.

> Teriberka is an extreme version of Vardø. According to Svein Harald Holmen, Pøbel's project partner and native of Vardø, Teriberka's history tells us what may happen in Norwegian coastal communities if nothing is done. Having seen the downward turn of his hometown, Holmen relates easily to how people on the Kola Peninsula feel: "People in Teriberka are disempowered, and we see the same thing happening at home in Vardø and the rest of coastal Norway. The people who live there have no influence. Local consultation occurs, but people are still not involved in decision-making. The situation in Teriberka is significantly worse than in Norway, but the communities and challenges they face represent two sides of the same coin. People in Vardø can learn from the story of Teriberka and vice versa," proffers Holmen.

Now, both Holmen and Pøbel have experience working with sleeping communities, rousing them from slumber. Painting art on abandoned houses gave buildings a chance for a new life, and through *Komafest* (an art project), they highlighted the issues surrounding Vardø's population decline. This philosophy also characterizes the *New Chapter*.

A NEW CHAPTER

> "We have met people who cannot understand why we were so smitten with Teriberka. My motivation for these past six weeks, and for working for two years without a salary, is that we want to reveal what is happening here now. This story is not unique. For me, Vardø and Teriberka are symbols of the deteriorating situation in Norway, especially along the entire coast."
> *Pøbel*

No one involved in the *New Chapter* thinks that additional bureaucracy will be beneficial on a local level. This is not how meaningful change happens. However, the transformed military truck is a visually striking object, screaming for attention. A similar construction is planned for Vardø and will be based on local culture and history. The vision is that these two art pieces will continue to reflect a cultural and actual exchange between communities, moving between the two places.

This project attempts to empower communities, and including local skills, crafts, manpower, and community engagement are essential components. Their Russian partner, Fridaymilk, facilitated and organized the project alongside the Norwegian crew. In addition, camp Lavvo Lavvo was visited by carpenters, welders, architects, researchers, cooks, librarians, mechanics, a stonemason, and a local painter. Members of the Teriberka Cultural Palace, as well as journalists, writers, photographers, and local families, all stopped by.

For years, Pøbel has been both enthused and incensed about Norwegian regional policies and development, especially concerning coastal communities. He wants to ignite a spark in the people of Teriberka. A spark that could turn into a light at the end of the tunnel. Together with Vardø Restored, Pøbel wants to create place-specific literature to record and disseminate local history, legends, and culinary traditions. To reveal the community's knowledge, diversity, power, and richness, Teriberka will be 3D-mapped, and the salvaged material that was transported from abandoned houses and incorporated into the library and banya will be cataloged and connected back to Teriberka.[2]

A stone's throw away from the Teriberka truck lies the Cultural Palace. Throughout the summer, the head of the palace, Olga Nikolaevna Nikolaeva, has kept an eye on the work at the campsite. She got involved and followed the project long before the first nail was hammered. She thinks that the *New Chapter* can help ensure the story of Teriberka never completely disappears, even if the houses are torn down and people move away. She has lived in the village almost her entire life, through hard times and good times. While Teriberka's future may look bleak, she is sure of one thing: no matter how long the fire rages, the village will always rise from its ashes.

2   All of the activities were also thoroughly documented on video and will hopefully result in a documentary film.

A father and his two boys (2017)
> Members of the Teriberka Cultural Palace—journalists, writers, photographers, and local families—stopped by during the building of the library and banya, including this father and his two boys.

Filming (2017)
> The crew followed an open and inclusive process together with local residents of Teriberka. The process has been thoroughly documented on film.

ТЕРИБЕРКА

Banya and library interior (2017)
The library and banya are places for conversations and exchanging ideas.

No Teriberka (2017)
According to the signs, the original Teriberka no longer exists.

Olga Nikolaevna Nikolaeva (53), Head of the Culture Palace

"Teriberka is now being overrun by people, entrepreneurs, and opportunists who want to make money. Some wealthy outsider investors want to get even richer by investing in tourism. Previously, there were no tourists here, but now there is an influx of people who want to see the northern lights and the ocean, catch and eat crab, and experience nostalgia. We don't have much to offer them, but tourists do not give us anything back either. More people leave Teriberka than come. I have to move to the neighboring village—this upsets and angers me. I want to stay in Teriberka. They can tear down the old wooden buildings; the love we have for our hometown is in our hearts, not in these buildings. But new houses should be built where the old ones stood. I will always live and fight for Teriberka. There are ups and downs, but I'm sure we'll see better days."

Igor Bernovsky (17), Construction worker on a new high-rise in Lodeinoe

"The people who move from Teriberka to Lodeinoe are so beautiful. I'm happy people are moving here, but it's too bad they are forced to do it. It's horrible how the government wants to ignore all the problems and move people to Lodeinoe or Kola. Lodeinoe has a bank, post office, several shops, and a bakery. This may make some people happy. But we have our share of problems. Our Internet connection is bad, there are not many workplaces, the roads are in poor condition, and there are no sports clubs. All the new arrivals will be housed in the same high-rise. This summer, I helped build what we call the 'new house' in Lodeinoe. It is poorly insulated, and the walls are paper-thin, so you can hear what people are saying at the opposite end of the building. Still, it's a good alternative to the old houses. In Lodeinoe we are happy that we'll have a new three-story building. And soon, we'll also have new neighbors."

Maria Ivanovna Kostina (83), Resident of Teriberka

"I moved from Karelia in 1950. Back then, we had many administrative buildings, a hospital, a kindergarten, a clubhouse—everything we needed. I worked as a baker and baked tons of bread for the people of Teriberka. There used to be a Soviet army presence here; they came and bought a lot of bread. Today, the military has left, and the closest bakery is five kilometers away, in Lodeinoe. Everything in Teriberka is different now, except the house I live in. We don't have anything anymore. Both my husband and my father were fishermen, but there's hardly anyone who still fishes. It is almost impossible to make a living as a fisherman now. We live right by the sea, but we hardly get to taste the fish. Luckily, I won't be moving to Lodeinoe, as I live in one of the two state-owned houses that will not be demolished. They said my house was "too beautiful." Unlike where I used to live in Teriberka, this house has both indoor plumbing and heating. I have no problem with houses being demolished, but it's not okay to force people to move to a completely different village. Many are too old for this. They should build new houses here instead, but I was told that it is not possible because of flood risk to the area from nearby dams. I don't know how that can be true, as they are building new hotels here. Either way, our life here is nearing its end."

Thomas Juel Clemmensen is a professor of landscape architecture at UiT The Arctic University of Norway, specializing in landscape transformation.

Landscape Architecture Education above the Arctic Circle
Thomas Juel Clemmensen

Above the Arctic Circle, at the Academy of Arts in Tromsø, a landscape architecture program specializing in arctic/subarctic conditions is being developed. This program is part of a joint five-year integrated master's in landscape architecture, comprising three years of primary education at the Oslo School of Architecture and Design (AHO) and two years of graduate studies at the Universitetet i Tromsø – Norges arktiske universitet (in Northern Sami, Romssa universitehta – Norgga árktalaš universitehta, and in English, UiT The Arctic University of Norway). The graduate studies at UiT are also available as an independent two-year master's in landscape architecture. The program was established in response to pressing societal challenges associated with climate change, the exploitation of natural resources, growing urbanization, and polarization. These challenges are particularly pronounced in arctic/subarctic landscapes, making them highly relevant for research and teaching. With a dedicated and continued focus on arctic/subarctic conditions and a unique opportunity to live and study under these conditions, the program aims to educate landscape architects who can contribute to sustainable societal development and design for landscapes undergoing rapid changes.

PROJECT-BASED TEACHING AND DESIGN-DRIVEN RESEARCH
Common to all five study years is an emphasis on design-driven research, which reflects the overarching objective of educating landscape architects with strong design competencies. Most of the program is devoted to project-

based teaching in studio courses, where design-driven research plays a central role. In these courses, students are introduced to a broad range of mapping methods and fieldwork techniques. The remaining part of the curriculum consists of supporting courses in landscape architecture history and theory, ecology, terrain modeling, and the advanced use of Geographic Information Systems (GIS) and Light Detection and Ranging (LIDAR).

The project-based teaching at the Academy of Arts in Tromsø is structured around three different perspectives on the broad spectrum of human practices that affect and shape arctic/subarctic landscapes. The three perspectives overlap but are thematized in separate studio courses: Studio 1 focuses on urban landscapes and complex results of contemporary urbanization. Studio 2 focuses on historical, cultural landscapes and their continuous transformation. Studio 3 focuses on larger territories and the processes driving their transitions. The individual studio courses often center on current issues or concrete projects, linking teaching to practice through collaborations with research institutions, public administrations, and advisors within landscape architecture and planning.

In 2019, Studio 2 used the Svea coal mine in Svalbard as a case study. This studio course exemplified essential aspects of project-based teaching in the program by linking teaching to practice in support of extensive fieldwork. Here, students engaged with the landscape through site-specific investigations, a form of research that involved sensory aspects in the reading and understanding of the landscape. This is a crucial component of all studio courses in the program. The fieldwork in the remote mining area at Svea was made possible only because the mining company Store Norske kindly provided air transport, overnight accommodation, catering, and safety equipment. Secondly, the course aimed to develop critical thinking in future landscape architects who will contribute to the profession's development. In this case, students investigated alternative transformation strategies for the official 'clean-up project,' raising fundamental questions concerning natural and cultural heritage management. Thirdly, the studio integrated ecological knowledge into the design research. The preliminary studies of the mining area's geological and biological processes, prepared by the Norwegian Institute for Nature Research, were an essential source of knowledge, supplemented by support from the landscape architecture program's ecologist.

A CRITICAL VIEW ON LANDSCAPE RESTORATION AND MINING RECLAMATION

Svea was chosen as a case study because the official project highlights dilemmas and paradoxes associated with landscape restoration and mining reclamation. Not only do the active geologic processes on Svalbard draw attention to the dynamic character of landscapes, raising questions about originality and what should be restored or reclaimed, but the project also underscores the artificial distinctions between natural and cultural heritage. Why are landforms and ground material conditions not necessarily considered part of cultural heritage? Should ecological niches that arise following

1   Photograph from the Svea area depicting a so-called kame and kettle topography, the result of a glacial surge approximately 600 hundred years ago.

2   Experiments between aesthetics and ecology from a workshop at Ramfjordmoen where drone imagery of the area was used as a landscape laboratory.

human interventions be protected or removed? Based on such questions, the main task of the course was outlined. Rather than focusing on how to clean the mining area, the task was to clarify existing nature-culture assemblages and to develop exploratory concepts for new, robust heritage 'naturecultures,' which exemplify how to live with the material legacy of coal mining at Svea in a meaningful way.[1]

> The alternative approach to landscape restoration and mining reclamation at Svea is evident in Driftscape by Aaron Feicht, a project proposal addressing the airstrip and the vast amount of material used to construct this anthropogenic landform. According to Feicht, the top layer of fine-grained crushed granite mixed with sand was imported from mainland Norway, while lower layers of gravel and rock were sourced locally at Svea. Rather than attempting to remove this agglomerate of material, Feicht proposed reorganizing it on-site, together with other material listed as 'anthropogenic material,' on the geologic map of Svea. The material would be sorted according to grain size and concentrated in circular mounds around a central part of the airstrip, preserved as a straight path running through a new topography. Over time, wind and water will be instrumental in transforming the new topography. As materials settle and finer sediments drift away, the mounds will change shape as they slowly morph under the pressures of shifting air currents. The mounds disrupt the laminar flow of wind to create eddies and turbulence where snow and sediment accumulate. These low-velocity areas are essential for developing a new hydrological system as accumulated snow and water collect in depressions. Through the collection of sediments and water, the new topography will define growing conditions for vegetation.

Maintaining part of the airstrip as a linear landscape element acknowledges the recent past, where humans have acted as geomorphic agents. In contrast, the surrounding dune-like topography references a more distant past shaped by glacial activities around Svea (↦ 1). In Feicht's work, these different historical layers coexist and intersect, highlighting how human practices and natural processes such as erosion and sedimentation shape the airstrip and more extensive parts of the landscape. Driftscape exemplifies an approach to landscape restoration and mining reclamation that, like the official project, is environmentally responsible, akin to the official project, but devoid of ideological underpinnings that reinforce the nature-culture divide. As a result, traces of mining activities are not viewed as obstacles to ecological improve-

---

1   The concepts of nature-culture assemblages and heritage 'naturecultures' in particular are borrowed from Rodney Harrison, Professor of Heritage Studies at the Institute of Archaeology at University College London. See Rodney Harrison, "Beyond 'Natural' and 'Cultural' Heritage: Toward an Ontological Politics of Heritage in the Age of Anthropocene," *Heritage & Society* 8, no. 1 (2015): 24–42.

ment but as integral to the process. Furthermore, the proposals do not idealize the pre-mining landscape, thus avoiding the illusion that mining processes are reversible. Instead, the proposal focuses on establishing nature-culture assemblages in the current landscape, exploring how these can be integrated into future landforms that benefit the local ecosystem, and acknowledging this place's unique heritage naturecultures.

The project employs an open-ended design concept without a pre-determined result. This approach aligns not only with the actual dynamics and uncertainties of this landscape following climate change but also reflects a specific attitude toward the design of land-scapes, treating the site as a kind of laboratory for gaining new aes-thetic and ecologic insights.

EXPERIMENTS BETWEEN AESTHETICS AND ECOLOGY

The emphasis on ecology in the program aims to elevate ecology from being considered merely essential knowledge to a potential conceptual driver in the development of landscape architecture. In primary education at AHO, there are three support courses in ecology for landscape architecture, where students are introduced to key ecological concepts that can promote dynamic and relational thinking within landscape architecture. In the graduate studies at UiT, ecology is integral to design research across all three studio courses. To support this critical teaching component, the program in Tromsø aims to work with a landscape laboratory format for research and teaching at the intersection between ecology and aesthetics. In this setup, designated sites are used for site-specific experiments over an extended period, preferably several years, making it possible to monitor how the experiments evolve and change character.

The landscape laboratory format was tested for the first time during a one-week workshop in the fall of 2021, where second-year students from AHO and fourth-year students from UiT experimented with landscape interventions aimed at promoting biodiversity and high-lighting aesthetic qualities in a landscape. This workshop was linked to the research project MONEC² at UiT, which investigates the negative impact of the native invasive crowberry (*Empetrum nigrum*) on bio-diversity and reindeer husbandry in northern Norway. Students were tasked with making landscape interventions that would, on the one hand, limit the growing dominance of crowberry and improve living conditions for other native plants while, on the other hand, enhancing the aesthetic qualities of the landscape. The workshop took place at Ramfjordmoen, twenty kilometers outside Tromsø, where UiT main-tains a research station dedicated to investigating and monitoring the highest layers of the Earth's atmosphere. This extensive area hosts a collection of advanced instruments, with the European Incoherent Scatter Scientific Association (EISCAT) radars being the most distinctive.

Geologically, the area is a sand and gravel plain composed of moraine material with a relatively smooth surface, formed in the sea by a slowly retreating ice front during the last ice age. The vegetation in the area, characterized by its porous ground conditions, is dominated by dwarf shrubs, lichen, and birch trees (↔ 2).

One group of students focused on the mosaic pattern of dwarf shrubs and lichens, which they identified as a striking aesthetic quality in this landscape. This pattern, in which patches of grey reindeer lichen (*Cladonia rangiferina*) stand out as an essential element, captured their attention. To highlight the mosaic character of the ground cover and enhance its qualities, the group opted to manipulate the existing pattern. In an open area devoid of birch trees, four patches of grey reindeer lichen were selected, cleared from their surrounding carpet of crowberry, and enlarged by transplanting lichen collected from the area. The crowberry was removed mechanically and burned on site, with the ashes subsequently used alongside chalk and seaweed to improve the bare soil, preparing it for the seeds of more than fifteen native flowering herbs. Whether the herbs can establish themselves more permanently and withstand the pressure from the crowberry remains to be evaluated (↔ 3,4). Meanwhile, the development of the landscape laboratory format continues in various contexts.

A LONG-TERM PIONEERING EFFORT

Developing a new landscape architecture program is a long-term endeavor that involves establishing a new professional environment centered around landscape architectural education and research. In this respect, it presents a challenge in that UiT offers no other architectural education and in that Tromsø is geographically distant from AHO and other institutions offering landscape architectural education and research. However, when it comes to knowledge and expertise in arctic/subarctic conditions, the program benefits enormously from its location and the diverse research environments found at UiT. Over the years, the program has engaged in many joint activities with other departments, including the Department of Arctic and Marine Biology and the Department of Social Science. These activities range from joint lectures and common workshops to research collaborations. The program continues to develop a close partnership with AHO and aims to strengthen its international research and teaching relations. To date, the program has entered into seven international student exchange agreements. After a long period of focus on developing the curriculum and establishing good administrative procedures, more attention will be paid to research and new research collaborations.

2   MONEC is an acronym for "To Manage Or Not: Assessing the Benefit of Managing Ecosystem Disservices." More information about MONEC can be found at monec.org/om.

3   Experiments between aesthetics and ecology from a workshop at Ramfjordmoen. Drone imagery of
       an intervention focuses on the mosaic pattern of dwarf shrubs and lichens, identified as a striking
       aesthetic quality in this landscape.

4   Experiments between aesthetics and ecology from a workshop at Ramfjordmoen. A photograph of the
       intervention, focused on the mosaic pattern of dwarf shrubs and lichens two years after its completion.

The year 2023 was a momentous year in the development of the program. In the summer of 2023, the first cohort of students graduated from the joint five-year integrated Master of Landscape Architecture (MLA). In January 2023, the final appointment was made to fill the last of the seven permanent positions (three full-time and four part-time) allocated to the program, marking a significant milestone. In addition to the permanent staff, the program aims to employ one or two PhD fellows continuously. In August 2023, the first PhD fellow to have completed the program was employed, marking another significant milestone. Finally, the program received international recognition in November 2023 when it was announced that it had won the prestigious Ribas Piera Landscape Architecture School Prize at the 12th Barcelona International Landscape Biennal. The landscape architecture program at UiT was selected as a winner by a professional jury in a competition with entries from seventy-two educational institutions across twenty-six countries. Each institution could submit up to five student projects, and the landscape architecture program at UiT submitted three projects from a studio course and two independent diploma projects. The studio course focused on developing mitigating measures in relation to potential conflicts between reindeer herding and other land uses in Finnmark, while the diploma projects addressed more-than-human marine spatial planning in the Fram Strait and a palliative design for the (after)life of Coal Mine #7 on Svalbard, respectively. According to the competition assessment, the jury was impressed by the program's commitment to a curriculum grounded in ecological, cultural, and economic realities. The studio work was noted for its excellence in design and methodology, with a design approach prioritizing processes over concrete outcomes.[3]

3   More information about the competition, the jury, and the submitted material is available at "UiT Arctic University of Norway Wins Prestigious International Landscape Architecture School Prize 2023," Barcelona International Landscape Biennal.

Snødepot
Akie Kono

This short photo series depicts snow deposits in the urban landscape of Tromsø, Northern Norway. The various mounds result from collecting snow from roads across the city. Snow removal is primarily done to ensure safe accessibility and transport for people walking, biking, or driving. Once the snow is removed, small gravel stones are often distributed over the road and pathway so that the ground does not get slippery when the snow is gone.

The snow mounds hold a strong presence within the city and are ever-changing urban forms. They are dynamic and temporary topographies, reshaping movement patterns, sightlines, and so much more. They are a prominent part of the aesthetic of an Arctic winter city such as Tromsø. Residents are proud of their winter city despite climate change slowly changing those conditions. For example, the city is dealing with increased precipitation and fluctuating temperatures in winter.

November 9, 2019, 13:30h. Central European Time (CET), GMT+1.
Strandgata 57 in Tromsø, Norway.

In Tromsø, snow removal, and maintenance in general, is a significant part of the
municipality's workload. Travel magazines may frame Nordic winter landscapes as
beautiful and Scandinavian architectures as charming and colorful, but there exists
a choreographed effort behind the scenes to maintain the image of Tromsø
as a desirable winter city.

November 9, 2019, 11:30h. Central European Time (CET), GMT+1.
Stortorget in Tromsø, Norway

The many snow mounds sometimes resemble the mountains surrounding the city.

November 8, 2019, 14:00h. Central European Time (CET), GMT+1.
Søndre Tollbodgate 5 in Tromsø, Norway

For now, huge amounts of snowfall and correspondingly tall snow deposits are still a common sighting in Tromsø. The deposits are scattered across the city, pushed onto forgotten plots, left at empty street corners, or, as seen here, in parking lots. Like many others, the scale of this particular snow mound can hide the usual inhabitants—the cars—of the parking lot.

November 8, 2019, 14:00h. Central European Time (CET), GMT+1.
Skansen in Tromsø, Norway

A snow-covered hill in the old part of town is topped up with the snow of its surrounding hard surfaces. The combination results in a new topography for the small hill, ranging from smooth to irregular snowy surfaces.

Dr. Marya Rozanova-Smith is a Research Professor at the George Washington University (Washington, DC) with expertise in Arctic affairs. Andrey N. Petrov is a Professor of Geography and ARCTICenter Director at the University of Northern Iowa, USA, with expertise in Arctic sustainable development, economic systems, and climate change adaptation.

"We Need Our Own Places": Paths for Indigenization in the Russian Arctic City of Naryan-Mar
Marya Rozanova-Smith and Andrey N. Petrov

This chapter describes the complex processes of Indigenous urbanization and government-driven Indigenization using the case study of the Russian Arctic city of Naryan-Mar. As many Arctic cities experience a postcolonial transition, Naryan-Mar is also undergoing multiple transitions from the Soviet and post-Soviet past to a city of the twenty-first century. Indigenization is part of this transformation, encompassing the urban built environment, culture, economy, and political sphere.

As a part of a global trend, the Russian Arctic is experiencing ongoing urbanization, with the majority of Arctic cities established on the lands of Indigenous Peoples. Many northern towns and cities in Russia are relatively young; they were built to play an important role in the national economic development agenda of the Union of Soviet Socialist Republics (USSR).[1] Similar to other Circumpolar regions, Arctic urbanization in the Nenets Autonomous Okrug (NAO, where Okrug is the equivalent of a District, in English) in Russia was not "a naturally driven result of the imminent development of traditional settlements,"[2] but rather, the result of a rapidly intensifying exploration of natural resources and industrialization of Indigenous lands. In contrast to other regions, the speed and scale of urban development in the Arctic were especially dramatic, and urbanization was seen as a necessary and desirable way to develop the Soviet North.[3] After the collapse of the USSR in the 1990s, the so-called Russian Arctic, including its cities, experienced a significant population outflow, with some urban places shrinking significantly.[4] In oil-rich regions, like NAO, this process was less pronounced and even reversed later in the 2000s.[5] However, Soviet-era population growth rates were never again attained, and sources of urbanization changed with more new urban residents coming from rural areas of the NAO, thus accelerating Indigenous urbanization.[6]

There is a growing volume of literature on various aspects of Indigenous urbanization in the Arctic, including cities in North America[7] and, to a lesser degree, in Greenland[8] and Fennoscandia.[9] The urbanization of the Indigenous Peoples in the Russian Arctic is a relatively new area of research. Most studies on Indigenous urbanization are conducted at the intersection of ethnology and social anthropology, such as: Lyudmila Khakhovskaya's case study on the urbanization of Indigenous Peoples in Magadan and their occupations in the urban labor market.[10] Olga Povoroznyuk's study of the industrialization and urbanization of the Evenki Indigenous community in the Baikal-Amur Mainline region.[11] Vera Kuklina and Natalia Krasnoshtanova's study of urbanization processes in Indigenous communities in the Tuva Republic, Sakha (Yakutia) Republic, and Baikal region, as well as Indigenous individuals' employment patterns.[12] Elena Lyarskaya's field research on the boarding school system for Nenets children in Yamal-Nenets Autonomous Okrug as a prerequisite for their cultural assimilation and adaptation to the urban environment.[13] Marjorie Balzer's studies of "Indigenous cosmopolitans," urban-based activism,

1   Marlene Laruelle, "Postcolonial Polar Cities? New Indigenous and Cosmopolitan Urbanness in the Arctic," *Acta Borealia* 36, no. 2 (2019): 149–65; Andy Bruno and Ekaterina Kalemeneva, "Creating the Soviet Arctic, 1917–1991," in *The Cambridge History of the Polar Regions*, ed. Adrian Howkins and Peder Roberts (Cambridge University Press, 2023), 462–86.

2   Viktor Martynov, "Urbanizatsiia Rossiiskoi Arktiki: Severnaia Gorodskaia Identichnost' Kak Faktor Razvitiia" [Urbanization of the Russian Arctic: Northern Urban Identity as a Development Factor], in *Rossiiskaia Arktika v Poiskakh Integral'noi Identichnosti: Kollektivnaia Monografiia*, ed. O. B. Podvintsev (Novyi Khronograf, 2016), 114.

3   Samuil Slavin, *The Soviet North: Present Development and Prospects*, trans. Don Danemanis (Progress Publishers, 1972); Colin Reisser, "Russia's Arctic Cities," in *Sustaining Russia's Arctic Cities: Resource Politics, Migration, and Climate Change*, ed. Robert W. Orttung (Berghahn Books, 2017).

4   A. Petrov and T. Vlasova, "Migration and socio-economic well-being in the Russian North: Interrelations, regional differentiation, recent trends and emerging issues," in *Migration in the Circumpolar North: New Concepts and Patterns*, ed. L. Huskey and C. Southcott (CCI Press, 2010); Nadezhda Zamyatina, Suter Luis, Dmitry Streletskiy, and Nikolay Shiklomanov, "Chapter 2. Shrinking Cities, Growing Cities: A Comparative Analysis of Vorkuta and Salekhard," in *Urban Sustainability in the Arctic: Measuring Progress in Circumpolar Cities*, ed. Robert W. Orttung (Berghahn Books, 2020), 49–73; Flera Sokolova and Wooik Choi, "The Russian Arctic in the Post-Soviet Period: Dynamics of Migration Processes," *Region* 8, no. 2 (2019): 197–226; and Timothy Heleniak, "Migration and Population Change in the Russian Far North during the 1990s," In *Migration in the Circumpolar North: Issues and Contexts*, ed. Chris Southcott and Lee Huskey (Canadian Circumpolar Institute Press, University of Alberta, 2010).

5   Timothy Heleniak, "Growth Poles and Ghost Towns in the Russian Far North," in *Russia and the North*, edited by Elana Wilson Rowe, University of Ottawa Press, 2009.

6   Marya Rozanova, "Indigenous Urbanization in Russia's Arctic: The Case of Nenets Autonomous Region," *Sibirica* 18, no. 3 (2019): 54–91.

and the Indigenous rights movements in the Sakha (Yakutia) Republic.[14] A case of creating a new image of the city of Yakutsk with visible Indigenous cultures by Indigenous university students and graduates is described by Kuklina et al.[15] At the same time, Solovyeva and Kuklina examined the circulation of goods, money, information, and people between Sakha cities and remote communities.[16]

Literature about Indigenous Peoples' institutions in Russia and their role in shaping urban Indigenous communities and relationships with regional/municipal governments is still scarce. New studies reflect on new processes of urbanization and (post)colonial trends in the Arctic regions of Russia[17] and NAO[18] on emerging urban Indigenous identities in Yakutsk (Sakha or Yakutia Republic) and Naryan-Mar (NAO),[19] future scenarios for the Russian Arctic and Indigenous Peoples in NAO,[20] cultural resurgence and postcolonialism in Kamchatka[21] and more. The literature on settler-colonial or decolonial or postcolonial studies regarding Russian Arctic cities is scarce, as these are "highly debated topics, particularly among Russian historians who at times admit the exploitation of non-Russian peoples, but not its colonial nature."[22]

The first part of the chapter presents the study's conceptual framework and describes the historical context of urbanization in the Nenets region and the preconditions for mass migration of the Indigenous Nenets People from rural environments, including semi-nomadic settlements, to the regional capital of Naryan-Mar. It analyzes key demographics, language proficiency, education level, and occupational characteristics of the Nenets Indigenous population. The second part (Results I) focuses on the process of "Indigenizing" Naryan-Mar as a part of the government-driven path for urban Indigenization in the key domains (political, economic, cultural, legal [land-related], and built environment, etc.) against the background of government policies at the regional and municipal levels, including practices of institutionalized Indigenous-based symbolism in urban political and cultural amenities and infrastructure. Finally, in the third part (Results II), we discuss complementary visions of Indigenizing Naryan-Mar that include bottom-up initiatives and contribute to empowering the local Indigenous community to define their rightful place in the future urban space. The study is based on observations, document analysis, and interviews with Nenets Indigenous urbanites, Nenets Indigenous leaders, and government officials.

THE CONCEPTUAL FRAMEWORK

Arctic cities became the points of contact between what were, in many aspects, inherently antagonistic Indigenous and urban settler ways of life. In an urban context, the Indigenous relations with political actors and broader society are constantly evolving and reconfiguring.[23] In this process, they are changing the concept of urban Indigeneity and the role of Indigenous Peoples in urban settings, broadening our perspectives on mechanisms of urban Indigenization and opening horizons for the new discourses on future (postcolonial) Arctic cities. The cities are also turning into points of Indigenous empowerment with potential political and economic capital growth.

7   M. Norris and S. Clatworthy, "Urbanization and Migration Patterns of Aboriginal Populations in Canada: A Half-Century in Review (1951–2006)," *Aboriginal Policy Studies* 1, no. 1 (2011): 13–77; S. Nejad, R. Walker, B. Macdougall, Y. Belanger, and D. Newhouse, "This Is an Indigenous City; Why Don't We See It? Indigenous Urbanism and Spatial Production in Winnipeg," *The Canadian Geographer / Le Géographe Canadien* 63 (2019): 413-424; Margaret Blackman, "Anaktuvuk Pass Goes to Town," *Études/Inuit/ Studies* 32, no. 1 (2008): 107–15; Nancy Fogel-Chance, "Living in Both Worlds: 'Modernity' and 'Tradition' among North Slope Inupiaq Women in Anchorage," *Arctic Anthropology* 30, no. 1 (1993): 94– 108; Nobuhiro Kishigami and Molly Lee, "Les Inuit Urbains," *Études/Inuit/Studies* 32, no. 1 (2008): 5–11; Donna Patrick and Gabriele Budach, "'Urban-Rural' Dynamics and Indigenous Urbanization: The Case of Inuit Language Use in Ottawa," *Journal of Language, Identity, and Education* 13, no. 4 (2014): 236–253; Donna Patrick and Julie-Ann Tomiak, "Language, Culture and Community among Urban Inuit in Ottawa," *Études/Inuit/Studies* 32, no. 1 (2008): 55–72; Julie Tomiak, "Contesting the Settler City: Indigenous Self-Determination, New Urban Reserves, and the Neoliberalization of Colonialism," *Antipode* 49, no. 4 (2017): 928–945; Laura C. Senese and Kathi Wilson, "Aboriginal Urbanization and Rights in Canada: Examining Implications for Health," *Social Science & Medicine* 91 (2013): 219–28; Lee Huskey, Matthew Berman, and Alexandra Hill, "Leaving Home, Returning Home: Migration as a Labor Market Choice for Alaska Natives," *The Annals of Regional Science* 38, no. 1 (2004): 75–92; Jacqueline Gillis, "'We Have a Very Colonial Way of Thinking...': Ontario Municipalities' Climate Collaborations with Indigenous Peoples," *Canadian Public Administration* 66 (2023): 496–513; Stéphane Guimont Marceau, Jennifer Buckell, Marie-Ève Drouin Gagné, Naomie Léonard, and Raphaëlle Ainsley Vincent, "Settler Urbanization and Indigenous Resistance: Uncovering an Ongoing Palimpsest in Montreal's Cabot Square," *Urban History Review 2023* 51, no. 2 (2023): 310–33; S. Nejad et al., "This Is an Indigenous City," 413–24; Mikkel Berg-Nordlie, "No Past, No Name, No Place? Urban Sámi Invisibility and Visibility in the Past and Present," *Aboriginal Policy Studies* 9, no. 2 (2021): n. pag.; Nobuhiro Kishigami and Molly Lee, "Les Inuit Urbains," 5–11.

8   Birgit Kleist Pedersen, "Young Greenlanders in the Urban Space of Nuuk," *Études/Inuit/Studies* 32, no. 1 (2008): 91–105; Jette Rygaard, "The City Life of Youths in Greenland," Études/Inuit/Studies 32, no. 1 (2008): 33–54; Klaus Georg Hansen and Rasmus Ole Rasmussen, "New Economic Activities and Urbanisation: Individual Reasons for Moving and for Staying–Case Greenland," in *Proceedings from the First International Conference on Urbanisation in the Arctic* (2012), 28–30; Lawrence C. Hamilton and Rasmus Ole Rasmussen, "Population, Sex Ratios and Development in Greenland," *Arctic* (2010): 43–52; Jens Dahl, Gail Fondahl, Andrey Petrov, and Rune Sverre Fjellheim, "Fate Control," in *Arctic Social Indicators: A Follow-up to the Arctic Human Development Report*, ed. Joan Nymand Larsen, Gail Fondahl, and Peter Schweitzer (Nordic Council of Ministers, 2010), 129–41; and Bert De Jonghe, *Inventing Greenland: Designing an Arctic Nation* (Actar, 2022).

9   Mikkel Berg-Nordlie, "The Governance of Urban Indigenous Spaces: Norwegian Sámi Examples," *Acta Borealia* 35, no. 1 (2018): 49–72; Torill Nyseth and Paul Pedersen, "Urban Sámi Identities in Scandinavia: Hybridities, Ambivalences and Cultural Innovation," *Acta Borealia* 31, no. 2 (2014): 131–51; Ludger Müller-Wille, "Precursors of Urban Processes in Finnish Sápmi in the 1960s," *Acta Borealia* 27, no. 2 (2010): 141–50; and Siv Eli Vuolab, "Negotiating an Urban Indigenous Identity. Expectations, Prejudices and Claims Faced by Urban Sámi in Two Contemporary Norwegian Cities," MPhil diss. UiT Norges Arktiske Universitet, 2016.

10   Lyudmila Khakhovskaya, "Aborigeny v Gorode: Etnokul'turnyi Oblik Zhitelei Magadana" [Aboriginal People in the City: Ethnocultural Image of the Urbanites of Magadan], *Sibirskie Istoricheskie Issledovaniia* 2 (2014): 39–59.

11   Olga Povoroznyuk, "Social dynamics and sustainability of BAM communities: Migration, competition for resources, and intergroup relations," in *New Mobilities and Social Changes in Russia's Arctic Regions* (Routledge, 2016), 149–173.

Postcolonial cities are characterized by Indigenous empowerment, self-determination, and cultural recovery and resurgence through the establishment of Indigenous government institutions and social economy, as well as community social and cultural infrastructure, including Indigenous community-based and -owned organizations.[24] Laruelle advances the idea that Arctic cities are now in a position to play a decolonizing role, as they are moving away from the purely Western nature by making urban places more postcolonial through being more "local and rooted (through Indigenous communities) and more global and multicultural (through foreign labor migrants)."[25] This argument places Arctic cities at the forefront of the urban postcolonial project and necessitates further elaboration.

Several key processes drive a transition to postcolonialism in Arctic cities. These processes manifest themselves in various aspects of urban life and urban space. The key drivers include Indigenization (recognition of Indigenous rights and knowledge as a part of urban life and governance), globalization and cosmopolitanism (multiculturalism, diversity, and openness to the outside world), environmentalism (focus on environment, recognition of nature as a part of urban fabric and dynamics), post-industrialism (development of a diversified, knowledge-based and equitable economy) and empowerment (the ability of all urban constituents to define a city's future and maintain their self-determination). In this chapter, we focus on the process of Indigenization and consider its current and possible pathways as a part of the twenty-first-century urban transition in the city of Naryan-Mar.

Although there is no broadly accepted definition of urban Indigenization, in this chapter, we understand it as the process of recognizing Indigenous urbanites as stakeholders and rights holders. This involves making meaningful changes in urban planning principles and decision-making practices by embedding Indigenous worldviews, traditions, and values into all urban domains—social, economic, civic, and political. Indigenization can be driven from the top, i.e., promoted by different levels of government, national and international NGOs, and sometimes industry. An administrative apparatus, abundant resources, and political support typically facilitate this top-down pathway. However, by its nature, it is not always based on the wishes and visions of urban Indigenous communities, and it can propagate political, economic, and cultural agendas that benefit political leadership and business elites (Indigenous and not). Top-down Indigenization can sometimes be construed as co-opting urban Indigenous communities, a way to earn 'political license' to govern and/or conduct business. It can even be seen as a tactic to subdue independent Indigenous voices. However, it is also true that top-down efforts may be a positive source of Indigenization if they are based on a true recognition of Indigenous rights and knowledge and involve urban Indigenous communities as equal partners. Bottom-up Indigenization in Arctic cities can be framed as a dimension of Indigenous resurgence. It is the process of reclaiming and restoring Indigenous cultures, Indigenous urban identities, and language to ensure the Indigenous urban communities' well-being and thriveability.

Urban Indigenization is most often propelled by the interplay of top-down and bottom-up processes and requires their synergy and co-existence to be successful. Enabling and reinforcing forces must come from multiple directions and be multi-level (i.e., communities, neighborhoods, municipalities, regions, and the nation) to move the process forward. Indigenization is also linked to Indigenous Peoples' empowerment, or more correctly, the concept of 'fate control' (within and outside of urban settings). The notion of 'fate control' has been pioneered by the Arctic Social Indicators Report as a key indicator

12   Vera Kuklina and Natalia Krasnoshtanova, "The Urbanization of Indigenous Peoples of Northeastern Siberia," in *New Mobilities and Social Changes in Russia's Arctic Regions*, ed. Marlene Laruelle (Routledge, 2016) 133–57.

13   Elena Lyarskaya, "'U Nikh Zhe Vse Ne Kak U Liudei …': Nekotorye Stereotipnye Predstavleniia Pedagogov Yamalo-Nenetskogo Okruga o Tundrovikakh" ["They Are Not Like Other People…": Some Stereotypical Ideas of Educators of the Yamal-Nenets Okrug about People Living in Tundra], *Antropologicheskii Forum* 5 (2006): 242–58.

14   Marjorie Balzer, "Korennye Kosmopolity, Ekologicheskaia Zashchita I Aktivizm v Sibiri i na Dal'nem Vostoke" [Indigenous Cosmopolitans, Environmental Protection and Activism in Siberia and the Far East], *Sibirskie Istoricheskie Issledovaniia* 2 (2014): 15–38.

15   Kuklina, S. Ignatieva, and U. Vinokurova. "Educational Institutions as a Resource for the Urbanization of Indigenous People: The Case of Yakutsk." *Sibirica* 18, no. 3 (2019): 29–53.

16   V. Solovyeva and V. Kuklina, "Resilience in a Changing World: Indigenous Sharing Networks in the Republic of Sakha (Yakutia)," *Polar Record* 56 (2020): e39.

17   Marlene Laruelle, "The Three Waves of Arctic Urbanisation. Drivers, Evolutions, Prospects," *Polar Record* 55, no. 1 (2019): 1–12.

18   Marya Rozanova, "Indigenous Urbanization," 54–91; M. Rozanova-Smith, "Stay or Leave? Arctic Youth Prospects and Sustainable Futures of the Russian Arctic Communities," *Sustainability* 2021, 13, 12058; Marya Rozanova and Valeriy L. Mikheev, "Rethinking Women's Empowerment: Insights from the Russian Arctic," *Social Sciences* 9, no. 2 (2020): 14.

19   Marya Rozanova-Smith, Stanislav Ksenofontov and Andrey N. Petrov, "Indigenous Urbanization and Indigenous Urban Experiences in the Russian Arctic: The Cases of Yakutsk and Naryan-Mar," in *Urban Indigeneities*, ed. Dana Brablec and Andrew Canessa (University of Arizona Press, 2023).

20   Andrey N. Petrov, Marya S. Rozanova Smith, Andrey K. Krivorotov, Elena M. Klyuchnikova, Valeriy L. Mikheev, Alexander N. Pelyasov, and Nadezhda Yu Zamyatina, "The Russian Arctic by 2050: Developing Integrated Scenarios" *Arctic: Journal of the Arctic Institute of North America* 74, no. 3 (2021): 239–417.

21   Tatiana S. Degai, "Places of Significance in Itelmen Country: Sacredness, Nostalgia and Identity in Kamchatka, Russia." PhD diss., 2009.

22   D. Schorkowitz, "Was Russia a Colonial Empire?" in *Shifting Forms of Continental Colonialism*, ed. D. Schorkowitz, J.R. Chávez, and I.W. Schröder (Palgrave Macmillan, 2019).

23   L. M. Furlan, *Indigenous Cities: Urban Indian Fiction and the Histories of Relocation* (University of Nebraska Press, 2017), 10.

24   L. M. Furlan, *Indigenous Cities*.

25   Marlene Laruelle, "Postcolonial Polar Cities? New Indigenous and Cosmopolitan Urbanness in the Arctic," *Acta Borealia* 36, no. 2 (2019): 151.

KEY DOMAINS OF URBAN INDIGENIZATION

POLITICAL

Recognition of Indigenous rights and knowledge as a part of urban life and governance; the ability of Indigenous communities to realize a political power and establish Indigenous community-based institutions to address their needs.

CULTURAL

Self-reliance of Indigenous urban communities to establish and maintain cultural infrastructure in the form of Indigenous community-based and -owned organizations; have a space for Indigenous cultural activities in all domains of city life; Indigenous language vitality.

PERSONAL

Ability to maintain resilient Indigenous urban identities through institutionalized mechanisms to keep a connection to land and participation in a mixed economy, keeping spiritual ties, and ability to learn and practice the Indigenous language.

ECONOMIC

Economic self-reliance of Indigenous communities and control over resources; well-established Indigenous-owned and -run businesses; workforce integration of Indigenous urbanites and ability to participate in "mixed" economy.

LEGAL (LAND-RELATED)

Recognition of Indigenous urbanites as Indigenous rights holders, cultural bearers, and knowledge-holders with full and unlimited access to their ancestral lands to practice traditional cultural activities.

BUILT ENVIRONMENT

Indigenous cultures' presence and visibility in urban built infrastructure; led by Indigenous communities and combined with institutionalized mechanisms build their own spaces.

1   The key domains of urban Indigenization as understood by the authors.

of well-being. It refers to the ability of Indigenous communities to realize "political power, economic self-reliance, control over land, and cultural empowerment" in order to thrive in the Arctic.[26] Without fate control and self-determination at the forefront of the Indigenization process, top-down and bottom-up forces will be severely weakened. It is also important to point out the barriers to urban Indigenization, as they are plentiful and often stem from colonial legacies, infrastructure violence, extractive capitalism, and entrenched inequities within Arctic polities. (Neo)colonialism is one of the most difficult obstacles to overcome. It may take different forms, either perpetuating past colonial relationships or creating new ones, but ultimately, it undermines urban Indigenization. In some cases, neocolonial forces can corrupt and co-opt Indigenization and even turn it into a (re)colonizing project. Other barriers include resource extractivism, which may impose economic and political strains on urban Indigenization. Isolationism and xenophobia, lack of diversity, and minority recognition substantially limit opportunities for Indigenous resurgence in urban communities. In the same way, disempowerment and political oppression that targets civil society and Indigenous movement may become a factor that obliterates Indigenization. Finally, the capacity of Indigenous urban communities, including their human, economic, political, and cultural resources, is an important factor in bottom-up resurgence, and a lack of capacity is often a problematic and persistent impediment to Indigenization in Arctic cities.

Laruelle considers two blocks of criteria for the 'success' of an Indigenous urbanness: 'objective' that includes the existence of Indigenous cultural organizations, self-governance, community solidarity opportunities, symbolic recognition in the urban landscape, public services using Indigenous languages, and workforce integration, etc., as well as 'subjective,' i.e., the emergence of Indigenous urban identities and subcultures.[27]

26   Jens Dahl et al. "Fate Control."
27   Marlene Laruelle, "The Three Waves of Arctic Urbanisation."

2   Situating the city of Naryan-Mar in the Russian Far North (scale 1:5,000,000).

A BRIEF HISTORY OF URBANIZATION IN THE NENETS REGION

The city of Naryan-Mar (67°38'N 53°03'E) is in the western part of the Russian Arctic. It is the administrative center and the only town in NAO.[28] The city is home to Arctic Indigenous Peoples, predominantly Nenets, and was founded on their ancestral lands. Today, NAO is the least populated region of Russia, with 41,383 people in 2023, of whom 30,832 were urban residents and 10,551 were rural. NAO urban communities consist of the administrative center, the city of Naryan-Mar, home to almost half the NAO population (23,579 in 2023), and the urban-type settlement of Iskateley (7,253 in 2023).

The city of Naryan-Mar was founded in 1931 as a part of the Soviet government's development initiatives in the Arctic in the 1920s and 1930s. Since the early days of Naryan-Mar, "the settlers became the majority, while traditional cultures and ethnic groups were forced to adapt to the de facto changed conditions of their existence."[29] Nenets culture, language, and values are deeply rooted in traditions of reindeer husbandry, fishing, hunting, and gathering. The urbanization processes led by a settler government agenda exposed the conflict between the political, economic, and societal domains of urban life that were in many aspects incompatible with the Indigenous traditional nomadic livelihoods and their traditional tribal structure. Urbanization was one of the most significant challenges to the Nenets People's Indigenous identity, culture, subsistence economy, tribal community structure, kinship ties, and nomadic way of life.[30] For the local Indigenous Peoples, the Nenets, urbanization was a sign of Otherness, despite initial attempts of the Soviet authorities to facilitate the korenizatsiia[31] (korenizatsiia *is* Indigenization or nativization, in English) in the form of affirmative action policies aimed at resolving the contradictions between the central government and the Indigenous Peoples by providing their representatives with educational opportunities and promoting them to leadership positions within the Soviet system.[32]

In NAO, the initial rural-urban migration was mainly triggered by the Soviet sedentarization policies that were complemented by education reform establishing a state-run boarding school system for Indigenous children, particu-

---

28   The Russian Federation presents a complex federal system, combining both models of territorial federalism (based on a strictly spatial division of power) and a national-territorial model (granting non-Russian peoples the right to some kind of statehood within the federation). The constituent units of the federation are divided into multiple types of regions: oblasts, republics, krais, autonomous okrugs, federal cities, and autonomous oblast. Republics and autonomous okrugs are homes to specific Indigenous peoples (often minorities) with their own culture, language, and traditions.

29   Viktor Martynov, "Urbanizatsiia Rossiiskoi Arktiki" [Urbanization of the Russian Arctic], 114.

30   See, for instance, Marya Rozanova, "Indigenous Urbanization."

31   George Liber, "Korenizatsiia: Restructuring Soviet Nationality Policy in the 1920s," *Ethnic and Racial Studies* 14, no. 1 (1991): 15–23.

32   Terry Martin, *The Affirmative Action Empire: Nations and Nationalism in the Soviet Union, 1923–1939* (Cornell University Press, 2001).

larly affecting Nenets women.[33] Over time, however, Nenets have begun to migrate to urban settlements and the administrative center of Naryan-Mar, mainly in search of jobs, education prospects, and more opportunities for children. In the post-Soviet times, during the transition to a market economy, the rural–urban migration intensified.[34] Rural residents, mainly Nenets, are semi-nomadic reindeer herders enrolled in wage and subsistence economic activities, including commercial reindeer herding, fishing, hunting, and gathering. However, these activities cannot support a prosperous life, especially in comparison with the income in urban households. Thus, there has been a significant influx of Nenets into the urban settlements. In 2022, about 700 Nenets, the majority of whom were male reindeer herders, were practicing nomadism in the tundra; there were also eleven traditional tribal families with women and children.[35] In addition, there are around 1,500 Nenets who live sedentary in villages, working in traditional subsistence roles mainly related to hunting and fishing.[36] In the near future, this Indigenous urbanization process is likely to accelerate due to the effects of climate change impacting permafrost thaw and increasing weather extremes combined with new extractive industrial projects affecting reindeer herding and other subsistence activities of Nenets People.

> Historically, urbanization in NAO has affected non-Indigenous and Indigenous communities to varying degrees. For instance, the ethnic Russian population dominating the urban settlements reached 70.7% of the total urban population.[37] Although the urbanization in NAO is continuing to increase, the pace of ethnic Russian inflows to urban settlements is slowing, with a slight increase of less than 7% over the last two decades.[38] This is in contrast with Nenets, who have been progressively urbanizing since 1935. Initially, it was at a much slower pace, but this process has recently intensified, with almost 30% of the total Nenets population now living in urban areas, compared to 20.4% in 2002. In the city of Naryan-Mar, Nenets comprise 6.6% of total city dwellers, while Komi, the second major Indigenous group, accounts for 3.8% of Naryan-Mar residents.[39] Indigenous urbanization has affected different genders in different ways, leading to a steady trend toward the feminization of Nenets' urban community: in 2010, the Nenets People were 61% women and 39% men. In 2020, 60% were women, and 40% were men.[40]

This gap is closely linked to the professional niches available in urban and rural areas. In the Western education system, Nenets men have a lower overall level of education than women and are inclined to traditionally 'male-specific' jobs in the tundra (reindeer herding, fishing, hunting, etc.), while women mostly work in 'female-dominated' spheres, like education, medicine, and culture, both in rural and, often even more successfully, in urban areas. Over time, the opportunities available to women in the rural environment become less attractive.[41]

Methodological Note

The research team consists of non-Indigenous scholars who have broad experience and long-term relationships working with Indigenous communities in Russia, including the NAO, and are committed to ethical principles when working with Indigenous Peoples.[42] In addition to lead researchers, an Indigenous community knowledge holder was enrolled to contribute to the recruitment process and scheduling of interviews, as well as to provide feedback on urgent community needs.

In this study, the research team relied on semi-structured interviews, as they provided a flexible, collaborative, and effective framework for collecting information from research participants. Special focus was placed on Indigenous youth in Naryan-Mar; young people are an important group since they experience the complex issues of identity and urbanity while representing the future of their Indigenous communities. In particular, we were interested in Indigenous urbanites who were born in urban areas or, at the very least, moved there at a young age in order to explore how they developed an Indigenous consciousness with little or no exposure to rural life.

33   Marya Rozanova and Valeriy L. Mikheev, "Rethinking Women's Empowerment."
34   Marya Rozanova, "Indigenous Urbanization."
35   "Doklad o Sostoyanii Olenevodstva v Nenetskom Avtonomnom Okruge na 2023 God [Reports on the State of Reindeer Herding in the Nenets Autonomous Okrug for 2023]." Naryan-Mar, 2023. Portal organov gosudarstvennoy vlasti [Portal of Government Bodies].
36   Administratsia NAO, "O korrektirovke Strategi i sotsial'no-ekonomicheskogo razvitiia Nenetskogo avtonomnogo okruga na perspektivu do 2030 goda."
37   "Russian Census 2002, 2010, 2020," Russian Federal State Statistics Service.
38   From 76.5 percent of ethnic Russian population in urban settings of total Russian population in NAO in 2002 to 80.3 percent in 2010, and to 83 percent in 2020 accordingly.
39   "Russian Census 2002, 2010, 2020," Russian Federal State Statistics Service.
40   Ibid.
41   Rozanova and Mikheev 2020.
42   IASSA 2020; Degai et al., 2022.

RESULTS I

Top-Down Pathways of Indigenization in Naryan-Mar The Russian Arctic urbanization project bears both resemblances and dissimilarities with urbanization in other Arctic contexts with colonial legacies. The settler urbanization in most places has been following the "urban nullius" strategy that others, hides, ignores or eradicate Indigenous rights, histories, voices, and physical and symbolic presence in a colonial city from its very foundation and throughout subsequent urban development.[43] A growing volume of literature on Indigenous urbanization emphasizes that this "invisibility [...] brings into play asymmetries of power"[44] while Indigenous Peoples and their cultures are not presented symbolically in various urban domains in many Circumpolar regions and beyond.[45]

In Russia, the urbanization processes in the Arctic have had their own unique feature in that regard. In contrast to settler urbanization in other Arctic states, where in the process of colonization, "the streets and schools and parks of settler-colonial cities were named during a time when most leaders and states were doing everything in their power to keep cities and nation as white as possible,"[46] since the beginning of active Soviet urbanization of the North, the authorities have been implementing a different model that included elements of the symbolic presence of Nenets culture and Nenets People in different domains of the city. The roots of this model come from Soviet federalism, which created several autonomous regions where Indigenous Peoples were assigned as "titular nations,"[47] including the NAO. Although the status of the "titular nations" did not necessarily translate into real power for Indigenous Peoples or recognition of Indigenous rights, there was a demand to incorporate Indigenous elements into physical and symbolic landscapes of a regional capital, such as Naryan-Mar. The symbolism inherited in modern Russia is continuing a top-down Indigenization project in a multitude of urban domains and is now interacting with other trends, such as an Indigenous resurgence, to produce a complex and contradictory nature of Indigenization.

POLITICAL DOMAIN

Government-Driven Recognition from the Top During the course of Soviet and post-Soviet history, government-driven "recognition from the top" promoted by settlers through the use of government institutions and political symbolism, including Indigenous visibility in urban landscapes, served different purposes. At different points in time, these were the idea of a "good governance" respectful to Indigenous Peoples, justification of the great Soviet past as a foundation for modern patriotism, political/geopolitical benefits coming from new expectations to create obligations on the part of governments towards emerging non-state actors in international relations, reshaping the Circumpolar political landscape, to name a few.

At the city level, political recognition and political symbolism can be manifested in various forms, including legislature (City Charter ensuring the special status of Indigenous Peoples in the city), Indigenous representatives at all levels of city administration and in all spheres of governance, elected Indigenous representatives at the City Council; Indigenization of official symbols of the city, e.g., flag and coat of arms, anthem, and its toponymic roots in the Indigenous heritage; various forms of support to Indigenous organizations.

As a part of a paternalistic tradition, in Naryan-Mar, top-down Indigenization is manifested in the official city symbols, such as flag and coat of arms, and Indigenous presence in the city toponymics is a well-established government-driven tradition. The city erected a number of prominent memorials commemorating the contribution of Indigenous residents. Out of the two city squares, one is the largest in the Nenets Region and the central place in the city for all major public events. It has a Nenets name, Marad Sey (Heart of the City, in English).

Government-Driven Glorification of the Past In Naryan-Mar, among sixty-one city streets, eighteen are named after famous individuals, with seven of those commemorating the Indigenous Nenets linguists, storytellers, writers, poets, pilots, political activists, and politicians whose significant achievements were recognized by settler authorities within their system of politically and culturally important activities.

In 2012, the NAO Administration erected a monument, *The Feat of the Participants of the Reindeer-Transport Battalions during the Great Patriotic War of 1941–1945* for the Day of Remembrance of the Reindeer-Transport Battalions,[48] celebrated on November 20. By highlighting the role of Nenets within the Russian grand narrative of World War II, this monument symbolically silenced the anti-Soviet (anti-collectivization) riots of the early 1940s, especially the main one,

43   Nursey-Bray et al., 2022.

44   D. Howard-Wagner, *Indigenous Invisibility in the City: Successful Resurgence and Community Development Hidden in Plain Sight*, Routledge, 2021, 12.

45   J. McElroy, "Who Owns This City? Why Debates Around Vancouver Place Names Are Divisive," CBC News, October 8, 2017; D. Howard-Wagner, *Indigenous Invisibility in the City*.

46   D. Howard-Wagner, *Indigenous Invisibility in the City*, 10.

47   Stanislav Kulchytskyi, "Building of the Soviet Titular Nations (1918–1938)," *Codrul Cosminului* 20, no. 1 (2014): 181–192.

48   During World War II, in November–December 1941, NAO provided over 7000 riding reindeer (almost 75 percent of the entire mounted reindeer corps) as well as soldiers for the battlefront. The reindeer battalions transported 8000 soldiers and 17,000 tons of ammunition to the front line. With reindeer transportation, 10,142 wounded soldiers were saved from the front line. From "Turizm," Nexplorer.

Mandalada (1943).[49] Thus, the city's government-cultivated cultural symbolism cherishes the idyllic narrative of harmonious, long-lasting co-existence of Indigenous Peoples and settler population, leaving latent political battles of memory about traumatic events of the past recognized but unreconciled.[50]

ECONOMIC DOMAIN

A Booming Indigenous-Inspired Economy In Naryan-Mar, there are clear signs of an emerging so-called Indigenous-inspired economy. The economic activities capitalizing on Indigenous culture and traditional subsistence activities are mainly presented by small businesses owned by Indigenous and non-Indigenous city dwellers, state-owned organizations, and Nenets urbanites enrolled in mixed economy activities. While local Indigenous non-profit organizations are not directly involved as part of the grant-reliance system, there is potential for diversification of their functions.

> A new trend of growing popularity and romanticization of Nenets culture has inspired many non-Indigenous-owned and -run small businesses to use Indigenous cultural rituals, symbols, design, and Nenets cuisine. Most of these commercial projects are developed without the consultation or participation of Indigenous People since no consent is formally required in Russia, and the concept of cultural appropriation is still not well known in the Russian Arctic outside of academic circles. For instance, Timan, the most prestigious restaurant-museum in the city, has Indigenous-inspired exterior and interior design imitating elements of chum (where chum is a tent, temporary dwelling used by the nomadic Indigenous Peoples, in English), displays Arctic ethnic artifacts, and cultivates elements of Nenets traditional cuisine, even presenting it at culinary competitions outside of NAO. Another example of a non-Indigenous-owned culturally oriented business is the Art Studio Narey (Nenets narey is spring, in English), which often collaborates with Nenets artists and uses elements of Nenets motifs in contemporary design.[51]

The booming tourism industry in the Arctic is becoming an important driver, increasing Indigenous visibility in the city. To promote Naryan-Mar attractions to tourists, the NAO Business Development Center initiated a graffiti campaign in public spaces, emphasizing a visual symbolic presence of traditional Indigenous culture as well as prominent Nenets artists. Although many Indigenous-owned small businesses and artists benefit from this growing market, these are not Indigenous community-driven initiatives and do not always correspond well to Indigenous cultural resurgence.

> Most Indigenous-led and -owned businesses are concentrated in rural areas and encompass reindeer herding, hunting, and gathering. Among them are eleven reindeer cooperatives (Yerv, Kharp, Indiga, etc.),

eight individual reindeer enterprises (farms like Nerm, Nyadei Ya, etc.), and eleven family (tribal) Indigenous obshinas (commune, in English, with Yamb To, Yalumd, Vark, and so on, among them) specializing in reindeer herding, five obshinas in fishing, three obshinas in Indigenous arts and crafts (for instance, Indigenous-owned and run handcraft and folk art center, Temboyko,[52] in the Indigenous village of Krasnoe), and one obshina in hunting.[53]

For these businesses, Naryan-Mar plays a crucial role in distributing and selling their products. For instance, the Yerv cooperative maintains reindeer products in grocery stores in the city, while many Indigenous artists bring their products to city exhibitions, expos, and so on. State-run Indigenous culture-oriented businesses include souvenir shops at the Ethnocultural Center and Nenets Museum of Local Lore, with most handcrafts designed by Indigenous professional artists following Nenets' traditional techniques using traditional materials.

These days, most self-organized Indigenous-owned culture-oriented organizations in Russia operate as non-profit organizations and not economically driven enterprises, serving a cultural function for their communities instead. One of the most significant challenges that many non-profit Indigenous organizations face to enter the economic mainstream is the reliance on the system of grants from the government and extractive industry companies' programs that are mainly accustomed to settler-oriented goals and overwhelming contractual obligations. The grant system does not allow overheads while paying the minimum and thus doesn't support business-oriented initiatives that may be capitalized into Indigenous enterprises, so "there is no way to generate a gain or profit to reinvest into the community, its development, and wellbeing."[54] Similarly, the Association of Nenets People "Yasavey," is also seen as an institution providing mainly cultural services for Nenets People

---

49   The Mandalada uprisings that took place in the eastern parts of NAO in 1943 were directed against the Soviet government's policies of eliminating the traditional socio-economic way of life and free use of tundra, Indigenous acculturation to Soviet society (especially against sending children to boarding schools), and economic exploitation during collectivization and World War II. For more, see: Podvintsev, O. B., ed. *Rossiiskaia Arktika v poiskakh integral'noi identichnosti: Kollektivnaia monografiia* [The Russian Arctic in search of integral identity: A collective monograph]. Novyi khronograf, 2016, 44; about Mandalada and contradicting narratives and the transformation of memory in Nenets communities, see R. Laptander, "Processes of Remembering and Forgetting," *Sibirica* 13, no. 3 (2014): 22–44.

50   Marya Rozanova, "Indigenous Urbanization in Russia's Arctic: The Case of Nenets Autonomous Region," *Sibirica* 18, no. 3 (2019): 54–91.

51   vk.com/narey.

52   taibarei.ru.

53   "Doklad o Sostoyanii Olenevodstva v Nenetskom Avtonomnom Okruge na 2023 God [Reports on the State of Reindeer Herding in the Nenets Autonomous Okrug for 2023]." Naryan-Mar, 2023. Portal organov gosudarstvennoy vlasti [Portal of Government Bodies].

54   D. Howard-Wagner, *Indigenous Invisibility in the City*, 162.

and not allowing them to accumulate enough economic capital to establish Indigenous-designed and -led enterprises with the potential of expanding their capacities by creating Indigenous cultural businesses, medical centers, preschool and childcare facilities, and social services.

Resilience of Urban "Mixed" Economies Many Indigenous People residing in Naryan-Mar are strongly connected with their ancestral lands. They are part of an urban "mixed" economy, i.e., they participate in subsistence activities in the tundra, helping their relatives with reindeer herding, fishing, hunting, or gathering, as well as in the urban economy by having jobs in the city. However, the ability to reconnect to nature and practice subsistence is becoming a privilege for some Indigenous urbanites who may experience difficulties related to the transportation costs to reach their ancestral lands. In addition, moving to a city may invalidate their "Indigenous Peoples" status that guarantees special quotas and licenses to hunt and fish in ancestral lands. In the Nenets region, the current struggle of Indigenous urbanites lies not so much in the legal framework of Indigenous land rights recognition and ownership or co-management but in the claims of total and free access to land to exercise traditional subsistence activities for all Indigenous People regardless of their place of residence and without restrictions imposed by federal and regional governments.[55]

CULTURAL DOMAIN

Increasing visibility of Indigenous culture in Naryan-Mar occurs through top-down government-driven processes and bottom-up emerging initiatives by Indigenous urbanites. State-sponsored ethno-cultural centers, craft studios, museums, and ethno-tourism centers promote Indigenous culture in state-supported yet predominantly Indigenous Peoples'-led ethnic music and dance ensembles.

Language Retention and Revitalization The ethnic imbalance (73.3% of the city population is ethnic Russian and 6.6% is Nenets) and the overwhelming dominance of the Russian culture and language, among other factors, contribute to significant language shifts among urban Nenets. In the region, only 36% of ethnic Nenets consider Nenets their native language, while almost 60% indicate Russian as their mother tongue.[56] These figures have been mostly stable over the last few decades. The most recent language data available for urban areas showed that only 25.3% of the city's Nenets population considered Nenets their mother tongue.[57]

Following the Soviet tradition of supporting minority languages, the NAO implements several top-down initiatives, including hosting the annual Days of Nenets Literature, a series of events aimed at preserving and popularizing the language, culture, and spiritual values of the Nenets People. Another form of language support is the state-funded main newspaper, *Naryana Vynder*, located in Naryan-Mar, which publishes materials in Russian with partial translation to Nenets. An example of an Indigenous community-driven bottom-up initiative with government support is the Nenets Language School Nenei' Vada (where Nenets word Nenei' vada is the real word in English). Initiated in 2018, the school offers (on an almost annual basis) classes throughout the year free of charge for city residents aged sixteen and older. Funded by the NAO's government, Nenei' Vada is a joint project between the Yasavey organization and the NAO's Ethnocultural Center.

BUILT ENVIRONMENT DOMAIN

The legacy of the Soviet state-orchestrated Indigenous Peoples' recognition from the top can be found in architectural manifestations in different periods of the city's history. Both in Soviet times and the post-Soviet era, the built environment with Nenets ethnic motifs, either in the form of architectural structures or exterior decor, is mainly presented in centrally located public buildings like the central post office, public schools, Nenets Museum of Local Lore, stadium (↪ 3). This creates visibility for Indigenous culture and heritage, but it is often implemented into the urban landscapes to promote different political agendas, for which Indigenous representation serves as a tool rather than a purpose.

Architects and designers of these buildings are not Indigenous, and Indigenous motifs used in these structures may be considered a form of cultural appropriation. At the same time, it is also true that the increasing visibility of the Nenets heritage and culture may lead to the reclamation of spaces in the city on their terms, which is something that Indigenous urbanites strongly desire and which, if it becomes a reality, will become a substantial contribution to urban Indigenization in Naryan-Mar.

LEGAL (LAND-RELATED) DOMAIN

Indigenous Reclamation of City Public Space(s) Only a few years ago, in 2020, the first steps towards reclaiming the rightful place for the Nenets People in urban public space were implemented in Naryan-Mar. Initiated by the Nenets

55   *Annual Report on the Observance and Protection of the Rights, Freedoms, and Legitimate Interests of Humans and Citizens in the Nenets Autonomous Okrug for 2019*. Naryan-Mar, 2020.
56   "Russian Census 2020," Russian Federal State Statistics Service.
57   "Russian Census 2002," Russian Federal State Statistics Service.

3   A sports stadium in Naryan-Mar references Nenets culture in its architectural design.

4   The post office of Naryan-Mar (April 2014).

Union of Reindeer Herders, Naryan-Mar's central cultural landmark is now a four-meter wooden idol of Semilikiy, which was created by Nenets sculptor Nikolai Vylka in accordance with Nenets People's cosmogonies and traditional beliefs. Symbolically, the idol was installed right in front of the building of the NAO Government Administration, i.e., next to the Governor's office windows. Near the idol in the central public location of Naryan-Mar, the Nenets People created a *chum*—a traditional Nenets dwelling.

The wooden idol of Semilikiy in Naryan-Mar is a part of a larger project of Indigenizing Nenets land. Other sacred idols are installed on Central Street in the Indigenous village of Krasnoe, thirty kilometers from Naryan-Mar. Organizers, like Vladislav Vyucheysky, Chairman of the Union of Reindeer Herders of the NAO, leave room for interpreting the meaning of these objects, giving importance to personal narratives: "These are art objects. But each person will see something different in them [...] For me, these are the guardians of the Nenets tundra, the Nenets People, our land, and reindeer."[58]

58   "Ustanovka derevyannoy skul'ptury v Nar'yan-Mare. Nebol'shaya fotoistoriya [Installation of a wooden sculpture in Naryan-Mar. A short photo story]," nao24.ru.

RESULTS II

POLITICAL DOMAIN

Bottom-up Pathways: Indigenous Urban Youth Voices The interview data revealed both advantages and limitations of the prevailing government-driven approach, especially when it comes to legal recognition of Indigenous urbanites and their rights in the city, support of their community-driven initiatives in the forms of grant proposals, or additional procedural hurdles that may become an obstacle for maintaining their cultural practices, pursuing traditional lifestyle, practicing reindeer herding, hunting, fishing.

> One of the possibilities for better addressing community needs is a more effective system of Indigenous Peoples' representation and their participation in government in all spheres and at all levels, with the prospect of creating Indigenous institutions based on the co-management model:[59]

> "Of course, the problem is that few Nenets work in the government."
> *Naryan-Mar, Nenets woman, 27*

In the situation when Indigenous youth needs are not fully addressed, this leads to further alienation from their Indigenous heritage and ancestors' lands, losses of Indigenous knowledge linked to traditional skills and language, and ultimately a widening gap between rural and urban Indigenous communities:

> "I grew up in the village, and I have relatives who are reindeer herders, so I went fishing and hunting all my childhood. My parents taught me. You can say that I was perfectly proficient in this. Now it is difficult because you need to get a hunting permit and a hunting rifle. These days, there is only fishing with friends. But it is happening more and more rarely."
> *Naryan-Mar, Nenets man, 28*

> The reliance on the paternalistic system of grants often creates tensions between government institutions/extractive companies and Indigenous communities when grantees provide funding for the projects that they find important:

> "The real preservation of our culture is possible through connection with the original way of life outside the urban environment. We have prepared a project of field events for young people. But we did not get funding for this project. The project proposed trips to nature in groups of about 30 people with an overnight stay at the base on Sokolinaya Gora and then by boat three to four hours closer to the sea to learn how to pick berries, how to go hunting, fishing. Plus, a trip to the tundra to the community, when someone nearby wanders near the city, necessarily with an overnight stay. It is an opportunity to practice the [Nenets] language. Master classes would include traditional lifestyle practices—how to assemble chum, how to heat a stove, etc."
> *Naryan-Mar, Nenets woman, 33*

> "We applied for a grant from Lukoil, a computer game in Nenets for the new
> generation of Nenets, but the proposal did not get funded."
> *Naryan-Mar, Nenets woman, 33*

CULTURAL DOMAIN

Our study participants pointed out that one of the crucial conditions for maintaining Indigenous urban identities is a developed cultural infrastructure and institutionalized Indigenous language support in Naryan-Mar. Both community- and government-led institutions appear to play a major role in creating such an enabling environment.[60] Thus, policies that strengthen these institutions and practices may yield positive results, particularly if co-designed with and led by the Indigenous Peoples. All research participants recognized the symbolic importance of the Nenets government-driven cultural institutions operating in Naryan-Mar. They also supported the idea of having more Nenets-oriented public events as a sign of the visibility (empowerment) of Nenets culture in the urban landscape:

> "In the city, it is still necessary to support [Nenets] cultural organizations;
> otherwise, everything will be forgotten."
> *Naryan-Mar, Nenets man, 28*

> "The [Nenets] culture in the city is modernized. Real preservation of culture
> is possible through familiarizing with the original way of life, outside the
> urban environment. On the other hand, regarding the city [cultural] clubs
> and studios of the Nenets culture and the Nenets theater: young people have
> started getting involved; through performances, they become familiar with
> the language and customs, and there is a good atmosphere. The same in the
> Ethnocultural Center. It turns out that these places of Nenets culture in the
> city are places of communication and memory."
> *Naryan-Mar, Nenets woman, 33*

The young urban Indigenous participants with a positive Indigenous identity were stressed about significant changes in self-identification they have experienced throughout their lives. They demonstrated a 'self-(re)constructed' positive Indigenous identity, which surfaced later in their lives when they 'rediscovered' their belonging through cultural learning available in the city (such as Indigenous language classes and ethnic studios):

59   See, for instance, Andrey Petrov, Dalee Sambo Dorough, Sweta Tiwari, Mark Welford, Nikolay Golosov, Michele Devlin, Tatiana Degai, Stanislav Ksenofontov, and John DeGroote, "Indigenous health-care sovereignty defines resilience to the COVID-19 pandemic," *The Lancet*, 401, 10387 (2023): 1478–1480.

60   For example, the Ethnocultural Center in Naryan-Mar mentioned below is one of the government-sponsored institutions in Naryan-Mar that serve as official recognition and manifest support of the Indigenous cultures of Nenets and Komi peoples in NAO. For more details, see Marya Rozanova, "Indigenous Urbanization in Russia's Arctic."

> "I am Nenets! And this is a conscious choice I made. In my childhood, in the "village" school, I had a different attitude towards my ethnicity, as special attention was paid to the Slavic culture only, and there was a feeling of unequal treatment. [...] We did not have Nenets classes in our school, and only later, when I started attending various Nenets cultural centers in college [in the city], I started to get into it."
> *Naryan-Mar, Nenets woman, 27*

There is a growing demand for greater visibility about the real lives of Indigenous urbanites, including high-quality feature films. Documentary movies focus on rural nomadic tribes living in tundra, reinforcing a one-sided vision of Indigenous cultures and leading to perpetuating the stereotype about what "authentic Nenets" are:

> "I would like them to start making feature films about the Nenets. So that they have a story, a life story. And now there are only documentaries."
> *Naryan-Mar, Nenets man, 28*

> "Films about Nenets are made, for example, on the TV channel North, but they are not very popular. They need to shoot well..."
> *Naryan-Mar, Nenets man, 21*

There are sometimes divergent views among young people on Nenets cultural heritage, involving a discussion on preserving traditions as static (considering them as authentic, 'real') or allowing traditions to develop with the understanding that they are likely to be influenced by changing surroundings around them:

> "...I rarely go to listen to our Nenets artists. I want something more modern..."
> *Naryan-Mar, Nenets man, 21*

> "...There should also be modern music with the Nenets language and motifs."
> *Naryan-Mar, Nenets man, 28*

> "The [Nenets] culture in the city is modernized. Real preservation of culture is possible through familiarizing with the original way of life, outside the urban environment..."
> *Naryan-Mar, Nenets woman, 33*

Language The ability to speak an Indigenous language is another indicator of resilient urban Indigenous identity. Native languages may be best preserved if they are widely spoken and/or traditional subsistence activities (e.g., reindeer herding, hunting, fishing, gathering) are well maintained.[61] However, some Indigenous young adults started actively partaking in their native language only after relocating to the city. One of the reasons is that the city often provides greater opportunities when it comes to language courses and diverse cultural activities:[62]

> "I speak a little Nenets. We did not have many Nenets lessons in primary
> school [in the village], and back then, it seemed that the Nenets language
> was unnecessary and unimportant. However, I started learning Nenets
> deliberately when the language courses were introduced in the city [of
> Naryan-Mar]. I will proceed to do so when the courses are held again."
> *Naryan-Mar, Nenets woman, 28*

> "It is necessary that the Nenets language courses be on a permanent basis
> and are free, as they are now."
> *Naryan-Mar, Nenets man, 28*

Interview participants also identified issues coming from 'refined' forms of
their native language. As some pointed out, the literary, or standard, Nenets
language that Western linguists developed in cooperation with Indigenous
folklorists and writers deviated significantly from local dialects used in
everyday life in different rural settings:[63]

> "There is a big difference between the literary and spoken Nenets languages.
> Original Nenets language mainly used simple formulations. While at school
> and in language courses, they teach a rather literary language, which is more
> difficult to learn and is little spoken on an everyday basis. For communication
> in everyday life, we need a more tundra-type conversational Nenets."
> *Naryan-Mar, Nenets woman, 33*

ECONOMIC DOMAIN

While there is no official data available on Indigenous-owned and -led businesses, the workforce integration of Indigenous urbanites in Naryan-Mar, or

61   A. A. Petrov and S. L. Chernyshova, "Cultural Heritage of the Indigenous Arctic Peoples of the Sakha
Republic (Yakutia)," *IOP Conference Series: Earth and Environmental Science* 302, no. 1 (2019): 12035–.

62   This Nenets Language School was initiated in 2018 by the local Nenets Indigenous Association 'Yasavey'
with the financial support of the NAO government in the form of grants to nonprofit organizations.

63   Nenets writing only appeared in the 1930s as a result of the joint efforts of Nenets scholars and
Western linguists of the Institute of the Peoples of the North in Leningrad (now St. Petersburg). Among
those who stood at the origins of Nenets literature were Nenets poet Nikolai Vylka and Nenets folklorist
Anton Pyrerka. They contributed to establishing Nenets literature and the first textbooks for Nenets
schoolchildren (for more, see O.I. Vorobyova, "Sozdatel' Bukvarya I Nenetskoy Pis'mennosti Pervyy
Nenetskiy Lingvist-Perevodchik Anton Petrovich Pyrerka" [The Creator of Orthography and Nenets
Writing First Nenets Linguist-Translator Anton Petrovich Pyrerka], *Vestnik Severnogo (Arkticheskogo)
Federal'nogo Universiteta* 2 (2014): 56–60). A literary—or modern standard—Nenets language
(Nenets-Yurak) is based on the Bolshezemelskaya tundra dialect. In the process of the codification of
Indigenous language, linguists had to overcome the challenge of the existing regional and local dialects
(nowadays, linguistic differences between local Nenets dialects are considerable, as seen in Johanna
Laakso, "Contact and the Finno-Ugric Languages," in *The Handbook of Language Contact*, edited by
Raymond Hickey, John Wiley & Sons Ltd, 2020), as well as making the Nenets language suitable for
describing various political, economic, social, and cultural developments of the modern world. The process
of the Nenets language codification was particularly damaging to the Forest Nenets by excluding and
marginalizing these small communities, putting them at a distinct disadvantage. For more, see Eva
Toulouze, "The Forest Nenets as a Double Language Minority," *Pro Ethnologia* (2003): 95–108.

income gaps between Indigenous and non-Indigenous populations, interviews indicated existing and ongoing issues with integration at the city labor market and the necessity of having Indigenous-oriented businesses:

> "Nenets People work in Naryan-Mar, wherever they take them. Some
> [Nenets] People cannot find jobs and find themselves in a new environment."
> *Naryan-Mar, Nenets woman, 33*

> "A venison processing plant is a great thing."
> *Naryan-Mar, Nenets man, 28*

All of our interview participants emphasized the importance of participating in an urban mixed economy. They found that opportunities to practice subsistence activities in the tundra are not only crucial to maintaining their ethnic identity but also a source of traditional food:

> "We try to have more fish in our diet, and it is preferable that we catch
> ourselves. Every year, we try to go fishing, especially for smelt, and we also
> collect goose and partridge eggs and pick cloudberries."
> *Naryan-Mar, Nenets woman, 33*

> "We pick the berries ourselves every year, then freeze them, make jam."
> *Naryan-Mar, Nenets woman, 27*

However, in the Arctic, many urban Indigenous residents live hundreds of miles away from their ancestral lands and do not have the physical and financial means to visit their native lands regularly:

> "I rarely pay a visit these days; I have not been there [in my village] in the last
> year. Only a one-way ticket costs 6,200 rubles [US $85]. We have our own hut in
> the tundra on Kolguev Island, where we used to go for two weeks in the summer
> with our relatives. And at this time, almost all the relatives live in Naryan-Mar,
> and on the whole, young people are leaving [the village] due to lack of jobs."
> *Naryan-Mar, Nenets woman, 33*

BUILT ENVIRONMENT DOMAIN

There is a growing understanding among Nenets youth of the importance of Indigenous-led built infrastructure in the city:

> "We need our own places in this city. Our idea is to create here a center for Nenets'
> youth. It can be based on the Native American model and designed as a single
> base with different workshops, crafts materials, language courses, movies,
> brochures, and teaching materials, and a place to have dinners with elders."
> *Naryan-Mar, Nenets woman, 27*

> "A Nenets Warm House for those who come to Naryan-Mar from the rural areas
> [...] the visitors can sit and relax after a long journey and have some hot tea [...]
> Often, those who come from the tundra to the city on business don't even have
> anywhere to stay [...] It will be a place for communication and watching films,

> and it can also provide advisory services on legal issues. It will also be
> a meeting place with elders to learn from them and practice the language.
> They speak the [Nenets] language, and the youth are already losing it."
> *Naryan-Mar, Nenets woman, 27*

Despite a general appreciation of Nenets symbolism in architectural structures, there are concerns about cultural appropriateness practices and no legal requirements of consent for the use of Indigenous symbols:

> "Architecture in the Nenets style is very cool. It would be better to have more
> buildings like this in the city [...] Yet, it also depends here [...] the Timan
> Restaurant is not part of our [Nenets] culture at all."
> *Naryan-Mar, Nenets man, 28*

LEGAL (LAND-RELATED) DOMAIN

All of our study participants emphasized the importance of connection to their ancestral lands presented through access to nature and nature-based traditional subsistence activities, such as reindeer herding, hunting, fishing, and gathering, as well as retaining strong ties to relatives living in rural communities and access to traditional food:

> "We need camps for children and youth in the tundra—immersion in the
> atmosphere of reindeer herders' life."
> *Naryan-Mar, Nenets woman, 21*

> "At present, it is getting more problematic to eat our traditional food
> regularly. Venison is very expensive in our stores, and I cannot afford it.
> That is when my relatives had their own reindeer herd on Kolguev Island;[64]
> they always used to send us venison."
> *Naryan-Mar, Nenets woman, 33*

In addition, a sedentary urban lifestyle is viewed by many older Nenets as less desirable, and some Nenets parents see it as important for their children to be in the tundra on a regular basis pursuing a (semi-) nomadic lifestyle:

> "Every summer, I go to the chum in the Bolshezemelskaya tundra for about
> ten days, where relatives have reindeer herding. And my parents also go to
> the chum and help with the reindeer. There, I also go fishing, picking berries
> [...] It happens to get out there only once a year. My parents want to send me
> to work in the tundra. And for me, ten days a year in the tundra is enough,
> and most preferably, not in winter."
> *Naryan-Mar, Nenets man, 21*

64   In 2014, Kolguev Island, located in the southeastern Barents Sea, witnessed one of the greatest tragedies in reindeer herding. Weather extremes with ice rains combined with oil-influenced grazing land grabs, the abandonment of traditional livestock husbandry practices, and over-exploited pasture lands led to mass reindeer death: within a three-year period culminating in 2014, reindeer livestock dropped from approximately 12,000 to less than 100 (some data varies). For more, see Alexey O. Pristupa et al., "Reindeer Herders without Reindeer."

Notably, a rural-urban food-sharing tradition persists, strengthening the links of urban communities to ancestral lands:

> "Relatives bring us meat from the tundra. It is important [to keep this tradition]. In our childhood, we did not get sick as we consumed our traditional food."
> *Naryan-Mar, Nenets woman, 27*

DISCUSSION AND CONCLUSIONS

Indigenous urbanization actualized and politicized a discussion on Indigenous "(in)authenticity"[65] and new types of Indigenous urban identities. While the colonial understanding of Indigeneity is limited to concepts of remoteness and wilderness and stagnant cultures reproducing customs and traditions,[66] the reality is much more complex. Jacobs pointed out that Indigenous identities are in constant transition as they attempt to reconcile dominant and Indigenous cultures, and this process greatly intensifies in diverse urban environments.[67]

> Our research in Naryan-Mar reveals that urban Indigenous identities are complex, hybrid, multifaceted, fractured, resilient, and thriving. Based on the interviews, we identified different types of Indigenous urban identities.[68] Among them are *positive* (an identity when a person feels joy, pride, confidence, kinship, and belonging to a particular ethnic group), *hybrid* (an identity when the global interacts with the local to create a new identity), *negative* (an identity when a person feels anxiety, uncertainty, discomfort with his/her own ethnic group and identity),[69] as well as an emerging *non-ethnic territorial identity* (an identity restricted to a specific place).[70] The study also identified key factors that support the resilience of an Indigenous identity of Nenets urban youth: connection to land and participation in a mixed economy, spiritual ties, and Nenets language use. Our research indicated that Indigenous experiences in cities can be less problematic if there are conditions and capacities to maintain stronger ties to rural communities, culture, and tradition while fully participating in an urban society.[71] Under such circumstances, Indigenous identities remain resilient, flexible, and complex.

Today, top-down (government-driven) and bottom-up (Indigenous community-led) urban Indigenization pathways co-exist in Arctic cities, and they encompass multiple domains, including personal, political, economic, cultural, legal (land-related), and the built environment. In Naryan-Mar, top-down Indigenization stems from historical Soviet legacies and the political interests of the current settler elites. While creating opportunities for visibility and representation of Indigeneity in the city, the top-down model alone cannot attain urban Indigenization. To be successful, it must coincide and develop synergies with bottom-up processes of Indigenous resurgence that enable Indigenous Peoples to exercise control in the urban environment and create their own spaces in the city. This can be achieved through the recognition of urban Indigenous Peoples as equal partners in city planning and development, capacity building among Indigenous organizations, and acknowledgment of both the historical trauma and Indigenous rights inherent to urban Indigenous communities.

It is evident that having these components in place may create settings in which Indigenous identities are able to be more resilient. Staying connected to rural communities and nature, keeping strong ties of kinship, and being regularly involved in traditional land- and water-based activities (hunting, gathering, fishing, reindeer herding, etc.) are some of the leading conditions of thriving urban Indigeneity. These are complemented by the consumption and sharing of traditional food and the ability to learn and use the Indigenous language.

Acknowledgments

We would like to express our deep gratitude to all interview participants in Naryan-Mar, who shared their perspectives on living in a city, visions of their Nenets culture, hopes, and concerns. Our deep appreciation goes to the editors of this volume, *Arctic Practices: Design for a Changing World*, Bert De Jonghe and Elise Misao Hunchuck, for their valuable comments. This research was supported by the US National Science Foundation (award number PLR 2127364 and PLR 2127366).

65   J. Coyle, "Where Are All the Koori Football Players? The AFL and the Invisible Presence of Indigenous Victorians," *Sport in Society* 18, no. 5 (2015): 604–13; and N. Lucero, "Being Indian in the City: Generational Differences in Negotiation of Native Identity among Urban Based American Indians," in *Indigenous in the City: Contemporary Identities and Cultural Innovation*, ed. C. Andersen and E. Peters (UBC Press, 2013).

66   D. Howard-Wagner, *Indigenous Invisibility in the City*, 14.

67   Curran Katsi'Sorókwas Jacobs, "Two-Row Wampum Reimagined: Understanding the Hybrid Digital Lives of Contemporary Kanien'kehá:ka Youth," *Studies in Social Justice* 13, no. 1 (2019): 59–72.

68   Marya Rozanova-Smith, Stanislav Ksenofontov and Andrey N. Petrov, "Indigenous Urbanization."

69   Valeriy Efimov, Alla Lapteva, and Ul'yana Borisova, "Problemy Vosproizvodstva Etnicheskoy Prinadlezhnosti Naroda Sakha (po Materialam Etno-sotsiologicheskikh Issledovaniy v Respublike Sakha-Yakutiya)" [Problems of Ethnic Belonging Reproduction of the Sakha People (Based on the Materials of Ethnosociological Research in the Sakha Republic (Yakutia))], *Problemy istorii, filologii, kul'tury* 2, no. 44 (2014): 333–49; Keri E. Iyall Smith and Patricia Leavy, *Hybrid Identities: Theoretical and Empirical Examinations* (Brill, 2008).

70   Anssi Paasi, "Territorial Identities as Social Constructs," *Hagar – International Social Science Review* 1, no. 2 (2000): 91–113; Alla Anisimova and Olga Echevskaya, "Siberian Regional Identity: Self-perception, Solidarity, or Political Claim?" in *Russia's Regional Identities*, eds. Edith W. Clowes, Gisela Erbslöh, and Ani Kokobobo (Routledge, 2018), 189–205.

71   Marya Rozanova-Smith, Stanislav Ksenofontov and Andrey N. Petrov, "Indigenous Urbanization."

Nan Niwhazheh ti'goonch'uu. The land is our home.
Arlyn Charlie

2023, Nij̀in ok nizii chihvyàh eenjit gwiinzii.
    Where there's an eddy, it's good for the net.

People travel from Teetł'it Zheh or the camps nearby to Nataiinlaii (8-Miles), where the nets are set. Oftentimes, people work together to fish during the fall freeze-up. In the winter, fishing nets are left submerged for hours at a time, only checked once or twice a day by being pulled to the surface. The trapped fish are removed, and the net is placed back under the water.

During the month of July, people begin moving to their camps along the Teetł'it Gwinjik (Peel River) to set their fishing nets to catch the Whitefish moving upriver. Today, the constant rise in temperature makes it a challenge to work with fish during the summer. People have to check their nets more frequently—every couple of hours—as the warmer waters cause the fish to drown more quickly.

People build smokehouses within their camps so that they have a place to smoke fish in the summer. While most of the fish is cut and processed into uutsik (dryfish), the remaining parts are often cooked over k'ill (dry willow) or driftwood so that nothing is wasted.

2020, Sreendit hee dinjii kat digakaii'k'it gwits'at nagadija.
In the spring, people travel back to their camps.

Today, some people still live off of or depend on the land, and cabins are built throughout the region by people with either logs or sourced lumber. Though not as prominent today, people used to travel to their camps before the spring break on the Teetł'it Gwinjik to spend a few weeks trapping muskrats and beavers.

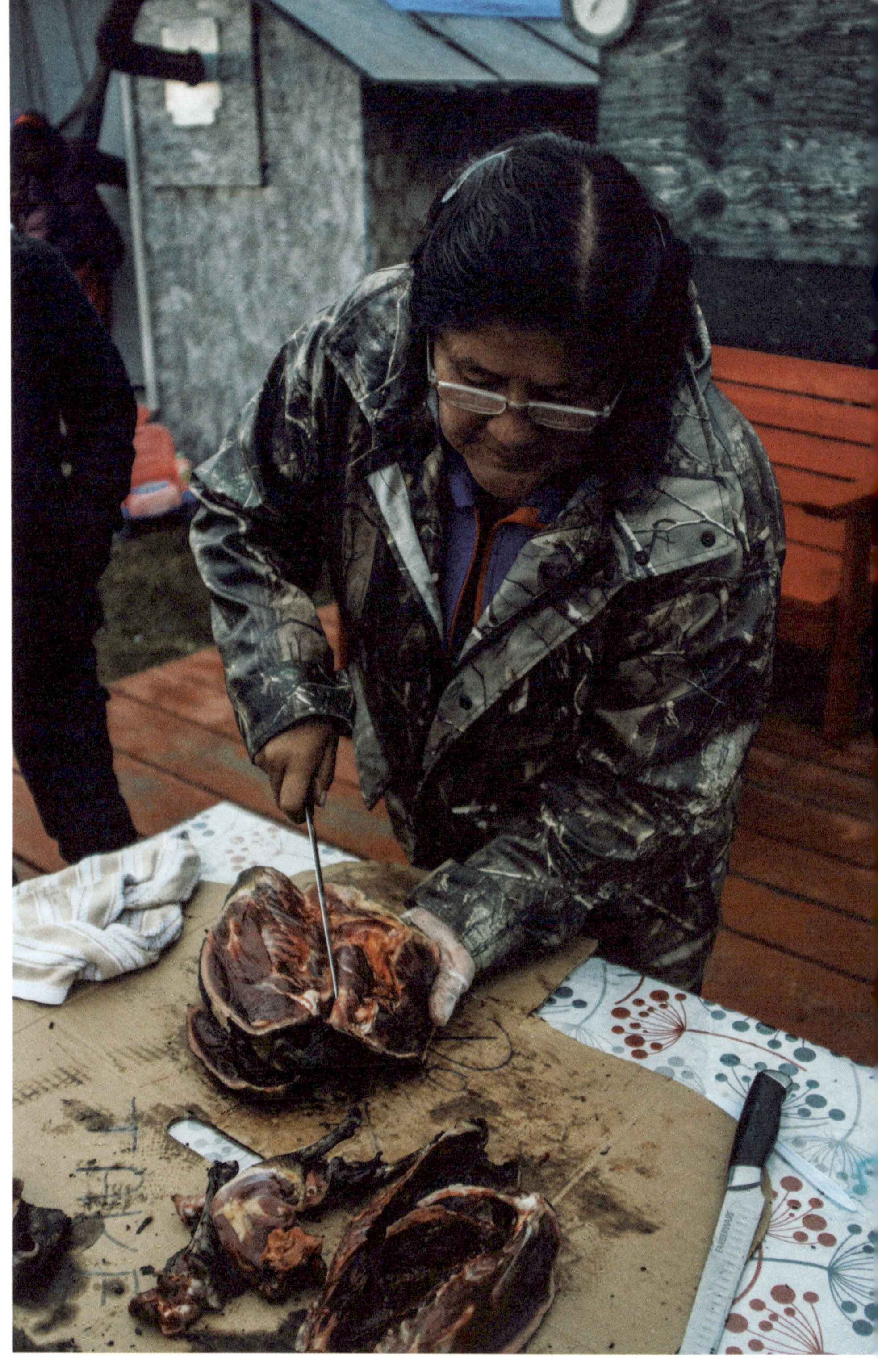

2019, Shootr'ih dats'an khadint'ii.
My Auntie is cutting a duck.

Migratory birds like ducks and geese such as the Njaa (White-winged scoter), Neet'aii (Mallard), or Kheh (Canada Goose), are often hunted in the spring as they travel back north. Before the spring break up of the river ice, people often travel along the river, out to areas of open water or on the lakes throughout the land to hunt the birds where they themselves congregate to eat and to hunt.

2019, Gwich'in shin hee uutsik gahtsii.
The Gwich'in people use the summer season to make dryfish.

Fish camps often have a designated area where people cut fish within the camp; grass is collected to cover the tables to ensure that the area is kept clean. The fish caught are often cleaned and cut with precision into dryfish where the fish is flayed and cut into narrow lines, which help in the drying process, ensuring that it doesn't spoil. Afterward it is placed under constant smoke for a few days. The end product is known as uutsik (dryfish).

2021, October nat tan t'eh chihvyah chitr'ahchuh.
In October, they set nets under the ice.

In the past, the river freeze up often occurred in mid-October; however freeze-up is sometimes remembered to occur at the end of September. Today the freeze up is occurring later due to climate change. After the river freezes over in November, people begin to set their nets under the ice as the Whitefish move downriver.

Though the fishing season has already begun in October and the fish have begun to move, people often have to wait for the river to freeze over. The fall river freeze-up tends to be unpredictable. Fishing nets are often held by wooden poles that are lodged in the ice, from where they are later pulled up to the surface to remove any caught fish.

2020, Shin hee nakal trinatsii gwiinzii.
In the summer, it's good to pick nakal (cloudberry).

Later in the summer, after the rain comes in, various kinds of berries can be found growing on the land. People like my Auntie, pictured here, often travel outside of Teetł'it Zheh (Fort McPherson) along the Dempster Highway. They park their vehicles along the road before walking to nearby patches of berries. People tend to spend weeks collecting and securing enough berries to last them through the winter.

2023, Khaiints'àn hee natł'at tri'natsii gwiinzii.
In the fall, it is good to pick cranberries.

Previous page: Come September, the fall weather begins to set in, and the temperature begins to drop slowly. Around this time—often towards the middle or close to the end of the month—the cranberries are ripe enough to be picked. September is when people spend their time collecting the berries.

Next page: Taken along the Dempster highway, roughly 30 kilometers (18.6 miles) outside of Teetł'it Zheh, people still utilize the far reaches of the land to a great extent. The Gwich'in people have a close and what is often considered a spiritual relationship to the land. Their traditional knowledge spans countless generations; thus, they have survived here for thousands of years.

Konstantin Ikonomidis is an architect whose work blends art, architecture, and scientific research, with a focus on extreme climates and cultural values.

Qaammat Pavilion
Konstantin Ikonomidis

Winter was approaching, and the days were growing colder and darker. Daylight faded into twilight earlier with each passing day. I went to the Qajaq club, where I spent my evenings learning how to build a qajaq (a Greenland-style kayak). To get to the community workshop from my home, I had to traverse a steep pass that separated the two neighborhoods of Nuuk's dramatic landscape. Guided by the faint glow of my headlamp, I could see where to place each foot as I walked up the rocky hill. Suddenly, the sky erupted in a mesmerizing display of the aurora borealis, its vibrant hues of green painting the darkness above. Amidst the chill and shadows, nature's light show brought awe and wonder to the wintry landscape. As I reached the top of the pass, I gazed down upon Nuuk's colorful houses in the historical area, a sight to behold even in the dim light. The community workshop was held on Nuuk's waterfront kolonihaven (a historic neighborhood at the harbor in central Nuuk) in a tiny yellow timber house, large enough to construct two kayaks at the time.

A traditional qajaq is tailored to the measurements of each individual and is constructed with timber, traditionally driftwood, and tightly stretched canvas or sealskin kept together with a sophisticated binding process. It makes the kayaks lighter, more portable (easier to carry), and requires less material. Tuiliks (waterproof jackets made of specially prepared sealskin), paddles, and finely carved harpoons of wood and bones, all associated with Qajaq culture, were lying around the cozy workshop. These functional tools were works of art themselves and reminded me of something Pia Arke wrote in her essay *Etnoæstetik (Ethno-aesthetics)*:

> Bodil Kaalund argues that art, far from being absent, is ubiquitous, that it is an integral part of every Eskimo product. The Eskimo, by constitution, is an artist, which is to say that in the Eskimo view of the world nothing and everything is art. A good harpoon is a beautiful harpoon.[1]

Just like the Greenlandic qajaq, which is very specific to its culture (not only is it an Inuit-style qajaq but can also be identified as a Greenlandic-style qajaq), perhaps the Greenlandic building culture could have evolved similarly,[2] as a piece of art with characteristics specific to its function and its culture, location, and environment.

SARFANNGUIT

On board one of Air Greenland's first flights to operate after the fleetwide grounding due to the COVID-19 pandemic, I flew to Sisimiut, this time to meet with the UNESCO Site Manager, Paninguaq Fleisher-Lyberth, who invited me to a first site visit to see Sarfannguit and to get started with the assignment of a monumental pavilion, a landmark for the newly announced UNESCO heritage site. Her and the UNESCO team's objective was to highlight and generate greater awareness for the recently announced UNESCO site and provide an architectural implementation with advantages for the residents and the tourism industry. They chose Sarfannguit, the only actively active site within the UNESCO area and one of the six key sites. Sarfannguit is located just north of the polar circle and southeast of Sisimiut. It is accessible by boat during the summer season and by snowmobile and helicopter during the winter. It's also accessible via a few days of walking and situated along a lesser-traveled section of the renowned Arctic Circle Trail that extends from the Sisimiut coast to the beginning of the inland ice in Kangerslusuaq.

I arrived at a deserted Copenhagen airport. On the several-hour flight, I watched *SUMÈ, The Sound of Revolution*, a documentary about the 1970's pioneering rock bands in Greenland. The charismatic front vocalist Malik Høegh and his band performed in the face of a glacier and the natural landscape of Greenland, singing about the country's identity and cultural independence. The first stop of the daily Boeing airplane was at Kangerslusuaq, Greenland's airport hub, and connected the smaller planes traveling between Greenlandic towns and settlements. After a few hours, I boarded a propeller aircraft carrying about fifty passengers en route to Sisimiut.

---

1   Pia Arke, *Etnoæstetik*. (ARK, 1995).

2   If the Danes hadn't introduced the Greenlandic Typehuse (a pre-fabricated house in Greenland) in the 1940s, would stone have been the most obvious material to construct? What would the Greenlandic architectural identity look like then? Today?

1   Snow and Ice road to Sarfannguit.

Flying at a lower altitude presented an unparalleled opportunity to witness the dramatic and natural environment where glaciers could be spotted from time to time. After a brief flight, we touched down at Sisimiut's airport, where Paninguaq whisked me away on a tour of the charming town. We explored the picturesque areas of Sisimiut before arriving at the Sisimiut Museum, where we enjoyed a cup of coffee with the museum director, Marie Bønløkke, who hosted me at the museum for the project's duration. Throughout the survey and construction phase, I embarked on a captivating tour of my temporary home. As we wandered through its two floors adorned with public exhibitions showcasing local artifacts, I marveled at the wealth of history; on the third floor was a guest room, hidden from public visitors; a kitchen was on the second floor. The room had spectacular views of the well-trodden 544-meter-tall Palasip Qaqqaa (Præstefjeldet, or Priest Mountain) and the bustling harbor below. I met Paninguaq at the harbor the following morning, ready for our adventure. Joining us on the boat was filmmaker Aannguaq Reimer-Johansen, bound for Sarfannguit to capture a series of interviews and stories from the settlement's residents. During the journey, Paninguaq pointed out the boundary of the UNESCO Heritage Site and the location of Nipisat, a significant archaeological site under excavation. After an hour of sailing, we arrived at Sarfannguit and were greeted by a colorful array of houses at the end of the fjord.

SITE AND INTERVIEW

During the survey's early stages of constructing the landmark (Qaammat), I engaged in numerous conversations with the village chairman, Aron Olsen, who shared stories and Greenlandic legends that strongly relate to the Greenlandic bond with nature. Based on this, I attempted to construct an atmosphere in a fictitious geometry that might convey the sensation of mystery as I heard his tales. Aron grew up in Sarfannguit and knew the area like the back of his hand. He proposed several locations, each presented to and discussed with the community, municipality members, and archaeologists. The first proposed option was atop the hill, with a spectacular view overlooking the two fjords at Sarfannguit's eastern tip. While hiking up to the highest point of Sarfannguit to explore pavilion site options, filmmaker Aannguaq, who made short films about Sarfannguit and conducted interviews with the community, pointed out the abandoned village of Saqqarliit on the horizon. He emphasized the value he believed it would have for the villagers to connect the two communities by positioning the pavilion to face Saqqarliit, especially considering that some families relocated to Sarfannguit when Saqqarliit was abandoned in the 1960s.

> Full of impressions and information, I packed my twelve-kilogram backpack as lightly as I could and prepared for the six-day walk from Sisimiut to the airport at Kangerslusuaq to reflect on the ideas and feel the natural scenery while walking across landscapes that changed from day to day.

DESIGN AND PREPARATION

It was essential to design a structure closely connected to the heritage and cultural values to minimize its impact on the topography while having a significant visual appearance in its location and serving as a landmark. It requires careful planning and involvement with the community, which is familiar with the conditions, possibilities, and limitations. The design process had to be adopted, and the following conditions had to be considered: Location inside the Arctic Circle, winter temperatures far below zero and frequent blizzard conditions. Topography with dramatic rocky terrain. The selected site required building materials to be transported by boat, ATW bike, and hand. Among the practical design criteria are developing a structure that could be easily packaged on pallets for shipment by ferry to Greenland and carried by one person. The narrow window of favorable weather during the summer months permits construction. Create a team of people who can assist during the construction phase.

> Glass is a highly versatile material with a rich historical lineage, tracing its origins to four millennia in the past. The choice to work with glass was a natural one due to its properties: it blends well into its environment thanks to its ever-changing reflections, transparency, and seasonal variations in appearance; it can be camouflaged

in nature, and it can give the appearance of clear ice. How the glass meets rock also plays an important role. As a material, glass also adds a sense of vulnerability to these lands surrounded by mountains. There are endless ways of utilizing glass from small pearls on an architectural scale; in this process, I was looking to find a kind of transparency so the surrounding area could be seen through the pavilion with a texture that let the glass reflect a variation of colors. After receiving a series of samples, one stood out: solid casted glass blocks, handcrafted by the Murano-based glass manufacturer WonderGlass using traditional methods: each block was cast in a metal mold that imparted a textured surface that created variability in the reflections of the surroundings.

The inussuk (like a cairn, a structure made of stones piled on each other) started to play an important role in the concept and representation of the pavilion. One of the significant features of UNESCO's Aasivissuit-Nipisat World Heritage Site is its inussuk, the extraordinary Greenlandic cairn systems, monuments manufactured in open environments. These were historically made to navigate people, indicate locations, and be used as a hunting tool to direct reindeer into a trap. The specific location played an important role; an inussuk needs to be strategically placed to meet its function and to be visible; in a way, this also works very well for a landmark.

I begin to compose a variety of circular geometries, envisioning the play of light and texture that solid cast-glass blocks could create within their surroundings, and memories of my early morning strolls across the rocky pass from my home in Nuuk flood back to me. I recalled those crisp winter mornings when the moonlight danced upon the thick blanket of snow, transforming the landscape into a mesmerizing spectacle. In those moments, especially when the moon was full, the combined radiance of the moonlight and the glistening snow rendered my trusty headlamp unnecessary. Instead, I found myself enveloped in a serene glow, navigating the darkness with ease. It was a reminder of the subtle yet profound ways in which light and environment intertwine, shaping our perception and experience of the world around us. It was then that the name *Qaammat*—meaning moon in Greenlandic—came to mind. It is a fitting tribute to the enchanting light that inspired the landmark's design.

The first-hand and digital sketches showed a circular bottom geometry tapering toward the top. With a space between each block that allows the wind to pass through, the design calls for the holes to get progressively smaller as the structure rises, culminating in a linear top. The digital model was based on mathematical equations. I created a physical timber model in 1:5 to get a feel for how each block was placed by "eye-and-glue" without any template that would guide each position of each block. From my experience constructing in rural areas of East and West Africa and developing typical architectural work in other remote areas of Greenland, I learned how important it is to keep it as simple as possible and use building methods familiar within the community. This gained experience had to be implemented in an early design phase, as well as considering smooth shipping options and minimizing construction time. I decided to use anchor post solutions (a drilled hole in the terrain and a rock anchor); that's how most typical homes are constructed in settlements. This method would also create a visually pleasing appearance for the glass blocks elevated from the ground. It was also important to design and pre-manufacturer elements; the horizontal metal bar was manufactured in smaller units with "puzzle" edges so the geometry could be guaranteed and easily assembled and welded together on-site in a shorter period due to the limited time window. Working with a block system was an obvious choice, as it offered a multitude of benefits. Not only was it easy to pack, transport, and carry, but it also allowed for the construction of larger objects from smaller units with remarkable efficiency. A modular approach would streamline the process, providing the practicality and flexibility to bring this vision to life.

CONSTRUCTION

The brick-laying procedure for the glass blocks is conventional mason work; however, I was unfamiliar with the adhesive that would bond between solid cast glass blocks and blocks to stainless steel. I had to understand the nature of glass, go in-depth with the material, experiment, and prototype to learn how to construct solid cast glass blocks in an Arctic environment. In this instance, the objective was to materialize a conceptual idea into reality: it's essential for each new undertaking to implement innovative construction techniques to go beyond the conventional. These are opportunities to set examples and to test and demonstrate alternative construction techniques that might inspire or encourage future creative construction practices in the Arctic region. I received a grant from the Dreyer's Foundation to learn more about the material and conduct experiments and prototyping. I was interested in trying out a variety of adhesives to find one that would be suitable for the Arctic climate, user-friendly, and have an appealing aesthetic. Being thoroughly prepared while working on a contract in such a remote location is essential. I had to do my best to foresee any possible obstacles from the limited resources available in this place. Constructing a 1:1 mock-up of a section of the design would enhance my familiarity with adhesive application, tool utilization, technique implementation, and process anticipation. I contacted a team of glass researchers from Delft University of Technology's glass department, Faidra, and Telesilla, who are known for their expertise with glass as a construction material and who advised and contributed with their knowledge about glass as a building material. A test-shearing machine was utilized at the Delft University of Technology's glass laboratory to evaluate a series of adhesives. This apparatus involved the bonding of two glass blocks with an adhesive. One part of the machine holds a block while the other presses the blocks apart. In this situation, we could determine the strength of each adhesive. Based on these results, two adhesives were selected and employed to create a mock-up of the pavilion in a simulated environment.

The summer months were approaching, and it was time to take advantage of the favorable weather conditions for construction. With the knowledge gained from the experiments, I traveled back to Sisimiut to get started with construction. I met a construction team the morning after. Qeqetta Kommunia's (Qeqetta municipality) building department supported the construction and installation of the stainless steel foundation and rock anchors since they were familiar with drilling in that terrain. A custom-made rock anchor was manufactured at the local metal shop in Sisimiut to connect the pre-manufactured stainless-steel bar that had recently arrived. Jakob Olsen from the municipality maintenance department looked through the workshop supplies and prepared boxes of tools that would be needed. As we disembarked at the Sarfannguit harbor, the current village chairman stood next to the five pallets of solid cast glass blocks that had also recently arrived. Since my last visit, the site of the proposed landmark had been reconsidered for practical reasons; instead of constructing it on top of the hill, a new location was at the village's end, where the two fjords met, on a cliffside.

2—3   The Qaammat under construction.

Upon visual inspection of the two sites, I noticed a significant difference in scale. The formation of the rock played a crucial role in the creation of the *Qaammat*. In the selected site area, I searched for a prominent rock formation, specifically identifying the locations where each rock anchor might be drilled. The selected rock formation was significantly smaller than the pavilion's diameters, and there was a variation in elevation on the landscape. Reducing the size and increasing the prominence of the pavilion would create the illusion of a larger structure. It would have more likely disappeared into the landscape if it had been built atop the hill. The new location was also closer to the water; the texture of the water would also add scale to the pavilion and create a relationship between the object and the fjord, blending into the surrounding scenery. The dark blue water would, at some angles, make the piece stand out. Another practical feature of the pavilion was its visibility as a landmark for ice and water traffic. It would function as a contemporary inussuk, indicating the position of Sarafannguit.

The municipal team in Sarfannguit arranged for assistance in transporting the heavy tools from the harbor through the rocky terrain at the settlement's edge. Five pallets of glass blocks required the efforts of seven people over a full day. The blocks were driven by ATVs for most of the way but had to be carried by hand for the last stretch, where the wheels could not traverse. Each box contained four blocks, four kilograms per block. One of the five women who helped carry the blocks was Kloe Andressen, who grew up in Sarfannguit. Kloe was very familiar with the area of Sarfannguit and the community; she was excited that this construction was beginning. She had seen drawings and visualizations of it earlier that the municipality had shared with the community. Kloe pointed out a carefully arranged pile of stones next to the site as we carried the blocks. Looking carefully, we could see it was a pre-Christian grave where bones could be seen between the stones. The grave was camouflaged and difficult to spot if one did not know to look for it.

4—5   Community glass workshop in Sarfannguit (2021).

Although it was summer, occasional, unexpected gusts of severe winds occurred. Constructing a custom-made tent to cover the Qaammat during the construction phase was crucial: to protect the construction from the weather, we had to protect the adhesive from dust, install a petroleum heater, and keep the Greenlandic summer mosquitoes out. In anticipation of challenging periods, each step needed to be executed seamlessly to avoid errors once the adhesive had bonded. The tent became like a pop-up studio, with shelves for storing the unique glass blocks and a working table with a smooth cloth to protect the glass from surficial scratches. The blocks were sorted based on their thickness. Since they were cast in metal molds, this meant that five of the surfaces of the

6   Qaammat, Sarfannguit.

glass blocks were completely flat, while the top surface held a gradual change in dimensions. The dimensions of each side of every block were individually measured using a digital caliper before being organized and placed on the shelf.

We formed a two-person team, one applying the adhesive while the other laid the glass blocks. Kloe of Sarfannguit assisted in the construction from the first to the last block. The glass researchers also visited throughout a five-day workshop, and friends from the community also came to help. I prepared CNC templates cut according to the digital model; these guided us as we placed each block in the same place as the digital model. After a few rows, I built up the pavilion without the templates to give it a more human touch. Even though the blocks would have a slightly different angle, the light would be reflected differently, which I presumed would have a positive effect. The large physical model we made earlier—the timber model—gave me the confidence to "eye-and-glue" without the templates; I felt like I could feel the geometry. Even though designs are usually communicated as a drawing, we used it as a guideline in this case, leaving space for improvisation and improvement. For the pavilion's final (top) rows, I wanted to balance the structure and the terrain. Should it be a flat line? A curve that follows the terrain? Or should the top edges rise towards the ocean? I set a few blocks in place without adhesive, stepped back, and mocked up a few variations until I was satisfied. Some things can't be simulated on a digital model and can only be done on-site.

Every project is an ongoing process where one can find new ideas. During the development of the Qaammat, I was intrigued by the potential to explore different visual characteristics, artistic qualities, and levels of translucency using printed glass. This technology has its limitations: the experimental glass 3D-printed model[3] was not intended to replicate the block system employed in the construction of the Qaammat, but to explore different aesthetics characterized by layers, patterns, and a surface amenable to 3D printing.

> In addition to the pavilion building, the organized glass workshop was held: "One person, one block." Each participant was given one block. Residents of all ages attended, and about one-third of the town's one hundred inhabitants participated. We made a "cairn" using the same construction technique as in the Qaammat to pass on the knowledge gained from the construction to the community. The word had spread in the greater Sisimiut area that a glass pavilion was under construction in Sarfannguit, and an increased number of visitors had already started to come to the construction site. For the glass workshop, the community constructed the cairn on the hilltop to indicate the way to the Qaammat pavilion for the visitors. The position of the small cairn was strategically placed; it can be seen from a distance, and then, as one approaches the cairn, the top of the Qaammat becomes visible.

OPENING

As winter's chill settled in, delicate snowflakes drifted from the sky, signaling the season's arrival. The transparent tent that had shrouded the pavilion during its construction was finally lifted, revealing a form that could now be seen from a distance. I walked further up the hill to take in the pavilion from a distance. In the Arctic's remote landscape, I discovered a profound appreciation for the block system's simplicity and the enduring strength of glass as a building material. Each architect's creative journey is deeply personal and influenced by diverse methodologies and project approaches. While the ultimate goal is the creation of tangible structures, it's the winding path we follow that holds the truest value.

> Amidst the challenges of the extreme conditions, community-based knowledge emerged as an invaluable resource, guiding each of us through unfamiliar terrain. As friendships developed, each connection became a testament to the shared experiences and collaborative spirit that defined our journey to the Qaammat.

---

3   A small 1:20 model was fabricated to test the technology and showcase Qaammat at Venice Glass Week.

Jessica MacMillan is an artist and amateur astronomer based in Oslo, Norway.

Time Line
Jessica MacMillan

There is a place in the night sky, between the constellations of Lyra and Hercules, where you can look to see where our planet is heading. Called the solar apex, this location marks the direction in which our solar system is traveling within the galaxy. *Time Line* was an outdoor installation of a single 10-watt green laser that pointed to and followed this coordinate in the sky. As the planet rotated and the stars moved overhead, a motorized telescope mount turned the laser to track this point. The line appeared to extend infinitely, reaching all the way to some future destination. With a solid line of light, *Time Line* projects the path our planet is taking.

> Longyearbyen was chosen as the site for this work because Svalbard and the Arctic, as a region, are experiencing the effects of climate change faster than the rest of the planet. Abnormal weather conditions are already changing the physical landscape. Excessive rain destabilizes the earth, creating landslides. Permafrost is thawing. Glaciers are melting. Winter sea ice no longer reliably fills the fjords. Unusually extreme winter storms create avalanches, taking lives and buildings. For those dependent on Svalbard, there is an urgency to consider the future when making decisions today. The future hangs heavy.

On the nights of November 30 and December 5, 2021, anywhere one stood in Longyearbyen, the laser was visible in the night sky. The light acted like a beacon: coal miners ending their late-night shift followed the light to see the source, and curious visitors gathered from across the town. Because of the minimal air traffic high in the Arctic, the laser could run uninterrupted through the evening and night.[1] *Time Line* used the very atmosphere as its medium: a laser beam is only visible because the concentrated light scatters off of particles—like water droplets, ice crystals, or dust—hanging in the air. As the beam travels past the atmosphere and extends into space beyond, it becomes invisible to the human eye simply because there is no longer anything for it to bounce off. The light continues indefinitely until it meets some interstellar dust or another planet, perhaps another galaxy, millions of years in the future. It is an act of art at the cosmic scale.

> The luminous line was our timeline, and for two nights, our future took the physical form of a thin green path laid out before us. How will our world transform as the Earth moves along this line? The future may be something we cannot know. But it is something we can imagine.

1   It was still necessary to stay in close contact with the airport's control tower. At one point on December 5, 2021, the laser needed to quickly be turned off while an emergency helicopter flew through the valley.

Note   *Time Line* was hosted by Artica Svalbard in 2021, curated by OCA: Office for Contemporary Art Norway, and funded by Norsk kulturrådet (Arts Council Norway) and Norske Billedkunstnere Vederlagsfond (Norwegian Visual Artists Fund).

This long-exposure image was taken as the laser slowly moved across the sky, showing several hours of the Earth's rotation and the path of the solar apex. Bright points within the fan of light are snowflakes caught in the laser's beam.

On December 5, 2021, *Time Line* was brought to Adventdalen, a valley adjacent to Longyearbyen. The color of the laser, a 532 nanometer-wavelength green, was chosen specifically because the human eye is most sensitive to colors in this range. Serendipitously, it is also nearly the same as the green of the aurora borealis at 557.7 nanometer-wavelength.

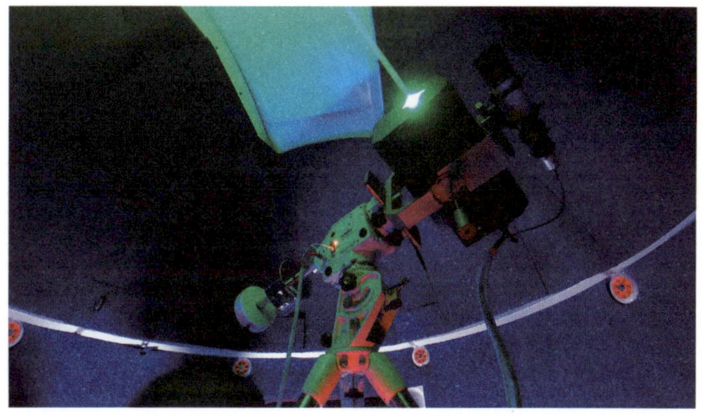

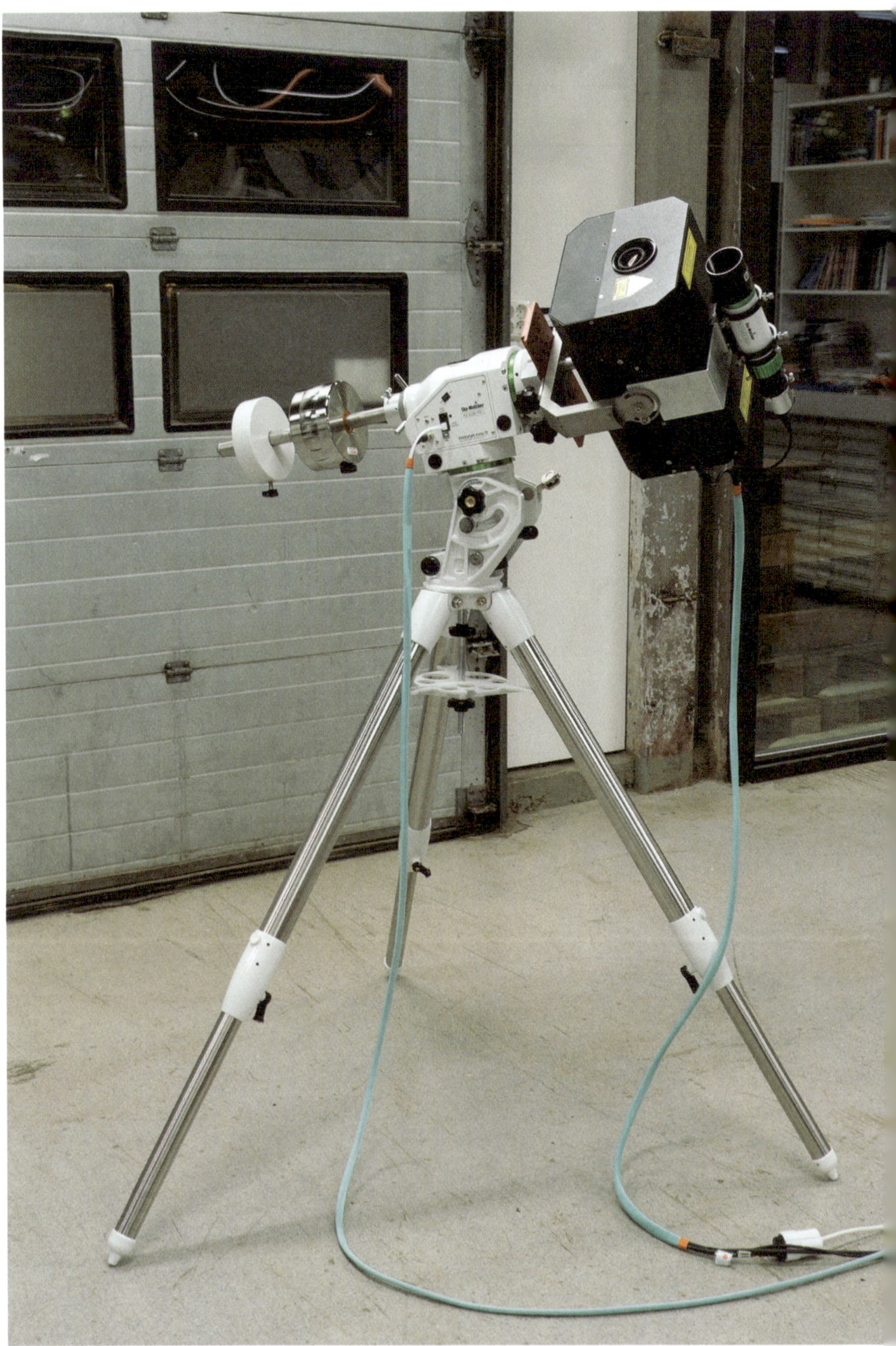

Time Line as seen from Sukkertoppen Mountain on November 30, 2021. On the first night of the project, the laser was set up at the north end of Longyearbyen along the edge of Adventfjord.

Anastasia Savinova was born near the Ural Mountains in the former Soviet Union and is currently based in the north of Sweden.

Genius Loci Norr
Anastasia Savinova

Genius Loci is an architectural collage project, a journey to a multitude of places in the world, urban and wild, crowded and uninhabited, accessible and remote. It explores the character and the spirit of places. Each work is a visual archive, where one picture concentrates a visited site's essence and feeling. Streets, mountain passes, and encounters on and off-road are all sources of visual information containing form, color, and texture; simultaneously, the environments encountered contain something incorporeal. Ancient Romans believed every place had a protective spirit: a *genius loci*. In contemporary usage, *genius loci* refer to a location's specific atmosphere and how it is experienced.

Each work in *Genius Loci* comprises numerous photographs of architectural and landscape forms taken during my travels. It is a common practice to take pictures of a place to help remember it. But the memory of a place doesn't come in the form of a single image. It usually assembles fragments—details, smells, colors, sounds, textures, and other haptic experiences. A memory is a world built from associations. As a method, collage helps bring together a multitude of different elements to call forth each memory, each world.

Genius Loci Norr is a chapter of *Genius Loci,* and it is dedicated to the towns, villages, and landscapes of Norrbotten County, the northernmost county in Sweden. The images take us from the industrial areas of Luleå to the seemingly abandoned villages in Tornedalen, from Riksgränsen with its ski-tourists to Kiruna with its open mine and unstable grounds, through the snowy views of Torneträsk and a lake that looks like the sea; from Nikkaluokta, where the public road ends to Kebnekaise and Tarfala Glacier Valley, where scientists measure the melting of ancient ice; from Jokkmokk, adorned with the skins and antlers of generations to Kvikkjokk with a population of nine people and further on still to Tarra Valley, embraced by their black and white mountains. Old wooden houses and barns, iron mines and towns built in the background of steelworks, hidden reindeer-herder houses, ice-fishing shelters, mountain huts, research stations, and magnificent landscapes. *Genius Loci Norr,* as a series of images, balances documentation and fiction with real and imaginary spaces to become a keeper of the memories and spirit of these places, reminding us that the North is vast and varied.

Somewhere in Swedish Lapland, scientists are watching glaciers melt. I traveled to the research station in Tarfala Glacier Valley in late September, at the end of the hiking season. I met no researchers, only a rabbit, who seemed to be the guardian of the place. You can see that rabbit at the bottom of the image. And, if you look closely enough, you can also see a poster I found on the door of one of the houses, which shows how Storglaciären has changed between 1910 and 1965.

Somewhere in the Swedish Lapland, I took a walk on the frozen river. Pictures for this work were taken during a multi-day walk on the frozen Tarra River in Padjelanta National Park. The house in the picture is a mix of a tourist hut on the route and a shelter of unknown purpose—perhaps a place to warm up for fishers or hunters. Long sticks with red crosses are the only colorful landmarks amidst the black-and-white landscape. They are used to mark the way.

Tornedalen. There are many abandoned places along the Torne River. This collage is comprised of pictures from an abandoned farm in Tornedalen. Small villages and farms are connected by the road and a bus that runs once or twice a day. The old buildings remain silent keepers of the place. How long will they stand?

NORTH ROCK
SUDVAS/MOOSE/REINDEER
BBQ SUBS

Kiruna. Kiruna is the northernmost city in Sweden, one hundred and forty-five kilometers above the Arctic Circle. The town, built in the 1890s to serve an iron mine, is currently—if not famously—being moved a few kilometers away due to the risk of unstable grounds posed by the still-expanding mining operations.
In the collage, photos of old Kiruna are assembled in a heap, not unlike the black slag heaps, left after mining. Texts from signs found across town—North Rock, Mine and the society—side by side, Reindeer BBQ—the poetry of a melancholic town with a challenging past, present, and future, can be seen throughout the collage, here and there.

Maureen Gruben is an Inuvialuk artist whose diverse multi-media practice incorporates organic and industrial materials salvaged from her local environment. Kyra Kordoski is a writer and photographer who has been working closely with Maureen Gruben since 2016.

Nakataq
Maureen Gruben and Kyra Kordoski

353   For the *Nakataq* series, Inuvialuk artist Maureen Gruben hand-etched repeated forms into a set of found photographic aerial survey prints using patterns based on her father's fox stretchers and traps. Eddie Gruben was renowned as the region's most successful trapper and is remembered as a generous supporter of his community. Orphaned as a young child by famine and the 1920s pandemic, he used his skills and efforts in trapping with a dog team over vast distances to eventually build the largest transportation company in the Northwest Territories.

The prints that form the material basis for these works were recently recovered from local work camps that oil companies set up and subsequently abandoned in the 1980s; they chart ice coverage in relation to oil wells in the Arctic Ocean surrounding the artist's home community of Tuktoyaktuk. Marks added by the artist converge with but are texturally distinct from the exposures, which themselves include surveyors' annotations—names and numbers added in the darkroom when they were printed. Maureen Gruben has added her father's Inuvialuk name, Kagisaluq, to *Nakataq IV*, for example, which also bears the darkroom annotation "Amundsen." Roald Amundsen was a Norwegian explorer; it can be presumed one of the oil wells was named after him. Varied representations of her father's tools occur throughout Gruben's practice. This ongoing process works to preserve not only the objects themselves but also reflects so many of the complex memories and values that can be sustained by a form.

The intersections of these inscriptions touch on markedly different but deeply entangled relationships to land and concepts of value, particularly with respect to tensions between home and resource extraction.

Following spread

Installation view of *Nakataq I* (2022) and *Nakataq II* (2022) at The Women's Darkroom + Gallery, Brooklyn, NY, US. October 2022.

Morgan Ip is an expert in place-based, human-centered architecture and urban design in polar regions.

Envisioning Urban Futures in the Arctic Borderlands of Norway and Russia
Morgan Ip

AN URBAN SCENE OVERLOOKING AN ARCTIC CITY

Ice crystals hover in the silent air as you ski along one of the culture-nature trails that spread out from the city center. Perched on stony outcroppings overlooking the urban landscape and nestled between stands of pine and birch are reconstituted relics from the war. Foxholes, pillboxes, and bunkers serve as resting areas and camping sites. Elsewhere along the paths are lavvus (Sámi temporary dwellings), gapahuker (Norwegian lean-to structures), banyas (Russian steam baths), and saunas, eagerly constructed by architecture students learning about local vernacular structures. You stop to rest at one of the shelters and warm in the crackling heat of its hearth...[1]

ARCTIC URBAN IMAGINARIES

Integrating the city with its natural environment is an essential element of Arctic urbanism found in the collective imagination of citizens in the Norwegian-Russian borderlands.[2] The vignettes in this chapter are a comprised of locally voiced ideas and concepts for how the urban future of the twin cities of Kirkenes and Nikel could be. They reflect abstract visions common on both sides of the border—a closeness to nature and culture—with concrete and locally specific ideas to suit community or individual aspirations.

What is the collective imagination, and how does it pertain to communities and the urban environment? Political scientist Benedict Anderson conceptualized an imagined community to understand the origins of nationalism; people share an idea of their nation and thus maintain a sense of belonging to a place even if they have never been to all parts of it or know all people within.[3] This community and sense of belonging, while largely oblique, consequently exists in the imagination of all the participants of that community. When imagining communities specifically through the built form, urban planner Kevin Lynch notably investigated the mental maps of Bostonians and consolidated five elements of the city: districts, landmarks, paths, edges, and nodes.[4] These were important physical features for residents to organize their community in their imaginations. Architects, planners, and urban thinkers have increasingly accessed the collective imagination of local inhabitants to gain relevant and deep contextual information for spatial design.[5]

In the Arctic, urbanization has occurred most densely in northern Norway and northwestern Russia. Where the cities of Kirkenes and Nikel meet provide a case study of how Arctic urbanism is expressed within different but proximate nation-states. The border zone is a particularly interesting location to access the collective imagination; such areas have been conceived of as third nations in that they maintain elements of both or multiple national identities.[6] They have also been described as liminal areas, with the concept of liminality a similar hybridity of the two realms on either side, and come from cultural anthropologist Victor Turner's concept of being in the "betwixt and between" state of childhood and adulthood, yet at once neither.[7] For those concerned with the city, such as urbanist Tom Avermaete, this notion of the limens is manifest in the built environment; spatial form and programming can be activated by various aspects of a diverse surrounding fabric of a neighborhood, for example as at the meeting of 'boundaries' between suburban and urban areas, or industrial, commercial or residential spaces.[8] How can an international urban neighborhood and the collective imagination of its people bear witness to the changing dynamics of respective nation-states?

1 This vignette and the two others in this chapter are adapted from one in the doctoral thesis by the author; Morgan Ip, 'Urban Futures in the North: A Collective Imagination of an Arctic Borderland' (Oslo, Norway, The Oslo School of Architecture and Design, 2022), 104.

2 Ip, 108.

3 Benedict Anderson. *Imagined Communities: Reflections on the Origin and Spread of Nationalism* (Verso, 1991).

4 Kevin Lynch, *The Image of the City* (MIT Press, 1960).

5 Nishat Awan, Tatjana Schneider, and Jeremy Till, *Spatial Agency: Other Ways of Doing Architecture* (Routledge, 2011); Eleftherios Pavlides and Galen Cranz, 'Ethnographic Methods in Support of Architectural Practice,' *School of Architecture, Art, and Historic Preservation Faculty Publications*, 1 January 2011; Jonathan Ventura and Jo-Anne Bichard, 'Design Anthropology or Anthropological Design? Towards "Social Design,"' *International Journal of Design Creativity and Innovation* 5, no. 3–4 (2016): 222–34.

6 Michael Dear, *Why Walls Won't Work: Repairing the US-Mexico Divide* (Oxford University Press, 2013).

7 Victor Witter Turner, *The Forest of Symbols: Aspects of Ndembu Ritual* (Cornell University Press, 1967).

8 Tom Avermaete, "The Borders Within: Reflections upon Architecture's Engagement with Urban Limens," in *Border Conditions*, ed. Marc Schoonderbeek (Architectura & Natura Press, 2009).

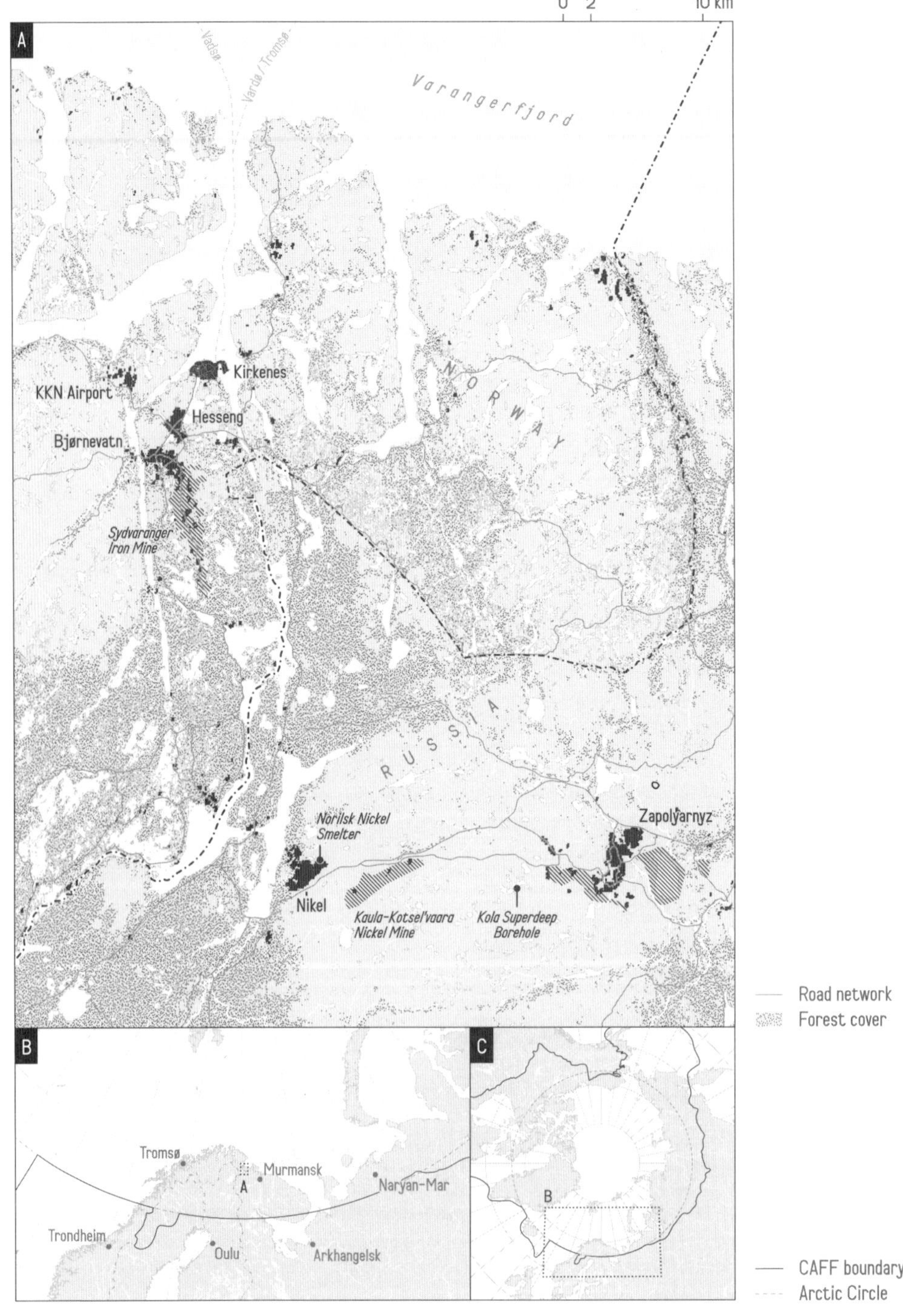

1   Situating Kirkenes and Nikel in relation to their respective mines (scale 1:500,000).

BORDERS THROUGH TIME: MARGINS OF MULTIPLE COLONIAL POWERS

To understand the present dynamics of the Arctic borderlands, it is useful to recognize their historical roots. The ancient cultural landscape is a part of Sápmi, the homeland of the Indigenous Sámi peoples. During colonial periods from the thirteenth century onwards, Norwegian people settled from the southwest, Finnish settlers in the south, and Russian people in the southeast. Each successive period of colonization left an indelible mark on the region and is reflected in its architecture and infrastructure.

> Vardø, across the Varanger fjord from Kirkenes, was the first city to develop in the area. It maintained a bastion, or star-fort, from 1739, replacing an earlier fort established at the beginning of Norwegian colonization in 1309.[9] Within the old fort's walls between 1621 and 1663, witch trials and executions unevenly affected women and Sámi people, but one chapter of the historical colonial violence in the area.[10] In 2011, a contemporary memorial designed by architect Peter Zumthor and artist Louise Bourgeois was built where executions took place, contrasting architectural expressions of state direction. The monument stands as a manifestation of dark heritage. It is not without controversy as a part of the contemporary Norwegian state's tourist routes and economic policy to promote areas of outstanding natural beauty.[11]

The Novgorod Republic, a predecessor state to Russia, also contested the region and established trade routes and religious missions. Pechenga Monastery was founded in the sixteenth century, just east of present-day Nikel. Another small orthodox church, the Chapel of St. George, was built near the Finnish border in Neiden, west of Kirkenes. The monastic buildings, though modest, were significant in spreading Eastern Orthodox Christianity and Russian influence in the region. Further, the presence of the church of Saints Boris and Gleb was significant in defining the present-day border; its small grounds on the west of the Pasvik River negotiated to remain Russian in exchange for a much larger coastal area east to Grense Jakobselv / Vue'rjemjokk, which went to Norway. The current border, which has been in place since 1940 and established with little consideration to Sámi sovereignty, has experienced an ebb and flow between openness and closure, with the recent and ongoing war in Ukraine ensuring a harder border. While the cultural and border infrastructure reflect the historical particularities of the region, other elements of the built environment strongly relate to corresponding national urban paradigms.

---

9   Gunnar Isaachsen Willoch, *Vardøhus festning 650 år* (Landstrykkeriet AS, 1960).

10   Liv Helene Willumsen, *The Witchcraft Trials in Finnmark, Northern Norway* (Skald, 2010).

11   Nasjonale turistveger, "Steilneset," Nasjonale turistveger; John Ødemark, "Cultural Difference and Development in the Mirror of Witchcraft - The Cultural Policy of Display at Steilneset Memorial," *Nordisk Kulturpolitisk Tidsskrift* 17, no. 2 (December 15, 2014): 187–209.

2–7   Typical housing in Kirkenes follows templates established for much of Finnmark following
        the large-scale destruction during the Second World War.

Finnmark and Troms Counties suffered incomprehensible ruin in the Second World War, and almost everything from the Norwegian border to Lyngenfjord was destroyed. The eastern towns of Kirkenes, Vardø, and Vadsø were damaged mostly through Russian bombardment of the area, with Kirkenes losing 450 of its 500 buildings in the campaign.[12] In response, the Germans retreated from Finnmark and parts of Troms in 1944 and evacuated almost the entire population, save for those who hid in the mountains. They employed scorched-earth tactics to burn to the ground everything crafted, maintained, or cared for by human hands, from houses and quays to telephone poles, sparing only a few small chapels or churches. The departing army dynamited concrete foundations of what remained and slaughtered all domestic livestock and half of the reindeer.[13] Considerable swathes of the old birch and pine forests were also burnt as smokescreens during the war. Reconstruction was organized by the Norwegian state, with town centers built from less flammable materials and residential areas reflecting wooden houses in the country's south. Much of the rebuilt housing stock adhered to standardized models, which resulted from an architectural competition.[14] The city of Kirkenes thus contrasted considerably with Nikel, on the opposite side of the border.

Nikel, eponymously named after its nickel ore, was, like Kirkenes, constructed as a mining town. It was initially developed in the 1930s during Finnish sovereignty in the area. The Pechenga area was returned to Russia in 1944, and while some of the housing from this era remained, subsequent development in the city followed Soviet urban principles deployed across its empire in mono-industrial Arctic cities in the Kola Peninsula and throughout the USSR.[15] The evolution of the residential block, for example, follows 'Stalinka' to 'Khrushchyovka' designs, so named after the ruling president of each era.

Like other Russian Arctic cities, the Soviet buildings are lined along treed boulevards, with main avenues leading to significant community centers like the cultural palace and the city hall. Large sections of the city are devoted to garage areas, a manifestation of heavily gendered spatial arrangements. The concrete city towers above the low canopy of the taiga reflect the political and cultural decisions made two thousand kilometers away in Moscow.

12   Diderich H. Lund, 'The Revival of Northern Norway', *The Geographical Journal* 109, no. 4/6 (1947): 185–97.

13   Lund, 13.

14   'Gjenreist Og Særpreget: En Planleggings- Og Utbedringsveileder for Hus Og Steder i Nord- Troms Og Finnmark' (Husbanken, November 2007); Norsk Folkemuseum, "Arkitektkonkurranser og typetegninger," accessed February 26, 2024, norskfolkemuseum.no/arkitektkonkurranser-og-typetegninger.

15   Peter Hemmersam, *Making the Arctic City: The History and Future of Urbanism in the Circumpolar North* (Bloomsbury Visual Arts, 2021).

8   Housing in Nikel reflects the state-building policies of successive Soviet governments.

The difference between the two cities' materiality and building typologies reiterates the power of architecture to embody societal visions for the present and future.

ACCESSING THE COLLECTIVE IMAGINATION

...Warmed by the fire, from the shelter you see Kirkenes huddled between weathered mountains before you: a brightly glowing, glass-covered pedestrian mall, a large passenger ferry berthed in the center, tourists and locals strolling along the boardwalk, a vast museum complex housed in the former iron ore processing plant, a striking wooden tower home to research institutions and diplomatic missions, a new oil transfer terminal, an eye-catching bridge connecting to the communities across the fjord, an observatory on the iron slagheap, a glittering opera house by the sea...

As Arctic urban centers navigate the complexities of economic development, environmental sustainability, and cultural preservation, the voices of the local communities are paramount. Local people know the contours of their neighborhoods most intimately and are the best arbitrators to contribute to future design considerations. Those who design and decide the future of Arctic cities, presently often from outside, can embrace the diversity of perspectives and incorporate local knowledge of place using an interdisciplinary toolbox drawing from architecture, design, and anthropology. Such methods should be engaging and encourage the participation of residents where possible, such as with public ideating workshops and mapping activities.[16]

The study that formed the basis for this chapter included physical collaborative mapping at local public fairs and events and a complementary online mapping application. Further, interviews with residents on both sides of the border were conducted, with ethnographic work including the use of photography and participant observation.[17] Accessing as many local concepts of place as possible can bring forth local specificity in the abstract (such as relationships between mines and towns, ideological cultural representation, and suggested policy directives) and concrete terms (like crossroads that require signage and neighborhoods that require renovation and upkeep). The collective gathering of voices regarding the built environment highlights nuances of how Arctic urbanism can be locally envisaged.

> The imagination of urban possibilities will inherently contain diverse ideas and visions, sometimes, if not often, in conflict with each other. With the swift expansion of digital space, including virtual and augmented realities, and the advent of artificial intelligence, space and place can be imagined and shared in increasing ways. The journey ahead is complex, but the voices of the residents of the Norwegian and Russian borderlands share a commitment to forging a future where the beauty of the landscape is preserved, the richness of culture celebrated, and urban centers thrive seamlessly within the Arctic environment.

DREAMING OF AN ARCTIC URBAN FUTURE

> …You take in the urban vista of Nikel bathed in steel-blue afternoon light: a thriving civic plaza, rejuvenated apartment blocks, and parks, a grand central park hosting a botanical museum and greenhouses, a shuttered metallurgical plant no longer belching soot across the snow, people gliding on a frozen lake by a lodge where one can rent skates, skis, and snowshoes (or canoes and kayaks in the summer), a striking new aquatics complex, a bathhouse where the birch branches redden one's skin.

The vignettes in this chapter illuminate some of the physical infrastructure residents envision that could improve their respective towns or cities. As Arctic borderlands continue to evolve, active input from local community members can play a pivotal role in shaping the trajectory of urban development. Research offers glimpses into the aspirations and dreams of those who call this Arctic home, with examples including sustainable architecture that harmonizes with the environment and community-led initiatives promoting cultural preservation. Sometimes the conversations reveal conflicting or

---

16   Paul Jenkins, "Concepts of Social Participation in Architecture," in *Architecture, Participation and Society*, ed. Paul Jenkins and Leslie Forsyth (Routledge, 2010), 220.

17   Morgan Ip, "Cultural Mapping and Digital Public Engagement in the Future North," *Nordiskturforskning* 30, no. 3 (2018): 81–106.

opposing visions. For example, the statue of Lenin in Nikel was a source of some friction, with one contribution recommending its removal, replacing it with more neutral cultural representations, and others who prefer it remain.

Further contestation extends to the ever-present resource sector, which, while providing economic sustenance, also brings forth challenges related to exploitation and environmental degradation. Striking a balance between economic prosperity and ecological conservation is imperative for the sustainable development of Arctic urban centers. Listening to the voices of those employed in the resource sector, one hears the echo of concerns from residents elsewhere in the Arctic. They want the ability to have a good quality of life, employment opportunities, and connections with nature. Although local people are strongly connected to their community, they are also connected to the world, with many having visited, worked, or gone to school in other parts of the country or the world.

The cities of Kirkenes and Nikel exist in countless iterations in the minds and dreams of their residents, deeply informed by historical and contemporary realities that shape their physical and cultural fabrics. The two cities are in constant dialogue, influencing and being influenced by one another to varying degrees contingent on the openness of the border at any given time. The creative energy of their inhabitants enriches the collective imagination and the potential for their urban futures. Despite the sometimes fantastical nature of these imaginings, they reflect the untapped possibilities inherent in the borderlands, with their unique blend of obstacles and prospects as they progress into the future.

Mari A. Aston Bergset, based at 69° North in Tromsø, is a landscape architect with a keen interest in understanding and embracing the positive design potential in challenging climate conditions.

Notes on an Arctic Landscape Architectural Practice
Mari A. Aston Bergset [1]

Lo:Le Landskap is a landscape architecture practice from Tromsø, Northern Norway. Drawing on their team's interdisciplinary and international experience,[2] Lo:Le seeks to address each new project with a place-specific perspective where the possibilities and challenges of a site are addressed in the larger context of the ecosystems it belongs to. Lo:Le relies on their spatial skill set, drawing upon historical and contextual knowledge, analytic capacities, empathy and agility in order to better understand any given situation, translating them into well-functioning public Arctic spaces. The following four projects provide the reader with insights into how our knowledge and beliefs manifest into built work and research endeavors.

MANAGING SNOW IN AN ARCTIC CITY CENTER

With approximately 78,000 inhabitants, Tromsø (Romsa in Sámi) is one of the larger cities situated in the Circumpolar North. Located well above the Arctic Circle, the city is an increasingly popular tourist winter destination—including many visitors from across Europe and Asia wanting to see the northern lights, go reindeer sledding, or explore its many restaurants and shops.[3] Due to the Gulf Stream that carries warm water and air from the Gulf of Mexico, Tromsø is fortunate to experience moderate temperatures and ice-free waters. Still, Tromsø is an Arctic city and receives significant snowfall each year. While having snow in the city center and maintaining a winter city experience is considered necessary, managing the volume of snow continues to be a challenge.

One place where these two demands meet is on Storgata, the main pedestrian street in the city center of Tromsø. It is a place bustling with shoppers, it is where to find good food and drinks, and it is also the venue for a range of public events, such as the annual reindeer race on Sámi National Day (February 6), the Tromsø International Film Festival (mid January), and Rakettnatt, an outdoor festival (August).

In 2020, the municipality of Tromsø commissioned an upgrade of Storgata, as the street had become worn down. The project's first part, located south of the town's old central church, was designed by Dronninga Landskap and was completed in 2018. The second part, continuing north from the church, is still under construction. Lo:Le Landskap and Verte landskap-arkitektur are designing this northern part of the city's central axis. The new segment may have its own identity, but it brings a unifying experience to the historic and new buildings along the street, including many different façade colors, textures, and materialities.

Part of the design upgrade to the central pedestrian street will secure universal accessibility for everyone: newly installed snow-melting equipment will be able to melt any snow that falls across the entire width of the street. The resulting melt water is directed towards large planters where it can infiltrate, leaving the street free of snow. Heated sidewalks in winter cities are not uncommon and usually take the form of tubes of hot water (heated with excess heat from waste incineration) underneath the street. The upgrade is also planned so that it will be possible to host the annual reindeer race. For that, there must be snow. The snow-melting infrastructure is therefore divided into zones, with a dedicated zone for reindeer racing that can be turned off for the annual Sámi week and the race. In this scenario, the center of the street (four meters wide) will be covered entirely in snow. There is also a zone for what has been termed a 'white street,' intended for events like the International Film Festival, when the city wants to enhance its character as a Winter City,[4] but at the same time also allows for sufficient pedestrian movement for the many visitors. This white street setting can be turned on and off to balance energy use for melting, to allow for winter activities (like ski or reindeer races), or to keep a sense of Arcticness in the main street while accessibility for all is ensured.

DESIGNING AN ARCTIC SCHOOL

Kautokeino (Finnmark County, Norway) is one of two cultural centers of Northern Sápmi, the other town being Karasjok. With approximately 3,000 residents, Kautokeino is a small but important town and is home to the Beaivváš Sámi Našunálateáhter (Sami National Theatre Beaivváš) and the Sámi allaskuvla (Sámi University of Applied Sciences).

As the world's largest Sámi school, programmed for between 270 and 350 pupils from grades one to ten, the Kautokeino school[5] has become a community center with several functions to be used by the entire town and wider region—including a swimming pool, volleyball hall, and Árran (a large indoor gathering place). This effort results from a closed design competition with a selection of pre-qualified design practices.[6] The project was finished in the autumn of 2023, with some completion works in the outdoor areas planned for the summer of 2024. The winning entry, *Luondu oahpaha (Nature teaches us)*, was made by Peab Bjørn Bygg, with Ola Roald Arkitektur and Lo:Le Landskap as the landscape architect.

The school site has a view over the Kautokeino River and consists of a western part with significant attention to green spaces, while the eastern part includes mostly hard but permeable surfaces. These complementary qualities of the site are woven together like ribbons. These braided ribbons are inspired by both Sámi textile art and design, as well as the waterways in the large open landscape around Kautokeino.

The school has a unique Sámi curriculum, which most schools in Norway don't have. The Sámi curriculum requires outdoor schooling in several subjects; a strong connection between inside and outside spaces is therefore crucial. The outdoor spaces include Sámi functions and traditional spaces such as luovvi,[7] lávvu,[8] lasso-pitch, and several campfires, tied together with play equipment along the ribbons. This collection of lines of movement, functions, and places references how the larger landscape is used in Sámi culture. The outdoor areas are connected to the building through a large central circle with fireplaces mirroring the indoor fireplace located in the Árran. Facing southwards, this is also where the first rays of the sun can be collected after the (almost two-month-long) polar night season, harvesting heat on the dark wood facade and wood deck to provide the best possible microclimate for outdoor activities.

NORTHERN NORWEGIAN VEGETATION: FROM NURSERY TO DESIGNED LANDSCAPE

Norway is a long country crossing a range of different climatic zones. Even though the country is well populated, there are fewer nurseries further up north, where there may be a commitment to using local plants in this region. However, a limitation exists, as there are no places to source or purchase

1   The author appreciates input from her colleagues, including Annie Breton and Beata Willman.
2   Six out of nine employees are international.
3   Elizaveta Vereykina, "Tourism is booming in northern Norway," *The Barents Observer*, January 4, 2024.
4   Such considerations are not new and can be traced back to the 1980s Winter Cities Movement.
5   The new school is replacing the old school, which consisted of many different buildings dispersed across the plot. For older high school children there is another new school being built in Kautokeino (designed by 70°N Arkitektur, Snøhetta, Joar Nango, and Econor).
6   The client was the Kautokeino Kommune, and as a result, there is a close connection to Sámi culture in the organization of the competition.
7   A luovvi is a raised construction to store foods and other goods.
8   A lávvu, in its most simple form, is a circular tent, often with a fireplace in the middle.

1   Reindeer racing championship at Storgata, Tromsø, Norway (February 2014).

those plants. The focus on using northern-specific plants in large-scale projects is relatively new (i.e., going beyond the species you might easily find in a southern nursery), as is the impetus to change the perceived value of local (northern) plants in an organized or designed landscape (i.e., seeing them as more than weeds).

> Northern landscape practices need a local nursery to address the needs of designing and planting large projects. Until recently, a nursery in the North was one of the few places to find specific local species, but it closed not so long ago. We rely on so few actors, so the closure of the only one has significantly impacted our ability to use northern-specific plants, which is crucial to counterbalance the spread of invasive species brought on by climatic changes and non-place-specific design traditions. To be able to use northern plants is a fundamental element in the restoration of natural and cultural landscapes.

The *Naturmangfoldloven (Nature Diversity Act)*, which applies to all activities in Norway, is an important document for us, published in 2009: "The purpose of this Act is to protect biological, geological and landscape diversity and ecological processes through conservation and sustainable use, and in such a way that the environment provides a basis for human activity, culture, health and well-being, now and in the future, including a basis for Sami culture."[9] This context spurred the need for a research and development project (led by Verte with Lo:Le part of the working group together with other collaborators) in northern Norwegian vegetation.

Northern Norway, encompassing the counties of Troms and Finnmark, has attractive plants that are naturally well suited to be implemented in design projects. A significant amount of open land is available and can be used to produce local plants and collect seeds. The entire value chain must be redesigned to function and achieve market-adapted production. In the past, plants used in designed landscape projects were produced from local trees and shrubs such as birch, rowan, and willow—as well as pine forest plants—but the industry has gone through a generational change, and the main part of this work has stopped. Several previously cultivated species are now on the alien species list and can no longer be used. In connection with the European Green Deal, there are new requirements for traceability and a reduced climate footprint, so there is an even greater need to ensure Troms and Finnmark's plant material meets future requirements.

Through this research and development project, we have worked to find solutions toward (I) strengthening and protecting northern Norwegian nature, our basis of life; (II) creating new practices within the green facilities sector in Troms and Finnmark; (III) increasing the knowledge and competence of participating companies and municipalities; (IV) contributing to a change of attitude in the industry by showing that local plants are not only a realistic but desirable alternative; (V) forming the foundation for future pilot projects with local vegetation in several municipalities; and (VI) contributing to new thinking and sustainable business development in Troms and Finnmark. Throughout 2024, the work will continue by planning pilot projects to test and practice some of the findings from work done in 2023, work that has been summarized above and published in *Bruk av Nordnorsk Vegetasjon i et næringsperspektiv (Use of Northern Norwegian Vegetation from a Business Perspective)*, a public report.[10]

VERVET: FROM SHIPYARD TO PUBLIC SPACE

Vervet is an urban transformation project that has transformed the old shipyard (situated in the center of Tromsø) into a new neighborhood with four hundred flats and generous public spaces. The old shipyard is central to the polar history of Tromsø, a city also known as the Gateway to the Arctic. Tromsø Skipsverft (Tromsø's Shipyard) was the city's first industrial workplace, established at Skansegata 1 in 1848. The last boat was repaired here as late as 2018. Tales of the shipyard's history are told through public spaces by the preservation of the boat slips and the main workshop building that now houses a popular restaurant that has kept its original name, Maskinverkstedet (Machine Hall). The newly designed public square within the Vervet project, called Slipptorget, has a paving inspired by the drift ice, which the

9   "Nature Diversity Act," Acts and Regulations, Government of Norway, effective June 19, 2009.
10   Verte Landskap-Arkitektur & Lo:Le Landskap, *Bruk av Nordnorsk Vegetasjon i et næringsperspektiv* (Troms of Finnmark Fylkeskommune, 2009).

2   A rendering in which Sámi functions and traditional spaces are woven together with play equipment.

3   The remains of Vervet's industrial history are balanced by the lush, successful plantings of Lo:Le's design. Vervet, Tromsø, Norway.

polar vessels would encounter on their adventures. The drift-ice sheets are cut in Cor-Ten steel to echo the steel of the boats, and many of the known names of boats that have been repaired at the shipyard are cut into these steel drift-ice sheets. The client wished to use Cor-Ten steel as they felt it related to the site's history as a place of ship repair. It went from a very dirty place to a very polished place; the Cor-Ten maintains a balance with the raw industrial qualities of the site. Cor-Ten is also low maintenance and can be cut in many ways. We also kept a selection of the equipment and machines on site.

The key here is identity, demonstrated through a careful, continuous mediation of polar history and the industrial history of the shipyard. This has been fundamental to the architecture of the buildings and the designed landscape features, where residents and visitors can come and feel connected to the town's polar history. In addition to referencing the past, the project resolutely looks to the future as outdoor spaces create a range of microclimates designed for a diversity of current and future public functions; for example, all outdoor spaces are designed to take advantage of the favorable location of the plot itself (i.e., that it can get a lot of sun during a significant part of the day). At the same time, the building masses are placed to protect the outdoor areas against the prevailing winds. The sun angle in Northern Norway is shallow, so all of the vertical surfaces—sun walls—have much to contribute when creating micro-climates. A well-positioned wall in the sun accumulates warmth, creating a comforting place to sit for residents and visitors. Like Storgata, snow-melting equipment is present at Vervet public space, but the project is right next to the ocean, where snow melts quicker, so the need for snow clearing is less acute. Finally, the project comes with a detailed light plan,[11] which is important for a city with a dark season that is two months long.

11   Zenisk AS both created the detailed light plan and designed the custom-made light fixtures.

Eimear Tynan is an associate professor of landscape architecture specializing in Arctic and sub-Arctic landscapes. Bert De Jonghe is a landscape architect studying and teaching Arctic design practices.

Designing with Coastal Change in the High Arctic: Pedagogic Perspectives
Eimear Tynan and Bert De Jonghe

The high-Arctic landscapes and oceans of Svalbard are undergoing significant changes attributed to a rapidly warming climate. Svalbard is warming three to six times faster than the global average, with Longyearbyen warming up to seven times faster.[1] Some observed changes to Svalbard's environment include melting glaciers, thawing permafrost, reduced sea ice, ecosystem disruptions, and increased risk of geohazards. According to the report *Climate in Svalbard 2100: a knowledge base for climate adaptation,*[2] changes to Longyearbyen's future climate include precipitation increases of between 20 to 40 percent, which will increasingly fall as rain in the winter months. Flooding events are also expected to increase due to local glacier melt and more rain. A third significant change that is expected is the acceleration of thawing permafrost. Currently, the presence of permafrost limits erosion. However, as the temperature of the active layer (the surface layer of permafrost) rises, more sediments become available for transport. These changes are already in motion and will play out over both long and short timeframes in the form of slow changes and sudden events such as rockslides or flooding. The consequences of these changes are most prominent along the coasts of Svalbard.

In order to understand and appreciate the diversity and complexity of change along these coasts, a territorial perspective was adopted as a starting point for the design and teaching of *Territorial Practices*, a Master of Landscape Architecture studio-based course at the Arctic University of Norway (UiT), taught in the autumn of 2023 by the authors with the participation of fourteen graduate students. The course focused on high-Arctic delta environments in the Norwegian archipelago of Svalbard, where delta environments are undergoing rapid change in high-Arctic regions primarily due to rising temperatures. A range of spatial and temporal views of territories was required to address the complex environmental changes. This incorporated the mapping of Svalbard's aerial, marine, and terrestrial territories from political, climatic, ecological, environmental, and cultural standpoints. It also required site-specific engagement on a human scale where graduate students were asked to design *with* a delta area in the town of Longyearbyen, Svalbard, to address the present and future needs of human and non-human stakeholders. By doing so, students developed a better understanding of the complex and entangled nature of the chosen delta landscape.

The study of territories was approached in two ways. First, territories in this study embraced environments above and below land and sea surfaces through frozen and unfrozen layers. This is very much inspired and informed by the work of geographers Kimberley Peters, Philip Steinberg, and Elaine Stratford, who argue that "the terrains of territory need to be understood as voluminous, elemental, fluid, and indeterminate: as spaces that challenge the 'grounded,' static world of solid surface (terra) that typically has informed political thought."[3] This is particularly relevant in the study of an archipelago such as Svalbard that encompasses large oceanic areas with extensive frozen environments alongside dynamic social and political histories. Second, although the term 'territory' is commonly associated with space, this studio course challenged how the term might be opened up to new meanings and interpretations when considered from different temporal perspectives. This required examining territories from political, climatic, ecological, environmental, and cultural standpoints, all of which have different temporal associations that shift and morph over time.

A study of spatial and temporal territories provided a strong foundation for understanding Svalbard's intertwining human and more-than-human activities. However, as landscape architects living and studying in the Arctic, it was necessary to explore how these larger territorial readings play out on a local scale and how this knowledge may be applied in the development of design proposals. A delta site was selected in Longyearbyen, Svalbard's largest settlement of approximately 2,000 inhabitants. The site is influenced by natural

1   Joseph Phelan, "Svalbard: The Arctic islands where we can see the future of global heating," *The Guardian*, May 13, 2013; Øyvind Nordli and Przemysław Wyszyński and Herdis M. Gjelten, et al., "2020. Revisiting the extended Svalbard Airport monthly temperature series, and the compiled corresponding daily series 1898–2018," *Polar Research* 39 (2020): 3614.

2   I. Hanssen-Bauer, E. Førland, H. Hisdal, S. Mayer, A.Sandø, and S. Sorteberg, eds. *Climate in Svalbard 2100: A knowledge base for climate adaptation.* Report no. 1/2019. The Norwegian Centre for Climate Services, 2019.

3   Kimberley Peters and Philip Steinberg and Elaine Stratford, eds. *Territory beyond Terra.* (Rowman & Littlefield, 2018), 5.

1   Between 1950 and 1960, heavy machines were deployed to manage rock along Longyearelva, Longyearbyen's river.
2   Aerial view of Longyearelva in 1936.

3   Aerial view of Longyearelva in 2021.

processes ranging from tides to the flow of sediments that enter the fjord from the adjacent Longyearelva River and Adventfjord Valley. This results in an environment that is ecologically rich and productive, and unlike many other coastal sites in Svalbard undergoing coastal erosion, this site is undergoing deposition through the accumulation of shifting spit systems. However, alongside these natural processes is significant human interference. Over the last one hundred years, Longyearelva has gradually been reduced to a single channel and is continuously managed by large machines that maintain a strict linear form, thus destroying the natural braided system of the river. Maintaining this channel remains challenging for the local authority—also known as Lokalstyre—which requires the annual restoration of the river's artificial embankments. Not only have humans shaped the river over time (↪ 1, 2, 3), but there is also an ongoing trend of building in the river's flood plain that extends towards Longyearbye's coastal edge. Longyearbyen's river and delta are representative of tensions between natural systems and intensive anthropogenic activity that are increasingly common in other coastal environments around the globe. In this high-Arctic site, students were asked to work with the dynamic conditions, materials, and processes that are expected to change over time. Over the course of the semester, students and teachers explored how the selected coastal site in Longyearbyen may operate on a number of different spatial and temporal scales. These explorations were investigated primarily, but not exclusively, through a design project located in or adjacent to Longyearbyen's delta.

TERRITORIAL PRACTICES AND PEDAGOGIC APPROACHES

This course implemented an iterative design approach whereby students experimented, developed, and tested design ideas throughout the course. This approach may be described as "the process of continual improvement, of a concept, prototype, design or product. It is a cyclic approach to the development of a product, whereby a design is improved by frequent testing, client feedback, focus groups, materials testing, prototype testing, design development and evaluation, until a final refined/developed design is reached."[4] Four iterations were applied to the course to help structure the students' design development: observing and mapping, imagining, speculating, and projecting. Within these iterations, each student tested, evaluated, and refined their design projects. Each iteration phase was followed by a review whereby students presented work to their peers and teachers.

In the early stages of the studio, students undertook a territorial mapping of Svalbard. This collective exercise documented the archipelago's terrestrial, marine, and aerial environments with attention to different types of human or more-than-human activity. All of the layers used for the maps were animated as a means to highlight the dimension of time relating to activity, change, and movement.

4   Students explored the materials and tidal movements along the spit systems of Longyearbyen's coast during a field trip (August 2023).

The first mapping exercise illustrated the migration patterns of different tracked species. This included two polar bears, a bearded seal, a fin whale, a bowhead whale, and a kittiwake. The findings of this revealed very different patterns of migration in different areas of the Arctic Ocean. Most of the activity, however, was located to the northwest, west, and south of Svalbard. The bowhead whale maintained the most remote and northerly location, while the kittiwake stayed close to Svalbard's western coast. The fin whale, meanwhile, was active to the west and south of Svalbard. A second mapping illustrated marine traffic comprising fishing, cargo, and passenger vessel activity from 2019 to 2020. This revealed intense activity along the west and south areas (Barents Sea) of Svalbard. A third mapping focused on ice—Svalbard's glaciers on land and the archipelago's seasonal sea ice extent, which reaches to the south of Svalbard in the late winter/early spring and retreats to the northeast during the summer months. While the glaciers gradually retreat over time, the sea ice mapping gave a more rhythmic, seasonal pattern of advancement and retreat. The fourth mapping exercise documented ocean infrastructures and activity relating to petroleum and mineral extraction. This included bore-hole locations, sea cables, petroleum activity, and zones that are deemed potential areas for sea-bed mining. Following on from these themed mapping exercises, the students started to overlap different layers. This helped to identify the extent, pattern, and scale of different activities corresponding to Svalbard's terrestrial and marine geographies. More importantly, tensions and conflicts, particularly in the marine areas, started to emerge. One prominent example was the organic migration patterns of the bowhead whale, which was directly crisscrossed with intense areas for fishing vessel activity. Due to the addition of time and animation in the mapping exercises, students could identify that the whales appeared to be most disturbed and threatened between late September and January. Rich discussions on these multilayered stories emerged between teachers and students. Questions arose relating to increased human activity and the need to respect and protect areas that other species need to live and survive. The intense mapping phase offered students different perspectives of what a territory can be, what it can encompass, and how it can change over different timeframes. It confirmed that activities operate at various spatial and temporal scales and with varying intensities. In addition, the voluminous aspects of territories, like activities above and below the land and sea, added complexity to this mapping and visualization exercise. By overlapping layers of data, conflicts and tensions became evident, particularly between human and more-than-human activity. In the end, students tied together their maps into an animated video. The video was projected on a three-dimensional terrain model—made collectively by the student cohort—of Svalbard's archipelago, including the islands of Bjørnøya and Hopen. These forms of representation were effective tools from which to discuss high-Arctic territories with students whilst also being beneficial in communicating the research to external reviewers and visitors.

Early in the semester, the cohort also conducted on-site fieldwork in Longyearbyen. The focus was primarily on the delta system. To understand this large system and associated processes, we traced the main water systems that started at Longyearbreen, the large glacier that feeds into Longyearelva, and followed the river to the coast. The rock, gravel, silt, and mud that are carried by the glacier and river result in a dynamic series of spit systems along the eastern side of Longyearbyen's coast (↔ 4). Due to the town's development over the last one hundred years or so, the delta area has been highly modified. The lower parts of the river are deemed a risk zone by the local authority. This has resulted in the construction of high gravel embankments with large rock foundations. Local rock is too weak for building purposes or for fortifying structures, meaning that more robust rock must be imported from mainland Norway.

4   V. Ryan, "How iterative designing works," *Technology Student*.

Restricting the river to a channel has meant that these gravel flood barriers have burst during sudden melting events that start upstream. The flow of water increases, and the river does not have the space that it requires. Anuradha Mathur poignantly asked, "Why do rivers flood? The simple answer is that they flood because water crosses a line drawn by humans."[5] The gradual destruction of the natural, wide braiding system by local authorities was challenged in some of the projects produced by students, who made strong arguments for allowing the river to return to its braided form, thus blurring the lines between alluvial processes and lines defined by the local authority to denote flooding risks. The main benefit of such interventions was to slow the movement of the river and reduce the damage caused by intense flooding events.

The course included weekly tutorials[6] and opportunities for students to reflect on their design approach and process. A useful framework that was used for such reflection was a series of design approaches proposed by landscape architect Catherine Heatherington "that can be used by designers to reveal change in cultural landscapes."[7] The approaches were retaining (and repurposing), exposing (and concealing), adding (and subtracting), substituting, extending (and withdrawing), doing little, and mythologizing. In its most basic form, simply mastering those terms during tutorials and informal conversations influenced a student's design process significantly. Moreover, students examined and discussed each other's work in small breakout sessions. They also reflected on how they would categorize and translate selected case study projects. Taken together, the combination of group work, breakout sessions, and individual tutorials encouraged the cohort to go through several design iterations in a short period of time.

DESIGNING AN ARCTIC DELTA

During the course, much of the time was dedicated to developing knowledge about the diverse conditions and processes that were integral to delta landscapes. In a high–Arctic context, the materiality of the delta transforms from fluid, muddy conditions during late spring and summer to more rigid, icy states that persist largely from fall to spring. Due to a warming climate, however, this pattern of seasonal freeze and thaw has started to change dramatically. Longyearbyen now experiences events of warmer temperatures throughout the year as well as more precipitation falling as rain. This has led to more landslides and flooding. Taking this into account, the students sought to develop designs that worked with these conditions rather than respond with interventions that tried to prevent hazards from occurring. Another approach taken by some students was to work within risk landscapes associated with Longyearbyen's river and delta areas. These students found qualities in these spaces that informed their designs, such as the diverse sounds of the river or different bird and vegetation habitats that needed protection and care. Such an approach challenged these spaces labeled as 'risk' and argued that, for most of the year, these were safe and peaceful spaces to be enjoyed rather than avoided. The following is a selection of student design proposals that collaborated with the site-specific conditions in or adjacent to Longyearbyen's delta landscapes for the benefit of human and non-human users.

Julie Hjelt Wold drew attention to Longyearbyen's former landfill site, which lies adjacent to Longyearbyen's vulnerable delta environment (↔ 5). Her project, *Curating a Landfill*, engages with the haphazard composition of this site by developing a series of design interventions that frame landfill objects and landfill strata in different ways. The project is a temporary design proposal that sensitively works with the site, recognizing that it is very much overlooked by the local authority and exudes a sense of being in limbo. The allegorical design approach borrows design techniques from eighteenth-century English gardens: framing views, focusing attention and views to ruins, and manipulating the boundaries within this high-Arctic context. The intention is to promote, if not insist on, local engagement with Longyearbyen's recent cultural heritage, which necessarily includes raising awareness of the production and use of local materials, the dispersal of waste along the town's coast, and the need for a circular economy in the town.

Tomine H. Furelid's *Choreographing Natural Processes: interplay with natural processes to create land for nesting birds in Longyearbyen's delta* prioritizes vulnerable bird habitats located along Longyearbyen's coast.[8] With the town's urbanization growing towards the coast, there is an increased intensity of human use that disturbs many bird species nesting in the dynamic sand and mud spit systems at the mouth of Longyearelva. An important part of Tomine's design development involved using a large physical model composed of wood and sand. To grasp the dynamic spit systems that characterize this site, water was introduced to simulate tide and river currents (↔ 7). As a result, Tomine's proposed design engages with the natural processes of alluvial sedimentation and longshore drift that break up the spit system to create a series of fortified islands, allowing the bird habitats to develop without human interference and gently but firmly reprogramming this coastal site.

Sofie Randall King made reference to the multiplicity of more-than-human flows that interact along Longyearbyen's delta. Their project, *Soundmarking the River*, emerged through the identification of the sonic dimensions of these flows (↔ 6). Sofie adopted Kevin Lynch's

5   Anuradha Mathur, "Terrains of Wetness," in *Delta Dialogues*, ed. Christophe Girot (gta Verlag, ETH Zurich, 2017), 62.

6   Tutorials during this course were conducted weekly and comprised one-to-one supervision between student and teachers to discuss the design progress of each student project.

7   Catherine Heatherington, "Revealing Change," in *Revealing Change in Cultural Landscapes: Material, Spatial and Ecological Considerations* (Routledge, 2021), 46.

8   Tomine Furelid's project, *Choreographing Natural Processes*, won the AHO Climate Shift Award, an honorary award established by Skift, a Norwegian business-driven climate initiative with the goal of stimulating societal shifts in accordance with the UN Sustainability Development Goals (SDGs) and the 2030 Agenda. The purpose of the award is to promote collaboration across sectors and disciplines that can further lead to innovation and new business opportunities for a low-carbon society.

5   An illustration of a set of design interventions at Longyearbyen's landfill site by Julie Hjelt Wold.

6   An illustration of designed sound experiences along Longyearbyen's delta system by Sofie Randall King.

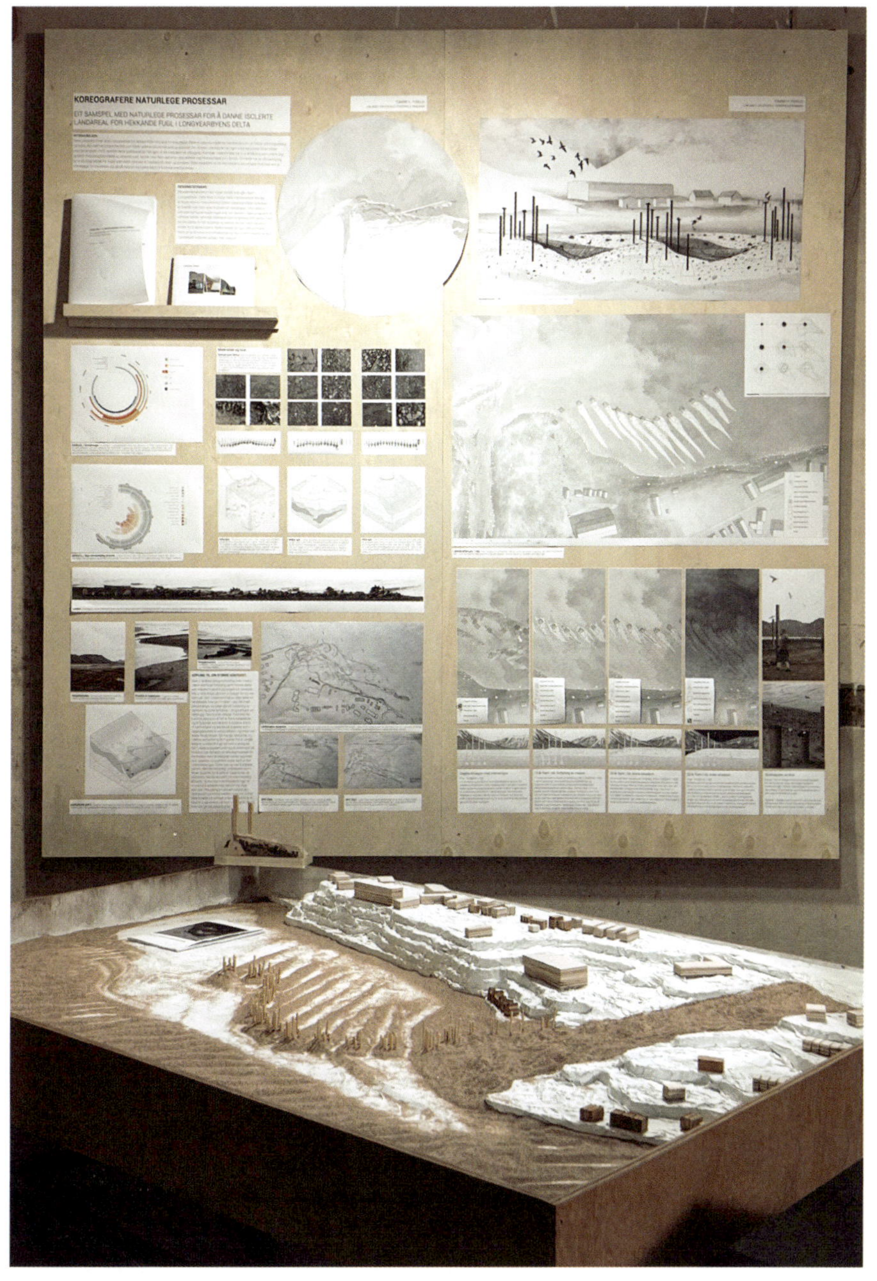

7   Tomine H. Furelid used model-making to simulate natural processes in order to develop design solutions.

concept of 'landmarks' and developed a series of 'soundmarks' as a means to draw the attention of the local community to the different sonic qualities of the delta area. The design curates these sounds by making the river quieter in some areas whilst amplifying sounds in other parts. The interventions utilize local materials, thus exerting minimal pressure on these vulnerable soundscapes.

The outcome of this studio course comprised an exhibition with fourteen individual landscape design projects that worked directly with Longyearbyen's delta and river. Situating a design-oriented course in Svalbard led to students thinking and working differently from what they were accustomed to. As the designers and instructors of this course, we observed three overarching considerations that also featured in our students' work:

First, the diverse temporal dimensions of this site and its location were crucial to consider from the early stages of the design process. We examined how deltaic environments have evolved over time, how they are changing today, and how they are expected to change in the future. Longyearbreen, the glacier adjacent to Longyearbyen, is expected to be largely gone by 2075. This will have significant impacts on the town, river system, and delta ecologies. Consequently, it was crucial to consider the delta landscape *through* time. Longyearbyen's delta area dramatically changes through the seasons, which directly affects the flow of sediments. In recent years, the river that leads to the delta has experienced sudden flood events due to spikes in temperature. The students responded to these learnings by considering and designing anticipatory, adaptive approaches. An additional consideration of time came through in student projects that worked closely with vegetation. In Longyearbyen, new species are not allowed to be planted. Instead, one must create conditions that favor specific plant species to grow. This required a new way of thinking for most students where the conventional luxury of importing soil and plants could not be implemented. Rather than develop precise planting plans, attention shifted to the creation or enhancement of soils and microclimates for the desired vegetation to be established. This meant that students proposed vegetated areas that could take many years to establish, whereby soil management, protection, and patience were required.

Second, designing with local materials sparked many challenging discussions with students. Although all students had a preference to work with local materials, it did not always align with the ambitions of the design project. This was particularly evident when students hoped to prevent flooding: local material is too weak to withstand the forces of the flooding events and geohazards that are specific to Svalbard, so a compromise was needed in some cases. For many, it raised the question of whether humans should really be living on Svalbard when so much disruption to natural systems is required, and the cost of living in high-risk environments is so substantial.

The final consideration evident in the students' work was the aesthetic dimension that was desired in each project. During the first days of the field trip in Longyearbyen, students observed and commented on the seemingly haphazard layout of the town and what appeared to be the random placement of objects, such as snow scooters and wooden pallets. However, after spending time photographing, sketching, and talking with locals, the students began to understand and discern the underlying organizing principles that determined the function of sites within the town. This local understanding and knowledge was adopted in many of the design projects where students wanted to integrate commonly used materials such as wooden pallets or large driftwood logs into their sites. Many discussions emerged on the subject of sustainability in Longyearbyen, where almost all materials have to be imported from mainland Norway. Students endeavored to use local materials where possible through the re-use of materials or driftwood that regularly beaches along Longyearbyen.

Taken together, these three considerations that underpin student work reflect how pedagogic competencies in an Arctic context can respond to the complexities embedded in rapidly changing environments. This course required students to operate on a number of spatial and temporal scales, which was demanding within one semester. However, creating group-work exercises allowed students to build confidence in their own skills whilst learning from one another—which was especially important at the early stages of the semester. The field trip to Longyearbyen marked the beginning of individual design projects. The trip lasted only five days, a very short time for students to become familiar with such new surroundings. A balance, therefore, had to be struck between students spending adequate time outdoors making observations and scheduling time with local experts to gain different perspectives. In a location that experiences extreme conditions, particularly with regard to light and temperature, students were limited in gaining a thorough understanding of life in Longyearbyen. A second trip later in the semester, when conditions were dark and frozen, would have been advantageous as it would have given students yet another perspective on how Longyearbyen operates during winter months and could have influenced different design outcomes.

Lola Sheppard is a founding Partner at Lateral Office and is Professor at the School of Architecture, University of Waterloo. Mason White is a founding Partner at Lateral Office and Professor at the Daniels Faculty of Architecture, Landscape, and Design at the University of Toronto.

Entangled Arctic: Home/Land in the House/Territory
Lola Sheppard and Mason White

ELASTIC SCALES OF ARCTIC INHABITATION

The Arctic region has been perceived as a frontier by colonial empires as early as the 1500s, when explorers sought control over the strategically advantageous circumpolar lands and seas, the promise of a shortened global passage, and, later, the bounty of resources that lay within and underneath its icy surface. The past two centuries have revealed an ever more layered and entangled complexity in Arctic politics and economics. This layering is temporal, such as shifts in ownership and stewardship, and physical in the sense of surface and subsurface rights. Today, extraction of minerals and hydrocarbons represents 31% of GDP in the circumpolar Arctic, activities that have been central to the development of, and tensions within, every Arctic nation—Canada, Denmark, Finland, Iceland, Norway, Sweden, Russia, and the United States.[1] While nation-states continue to contest boundaries, resource claims, and navigation routes, Indigenous groups continue to assert land and governance rights through regional and territorial governments as well as the Arctic Council, with its permanent participants represented by the Aleut International Association, the Arctic Athabaskan Council, the Gwich'in Council International, the Inuit Circumpolar Council, the Saami Council, and the Russian Association of Indigenous Peoples of the North. The Arctic Council represents people and regions by Indigenous governance rather than nation-state borders. The movement toward increased sovereignty of Indigenous rights and land governance has gained momentum in the region.

Events as recent as January 2024, when the government of Canada signed the Nunavut Lands and Resources Devolution Agreement with the government of Nunavut, becoming the largest land transfer in Canadian history, support this recent shift.[2] However, considerable conflicts persist between the assertion of Indigenous rights to traditional lands and the capitalistic drive of nations and corporations to exploit resources. It is important to note that much of today's complexity of the Arctic regards navigation, extraction, and governance as embodied in notions of home and land versus house and territory. This seemingly subtle distinction is central to how the region is viewed, as either home or territory and by whom. Home and land are concepts aligned with Indigenous values; house and territory represent concepts held by colonizers, nation-states, and extractive corporations. Home and land are sometimes interchangeable among Indigenous worldviews, while house and territory reinforce notions of property and ownership.

> The establishment of most Arctic villages and urban development has been driven by resettlement, sovereignty, and strategic access to resources. These motivations have significantly influenced employment patterns, infrastructure, mobility, and growth, making the daily patterns of inhabitation tethered to territorial inhabitation in ways far more intricate and immediate than in other global regions. If the Arctic territory is at the fringes of the global logistical network and planetary urbanization and it is the physical site of geopolitical contestations, it also represents a unique geographic shortcut in the very network.[3] The Arctic house crystalizes these territorial tensions in how they make complex connections to energy, food, water, and waste networks in each of its various localities (as determined by both local traditions and national governance).

Typically, inhabitation (particularly urban inhabitation) is considered within a linear scalar relationship, moving from the house to the neighborhood, the town, the region, and the nation in nested sequential scales. Geographer Erik Swyngedouw notes that, until the 1980s, "space was considered given and fixed and spatial scale was one of the given Cartesian attributes of spatial organization that permitted moving up and down dimensional ladders, depending on the type of enquiry or object of study. Neighbourhoods, ecosystems, cities, regions, river basins and states were considered given."[4] Swyngedouw further goes on to observe that scale is often a foregone conclusion that provides "a geographical frame and container in which to situate a set of processes which as such were not scale-dependent or scale-forming."[5]

1   Gérard Duhaime and Andrée Caron, "The Economy of the Circumpolar Arctic," in *The Economy of the North: ECONOR 2020*, ed. Solveig Glomsrød, Gérard Duhaime, and Iulie Aslaksen (Arctic Council Secretariat, 2021).

2   "Nunavut Lands and Resources Devolution Agreement," Government of Canada.

3   Neil Brenner, ed., *Implosions/Explosions: Towards a Study of Planetary Urbanization* (Jovis, 2014).

4   Erik Swyngedouw, "Place, Nature and the Question of Scale: Interrogating the Production of Nature," *Diskussionspapier 5*, Berlin-Branderburgische Akademie der Wissenschaften (July 2010): 7.

5   Ibid.

However, the radical transformations caused by global and environmental processes and the "recognition that local or regional configurations matter significantly in shaping national, supra-national or global processes"[6] have challenged our linear, nested understanding of scale.

The Arctic is a region where the nested "dimensional ladders" of scale are subverted; there is often no middle scale, and, in some instances, scales might be non-sequential and non-nested. Arctic inhabitation is increasingly governed by the resources (from caribou to diamonds) embedded in the territory, driven by extractive corporations tending towards monetization and Indigenous people asserting self-determination. It is the tension between understanding the Arctic as a place defined by house/territory versus home/land that makes the typology of the Arctic house (and home) relationship to the territory (and land) so layered and entangled.

Bruno Latour's "actor-network theory" as a paradigm for understanding social and spatial relations also suggests the possibility of collapsing the near and the far, offering that "the first advantage of thinking in terms of networks is that we get rid of 'the tyranny of distance' or proximity."[7] Further, Latour suggests that "elements which are close when disconnected may be infinitely remote if their connections are analyzed," and vice versa.[8] In this understanding, local and global scales can collapse and become entangled; the near and far are relative and interchangeable, and the remote and immediate can be understood as relational and adjacent once their connections are analyzed. Latour's tyranny of distance might also be expanded to include the tyranny of linear scalar relationships and the assumption that all things spatial can be measured, mapped, described, and framed objectively.

Anthropologist Anna Tsing similarly argues against the dogmatism of scalar precision, suggesting that it blocks our ability to understand heterogeneity and complexity. Tsing's non-scalability theory enables one to account for contingency and failure, claiming that "it shows us the architecture of non-nesting, which is key to the (re) making of cultural diversity, capitalist and otherwise."[9] How do we understand and visualize the material consequences of capitalism, the cultural consequences of colonialism, or the imprint of Indigenous practices? In the Arctic, conventional scalar thinking and representation fail to describe the entanglements of both the local and the global. Instead, spatial understanding requires an elastic and non-nested scalar approach in terms of dimensions but also with respect to the socio-cultural, economic, or political influences. This approach focuses on revealing object-to-territory relationships, such as a traditional object in a room and its immediate ties to the global infrastructure in the territory.

In the same way house and home should be differentiated, territory and land should be distinguishable. Geographer Stuart Elden notes: "Territory is itself a process, made and remade, shaped and shaping, active and reactive."[10] Territory is often associated with state actors, control, boundedness, and sovereignty. Much of the shaping of the Arctic territory is the ongoing negotiation for resources, the assertions of nation-states, and claims made on behalf of Indigenous sovereignty. Conversely, Indigenous conceptions of land are tied to stewardship, not control, and are deeply embedded with Indigenous values and world-views.

ARCTIC DOMESTICITY

In many regions of the Arctic, where assertions of sovereignty and colonization have significant impacts, the physical house did not necessarily provide a sense of home but was imposed, in its form and location, as a planned cultural change that often became the site of cultural trauma.[11] For Indigenous peoples, home extends beyond the interior of the house; the land is seen as home, family is home, and home was often made and re-made. The physical house, instead, often embodied a "cultural erasure" of home. It still does today.[12] The history of Arctic housing is littered with ill-conceived, one-size-fits-all solutions largely developed by bureaucrats seeking (and failing) to address only the technical challenge of construction in the Arctic.[13] All Arctic nations, except Iceland, participated in assimilation or relocation projects, visited upon Indigenous communities through architecture and settlement projects. These projects, often funded by the state, used the house and its bound spaces (rooms) such as bedrooms, kitchens, and living rooms to import colonial notions of home that partition the idea of domestic life into distinct prescribed interior zones, whereas Indigenous uses of spaces are more multivalent, ad hoc, and fluid with the land. Simultaneously, thousands of workers are employed in the extractive industries across the most remote parts of the Arctic, often in temporary work camps with cycles of fly-in-fly-out inhabitation. In these instances, the house is reduced to a basic

<table>
<tr><td>6</td><td>Ibid.</td></tr>
<tr><td>7</td><td>Bruno Latour, "On Actor-Network Theory. A Few Clarifications Plus More Than a Few Complications," (English version), Soziale Welt 47 (1996): 4.</td></tr>
<tr><td>8</td><td>Ibid.</td></tr>
<tr><td>9</td><td>Anna Tsing, "On Nonscalability: The Living World Is Not Amenable to Precision-Nested Scales," Common Knowledge 18, no. 3 (Fall 2012): 522.</td></tr>
<tr><td>10</td><td>Stuart Elden, The Birth of Territory (University of Chicago Press, 2013), 17.</td></tr>
<tr><td>11</td><td>Frank Tester, "Iglutaasaavut (Our New Homes): Neither 'New' nor 'Ours': Housing Challenges of the Nunavut Territorial Government," Journal of Canadian Studies/Revue d'études canadiennes 43, no. 2 (Spring 2009): 138.</td></tr>
<tr><td>12</td><td>Frank Tester, "IGLUTAQ (in my room) The Implications of Homelessness for Inuit: A Case Study of Housing and Homelessness in Kinngait, Nunavut Territory," A Report Prepared for The Harvest Society, Kinngait, Nunavut Territory (April 2006): 41.</td></tr>
<tr><td>13</td><td>In Russia, the Khrushchyovka became the default housing type; in Arctic Canada, the Federal and Territorial governments developed prototypes deployed by the hundreds, across the Arctic. In Greenland, the Danish government deployed large, culturally ill-adapted housing blocks in Nuuk, which famously housed one percent of the entire country in a single building.</td></tr>
</table>

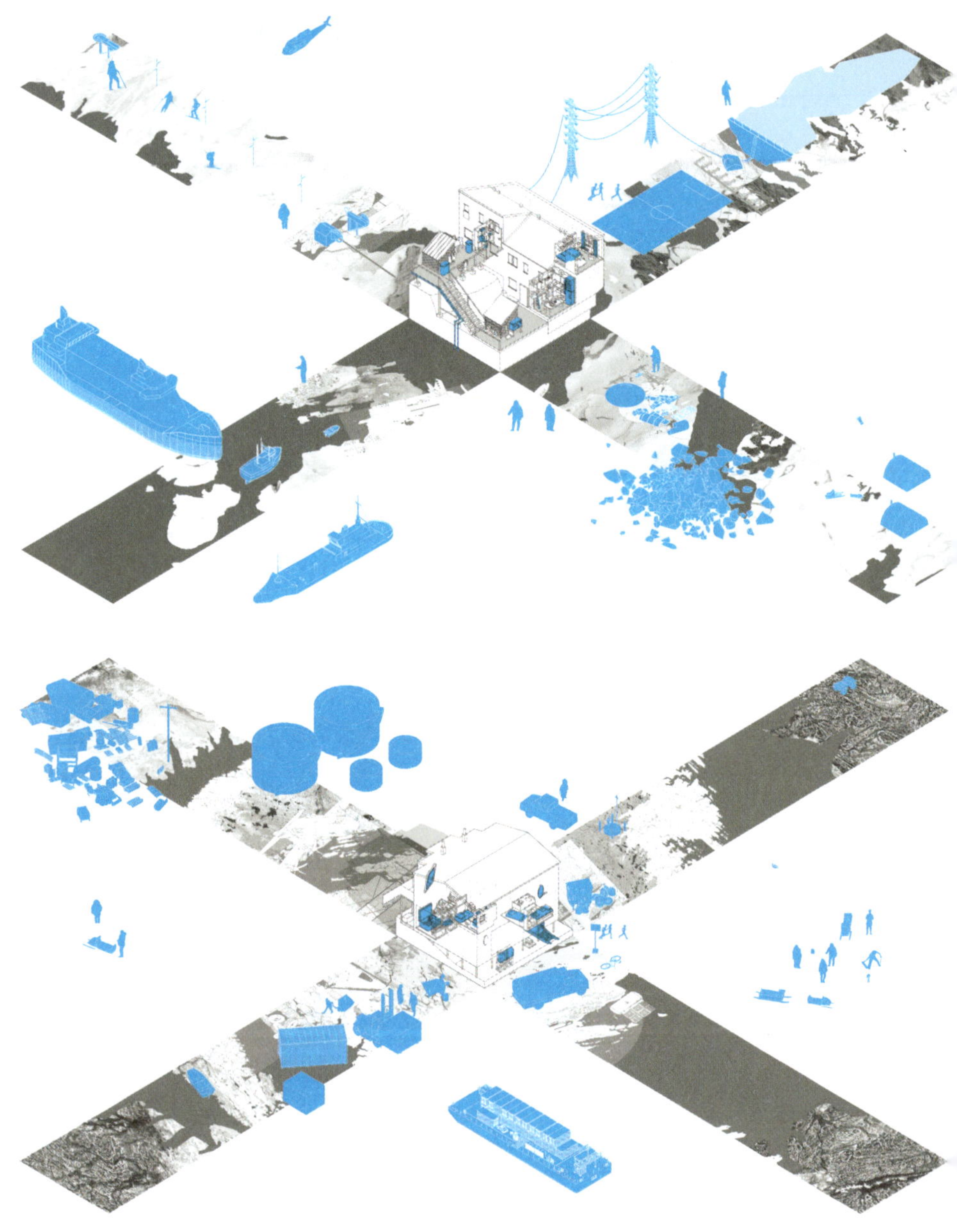

1   Nuuk, the world's largest Inuit capital city, is a hybrid of Danish housing influences and traditional
        Inuit practices. Evidence of country food harvesting appears in freezers on balconies and in living
        rooms. Cruise ships, hydropower plants, and mining reveal the extractive pressures on the land.

2   Typical rental housing in Resolute and other Nunavut communities are sites of extreme
        overcrowding, with snowmobiles, boats, and other objects stored on site. Barges delivering the
        annual sea lift remind one of the tenuous infrastructural links to territory, while residents
        traveling on the land remind one of profound connections between the domestic and the territory.

shell perpetuating the idea of protecting inhabitants from the harsh climate and failing as any kind of cultural or social interface situating Arctic domestic life within Arctic land beyond.

If the Arctic home is approached through a colonial lens—not dissimilar from how cultural theorist Dolores Hayden examined the home through a gendered lens or her contemporary Dianne Harris examined the home through a racial lens—the house becomes a forensic tool by which to understand local histories and serves as a magnifier of forces shaping the larger territory in which both house and home are situated.[14] What might the Arctic home reveal about these histories through its occupation, use, and adaptation? The research documents the evidence of spatial practice inside and out—tools, objects, equipment, adaptations—to respond to the climatic and geographic realities of everyday life in the Arctic.

The Arctic home, as a physical and conceptual space, oscillates between the local and the global, between Indigenous traditional practices and colonial extractive practices. The interplay between these scalar opposites of house and territory unfolds while negotiating extreme climate, remoteness, and land claims. *Contested Circumpolar, Domestic Territories* (CCDT) is a series of eight scaled domestic 'core samples' that collapse scales of house/home and territory/land in the Arctic. Each core sample tells a specific story of Arctic inhabitation, one for each circumpolar nation. Together, they represent a diversity of sites across the circumpolar region. In addition to the entanglement of scales, the models also entangle the medium of drawings with physical models. Regional infrastructure serving planetary urbanism is represented as a network wrapping multiple sides of the podium, while the smallest of objects and furniture are modeled to the scale of the house. The juxtaposition of scales is echoed in the juxtaposition of media: models with drawings. The methodology of CCDT embraces multi-scalar and non-nested documentation of inhabitation to understand evolving patterns of living in the circumpolar region.

CORE SAMPLING

While in no way totalizing or comprehensive, the CCDT model-podiums function in a manner similar to an ice-core or earth-core sample, which privileges data from a single point in greater depth over broad, shallow data-gathering techniques. Glaciologists and geologists use core samples to understand climate and soil composition through time at a single point.

---

14   Dolores Hayden argued in *The Grand Domestic Revolution* (MIT Press, 1982) that the form of the city and the house helped reify the gender roles, which corporate America sought to maintain to build a consumer base for domestic objects. Dianne Harris similarly explored in *Little White Houses* (University of Minnesota, 2012) how the desire for an "iconography of whiteness" influenced the design and representation of the postwar American house.

3   Domestic spaces in Sámi territory of Finland are often composed of ingenious repurposing of found elements; in this case, an upturned boat hull becomes a workshop.

4   Eight core samples, one for each circumpolar nation, are arranged in a circle, recalling the Circumpolar Council. Each one tells the story of domestic life and territorial geopolitics.

The domestic core samples in CCDT revel in the scalar entanglements and intertwined narratives of Arctic inhabitation found at each of the selected sites of their extraction. Collectively, the eight models reveal stories of movement, relocation, climate change, housing inequality, and overcrowding, as well as Indigenous ingenuity, spatial practices of food harvesting, daily life, and community gathering, among others. In each core sample, the house describes the spatial practices of residents at a domestic scale, while the podium describes the geology, infrastructures, and logistics across the land and territory. By connecting and entangling these scales, Indigenous notions of home and land remain in tension with colonial impositions of house and territory.

The CCDT models are presented with articulated detail only in specific rooms of each house—bedrooms and kitchens in some, bathrooms and living rooms in others. Degrees of articulation are used to focus only on objects relevant to each narrative. Select objects are highlighted in blue as primary actors, which reveal adaptations dealing with the specificity of Arctic climate, remoteness, environment, and daily life. Only the rooms that contain the sample highlighted objects are exposed to the viewer and given the level of detailing appropriate to the scale. Rooms that are not primary actors in the stories are left solid and unarticulated. The model podiums, which complete the depth of the "core sample," describe territorial infrastructures, landscapes, and geopolitical forces shaping each community unfolding from the house out into the territory. The land and oceans are not merely surfaces to inhabit but represent a thick, animated geological layer of resources and energy, as well as hunting and camping grounds. Mines and rigs extract from their depths; thermokarst and permafrost layers shift and heave under the forces of climate change; water bodies freeze and thaw, connecting and separating communities and regions across the seasons. Again, the primary actors in this network are highlighted in icy blue. All of these activities extend outward from the house, sometimes passing through or by foundations or walls of houses.

DOMESTIC & TERRITORIAL OBJECTS

Although the method of highlighting a domestic object and a territorial infrastructure in the same representation might create scalar friction, this is the very condition that Arctic citizens continue to negotiate. Material culture is a field that examines the relationship between objects and people, resources, and spaces to understand how they reflect and define different societies. Anthropologist Arjun Appadurai, in *The Social Life of Things*, argues that: "things have no meanings apart from those that human transactions, attributions, and motivations endow them with [...] we have to follow the things themselves, for their meanings are inscribed in their forms, their uses, their trajectories."[15] These objects that populate the domestic often represent the one realm in which residents retain agency over their environment. The expression of the domestic can be seen as a form of critical resistance against the impositions of the house, the manifestation of local cultures percolating up despite the orthodoxy and colonialism of so much of Arctic architecture. Conversely, territorial objects are often the evidence of extractive practices, assertions of sovereignty, scientific exploration, or urban and rural infrastructures. Unlike domestic life, which responds to seasonality, territorial objects seek to defy either seasonal changes or more long-term changes in climate. *Contested Circumpolar, Domestic Territories* (CCDT) seeks to reveal the complex linkages between the house and the territory, the home and the land.

> In asking these questions as visitors to the region, we relied heavily on interviews with knowledge holders, local residents, and planners, as well as first-hand observations of homes, film archives, historical and contemporary photography, as well as analytic spatial drawings and maps at various scales. The collected research of CCDT synthesizes these spatial stories into three-dimensional models that document the spatial connections between the domestic and territorial scales. The Arctic home is the house on the land in the territory.

UNRAVELLING ENTANGLED ARCTIC STORIES

Each of the eight core samples tells a specific story of Arctic inhabitation, one for each circumpolar nation. Recurring themes appear, such as stories of extraction, monitoring, and Indigenous traditions, yet each has a distinct voice to express an emerging circumpolar vernacular of home.

> The conflation of scale between the domestic and the territorial is uniquely apparent in Norilsk, Russia, where the khrushchevka apartment block that was once deployed with almost ruthless efficiency in the early 1960s is now aging concrete panels and foundations that are cracking and failing.[16] Climate change and thawing permafrost are accelerating building stock failure. Blind faith by state agencies in prefabrication, standardization, and efficiency in housing construction was meant to support the rapid growth in the copper and nickel mining and smelting industries. To combat the long, dark winters and grim urban conditions of Norilsk, residents maintain ultraviolet lights and greenhouses in their apartments. Outside, the surrounding landscape reminds citizens of the extractive foundations of the town, which is one of the most polluted places on earth.[17] Both the khrushchevka blocks and mines are supported by a complex network of pipes, rail lines, and electrical grids, although only resources are able to move into this closed city since no one is allowed to enter—or leave—without government permission.

In Inari, Finland, evidence of Indigenous ingenuity, as described by Sami artist-architect Joar Nango, is legible in various domestic adaptations such as the repurposing of old boats for temporary shelter, the craftmanship of traditional cooking tools from local wood, and the resourceful transformation of sleds.[18] These adaptations are part of being out on the land to support traditional cultural practices as well as reindeer herding. Simultaneously, the local ecology is under threat from rail lines built to support ever-encroaching mineral extraction, a reminder of the friction of global capitalism on the hyper-local.[19]

The core sample of Reyðarfjörður, Iceland, reveals the reality of mining work camps that are so familiar to the thousands of fly-in, fly-out workers employed across the Arctic. In Reyðarfjörður, the work camp served the construction of the nearby Alcoa Fjarðaál aluminum smelting plant (completed in 2008), which depends upon the massive Kárahnjúkar hydropower plant and dam, both of which have had significant environmental impacts on local waterways. As in many instances globally, worker housing is made of repeatable modular units linked together, offering minimal amenities and compact living units to its foreign worker majority.[20] In a remote and rural region traditionally dependent on fish processing, the plant and dam initially held the promise of additional local employment.[21]

The story of Longyearbyen, Norway, is centered on the impact of climate change in this former coal-mining town on Svalbard Island in the North Atlantic. Longyearbyen owes its existence largely to coal extraction and is now transitioning its economy to research, education, and tourism. Warming climate is causing permafrost to shift, and increased moisture in the air is augmenting the risks of avalanches, such as a 2015 event that buried ten historic houses and a 2017 event that damaged another four houses. The houses most at risk have been removed, and avalanche protection fences have been installed near the ridge above other threatened houses. As a former company town, most of the existing housing stock is owned by either Store Norske, the mining company, or Statsbygg, the Norwegian government's developer.

Kiruna, in the heart of Sámi territory in Sweden, similarly speaks to the voracious appetite of extractive corporations, in this case, the state-owned Luossavaara-Kiirunavaara Aktiebolag (LKAB). Founded in 1900 for iron ore extraction, Kiruna was the subject of a visionary Arctic town plan by Ralph Erskine in the 1960s. However, one

15   Arjun Appadurai, "Introduction: commodities and the politics of value," in *The Social Life of Things: Commodities in Cultural Context*, ed. Arjun Appadurai (Cambridge University Press, 1986), 5.

16   Vitaly Mikhayluk, "The Condemned: Living in a Khrushchyovka," *Russia Beyond the Headlines*, ed. P. Kortin, M. Korshunoc, L. Bellinello, 2017.

17   "Indigenous groups paying the price for Russia's massive Arctic fuel spill," *CBC News*, July 13, 2020.

18   Eilís Quinn, "The Arctic railway," *Eye on the Arctic*, September 22, 2019.

19   Miriam Rose, "A nice place to work in? Experiences of Icelandic Smelter Employees," *Saving Iceland*, February 20, 2017.

20   Hjalti Jóhannesson, "Lessons from Alcoa in East Iceland," *Nordregio* 2 (2007).

21   Elin Bäckström, "Transforming space and society in Kiruna," *Uppsala University: News*, March 24, 2022.

hundred years after its establishment, 6,000 of the 23,000 inhabitants are being relocated to extract additional iron ore directly beneath a portion of the town. The town and mine have infrastructures, including rail lines, in Sámi territory, disrupting and fragmenting traditional rcindccr grazing lands.[22] Quality of life in Kiruna is quite high, with residents partaking in outdoor recreational activities and benefiting from high-quality urban infrastructure and housing.[23] Most buildings in the town center will be demolished, while twenty key historic civic buildings are being relocated to the newly planned town. Kiruna is a reminder that resource extraction is a primary economic driver and colonizing force, producing the complex condition of a company-owned Arctic town.

Nuuk, the capital of Greenland, is home to a third of this small nation's population, and 90 percent of the residents are Greenlandic Inuit. Many Nuuk residents arrived in the settlement due to forced relocation in the 1960s as the Danish government sought to consolidate settlements. The city has been rapidly growing, creating an acute housing crisis with decades-long wait lists. As Greenland moved toward political devolution from Denmark, it faced decisions between economic independence, questions of environmental stewardship, and the need for transparency about decision-making demanded by its constituents.[24] Nuuk, like many Inuit cities, navigates a rapidly growing resource economy with traditional subsistence harvesting. Hunting and fishing are still regularly practiced by residents, as evidenced by freezers found in apartment hallways and living rooms, and on balconies.[25] The town and buildings navigate rocky terrain and are organized infrastructurally around utilidors and the network of elevated water and sewage pipes found in many Arctic cities.

Here, the utilidors often pair with elevated walkways, which offer an alternative, informal way of moving through the city, over and through the dramatic rocky landscape and terrain of the city. At a territorial scale, a large hydro powerplant supports energy needs, and a deep-sea port enables year-round delivery of products, making Greenland much more infrastructurally developed than Nunavut, its northern Canadian counterpart.[26] The nation is also home to vast amounts of surficial metals and rare earth metal reserves, which global corporations are actively seeking out as climate change thaws the ice above.

In Qausuittuq (Resolute), Canada, government rental units reveal the story of overcrowding and a hidden homeless population. Houses are being asked to sustain more residents than ever intended. In some cases, three-bedroom apartments accommodate up to twenty family members, revealing the scale of the housing crisis unfolding across Nunavut.[27] Everyday life of Nunavummiut is as much 'on the land' as 'in the house,' with snowmobiles, boats, quads, and other objects stored around and under the house.

Residents traveling out on the land to seasonal camps mark the importance of the land as an extension of the home and a space to reaffirm Inuit traditional life. Barges delivering the annual sealift (including fuel) recall the tenuous infrastructural links to global supply chains. Nunavut houses have their fuel and water tanks attached to the house outside, with either utilidors or trucks re-supplying them from municipal fuel farms and water reservoirs at the edge of town.

Utqiagvik, Alaska, is home to a majority of Inupiat people in one of the northernmost towns in the world. The United States Army established a meteorological research station there in 1881. Today it is a major service hub for the North Slope of Alaska. The region's oil and gas are important to the economy, but many residents continue to rely on traditional food harvesting, including whale, seal, polar bear, walrus, caribou, and fish. The town's buildings and land continue to be home to significant research and monitoring on climate change, in particular because it is the site of coastal erosion, community relocation, and changing animal migration patterns.[28]

MAPPING CIRCUMPOLAR STORIES

While the eight core sample models tell stories of local domestic entanglements, a circumpolar map shifts our conventional reading of the region from geopolitical boundaries to describe the multiple interconnected territorial stories of ways of life on lands and ice, but also food and resources and their infrastructures negotiating this shifting terrain. The circumpolar map documents the numerous and overlapping colonial practices in the name of extraction, shipping, exploration, and research, as well as Indigenous practices of hunting, fishing, and moving across the land, ice, and water. In addition, military stunts and monitoring exercises stake claims on land (and underwater), serving national and transnational actors. While these actions are localized, they tie into global flows and regional geopolitics, evoking Swyngedouw's process of "glocalisation," which argues that social life is "process based," always in a state of reconfiguration and that understanding economic networks and models of bottom-up resistance requires greater attention to engaging a "politics of scale."[29] In the circumpolar map,

22   Authors' interview with Nina Elisasson, Kiruna Planning and Development Manager. February 17, 2021.

23   Erica M. Dingman, "Greenlandic Independence: The Dilemma of Natural Resource Extraction," *Arctic Yearbook 2014* (2014).

24   Authors' interview with Runa Sværd, Nuuk City Planner. February 16, 2021.

25   John Thompson, "Greenland capital boasts deep-water port, hydro-electric dam and much more," *Nunatsiaq News*, July 19, 2007.

26   Tester, "IGLUTAQ."

27   Anne Garland, Anamaria Bukvic, and Anuszka Maton-Mosurska, "Capturing complexity: Environmental change and relocation in the North Slope Borough, Alaska," *Climate Risk Management 38* (2022).

28   Erik Swyngedouw, "Globalisation or 'glocalisation'? Networks, territories and rescaling," *Cambridge Review of International Affairs*, 17:1 (2004): 25–48.

scale dissolves and is elastic, allowing micro-narratives on equal footing with large, transnational economic forces.

In a context where so much of social and economic daily life happens both in the home and out on the land, *Contested Circumpolar, Domestic Territories* exposes the linkages of the near and far, the local and the global, the house and the land as sites of colonial contestation and local sovereignty. These disparate linkages seek to reveal an elastic middle scale, snapping between the objects of home-life and the territory of house-life. Accepting its elasticity is an opportunity to negotiate the impacts of the global and the needs of the local. CCDT is an exercise in thickened spatial storytelling. It argues that an emergent, hybrid understanding of domesticity and territory is needed. The Arctic home negotiates the powerful spatial practices of residents and the inevitable reality of architecture as an imposed colonial force. Home/land and the house/territory are a crystallization of competing visions of an Arctic way of life informed by thousands of years of spatial practice with the imposed settler-colonial forces of extraction, property, and capital.

29   Ibid.

Note   *Contested Circumpolar, Domestic Territories* (CCDT) was a collaboration between Lateral Office and Arctic Design Group, led by Lola Sheppard, Mason White, and Kearon Roy Taylor, and Leena Cho and Matthew Jull, respectively. CCDT was exhibited at the 17th Mostra di Architettura di Venezia (Venice Biennale of Architecture), entitled *How Will We Live Together?*, curated by Hashim Sarkis. Due to the COVID-19 pandemic, the biennale took place in 2021 instead of 2020.

Caitlin Jakusz Paridy is a landscape designer and researcher investigating landscapes of extraction.

Palliative Design for a High Arctic Landscape
Caitlin Jakusz Paridy

As the forthcoming closure of Gruve 7, Longyearbyen's last operational coal mine, in 2025[1] coincides with increasing temperatures and glacial melt, creating new landscapes across the island,[2] Svalbard is witnessing a rapid transformation of its cultural landscapes. With their disappearance, historical methods of relating to the landscape through this extractive practice[3] call to question how these spaces should be remembered and understood moving forward, given their lasting influence on the Arctic's cryosphere and the uncertain environment ahead.

> This paper project proposes a strategy for mine decommissioning that embraces the entropy of these changing Arctic landscapes.[4] Presently, the mine's decommissioning will likely follow historical closure methods such as abandonment, preservation, or, natural restoration, erasing the site's surface imprint.[5] However, historically, these practices have rarely considered the changing glacial landscape or the establishment of new relationships to the site.

To embrace these fluctuating landscapes and the site's human-geological relationship, a palliative design strategy for the decommissioning of Gruve 7 is proposed. This method adapts geographer Caitlin DeSilvey's concept of "palliative curation"[6] to landscape architecture, disrupting preservation to embrace the entropy of decay. Within the shifting landscapes of Gruve 7, an incremental land art intervention is proposed, a means of caring for and transitioning the site through the agency of its natural processes, leaving room

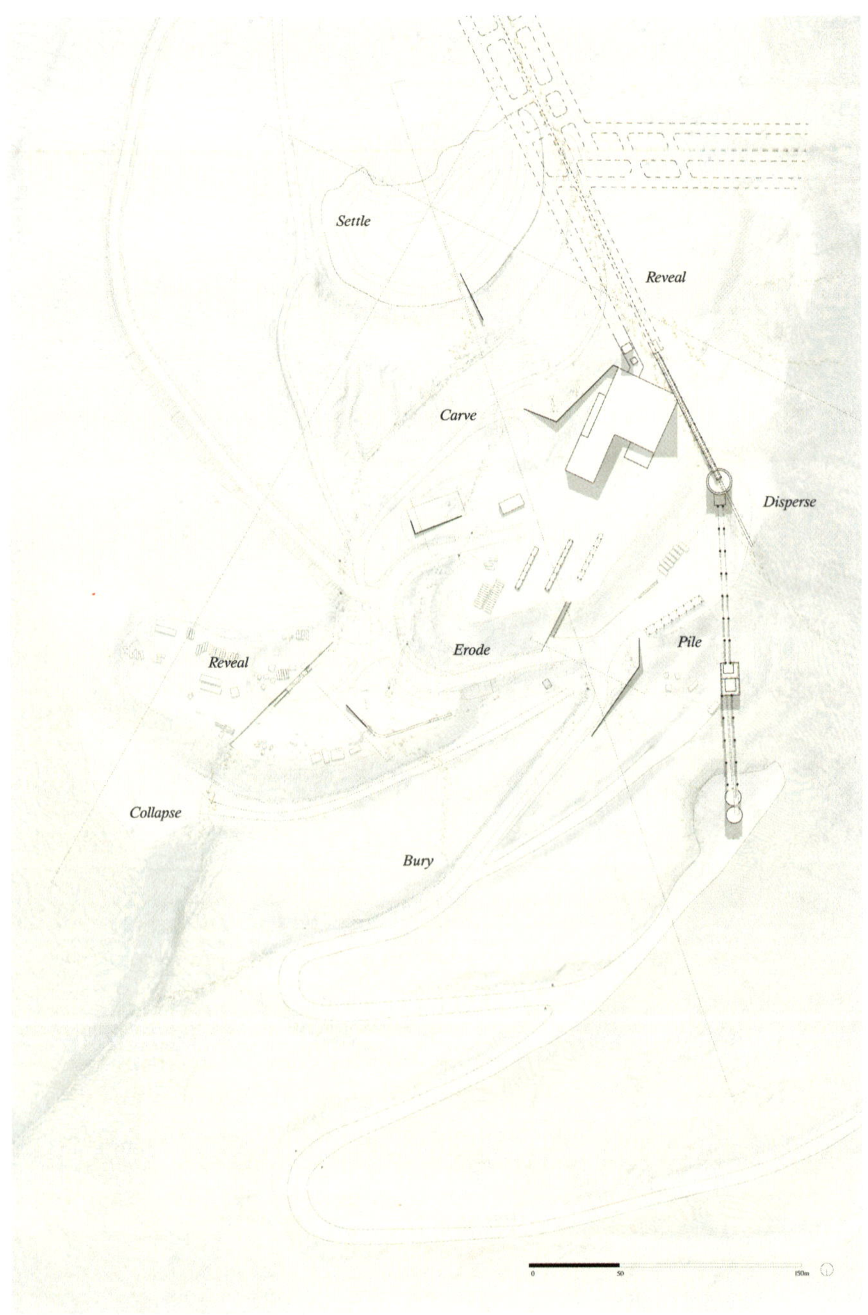

1   Plan showing the cryogenic processes shaping the land art intervention and the surrounding landscape after two years of palliatively opening up the site to decommissioning (May 2023).

for the surrounding community to come to terms with growing feelings of solastalgia as the familiar glacial environment melts away.[7]

This intervention was developed following a study of the site's anthropogenic and other-than-human materials, including how cryogenic elements such as rainfall, snow, and glacial melt manipulate Arctic landscapes.[8] These processes are harnessed and accentuated through a series of landscape features that repurpose the mine's infrastructure into the axis and contours of the site, foregrounding the entropy created from its decay. The catalyst for this movement arises from the carving of the water retention pond at the top of the site. Designed as a public event, the water gathered within the pond is released and channeled down the site through a series of irrigation ditches and steel retaining walls. As it flows down the steep plateaus of mine tailings, the water slowly erodes the ditches' sides, growing over the years to accommodate the increased rainfall and melt expected to arise.[9] Once the flow approaches the lower plateau, the rainwater is funneled through an embedded steel passageway connecting the upper and lower sites. Here, the movement of water is amplified as it echoes off the walls, marking times of heavy rain or melt with overwhelming waves of noise, and other times with faint smacks and trickles as the melt drips through.

1	"Gruve 7 har kull til sommeren 2025 — sa er det tomt," Line Nagell Ylvisaker, *Svalbardposten*.
2	Situated directly above Gruve 7 is the Foxfonna Glacier. As temperatures across the island have increased, the glacier has slowly started to melt. This meltwater permeates the underground chambers, creating underground lakes forced out of the mine's entrance using a system of pipes and pumps. This melt is expected to increase with each passing year. Researchers have predicted the complete disappearance of Foxfonna by 2050. From Wayne Cheung, "Surface and bed topography mapping of Foxfonna & Rieperbreen glacier, Svalbard, 1936–2020" (Master's thesis, Saint Petersburg State University and Hamburg University, 2020): 50–51.
3	Dina Brode-Roger, "Mining, Materiality and Memory: Lingering Legacies in Longyearbyen," *Journal of Contemporary Architecture* 9, no. 1 (2022).
4	This MLA student diploma project (entitled *A palliative design for the (after)life of mine #7* under teaching staff Mari A. Aston Bergset, course leader, and Eimear Tynan, student supervisor) was awarded the TERRA NODA prize by the Nordnorsk Design- og Arkitektursenter (Northern Norway Architecture and Design Center) as well as the Ribas Piera International Prize as one of five representatives from the University of Tromsø — The Arctic University of Norway (Norwegian: Universitetet I Tromsø — Norges arktiske universitet, and in Northern Sami: Romssa universitehta — Norgga árktalaš universitehta). It was also supported by the Canadian Center for Architecture (CCA; in French, Centre Canadien d'Architecture) and the Norges forskningsråd (Research Council of Norway).
5	Ove Haugen (Store Norske) in discussion with the author, March 14, 2023; Lili Wikstrom (LPO Architects) in discussion with the author, March 12, 2023.
6	Caitlin DeSilvey, *Curated Decay: Heritage beyond Saving* (University of Minnesota Press, 2017).
7	DeSilvey explores solastalgia through the study of a lighthouse in Orford Ness on the rapidly eroding Suffolk, UK, coast where the community participated in grieving practices for the structure with artwork, events, and documentation.
8	These elements and processes observed at sites of extraction in Longyearbyen and Tromsø from January to May 2023 were documented and collected into a series of zines and displayed in the final diploma exhibition *Ephemeral Edges*, at the Art Academy in Tromsø.
9	Inger Haseen-Bauer et al., *Climate in Svalbard 2100* (Norwegian Environmental Agency, 2019).

2   A view from inside one component of the land art intervention. Here, meltwater is channeled through an underground passage, echoing off the steel containers embedded in the site's mine tailings (May 2023).

3   Film photograph taken from the edge of Gruve 7 with a view towards Longyearbyen as coal dust envelops the snow piles (March 2023).

The water is then pushed off the side of the cliff, eroding the surface as it continues the journey down towards the fjord and warming Barents Sea below.

As natural processes such as meltwater move through the intervention, the site is decommissioned around them, re-framing the landscape around their agency in shaping the future of this site. Events such as the carving of the retention pond or the seasonal expulsion of underground glacial melt make space for visitors to witness change. As DeSilvey reflects within her research, these kinds of gatherings allow communities to become better equipped to come to terms with these changes "and to understand palliative care not (only) as an ending, but (also) as an opening to many possible futures."[10] In this way, the community's relationship to the site may move beyond grief for the loss of its cultural landscapes or the perpetual preservation of the coal mining heritage. Instead, this palliative approach to the decommissioning of Gruve 7 embraces the fluidity of the High Arctic and the future of Svalbard's rapidly evolving landscapes.

To accompany the design proposal, soundscape compositions were created for each perspective using field recordings of cryogenic processes from Longyearbyen and Tromsø as a way to depict the design at key points over fifty years. These sounds and images further emphasize the agency of the site's processes to shape the landscape as the design continuously evolves with the changing climatic conditions of the Arctic (May 2023).

10   Caitlin DeSilvey, "Palliative Curation and Future Persistence: Life after death," in *Cultural Heritages*, ed. Cornelius Holtorf and Anders Hogberg (Routledge, 2020), 227. Parentheses are by the original author.

Evolution and Activity of Mine #7's Materials

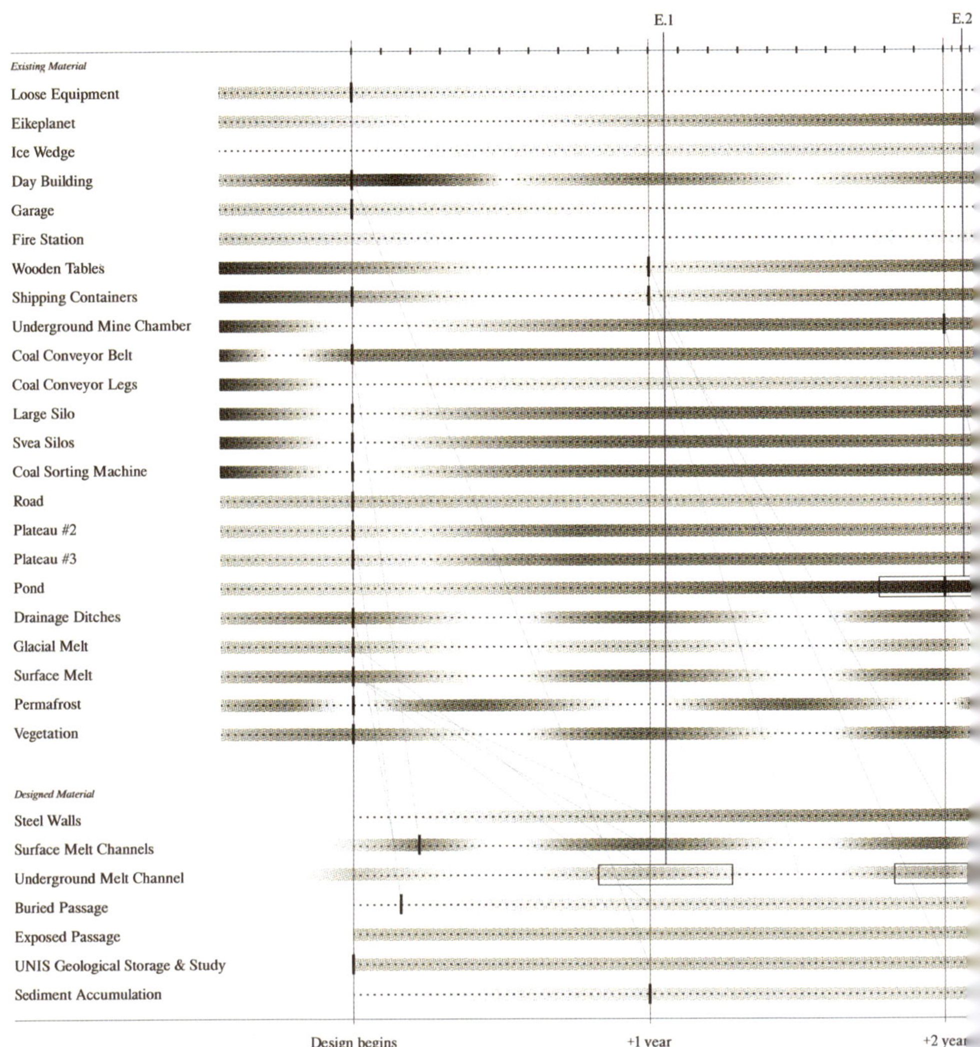

4   A temporal-material mapping of the cryogenic processes connecting and transforming Gruve 7 and Foxfonna Glacier over time (May 2023).

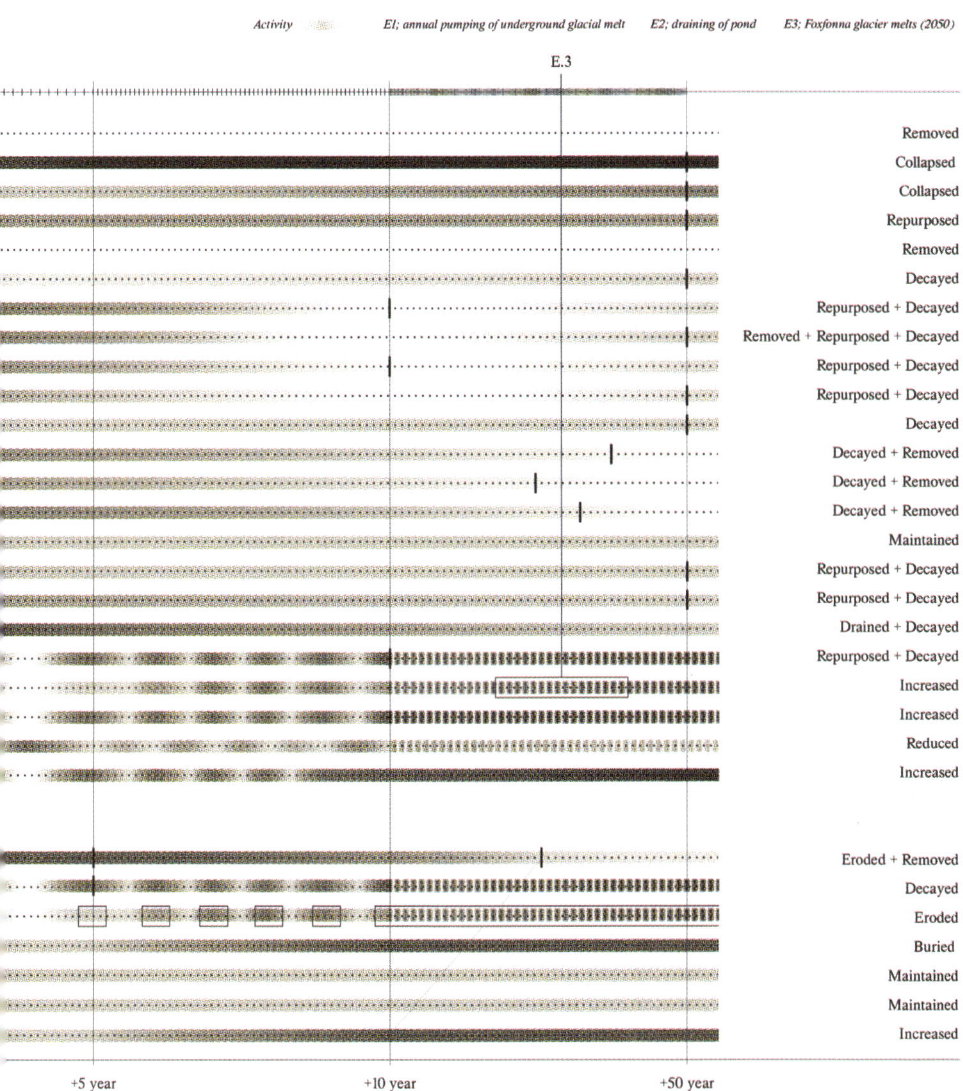

Activity
E1; annual pumping of underground glacial melt
E2; draining of pond
E3; Foxfonna glacier melts (2050)
E.3
Removed
Collapsed
Collapsed
Repurposed
Removed
Decayed
Repurposed + Decayed
Removed + Repurposed + Decayed
Repurposed + Decayed
Repurposed + Decayed
Decayed
Decayed + Removed
Decayed + Removed
Decayed + Removed
Maintained
Repurposed + Decayed
Repurposed + Decayed
Drained + Decayed
Repurposed + Decayed
Increased
Increased
Reduced
Increased
Eroded + Removed
Decayed
Eroded
Buried
Maintained
Maintained
Increased
+5 year
+10 year
+50 year

Sofia Singler is an Assistant Professor of Architecture at the University of Cambridge.

When Is Now? The Case for Temporal Ambiguity in Critiques of Sámi Architecture
Sofia Singler

The evidence was always hiding in plain sight: modern architecture was not about rejecting the past as much as selectively appropriating and manipulating it, swapping the burdens of recent history for a more ancient past. Tellingly, the cover of the Bauhaus manifesto depicted not a heroic factory but a cathedral.[1] The Alberses' studies in color and textile drew from the messianic formal purity of pre-Columbian temples and miniatures rather than transport terminuses.[2] Despite declaring war on an antiquated "consciousness of time," even De Stijl turned to methods borrowed from art history in its zeal to dismantle the "old world with its contents."[3] A Classical statue lay in observation at the foot of Walter Gropius and Adolf Meyer's Motorworks Pavilion at the Werkbund Exhibition of 1914, her relaxed pose communicating calm contentment: the authority of the past keeps its gaze on the modern, yet offers a relaxed acceptance of the novelty being celebrated.[4]

Still, a temporal bias persists in many accounts of the modern movement of the twentieth century. Awareness of modernists' simultaneous and mutually reinforcing interest in ancient history, on the one hand, and techno-scientific modernization, on the other, has grown considerably in the last few decades and remains the subject of scholarly interest today.[5] Yet it has not managed to extinguish the assumption that modernism was primarily, if not fundamentally, about rejecting the past. Modern architecture is, to this day, often understood as an architecture that unidirectionally positions itself toward the future—at the cost of the past.

The opposite bias lingers in accounts of Sámi architecture in the sub-Arctic and Arctic. As with many other Indigenous architectures and cultural practices, Sámi architecture is often assumed to be unidirectionally oriented toward historical origins: a vernacular that comprises moveable, modest, and momentary familial dwellings, such as the goahti and lávvu, built of timber, mosses, and reindeer hides. Although the Sámi have moved and been forced to move into permanent dwellings since the nineteenth century, particularly intensely from the 1950s and 1960s onward (as a result of which nomadic and semi-nomadic lifestyles have largely been replaced by sedentism), the lávvu, in particular, persists as an ethnopolitical symbol of resistance and as architectural shorthand for Sámi culture more generally.[6]

While the 'orthodox' modern architecture of the twentieth century has been narrated simplistically as rejecting history, 'authentic' Indigenous architecture is often deemed to indiscriminately belong to or perpetuate the past.[7] In critiques of Indigenous architecture, 'authenticity,' more often than not, describes an allegiance to historical precedent and tradition, a state of uncorrupted originality and primordiality that is fundamentally at odds with contemporaneity. Analyses of Aboriginal architecture, for instance, remain constrained to a framework wherein "representations have a tendency to simplify and romanticise ideas of 'Aboriginality' and 'authenticity' that are framed within readings of the historic past, the Dreaming or a connection to country. From the point of view of this colonial framework, Aboriginal cultures are fixed in an unchanging past and delineated by a singular set of values."[8]

1 Magdalena Bushart, "Am Anfang ein Missverständnis. Feiningers Kathedrale und das Bauhaus-Manifest," in *Modell Bauhaus* (Bauhaus-Archiv, Museum für Gestaltung, Stiftung Bauhaus Dessau und Klassik Stiftung Weimar, 2009), 29–32.

2 Lauren Hinkson, ed., *Josef Albers in Mexico* (Guggenheim Museum Publications, 2017).

3 Theo van Doesburg et al., "Manifest I of 'The Style', 1918," *De Stijl* 2, no. 1 (1918): 4.

4 William J. R. Curtis, *Modern Architecture since 1900* (Phaidon, 1996), 104–06.

5 Kenneth Frampton, *The Other Modern Movement: Architecture, 1920–1970* (Yale University Press, 2021).

6 A "symbolic breakthrough" has been pinpointed to the early 1980s, when Sámi hunger strikers constructed a lávvu outside the Norwegian Parliament building in protest of the hydroelectric development of the Alta-Kautokeino river valley. Ivar Bjørklund, "The Mobile Sámi Dwelling: From Pastoral Necessity to Ethno-political Master Paradigm," in *About the Hearth: Perspectives on the Home, Hearth, and Household in the Circumpolar North*, ed. David Anderson, Rob Wishart, and Virginie Vaté (Berghahn Books, 2013), 69–80.

7 In this regard, the criticism of Indigenous architecture parallels and indeed overlaps with that of 'historical,' 'traditional,' and 'vernacular' building practices. Marcel Vellinga, "The Inventiveness of Tradition: Vernacular Architecture and the Future," *Perspectives in Vernacular Architecture* 13, no. 2 (2006/2007), 117.

8 Tara Mallie and Michael J. Ostwalf, "Aboriginal Architecture: Merging Concepts from Architecture and Aboriginal Studies," in Liam Fennessy, Russell Kerr, Gavin Melles, Christine Thong and Emily Wright, eds., *Cumulus 38º South: Proceedings of the Cumulus Conference, 'Hemispheric Shifts Across Learning, Teaching and Research', Swinburne University of Technology and RMIT University, Melbourne, Australia, 12-14 November 2009* (Swinburne University of Technology and RMIT University, 2009), 483.

1   A slide from the teaching collections of the Helsinki University of Technology, illustrating modern architecture's complex relationship to history: a Tuscan charterhouse (from the fourteenth to sixteenth century) juxtaposed with Le Corbusier's Villa Savoye in Poissy (1929–31).

Assumptions of such definitive temporal orientations both underpin and bolster historiographical patterns of marginalization. Qualities deemed to contradict the assumed temporal disposition of an architectural ethic are cited as evidence of inauthenticity. Modern architecture that draws from craft rather than mechanized mass production or from stylistic precedent rather than abstracted expression is deemed 'backward-looking' and there-fore not truly modern; its belonging to the past becomes an affront to its purportedly future-oriented disposition and thus disqualifies it from the canon of modernist orthodoxy.[9] "Pervasive anomalies" that are detected in modern architecture—such as undeniably influential projects that come with a dubious whiff of history—may be categorized as "anachronistic hold-overs from defunct proto-modernist trends, or as successors challenging an already-codified modernism."[10]

The same dynamic, in reverse, is at play in analyses of Sámi archi-tecture. Sámi projects that concern themselves with the 'materials of modernity' (steel, concrete, plastic) rather than 'vernacular' natural materials (timber, moss, reindeer hide) or that address conditions of the contemporary city rather than nomadic life in ancestral land-scapes sit uneasily within what is perceived to be the authenticity of Sámi building tradition. Such designs are, therefore, often dismissed as exceptions to the rule or marginalized as something wholly Other. Categorizations such as 'Indigenous,' 'folk,' 'primitive,' or 'vernacular' architecture serve to "help define and legitimise the exclusive domain of what may be called 'high design' or 'capital A' architecture [...] by representing those architectural traditions that are not seen to be part of it in a way that emphasises their Otherness."[11]

Both modern and Sámi architecture have suffered from being tethered—too strictly—to opposite ends of the same linear teleology. The false dichotomy that fuels patterns of Othering in both cases—that an architecture can only ever reject or accept history—is particularly pernicious in the Indigenous context. Assigning Sámi architecture exclusively to the past continues to constrain its analysis to a colonial framework of interpretation, wherein modernity and contemporaneity are considered the realm of the sovereign Nordic nation-states (the future) and ancient history that of Sámi architecture (the past).

This framework relegates Sámi architecture to an interpretive schema of nostalgia. Since it dwells in the past, it can never quite manage to realize itself in the current moment; 'authentic' Sámi architecture cannot be retrieved or revived in the present. Sámi new-build commissions are thus stuck treacherously between Scylla and Charybdis. They may enter modernity by aligning themselves with the Nordic mainstream and thus accept a degree of inauthenticity in exchange for contemporary relevance, or they may maintain distance to their Nordic counterparts but, in so doing, surrender to becoming something Other, un-contemporary, and therefore nostalgic. Especially in Indigenous contexts, such "claims for authenticity and fulfilment of identity through the invocation of memory are normally the rhetoric of dogmatists who would lead us, individually and collectively, into desperation."[12]

The discourse surrounding the major public buildings erected in Sápmi from the 1970s onward testifies to the limits of such temporal determinism. Designed to give a contemporary form to an ancient nomadic Indigenous culture, the central attributes of publicness and permanence are foreign to the architectural tradition that newly built Sámi public buildings seek to represent. The museums, cultural centers, and parliamentary assemblies built in Sápmi in the last half century have been critiqued in light of an ostensible contradiction: their very existence, as manifestations of ancientness in the contemporary moment, is seen as inherently paradoxical. They appear to simultaneously

9   After all, the condition of modernity comes with a fundamental "orientation toward a future that will be different from the past and from the present," and modernism, as a set of responses to the condition of modernity, declares "sympathy with the orientation toward the future and the desire for progress." Hilde Heynen, *Architecture and Modernity: A Critique* (MIT Press, 1999), 9–10.

10   Sarah Williams Goldhagen, "Something to Talk About: Modernism, Discourse, Style," *Journal of the Society of Architectural Historians* 64, no. 2 (2005): 149.

11   Marcel Vellinga, "The End of the Vernacular: Anthropology and the Architecture of the Other," *Etnofoor* 23, no. 1 (2011): 172.

12   Stanford Anderson, "Memory without Monuments: Vernacular Architecture," *Traditional Dwellings and Settlements Review* 11, no. 1 (1999): 21.

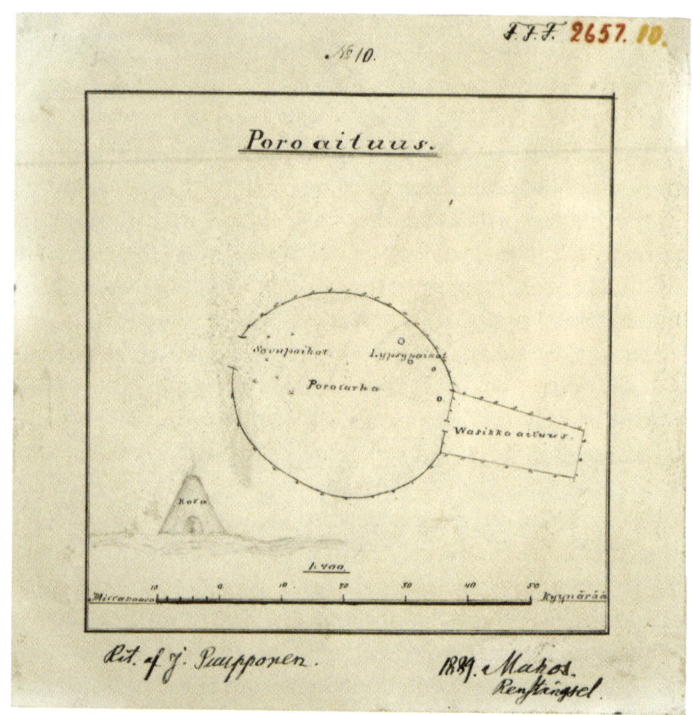

2   *Reindeer enclosure, plan* (1889), by Jaakko Puupponen.

occupy the ancient and future poles of the timeline of history, thereby violating the presumed belonging of Sámi architecture to the past.

Subsequent scholarly insistence on the 'contradictory contemporaneity' of Sámi public buildings has fueled a contrived hybridity wherein qualities perceived as 'ancient' are deemed Sámi, whereas 'contemporary' facets are considered Nordic.[13] Elements read as references to the past—semiotic citations of vernacular craft traditions or the employment of pre-industrial natural materials—are deemed Sámi, but elements considered decidedly contemporary—prefabricated concrete frames or triple-glazing—are judged inherently Nordic. In the case of the Sámi Parliament Building in Karasjok, for instance, designed by Stein Halvorsen and Christian Sundby and inaugurated in 2000, the exterior cladding in Siberian larch "ties the building to its specific location history, while steel, glass and concrete herald the modern and new."[14]

The Sámi Parliament and Cultural Centre Sajos, in Inari, designed by HALO Architects and completed in 2012, has been described in similar terms as a crossbreed. On the one hand, its morphological references to duodji, Sámi handcraft, are credited as authentic Indigenous elements: "The auditorium is shaped like a *kiisa*, an oval-shaped wooden container, like a small chest.

The conference room of the Sámi Parliament resembles a *risku*, a rounded piece of jewelry. Both spaces may also be conceived of as transformations of the shape of the traditional drum."[15] On the other hand, its overlaps with Nordic counterparts are perceived as threats to its Indigenous identity. "The authenticity of Sajos can justifiably be called into question: the building represents the mainstream of young Finnish architecture with its curved forms and minimalist, airy central space. Moreover, the topological quality of the roof surface and plasticity of form also associate the building with its contemporaries."[16]

Čoarvemátta, a cultural complex home to the Beaivváš Sámi Našunálateáhter (Sámi National Theater) as well as Sámi Joatkkaskuvla ja Boazodoalloskuvla (Sámi High School and Reindeer Husbandry School), set to open in 2024, is another case in point. Designed collaboratively by Snøhetta, 70°N arkitektur, Econor, and Joar Nango, the scheme is seen to embody ancient tradition both in terms of its program (reindeer husbandry, oral histories, performance, crafts) and its massing, which purportedly draws from the geometry of reindeer antlers.[17] Yet the technological sophistication of its structural system, environmental control, and construction is typically seen as Nordic. The design, therefore, appears to embody an inevitable concession Sámi culture is forced to make to its Nordic colonizer—a conclusion not limited to Čoarvemátta but endemic to much of the criticism of architecture in Sápmi. These hybrid categorizations, rooted in the perceived conflict between ancientness and modernity, generate ever-recurring conclusions of Sámi architecture being stuck in a purgatory between Indigenous authenticity and contemporary relevance. New-build Sámi buildings, as an architectural genre, are condemned to be never quite authentically Sámi.

What happens if we reject a teleological account of history and move away from the historiographical dichotomy in which Sámi architecture is exclusively oriented to the past? If we accept that Sámi architecture can simultaneously seek to reject and reprise facets of history and, similarly, that it can both claim and resist aspects of contemporaneity, we may find the tools to interpret it beyond the colonial frameworks that have defined its study for so long. Acknowledging a more ambiguous approach to time promises to expand critiques of Sámi architecture beyond the insipid constraints of comparative analyses of the architecture of the Nordic nation-states.

13   Sofia Singler, "Contradictory Contemporaneity? Sámi Building in Nordic Architectural Discourse," in *Joar Nango*, ed. Axel Wieder (Sternberg Press), forthcoming.

14   Elin Haugdal, "'It's Meant to Decay': Contemporary Sámi Architecture and the Rhetoric of Material," in *The Handbook of Contemporary Indigenous Architecture*, ed. Elizabeth Grant, Kelly Greenop, Albert L. Refiti, and Daniel J. Glenn (Singapore: Springer, 2018), 818.

15   Lauri Louekari, "Sámi Cultural Centre Sajos, Inari," *Arkkitehti*, no. 5 (2012): 30.

16   Ibid., 30.

17   Statsbygg, *Detaljregulering for Beavváš og Samisk Videregående Skole og Reindriftskole*, planbeskrivelse til detaljregulering (Statsbygg, 2021).

3   Shared Sámi Theater and Reindeer Husbandry School, Guovdageaidnu / Kautokeino by Snøhetta Oslo,
         70°N arkitektur and Joar Nango with Econor, Čoarvemátta (2020–2024).

Given the inherently interdisciplinary nature of architecture and ever-changing definitions of what constitutes the architectural field, the theoretical and methodological frameworks employed to analyze the histories and present of the built environment "need to keep changing, too, in order to keep pace with the permanent reconfiguration of our object of study. An eclectic approach to interdisciplinarity is the almost inevitable consequence of this state of affairs."[18] Taking a cue from other disciplines, it becomes immediately apparent that bells announcing the necessity of non-linear understandings of history are sounding loud, echoing rapidly into architecture.

Scholars of Sámi religious history underscore that narratives surrounding the Christianization of the Sámi have been unduly constrained by the assumption that historic Indigenous religious practices were simply substituted by new Christian dogma. Rather than the ancient being replaced by the new, Sámi and Western religions interacted and overlapped in complex and sometimes contradictory ways, ultimately melding into an "increasingly syncretic belief system."[19]

Sámi pastoralism, similarly, has long been considered a paradigmatic shift from traditional hunting to modern pastoralism. The dominant narrative is of an ancient past being replaced by a new life-form, of Sámi livelihoods switching their orientation from history to the future. Researchers have therefore tended to focus on identifying the precise timing and mechanisms of the pivotal change at the expense of considering its character. Increasingly, scholars now recognize that "there has probably never been an abrupt change; hunting and herding have both been parts of a multifaceted adaption existing up to the nineteenth century."[20] A novel era did not replace a previous history in a singular temporal fold, but rather, the reverberations between pasts and futures were—and remain—tangled, dynamic, and synergistic.

Anti- and non-teleological readings of Sámi architecture pave the way toward productively ambiguous interpretations that, rather than imposing a predetermined temporal orientation on Sámi buildings, recognize both the fragility and vigor with which pasts and futures meld in them. Elin Haugdal offers a provocative and nuanced analysis of the complexities of material use in modern and contemporary Sámi architecture. Her interpretation avoids the pitfalls of reductively defining 'old' materials as Sámi and 'modern' as Nordic and thereby illustrates the value of moving beyond the historiographic dichotomy that constrains so much of the discourse on Indigenous architecture.

On the one hand, in line with the typical understanding of Sámi architecture's orientation to the past, materials such as untreated timber are seen to communicate "an aesthetics of decay that contemporary observers see in the ephemerality of traditional Sámi building practices," especially the ideal of never leaving permanent physical traces in the land, associated with mobile Sámi dwellings such as the lávvu.[21] On the other hand, non-decaying materials, which resist the effects of time, may be interpreted as cultural defiance—not products of a vernacular tradition, yet equally if not more 'Sámi.' Rather than invasively parasitic Nordic elements that corrupt Sámi authenticity, materials such as steel and concrete may be read as vessels of Sámi meaning that declare: "This building is decidedly *not* meant to decay."[22]

What anchors Joar Nango's practice in Sámi culture is not merely an interrogation of local materials, traditions, symbolisms, or tectonics—qualities recognizably linked to a Sámi past. Its embrace of the contemporary and the future is of the essence, epitomized by a design attitude or method Nango and Silje Figenschou Thoresen describe as 'indigenuity,' a portmanteau of

18   Mario Carpo, "Architecture: Theory, Interdisciplinarity, and Methodological Eclecticism," *Journal of the Society of Architectural Historians* 64, no. 4 (2005): 426.

19   Tiina Äikäs and Anna-Kaisa Salmi, "North/South Encounters at Sámi Sacred Sites in Northern Finland," *Historical Archaeology* 49, no. 3, "Contemporary and Historical Archaeology of the North" (2015): 90–109 (100).

20   Ivar Bjørklund, "Domestication, Reindeer Husbandry and the Development of Sámi Pastoralism," *Acta Borealia* 30, no. 2 (2013): 174–189 (174).

21   Haugdal, "It's Meant to Decay," 823.

22   Ibid., 812.

'Indigenous' and 'ingenuity.'[23] Temporally, indigenuity might be understood as operating beyond a dualistic dialectic between history and the future; it draws from both in tandem. While the Sámi vernacular may draw from natural materials, ancestral landscapes, and semi-nomadic livelihoods, contemporary Sámi material culture "includes Euro pallets and Coca-Cola bottles, plastic ropes, and other leftover consumer goods."[24] Projects of indigenuity resist being read as emblems of loss. Mass-produced Western commodities, consumer goods, or building systems are not evidence of colonial contemporaneity assuming a chokehold over Indigenous tradition as much as an instance of redefinition, reclaiming, and resistance. "The creation of an autonomously programmed object that distorts capitalist material flows" is subversion rather than surrender.[25]

> Resisting the urge to pinpoint Sámi architecture to the historic end of an imaginary architectural timeline liberates analyses of contemporary Sámi buildings from the typical conclusion that they represent a sorry compromise between Sámi pasts and Western futures. Forms and types of Sámi architecture that have previously been marginalized because of their incongruity with an assumed orientation to the past might come to represent a wholly novel category of authenticity, which gains legitimacy not from the authority of the past but from refusing to be pigeonholed to a strict teleology. What was previously narrated as a misfit now stands to be viewed as defiantly and presciently Other. This is a historiographical framework in which "accident, contingency, and human universals—fluidity without inevitability—offer the raw materials for a better model of architectural historical process than the static idea of culture (with either a capital or lower-case c)."[26]

In modern architecture—similarly appointed to one extreme of an assumed timeline of existence, albeit the opposite end—the "Other tradition" of modern architecture has been theorized as an ethic that transcends simplistic dualisms of past and present. The Other tradition, as described by Colin St John Wilson, gains its potency from its refusal to address time in dialectically opposed terms. It embodies "a dynamic relationship in which not only is the new derived in part from the past but, by extending the scope of the traditional, changes (in turn) our understanding of the past."[27] It consciously collapses pasts and futures into one another, resulting in a "true modernism not only of Eliot and Joyce but also of Matisse and Picasso, in which dazzling powers of invention jostle with ancestral figures."[28] The result is an architecture that cannot be considered in exclusively historical or contemporary terms. "The point of history was no longer to give triumphalist, teleological accounts of modernism's seemingly inevitable rise"—instead, linear accounts of history's triumphant march from the past to the future were substituted by an invocation of "its multiplicity, its variability and its unexpected shifts or reversals" in time.[29]

> Similar conceptions abound beyond St John Wilson's thesis: many ways of verbalizing ambiguity exist. Svetlana Boym's characterization of a "History Out-of-sync" and "Architecture of the Off-Modern" speaks to history writing, which evades a clear historical narrative arch. "Off-modern," she defines as "a detour into the unexplored potentials of the modern project. It recovers unforeseen pasts and ventures into the side alleys of modern history, at the margins of error of major philosophical, economic, and technological narratives of modernization and progress. It opens into the modernity of 'what if,' and not only postindustrial modernity as it was."[30]

More recently, Eeva-Liisa Pelkonen has continued challenging the presumed future-orientedness of modern architecture, arguing that "temporal disorientation was a hallmark of twentieth-century architecture, and that, while we often think that being modern means aspiring to leave the past behind with every tick of the clock, a disregard for chronological time was, in fact, an integral aspect of modernity."[31] Her characterization of "untimely" modernists explicitly foregrounds "the far-reaching intellectual legacy of questioning linear historical time and the impact it had on twentieth-century intellectual and artistic culture."[32] Hitherto Sámi architecture has been predominantly conceptualized as an aspiration to return to historical origins—what about an 'out-of-sync' or 'untimely' Sámi architecture?

> Interrogating Sámi architecture with reference to a productive Othering or untimeliness, in which time is viewed in non-linear terms, helps transcend the limitations of colonial interpretation. It frees the criticism of contemporary Sámi architecture from facile conclusions of hybridity. If a given project's ostensibly modern or futurist elements are interpreted as Sámi rather than Nordic, what might otherwise be interpreted as a cultural concession or submission may now be read as defiance, authenticity, and critique.

As Hirini Matunga notes: "Indigenous architecture is both *position and opposition* and *acceptance and resistance* [...] Given that it continues to evolve as a

23   Joar Nango and Silje Figenschou Thoresen, ed., *The Indigenuity Project* (Motto Books SA, 2013).

24   Joar Nango, "In practice: Joar Nango on building a library of Sámi architecture," *Architectural Review* (2022).

25   Ibid.

26   Dell Upton, "Starting from Baalbek: Noah, Solomon, Saladin, and the Fluidity of Architectural History," *Journal of the Society of Architectural Historians* 68, no. 4 (2009): 465.

27   Colin St John Wilson, "The Other Tradition," *AA Files*, no. 24 (1992): 3–6.

28   Ibid.

29   Anthony Raynsford, "Provoking the 'Thingness' of History: The Anti-Teleological Hermeneutics of Steen Eiler Rasmussen," in *104th ACSA Annual Meeting Proceedings: Shaping New Knowledges*, eds. Robert Corser and Sharon Haar (ACSA Press, 2016), 543–48.

30   Svetlana Boym, *The Off-Modern* (Bloomsbury Academic, 2017), 3.

31   Eeva-Liisa Pelkonen, *Untimely Moderns: How Twentieth-Century Architecture Reimagined the Past* (Yale University Press, 2023), 1.

32   Ibid., 12.

4   *Utsjoki* (1960) by U. A. Saarinen.

design and built response to an ever-changing context, it should also resist the pejorative labels that in the past have tried to marginalise it, render it invisible or minimise it as a 'legitimate' architecture. These have ranged from labels such as primitive and savage to folk and traditional, 'rough' or 'just buildings' through to the vernacular, pastiche or 'just a little bit too local'."[33]

The "Other" approach has far-reaching consequences in light of green colonialism and other issues. Exploiting land areas in Sápmi is easier to justify if the Sámi built environment is defined in terms of ancientness. So long as patterns of reindeer herding or fishing are not directly impacted, the effect of large-scale infrastructural interventions such as wind farms and new railways are said not to threaten Sámi dwelling. From the Nordic states' perspective, 'unbuilt' and 'underused' Lappish territories represent an empty canvas on which to build sustainable architecture. If we accept that Sámi architecture, as an 'untimely' mélange that comprises not just structures and lands that support ancient livelihoods and patterns of dwelling but also modern life forms from 'snowmobilescapes' to commercial infrastructures via which Sámi artisans serve tourist populations, the threats posed by such megaprojects become more difficult to neglect. These megaprojects may, at best, avoid disrupting vernacular Sámi lives, but they also upset modern, sedentary, and urban patterns of dwelling—which an untimely understanding of Sámi architecture compels us to view as just as relevant.

Embracing Otherism also broadens the scope of analysis to issues typically glazed over in the criticism of contemporary Sámi architecture. Hitherto, criticism has been limited predominantly to major new-build commissions of a public genre: civic, artistic, and political complexes that seek to serve Sámi communities. The politico-cultural burdens of such commissions—to celebrate or even represent an Indigenous people within the borders of a sovereign state—make them obvious targets for analyses rooted in the perceived conflict between Sámi pasts and Western futures. Yet little has been remarked on spaces and places that do not as explicitly straddle ancient pasts and presumed futures, and whose designs do not as straightforwardly carry responsibility for cultural representation. Although awareness of urban indigeneity is growing rapidly, architectural discourse has yet to interrogate the problems of the contemporary city in light of Sámi architectural practice.[34] Housing, for instance, is rarely addressed explicitly as Sámi architecture, nor has much been said of major Nordic cities south of Sápmi being home to sizable Sámi communities; for instance, the largest Sámi community in Finland is in Helsinki rather than the Arctic.[35] Architectural discourse remains complicitly silent on the situation faced by towns in Sápmi, such as Inari, which suffer from severe housing crises.[36]

Future scholarship on Sámi architecture ought to root itself in a critical re-evaluation of its relationship to history. Looking and seeing beyond Sámi architecture's assumed exclusive belonging to the past—via off-modern or untimely paradigms of historical interpretation—promises to expand and enrich the analysis of Sámi built environments manifold. After all, to borrow Stanford Anderson's reading of Banni architectural traditions in Gujarat, "despite its presence from time immemorial, this art of building [...] is very much a matter of the present."[37] Many Sámi individuals have "dual" or even "plural" identities through which they identify with the Sámi nation as well as the nation-state(s) in which they live; analogously, much of the architecture in Sápmi straddles ambiguous hybridities between nation-states and Indigenous communities, as well as between pasts and futures.[38]

33   Hirini Matunga, "A Discourse on the Nature of Indigenous Architecture," in *The Handbook of Contemporary Indigenous Architecture*, ed. Elizabeth Grant, Kelly Greenop, Albert L. Refiti and Daniel J. Glenn (Springer, 2018), 304.

34   Dana Brablec and Andrew Canessa, eds., *Urban Indigeneities: Being Indigenous in the Twenty-First Century* (University of Arizona Press, 2023).

35   Jenni Hakovirta, "Building a Case for Indigenous Architecture with Mixed-use Anarâškielâ Language Nest and Home for Elderly," MArch thesis, University of Oulu, 2021.

36   Reetta Lehtiranta, "Kotiin? Paikallisten suhde arkkitehtuuriin Inarissa," MArch thesis, University of Oulu, 2022.

Modernist architects who viewed time in kaleidoscopic rather than telescopic terms found meaning in the process more than periodization. Their interest in select moments of history was rooted in an appreciation of socio-cultural context and method: the medieval church-building as a paragon of collective labor, or the Mesopotamian house-temple as a perfect translation of ritual movement into built form. Calls for questioning or even collapsing strict temporal orientations in the interpretation and criticism of Indigenous architecture similarly suggest an "approach that explicitly focuses on building traditions rather than buildings," on process rather than product, as a method of avoiding the pitfalls of "historical entrapment."[39] In the context of Sámi architectural scholarship, a non-linear temporal foundation is not a novel framework of historical analysis as much as a re-acknowledgment of architecture as a timeless, immediate encounter with the meanings one can create and encounter through the manipulation of materials and space.

37   Stanford Anderson, "Memory without Monuments: Vernacular Architecture," *Traditional Dwellings and Settlements Review* 11, no. 1 (1999): 15.

38   Mikkel Berg-Nordlie, "The Governance of Urban Indigenous Spaces: Norwegian Sámi Examples," *Acta Borealia* 35, no. 1 (2018): 53.

39   Vellinga, "The Inventiveness of Tradition," 118.

Brandon Bergem and Jeffrey Garcia are principals of Office In Search Of (OISO), an interdisciplinary and collaborative design and visualization practice, and educators at the University of Toronto.

Ultima Thule Museum of Natural History: Containing the Full Reconstructions of the Landscapes of Svalbard, of Instruments of Prophecy, and of Accidental Monuments with an Account of its Architectural Oddities: With a Repository Containing some Important Historical Artifacts Salvaged prior to the Disappearance of the Arctic
Brandon Bergem and Jeffrey Garcia

INTRODUCTION

In the fourth century, Before the Common Era (BCE), the Greek explorer Pytheas of Massilia, searching for new trading opportunities, discovered a mythical island, Thule, in the most extreme—ultima—remotest Far North.[1] The exact location is unknown because the account of his voyage, *On the Ocean,* perished when the Library of Alexandria was consumed by fire. As centuries passed without a documented reference, Ultima Thule became more of an idea than an actual place. It was simultaneously of the world and a mythical symbol of the edge of an unknown world to cartographers, explorers, and poets.[2] It represented an unexplored northern frontier with unlimited fantastical possibilities. It is imagined that in the twenty-first century, Ultima Thule embodies the uncertain future facing the arctic archipelago of Svalbard, a unique territory with intricate sovereignty aimed at safeguarding the resource extraction interests of multiple nations.[3] The area contends with environmental degradation as a consequence of climate turmoil.[4] This tundra hosts centuries-old remnants and fossilized imprints, juxtaposing resource exploitation with prolific scientific monitoring done by researchers worldwide. Svalbard has an idiosyncratic identity: it is simultaneously a place that was unnecessary to define because, already before the treaty, it was deemed terra nullius and the most advantageous place in the world to best help us understand the deleterious consequences of the ways we have chosen to inhabit our planet.[5]

Several drawings from the *Ultima Thule Museum of Natural History* (UTMNH) research project portend grounded speculations on the islands' disappearance.[6] The architectural scenarios depict conjectured mythology intertwined with empirical data. The project anticipates the continuous necessity of a repository where physical remnants are exhibited in mise-en-scènes that interpret moments in time. The fantastical narratives can be misleading because they are located in a fictional museological setting in an indeterminate future. Although the scenarios may seem exaggerated, they fulfill the purpose of storytelling, whether meant to entertain, inform, and inspire or caution and cause alarm.

ON IMAGE CREATION: DRAWING REALITY AND CONSTRUCTING ILLUSIONS

For centuries, unprecedented devices have been used to aid in representing reality. The Hockney-Falco thesis posits that advances in realism and accuracy since the Renaissance were primarily the result of optical instruments such as the camera obscura, camera lucida, and curved mirrors, more so than any single artistic technique and skill.[7] Albrecht Dürer's door, evident in the sixteenth-century woodcut *The Draughtsman of the Lute*, constitutes the first example of ray tracing.[8] Albeit analog, it was the precursor to a fundamental technique for computer rendering.[9] The limits of photorealism now depend on a render engine's capacities—like Chaos® V-Ray®—which simulates photorealistic lighting and physical material properties in 3D digital models.

The contrivance of a natural history museum diorama harkens back to 1822, when Louis Jacques Mandé Daguerre and Charles Marie Bouton opened the Diorama in Paris that simulated realism using visual tricks like multilayered paintings, light projection, and shutters.[10] The mastery of evoking immersive environments for mass audiences became elevated due to Frank M. Chapman, who joined the American Museum of Natural History (AMNH) as its first bird curator in the late nineteenth century. Chapman is credited as the person who brought dioramas to the AMNH and instituted its practice of sending teams of artists, taxidermists, and naturalists to the habitats they were recreating so that everything from the vistas to the vegetation was rigorously documented, with scientific accuracy inextricable from the artistry.[11] According to Steven Quinn, who oversaw the creation of dioramas at the AMNH, Carl Akeley (taxidermist and inventor) and James Perry Wilson (painter and architectural designer) continue to be considered the esteemed pioneers and masters of the diorama because of the remarkable verisimilitude of the landscape depictions they created.[12] Their coordinated compositional interface between photorealistic paintings, taxidermy animals, and three-dimensional dioramas and their elements have been compared to virtual reality.[13]

1   Ian Whitaker, "The Problem of Pytheas' Thule," *The Classical Journal* 77, no. 2 (December 1981): 150. Pytheas reported that the coastline of the island was more than forty thousand stadia, and Thule was not composed of land, sea, or air, but a substance concreted from all those elements, a thing in which he says: "[T]he earth, the sea, and all the elements are held in suspension… a sort of bond to hold all together which you can neither walk nor sail upon."

2   F. Salazar, "Claiming Ultima Thule," *Hakai Magazine: Coastal science and societies*, September 8, 2020, hakaimagazine.com/features/claiming-ultima-thule. Ultima Thule was poised at the edge of the known and unknown Earth and functioned as an emblem of mystical isolation, liminal remoteness, and a place truly unknown. To quote Edgar Allan Poe's allusion to the island in his poem *Dream-land*: "I have reached these lands but newly / From an ultimate dim Thule – / From a wild weird clime that lieth, sublime / Out of SPACE – out of TIME."

3   "The Spitsbergen Treaty," *Spitsbergen Svalbard*, accessed May 2, 2024. The Spitsbergen Treaty was signed on February 9, 1920, in Versailles, France. Although it is commonly referred to as the Svalbard Treaty, this is incorrect because the term "Svalbard" was not used until August 14, 1925, when the treaty was enforced and included in Norwegian law. Prior to the nineteenth and twentieth centuries, several nations in Northern Europe did not believe it was necessary to claim sovereignty of a so-called no man's land. This concern was rescinded when mining became the dominant field of economy in Spitsbergen. The treaty defines several framing conditions, such as 1. Spitsbergen was under Norwegian administration and legislation, 2. Citizens of all signatory nations had free access and the right of economic activities, and 3. Spitsbergen remained demilitarized with no nation (including Norway) being allowed to permanently station military personnel or equipment.

4   "While the Arctic is warming about four times faster than the rest of the world, in Svalbard, temperatures are climbing even faster — up to seven times the global average." From Lisi Niesner and Gloria Dickie, "Climate Change Thaws World's Northernmost Research Station," *Reuters*, April 19, 2023.

5   Ibid.: The northernmost year-round research station is in close proximity to Ny-Ålesund (New Ålesund) on the island of Spitsbergen in Svalbard, which is above the Arctic Circle. Researchers have been studying the polar region for over forty years. A comprehensive study is possible because of the cross-disciplinary collaborations. François Burgay, a chemist from the Paul Scherrer Institute (PSI) in Switzerland remarked that "one of the special things about this place is there are a lot of different scientists [including] biologists [and] geologists."

6   Known for his writing on climate change, David Wallace-Wells, in his chapter titled "Drowning," warns that sea-level rise would continue for millennia with approximately 444,000 square miles of land lost. He reminds us that nearly two-thirds of the world's major cities are on the coast. In addition to rising sea-levels, there is a major concern of the methane that will be released by a melting Arctic, where permafrost contains up to 1.8 trillion tons of carbon. When it thaws, some of it will evaporate as methane which can be at least several dozen times more powerful a greenhouse gas than carbon dioxide. Found in David Wallace-Wells, *The Uninhabitable Earth: Life after Warming* (Tim Duggan Books, 2019), 61–62, 66.

7   The Hockney–Falco thesis is a theory of art history advanced by artist David Hockney and physicist Charles M. Falco that elicited interest by scientists, historians, science historians, and art historians. Hockney and Falco claimed that "advances in realism and accuracy in the history of Western art since the Renaissance were primarily the result of optical instruments such as the camera obscura, camera lucida, and curved mirrors, rather than solely due to the development of artistic technique and skill." "Hockney-Falco Thesis," *Hockney-Falco thesis – Harvard Canvas*, accessed January 18, 2024. In an article titled "Secret Knowledge: Rediscovering the Lost Techniques of the Old Masters," written by Jane Partner in 2002 for the *Cambridge Quarterly*, Hockney offers evidence for their conceit: "Early Renaissance artists such as Jan van Eyck and Lorenzo Lotto used concave mirrors; as evidence, he points to the chandelier in Van Eyck's Arnolfini Portrait, the ear in Van Eyck's portrait of Cardinal Albergati, and the carpet in Lotto's *Husband and Wife*. Hockney suggests that later artists, beginning with Caravaggio, used convex mirrors as well, to achieve a large field of view."

8   Ray tracing digitally emulates how light reflects and refracts to create more realistic objects and environments.

The diorama is a unique evidentiary typology bound to the accuracy of a specific location in a moment, depicted to be remarkably measured with scrutinized precision. Yet, its fidelity to reality often relies on special effects and illusions. With Carl Akeley's innovation in taxidermy, known as The Akeley Method, animals, regardless of being faultlessly sculpted and posed in perpetual stasis, became lightweight papier-mâché figurines (called manikins) tautly sheathed in their respective hides, pelts, or fur.[14] James Perry Wilson's contribution to background painting corrected distortion by devising an irregular grid that could be applied on a curved surface.[15] The legacy of their contributions to diorama construction is evidenced in *The Wolf Pack*, the famous wolf diorama at the AMNH. The back leg of one of the two wolves is about to propel its body into the air, while a front paw on the other hovers slightly over the snow in anticipation of landing. They are accompanied by a background that documents the sky above Gunflint Lake, Northern Minnesota, at 3:00 a.m. on December 7, 1941, with the constellations perfectly placed. However, the precision of the demonstration required a modest deception. A mixture of marble dust and mica chips needed to be sprinkled to achieve the shadows of the running wolves that were faked.[16]

All the depicted dioramas at the UTMNH are in an in-production state that parallels their making as a digital construct. Unlike the examples in the AMNH, where concerted efforts to minimize obvious visual trickery are the ambition, the explicit exposition of its mimicry is the goal. While dioramas are constructed with a particular vantage point in mind for museum visitors, the drawings only make sense to us as viewers of the images.[17] One cannot be fooled because the reality shown is heavily stylized. The weight of the stacked house-sized models seems negligible compared to the meager scaffolding supporting them. The plywood panels used for the topography are too pristine for a surface that would be constantly stepped upon when installed. The height necessary to suspend objects from the ceiling exceeds the reach of the tallest tower cranes. The uncanny lighting is consistent in all the scenarios because the amount that enters a scene suggests non-existing light fixtures and dubious installation distances. Even the puddles, ladders, and work surfaces are pictorially composed and not appropriately haphazard for how an undepicted workforce would abandon their tasks.

The foundation of diorama making has been upgraded with software. Individual props can be acquired as pre-made models shared by their authors in a voluminous online warehouse. The hollow taxidermized manikins sheathed in their original hides are digital models wrapped with material textures provided by a photographic database. An undulating, sloped, textured, or smooth landscape depicted like an assemblage of individual plaster tiles or wood planks can result from a visual programming language that generates geometries by linking data to functions. Detailed examples of architecture,

9   Steve Luecking, a professor of art at DePaul University postulates that Albrecht Dürer made an analogue apparatus, Dürer's Door, that employed principles shared with the most common method of rendering 3D objects in a computer. The woodcut depicts Dürer's method of using a square to measure the horizontal and vertical position at which the thread passed through the door. Creating an image required the thread to be attached to the end of a stylus while an assistant moved it, creating a series of dotted lines along an object's contours. The thread passed first through the door's frame and then through a hook on the wall. Ray-tracing software is similar in principle, where it measures the raster position of a ray emanating from a point on a virtual object to the position of a virtual camera as a ray that passes through a virtual screen. Like Dürer's Door, the sum of these points creates an accurate 2D perspective. Steve Luecking, "Durer, Drawing, and Digital Thinking," in *Leonardo's Legacy* (FATE, Savannah, Georgia, USA, 2023), brian-curtis.com/text/conferpape_steveluecking.html.

10   There were no live actors or conventional scene changes. Transforming impressions, mood changes, and movement were produced by a system of shutters and screens that allowed light to be projected from behind on alternately separate sections of an image painted on a semi-transparent backdrop. According to historians of photography, it was Daguerre's efforts to improve technology of the diorama that led to his investigations of light-sensitive materials and eventually the invention of the daguerreotype, the first photographic technology. Eszter Szalczer, "Nature's Dream Play: Modes of Vision and August Strindberg's Re-Definition of the Theatre," *Theatre Journal* 53, no. 1 (2001): 50.

11   Andrea DenHoed, "The Making of the American Museum of Natural History's Wildlife Dioramas," *The New Yorker,* February 15, 2016.

12   Steven Quinn worked at the AMNH from 1974 to 2013, Carl Akeley joined the AMNH in 1909, and James Perry Wilson joined in 1934. Elizabeth Barlow Rogers, "Representing Nature: The Dioramas of the American Museum of Natural History," *SiteLINES: A Journal of Place* 8, no. 2 (Spring 2013): 10-13.

13   At the turn of the nineteenth century, museums catered primarily to upper class visitors who did not require didactics because they would be accompanied by guides. A step towards inclusion resulted in the emergence of the self-tour in the late nineteenth century. Menachem Wecker quotes David Skelly, who directs Yale University's Peabody Museum of Natural History, saying: "[Dioramas] were the virtual reality machines of their age, the pre-television era." Citing the African savannah or the mountains of western North America dioramas at the AMNH, he continued: "[Dioramas] gave them a sense of what wildlife looked like there, and what the world was like in the places where they'd never been and likely would never go." Menachem Wecker, "The History and Future of the Once-Revolutionary Taxidermy Diorama," *Smithsonian Magazine*, October 11, 2016.

14   Akeley's Method involved taking extensive field measurements and modeling clay around a skeletal armature to create a detailed sculpture of the animal. He then covered the clay with its hide, which he would ensure had been processed at a tannery to make it supple and insect-proof. He would further manipulate the wet clay within the now-skin-clothed animal to ensure subtler detailing of the musculature, wrinkles, and folds to perfect the imperfect lifelike pose he conceived for the manikin. When Akeley was satisfied, a plaster cast encased the entire hide-covered clay sculpture. Once hard, the plaster and underlying pelt were incised and separated into two halves. The hardened clay was removed from the molds and the skeleton was sent back to the Department of Mammalogy, after which Akeley's team filled the plaster shells with papier-mâché. Once it was dry, they reunited the two halves of the animal, removed the plaster from the exterior, sewed the skin together again at the seams, and concealed the stitching where the specimen had been cut apart. Steven Quinn from the AMNH has conceded they are essentially lightweight papier-mâché figurines. For more, please see Elizabeth Barlow Rogers, *"Representing Nature,"* 10–11.

15   James Perry Wilson developed a method of painting that considered perspectival optics (based on the physiology of human binocular vision). He began his process by using a grid he could geometrically alter so that the grid would appear orthogonal when viewed from a central position, while the squares of the grid changed in size and shape toward the edges of the diorama's curved background wall. Wilson used panoramic stereoscopic photographs as references to place the horizon line at exactly five feet two inches from the ground (which he considered to be the average viewing height of a museum visitor). Once the preliminary scenery was sketched onto the surface, he referred to plein-air paintings he himself had completed on site to ensure that the color and values of the diorama's background approached those seen by the naked eye when looking into the distance out of doors (for more, please see Elizabeth Barlow Rogers, *"Representing Nature,"* 11–12).

towers, and scaffolding are made with rudimentary 3D modeling software. Replacing each brushstroke loaded with paint are individual pixels that are assigned a single color. What would take months to produce in analog can be conjured within an hour using an entry-level laptop computer. At the *Ultima Thule Museum of Natural History*, facsimile and facts are reconciled in high-resolution fidelity.

CONCLUSION

The *Ultima Thule Museum of Natural History* engages the histories of two Arctic islands. One is ethereal and untouched, and the other is Svalbard, Norway, the canary in the coal mine because it experiences the effects of climate change before anywhere else in the world. In the twenty-first century, in addition to the numerous research outposts, it is populated with a taxonomy of measuring devices—thermometers, anemometers, hygrometers, barometers, heliometers, pyrometers, Mesosphere-stratosphere-troposphere radars, and atmospheric radar—that have become instruments of prophecy, assiduously monitoring the health of an increasingly vulnerable archipelago.[18] In the sixteenth century, the certainty of its actuality was disputed. Thule was simultaneously fiction and fact, ethereal and tangible, real and imagined.[19] Rather than Svalbard being frequently defined by data as the effects of climate change are measured and anticipated, Thule's identity was dependent on chronicles of its existence.

The representation of these three dioramas can be appreciated as visually entertaining. However, the content of the drawings reflects the efforts enacted by Alvin Boyarsky at the Architectural Association, where it is posited that "[the] efflorescence of interest in [drawings] reflect not only the growing prominence of drawing as a medium of discourse but also the centrality of discourse itself."[20] Deploying rendering applications as a visual storytelling substrate shows it in a perpetual state of incomplete assembly, where this collection of digital renderings are situated as stories in which the past represents an imagined future (with sources, from scholarly to speculative). The depiction of the *Ultima Thule Museum of Natural History* is sui generis compared to how most architectural spaces are digitally manifested as fait accompli. On their own and together, *Lifting Longyearbyen*, *Seismographic Surveyors*, and *Primordial Pyramiden* suggest the effects of the climate change crisis have approached maximum devastation, with one of the few lingering cultural artifacts being architectural narratives.

16   The low-level fluorescent lamps with blue filters used to simulate nocturnal light are incapable of casting the stuffed wolves' shadows, which fall according to the position of the full moon and cannot be seen but can be imagined to be outside the diorama. For more, see Elizabeth Barlow Rogers, *"Representing Nature,"* 13.

17   James Perry Wilson's devised grid was manipulated so that from the vantage point of a visitor (of average height and eye level), the grid would appear straight and its units would appear square. Some of the steps involved were to establish an eye-level line, locate the center of the opening of the curved diorama shell, locate the central viewing point, project a line from the central viewing point through the center of the diorama opening and onto the interior of the diorama shell, inscribe on the floor the largest arc that could fit within the confines of the diorama shell, determine and mark several reference points from the floor to the eye-line, calculate and mark the horizontal spacing, and connect the vertical and horizontal points. Ruth Morrill, "A Dual-Grid System for Diorama Layout," *Curator: The Museum Journal,* vol. 39, no. 4, 282-284. Accessed May 20, 2024, onlinelibrary.wiley.com/toc/21516952/1996/39/4.cc

18   An example of an integrated network is the Svalbard Integrated Arctic Earth Observing System (SIOS), a collaborative effort to develop and maintain a regional observational system for long-term measurements in and around Svalbard, addressing Earth System Science (ESS) questions related to Global Change. The observing system and research facilities offered by SIOS build on the extensive observation capacity and diverse research infrastructure provided by institutions already established in Svalbard. This includes a substantial capability for utilizing remote sensing resources to complement ground-based observations. SIOS focuses on processes and their interactions between the different spheres of the Earth, i.e., biosphere, geosphere, atmosphere, cryosphere, and hydrosphere. *"Svalbard Integrated Arctic Earth Observing System — the Current State,"* Svalbard Integrated Arctic Earth Observing System (SIOS), February 20, 2024.

19   The *Carta Marina map* was created by Olaus Magnus, an exiled Swedish priest living in Italy, and published in 1539. The scope of information was so complete that it established a standard of comprehensiveness and accuracy, especially the geographic outline of the Nordic countries. It is notable that this document with empirical authority includes Thule (labeled Tile). H. Thomas Rossby and Peter Miller, "Ocean Eddies in the 1539 Carta Marina by Olaus Magnus," *Oceanography, The Oceanography Society* 16, no. 4 (2003), 77.

20   As director of the Architectural Association from 1971 to 1990, Alvin Boyarsky, instituted the prominence of drawing in the studio unit system as a process, methodology, and pedagogy. Igor Marjanovic and Jan Howard, *Drawing Ambience: Alvin Boyarsky and the Architectural Association* (Mildred Lane Kemper Art Museum and Museum of Art, Rhode Island School of Design, 2014), 29.

The *Ultima Thule Museum of Natural History* is an ongoing project where curators and workshop artisans meticulously craft miniatures to envision vast dioramas. The installations recall a vanished world that reflects Svalbard's near certainty of vanishing.[1] Each tableau is akin to a story, where the aggregation completes the tale. Optimism and environmental distress congregate, oscillating between collective hope and shared defeats. Notably, the guilt of being unable to defy cataclysmic climate change, regardless of our efforts to be environmental stewards. The seam between the beginning and the end is tenuous and imperceptible, merely a remnant of a world consigned to folklore by our negligence.

1   In *The Uninhabitable Earth: Life after Warming*, David Wallace-Wells warns that in addition to rising sea levels, many climate scientists hold a more immediate concern: the albedo effect, which is that ice is white and reflects sunlight back into space rather than absorbing it. Peter Wadham, a professor of ocean physics and head of the Polar Ocean Physics Group at the University of Cambridge, UK, concludes the total disappearance of ice could mean a massive warming equivalent to the entire last twenty-five years of global carbon emissions. Wallace-Wells reminds us that the previous twenty-five years of emissions are about half of the total that humanity has produced. He considers it "[a] scale of carbon production that has pushed the planet from near-complete climate stability to the brink of chaos."

The mayor urgently exclaimed: "The ground is melting! We can no longer trust the permafrost!"[2] The town was experiencing, more and more frequently, melting glaciers, precipitation-induced landslides, coastal erosion, and rising sea levels. Over time, as these disastrous events occurred, they were increasingly damaging. Any solution was sought to simultaneously mitigate the bombardments of natural forces and save the cheerfully painted gable-roofed houses that the citizens were so proud of. The first bold response was to extricate their residences from their foundations, inserting them into a megastructure tall enough to stand above impending floods.[3] The townsfolk were relieved to see their homes unharmed. Consequently, the community renamed their town from Longyearbyen to Askeladden, after the cunning child from Norwegian folklore who succeeded when others failed.[4] He personified the citizens' joyful optimism, steadfast adaptability, and uncompromising conviction.

2   The story depicted in the award-winning BBC-produced documentary "Frelsen til Longyearbyn" [The Salvation of Longyearbyn] about Mayor Bertine Berg warning the townspeople by circling the town in a helicopter with loudspeakers is highly plausible but fictitious. Ms. Berg was formerly a Nordic scientific expeditions pilot and immediately rallied various communities into taking action after meeting with a coalition of climatologists. However, the news was disseminated primarily in simultaneous social media posts on Facebook, Instagram, X (formerly Twitter), and TikTok.

3   K. Breili et al., "High-Accuracy Coastal Flood Mapping for Norway Using Lidar Data," *Natural Hazards and Earth System Sciences* 20, no. 2 (2020): 673–94. Using high-accuracy light detection and ranging (lidar) elevation data coastal flooding maps for Norway, approximately 80 percent of the coast was mapped, providing sufficient accuracy for analysis. The researchers observed that generated maps showed that many parts of the coast are vulnerable to flooding.

4   Jan Brunvand, "Norway's Askeladden, the Unpromising Hero, and Junior-Right," *The Journal of American Folklore* 72, no. 283 (1959): 14. In Norwegian folklore, Askeladden is one of the most prominent heroes. He was known as "the ash-lad" because, as the weakest member of his family, he was made to sit in the ashes on the hearth. Although his brothers despised him, he remained humble and was eventually able to use his natural gifts to acquire wealth and esteem. Stories characterized him as "clever, bold, patient, and successful against all odds." Askeladden was regarded as a model of courage and perseverance. The American folklore researcher Jan Brunvand notes he was widely regarded in Norway as "a remarkably complete personification of [its] national traits."

SYS1-PHOS

Perched atop several watchtowers are beacons where statistics from surveyed data are connected with field studies. Flocks of drones ensure the governor's *Environmental Protection Act* is maintained throughout Svalbard, Norway.[5] Half of them scan the landscape to detect and record the constant rumblings of debris, slush, and quick clay landslides. The second half performs ecological life support by returning pebbles dislodged from seismic shifts back into position. The island's resilience diminishes daily as more geological material is lost. The endeavor is as futile as the enchanted boulder Sisyphus pushed up a hill, only for it to roll back as soon as the summit was reached. The cycle of exasperation and frustration is self-inflicted by the optimism that the island can be saved by returning dislocated sedimentary rock *ad infinitum*. Inevitably, what gets displaced will outpace what can be recovered: there will be no rocks left to grab and nowhere to deposit them.[6] Svalbard will spill into the ocean, where the booming sounds of a crumbling island will, eventually, be replaced with a disconcerting stillness.[7]

5   "Svalbard Environmental Protection Act," Norwegian Government Security and Service Organization (G.S.S.O.), April 12, 2012. "The Svalbard Environmental Protection Act relates to the Protection of the Environment in Svalbard. It states, "The purpose of this Act is to preserve a virtually untouched environment in Svalbard with respect to continuous areas of wilderness, landscape, flora, fauna and cultural heritage."

6   When the drones returned to the research station to be cleaned and emptied, Dr. Barrett Berg from the Nordic Unmanned Aerial Vehicle Reconnaissance Initiative discovered that random detritus was gathered and contained in their storage cavity. In his field notes, he laments that the physical evidence of Svalbard's existence amounts to a few meager handfuls of rocks and soil.

7   During a panel discussion at the Dronesphere symposia held in Toronto, Ontario, Dr. Simon Weise, a UAV Anthropologist, recalled when his team downloaded surveillance records from the fleet of drones assigned to Nordland. They had to refer to satellite data to verify the flight path coordinates were correct because there was no video footage or audio recordings of Svalbard or the surrounding islands. He said: "We were initially perplexed that nothing was documented except the surface of the ocean and the sound of nothing but seagulls in the distance. The silence was horrifying because it confirmed our prediction that the existence of Norway was in jeopardy."

At the once-thriving mining town of Pyramiden, the Soviet Union asserted dominance over the tundra by superimposing the fertile soil of Ukraine and, with it, its robust grasses.[8] The settlement is not abandoned; it is merely in cold storage. This post-human town is not deserted; it is in perpetual stasis. The library shelves are stocked with 60,000 untouched books and 1,000 sealed movie reels. In empty homes, dozens of porcelain cups wait to be filled with warm tea. The northernmost bust of Lenin stands alone in the central square, watching the sun set and rise on the horizon.[9] Kittiwakes inhabit building façades like nesting cliffs and have become custodians to an inadvertent arboretum. Climate change invited a previously impossible forest to grow, shrouding the town with an unsettling grove.[10] Like a specter seeking retribution, this supernatural landscape is slowly encroaching.[11]

8   Jiří Schlaghamerský et al., "Enchytraeids in Imported Soil and Organic Deposits in Pyramiden, an Abandoned Mining Town on Spitsbergen in the High Arctic," *Elsevier Science BV*, vol. 192 (2023). "[I]n 1998, Chernozem soil from southern Russia or Ukraine had been imported to create lawns. Today, the town's long central lawn presents an environmental gradient: on one end rather shallow humus-rich soil is fertilized by a sea bird colony on an adjacent building, the central part has a rich organic horizon topping humus-rich mineral soil whereas on the other end, humus-rich soil is covered by deposited mineral soil."

9   In July 2006, Elin Andreassen, a photographer and two professors of archaeology, Hein B. Bjerck and Bjørnar Olsen, conducted a field study of Pyramiden. When they arrived at the Hotel Tulipan [Hotel Tulip], they encountered Sofia Mikhailovic, a nine-year-old girl whose parents operated the hotel, who offered to take them to her favorite place, the Pyramiden Museum. Sofia pointed out the massive stuffed polar bear as they wandered through the exhibits. When they asked her why it was growling, she said, "The bear is angry because he expected the curators who left to return and take him to Russia. He is waiting for a future that will never arrive."

10   As the planet warms, the Arctic treeline is turning white landscapes green. Trees used to creep forward a few centimeters yearly, but they are accelerating toward the pole at a rate of 40 to 50 meters a year. In "'The Treeline Is out of Control': How the Climate Crisis Is Turning the Arctic Green," *The Guardian*, January 20, 2022, Ben Rawlence concedes that more trees may seem like a good thing, however, the problem is that the greening of the tundra further accelerates the warming process, as the birch improves the soil and warms it with microbial activity, melting the permafrost and releasing methane, a greenhouse gas 85 times more powerful than carbon dioxide in its warming effects over a shorter timeframe.

11   Elin Andreassen, Hein B. Bjerck, and Bjørnar Olsen, the authors of *Persistent Memories: Pyramiden – A Soviet Mining Town in the High Arctic*, observed: "Nature was intruding and mingling. Nesting gulls competed over cramped spaces on window ledges, while rivers and streams, once held in check by dikes and dams, had reclaimed their original delta space taken over by the town."

Biographies

(68)

Claudio Aporta is Professor and Canadian Chair (Marine Environmental Protection) at the World Maritime University in Malmö, Sweden. He completed a BA in Communications at Universidad Nacional de Cuyo (Mendoza, Argentina) and a PhD in Cultural Anthropology at the University of Alberta (Edmonton, Canada). Before moving to Sweden, he was a faculty member at Carleton University and Dalhousie University in Canada. In 2012, he held the Canada-US Fulbright Chair at the University of Washington. His research is at a crossroads between Marine Management, Anthropology, and Geography. Claudio has done ethnographic research in the Canadian Arctic since 1998. He has documented Inuit knowledge and use of marine and coastal areas in all regions of the Canadian Arctic. His current teaching (41) and research interests are connected to co-management, Marine Spatial Planning, Indigenous and local coastal communities' knowledge, and knowledge mobilization in cross-cultural settings.

(417)

Brandon Bergem is a principal of Office In Search Of (OISO), an interdisciplinary and collaborative design and visualization practice, and a sessional lecturer at the University of Toronto John H. Daniels Faculty of Architecture, Landscape and Design. Brandon holds a bachelor of environmental design (University of Manitoba Faculty of Architecture) and a master of architecture (University of Toronto Daniels Faculty). He received the Kuwabara-Jackman Gold Medal for the most outstanding graduate thesis and a Canadian Architect magazine Student Award of Excellence. His interests include exhibition design, environmental installations, narrative-centric architectural representation, and research-based speculative design. Notable OISO collaborations include the *Beneath the City: Rivers* exhibition for the Seoul Biennale of Architecture and Urbanism 2021 and *Boom Town* for (302) Toronto WaterFront ReConnect.

(365)

Mari A. Aston Bergset is the founder of Lo:Le Landskap. She is from an island on the western coast of Norway and is particularly fond of nature's wide range of expressions: everything between stillness and storm. This dramatic variation has also given the company its name. Lo is a nautical term that describes where it is windy, while Le (lee) is known to be where it is warm and sheltered. Mari has twenty years of design experience, and for the last nine years, she has been teaching in the landscape architecture program of the University of Tromsø – The Arctic University of Norway (UiT/ AHO) in Tromsø, Norway. She focuses on designing with empathy. In every project, she aims for both the functional and that which enriches people's everyday lives by embracing the experience of both storms and calm in the conditions of the local ecosystem and cultural context.

Caitlin Blanchfield is a historian of architecture and landscape whose work examines the infrastructures of settler colonialism and material practices of resistance. Her research addresses the role of modernist land management and design practices in projects of dispossession and colonization in North America and across the reaches of US empire, as well as the anticolonial architectures that unsettle them. Her collaborative and creative work includes cartographic investigations into the impacts of border infrastructures on Indigenous lands and multimedia projects on the geopolitical management of architectural value. Blanchfield received her PHD from Columbia University in 2024 and is currently a Princeton-Mellon Postdoctoral Fellow at Princeton University. She was a founding editor of the *Avery Review*, a digital journal of critical essays on architecture, and the coauthor of the book *Modern Management Methods: Architecture, Historical Value, and the Electromagnetic Image* (Columbia University Press, 2019).

Arlyn Charlie is a Teetł'it Gwich'in multidisciplinary artist based out of Teetł'it Zheh (Fort McPherson, Northwest Territories, Canada). A published writer and photographer, his work is based solely on documenting and preserving traditional knowledge pertaining to the Teetł'it Gwich'in People. Guided by the belief that language and culture are the foundations of one's identity, his work stresses the importance of preserving both, for one cannot exist without the other. Though he does not subjugate himself to one art form, he gravitates to photography and writing. In his exploration of the arts, he believes that story is a fundamental foundation for his work and the culture of his people.

(179) In believing that, he uses the tools of the arts to continue to share the stories of the elders, Gwich'in culture, language, customs, and history by observing and capturing the Gwich'in people and their interaction with the land. Throughout the year, he tries to return to the land as much as possible to learn the cultural and traditional skills of his people and to maintain a connection to the land of his people. He often spends the summer weeks at his family's fish camp located upriver from Teetł'it Zheh, at a place known as Dèeddhoo Gòonlii (Scraper Hill). It is here that his family engages in summer fishing along the Teetł'it Gwinjik (Peel River) with nets. Afterwards, during the fall,

(176) while the river begins to freeze, nets are set under the ice, and for a few weeks in November, they continue to fish. However, due to climate change, the simple act of fishing is being disrupted by rising temperatures that cause the summer waters to be far too hot, and the

(160) winter freeze happens later and later in the year. However, the root of his work tries to convey that the Teetł'it Gwich'in still utilize the land to a remarkable extent and to them, the land is thought of as home.

(260) *Thomas Juel Clemmensen* is a professor of landscape architecture at UiT / The Arctic University of Norway and the former head of its landscape architecture program. He trained as an architect at the Aarhus School of Architecture in Denmark, where he also earned his PhD. He has over twenty years of experience in landscape architecture and urban planning and is a member of the Association of Danish Landscape Architects. His primary research interest lies in the transformation of landscapes, focusing on nature-culture heritage and how landscape architecture can facilitate landscape transformations. Additional research interests include the roles of geology and ecology in landscape architecture, the interrelationship between infrastructure and landscape, urban-rural dynamics, and new public domains in urban landscapes. He teaches landscape transformation at the master's level and supervises PhD students.

A K Dolven is a Norwegian artist. She works across painting, film, sound, sculpture, and interventions in public space. Recurring themes in her production are the representation of natural forces and their resonance with human sensibilities. Her work alternates between the monumental and the minimal, the universal and the intimate. Interpersonal relations and interactions are central to her practice, and many of her performance-based works involve collaborations with other people. She lives in Kvalnes, Lofoten, Norway. In 2025, Oslo Nasjonalmuseet will exhibit *A K Dolven amasone*, a retrospective of her body of work.

Jakob Exner is an architect, CEO, and partner at the Greenland-based design office TNT Nuuk. He studied at the Kunstakademiets Arkitektskole, an institution of higher education in Copenhagen, Denmark.

Nadezhda Filimonova is an associate researcher at the Belfer Center's Arctic Initiative, Harvard University. She is also a postdoctoral researcher at the Arctic Centre, University of Lapland. Filimonova completed her PhD at the University of Massachusetts Boston in Global Governance and Human Security. She has been the recipient of numerous fellowships and grants and an author of several peer-reviewed publications. Filimonova has taught courses on international relations, Arctic studies, and daily life in Soviet Russia. Her research explores environmental governance and urban sustainability in the Arctic.

435 (417) *Jeffrey Garcia* is an educator and principal of the Office In Search Of (OISO), an interdisciplinary and collaborative design and visualization practice. He holds a bachelor of interior design (University of Manitoba Faculty of Architecture) and a master of design (OCAD University). He is a sessional lecturer at the University of Toronto John H. Daniels Faculty of Architecture, Landscape and Design. Jeffrey previously taught at the University of Manitoba Faculty of Architecture, where he received the Carl Nelson (224) Teaching Award and distinction from the University of Manitoba Centre for the Advancement of Teaching and Learning. His research focuses on experimental preservation and narrative-centric speculative design. Notable OISO collaborations include the *Beneath the City: Rivers* exhibition for the Seoul Biennale of Architecture and Urbanism 2021 and *Boom Town* for Toronto WaterFront ReConnect.

(81) *Aniella Sophie Goldinger* is a landscape architect and transdisciplinary spatial researcher based in Berlin. Her research is centered around oceanic hinterlands and the extended urban fabric of the polar territories and works to render visible the interplay between structures of power, ecologies, and more-than-human stakeholders across critical urban theory, political ecology, and science and technology studies. She is a PhD candidate in urbanism, a research and teaching associate at the Institute of Architecture, Technische Universität Berlin, and a member of the Architectural Association's Terrain Lab. She holds a master's degree in landscape architecture, specializing in Arctic and sub-Arctic territories, from (126) the Oslo School of Architecture Campus Tromsø, and a BA from the Royal Danish Academy. She participated in the Norwegian Marine Research Institute's 2023 winter expedition to the Barents Sea ice edge and continues to be drawn towards the viscous territories of the polar regions.

(352) *Maureen Gruben* is a multimedia artist whose practice incorporates organic and industrial materials that are often salvaged from her local environment. Based in the Inuvialuit Settlement Region of the Western Arctic, Maureen was born and raised in Tuktoyaktuk, where her parents were traditional Inuvialuk knowledge keepers and founders of E. Gruben's Transport. Gruben holds a BFA from the University of Victoria and a Certificate in Indigenous Political Development & Leadership, En'owkin Centre, Penticton. Her work has been exhibited internationally and is held in numerous public and private collections.

Nicholas Gulick is an American-Swedish landscape architect with over ten years of experience in landscape architecture and computational design. Based in Stockholm, he has worked across Sweden, Northern Norway, and the United States, specializing in designing didactic landscapes that highlight natural processes within urban environments. He is dedicated to advancing landscape architecture through the codification of design processes. His meticulous craft ensures the integrity of the landscape while elevating the ideas and stories that drive form-making, thoughtfully weaving narratives into the built environment. Nicholas holds a master's degree in Landscape Architecture and Territorial Studies from the Oslo School of Architecture and Design and a bachelor's degree in landscape architecture and environmental studies from Iowa State University. His master's thesis investigated the evolution and ephemeral qualities of the ice road over the Northern Dvina River in Arkhangelsk, Russia, and its historical and future role in the city's urban infrastructure.

Magdalena Haggärde is an architect and partner of 70°N arkitektur (Tromsø, NO) and a university lecturer in landscape architecture at the Kunstakadmiet (Academy of Arts at the Arctic University of Norway, Tromsø). She previously taught at the Bergen School of Architecture and was a visiting Professor at the Azrieli School of Architecture & Urbanism, Carleton University (Ottawa, CA). With an educational background in Sweden

436

and Paris, her engagements range from exhibitions and architectural design to urban and regional planning, with an experimental, participatory, research-based approach. Recently, a special focus has been on Arctic landscapes, Indigenous knowledge, and artistic means. In this work, methods, investigations, and proposals are centered on notions of openness (320) and planning for unknown futures, encompassing issues of multiplicity and indeterminacy.

(20) *Peter Hemmersam* is a Professor in Urban Design at the Oslo School of Architecture and Design, where he directs the Centre for Urban and Landscape Studies. He has a PhD in architecture and researches circumpolar cities. He has lectured widely on Arctic urbanism. Recent publications include "Comfort and discomfort - Conflicting concerns in Arctic urban planning and design," in Leena Cho and Matthew Jull's *Design and the Built Environment of the Arctic* (Routledge, 2023); "Svalbard's Urban Imaginaries," in Mathias Albert, Dina Brode-Roger, and Lisbeth Iversen's *Svalbard Imaginaries - The Making of an Arctic Archipelago* (Palgrave Macmillan, 2023); "Arcticness and the urbanism of the North," in *The Arctic Yearbook* (Arctic Institute, 2021); J.K. Larsen and P. Hemmersam, "Landscapes as Archives of the Future?" in *Arctic Archives: Ice, Memory and Entropy* (Transect, 2019).

(356) *Morgan Ip* is a researcher and institute associate at the Scott Polar Research Institute, Department of Geography, University of Cambridge, and worked (179) on the ERC Arctic Cultures project investigating how material culture informs Arctic narratives. Ip has a background in architecture and urbanism, with a focus on cultural landscapes, urban displacement, placemaking, and the future of Arctic communities. He uses interdisciplinary methods, including ethnography, collaborative mapping and design, to explore how local imaginaries shape the built environment. Ip attained his master of architecture at Carleton University in Ottawa, Canada (2009). He completed his PhD at the Institute of Urbanism and Landscape at the Oslo School of Architecture and Design (AHO, 2022), with a dissertation on a collective imagination towards civic futures in the Norwegian-Russian borderlands. He has taught architecture, urbanism, and landscape architecture studios at AHO and taught as a supervisor and seminar leader at the University of Cambridge.

Konstantin Ikonomidis is an architect whose work blends art, architecture, and scientific research with a focus on extreme climates and cultural values. After graduating from the Royal Danish Academy of Fine Arts, School of Architecture in 2014, Konstantin gained recognition for transformative projects such as the Qaammat Pavilion in Greenland, a landmark for the UNESCO World Heritage site that has been internationally awarded and exhibited. Drawing inspiration from diverse cultures, Konstantin bridges research and practice by developing glass block systems and exploring 3D-printed recycled glass to create novel construction methods tailored to each project's unique environment. He collaborates closely with local communities and specialists in each field to ensure his designs are both culturally sensitive and technically innovative. He played a key role in advancing malaria prevention and sustainable housing solutions in sub-Saharan Africa. Konstantin has lectured internationally, including to graduate students at Harvard University, where he shares his distinctive approach to designing in challenging environments.

Maaretta Jaukkuri is a curator and professor of contemporary art who has, throughout her career, influenced students, theorists, artists and the public. It is in her name, and supported by those whom she has touched, that the Maaretta Jaukkuri Foundation was initiated and led by the collaborative effort of Antony Gormley and A K Dolven. The Maaretta Jaukkuri Foundation (MJF) is a not-for-profit organization founded on August 10, 2014. She spends her time between Helsinki and Kvalnes, Lofoten, Norway.

(268) *Akie Kono* is a landscape architect based in Norway. She works at Grindaker in Oslo and previously worked at Snøhetta (Oslo), Lo:Le Landskap (Tromsø), and Sola Associates (Tokyo, Japan). She (176) holds a master's degree in landscape architecture (MLA) from the Oslo School of Architecture and Design and a bachelor's degree in the arts (BA) from the architecture department at Musashino Art University in Tokyo. (126) During her MLA studies in Tromsø, she was inspired by Sámi Indigenous culture and Arctic landscapes, and her diploma project, REINDEER, was published in 2022 after receiving funding from TVIBIT stigen by the municipality of Tromsø. Her practice includes photography, and her work has been featured in several exhibitions like Fotofever Paris 2018 - EINSTEIN STUDIO at Carrousel Du Louvre, Paris, and she has contributed to a range of publications, including Einstein Studio's TOKYO/JAPAN July 2018 (Tokyo, Japan).

(352) *Kyra Kordoski* is a writer and photographer who has been working closely with Inuvialuk artist Maureen Gruben since 2016. She holds an MA from University of Leeds and an MFA from Goldsmiths, University of London. Her art writing and documentation have been published in periodicals including *esse arts + opinions*, *C Magazine*, *White Fungus*, *Canadian Art*, *BOMB*, *Inuit Art Quarterly*, (100) CBC, and *The Globe and Mail*; and in exhibition catalogs including those published by Emily Carr University Press, grunt gallery, National Gallery of Canada, and Vancouver Art Gallery. She spends three to four months of the year at Maureen's home in Tuktoyaktuk.

(224) *Elena Krapivina* is an Arkhangelsk area native currently based in Stockholm. She is pursuing her interests in ecology and statistics through studies in landscape ecology with a focus on GIS mapping and analysis at Stockholm University. She recently completed a bachelor's degree in environmental science at Södertörn University in addition to her master's in Arctic ecology and bachelor's in linguistics at the Northern (Arctic) Federal University in Arkhangelsk, Russia. Previously, she worked as an English language teacher. Currently, Krapivina is assisting in developing GIS course materials at Södertörn University.

Helena Lennert is an architect, creative director, and partner at the Greenland-based design office TNT Nuuk. She studied at the Århus Arkitektskole, Denmark.

Gisle Løkken is an architect, founding partner, and manager of 70°N arkitektur, Tromsø, and currently a research fellow at the Department of Architecture and Planning, NTNU, Trondheim. He has previously taught at the Bergen School of Architecture and was a visiting professor at the Azrieli School of Architecture & Urbanism, Carleton University (Ottawa, CA). Through architecture practice, research, teaching, and writing, he takes a critical and experimental position in the public debate concerning architecture, urban development, and regional planning locally and in a broader Scandinavian and Circumpolar Arctic context. Løkken regularly teaches and is a lecturer, assessor, and jury member in national and international competitions and prize committees. Until recently, he was the president of the Norske arkitekters landsforbund (NAL, National Association of Norwegian Architects).

Nicole Luke (BEnvD, MArch) is an emerging Indigenous designer passionate about culture and design. Born on the territories with family residing in the Kivalliq region of Nunavut, she is one of the first Inuk architectural graduates in Canada and the first Inuk to receive her bachelor's and master's degrees from the University of Manitoba. Due to her wide exposure to urban and non-urban areas, she focuses on the design realities that communities face throughout the architecture and construction processes. She is committed to understanding her role as a designer. She aspires to be one of the first Inuit architects in Canada. Luke works to involve herself in projects that will inspire youth in northern communities to pursue an education in the design field. She believes that the built environment is a critical factor to developing socioeconomic agency and is dedicated to Indigenous initiatives as well as learning sustainable building practices.

(330) *Jessica MacMillan* (US) is an artist and amateur astronomer based in Oslo, Norway. Through kinetic sculpture, light, installation, and 3D animation, MacMillan's work investigates concepts in astronomy and planetary science and the relationship between our everyday lived experience and the astronomical timescales and structures of the cosmos. MacMillan holds an MFA in fine arts from the Academy of Fine Art in Oslo, a BFA in sculpture and art history from the Massachusetts College of (31) Art and Design in Boston, and studied astronomy at Arizona State University.

(116) *Dorte Mandrup*, Danish architect, founded her eponymous studio in 1999, eight years after graduating from Aarhus School of Architecture. Studies in both sculpture and natural sciences have influenced her approach, which is hands-on, materializing in deep contextual analysis and explorative prototyping. Her Copenhagen-based studio employs an artistic, humanistic, and scientific approach to create playful, original, and poetic designs that enhance the awareness and experience of each place. As a consistent critic, Dorte Mandrup is well known for her commitment to developing the architecture profession. She headlined the curated international exhibition at La Biennale di Venezia in 2018, is vice chairman at Louisiana Museum of Modern Art, member of Akademie der Künste in Berlin, honorary professor at the Royal Danish Academy of Architecture, adjunct professor at Accademia di architettura di Mendrisio, and is decorated with the Order of Dannebrog by the Danish Royal House (274) and the Prince Eugen Medal by the Swedish Royal Court.

(397) *Caitlin Jakusz Paridy* is a designer and researcher exploring landscapes of extraction, from conception to decommissioning. Presently, she is focused on spatializing the colonial impact of free-entry mining claims on Indigenous sovereignty and sub-Arctic landscapes of so-called Canada. These themes developed throughout her master of landscape architecture at the Oslo School of Architecture and Design - Campus Tromsø through spatial proposals, material experiments, and soundscapes for landscapes across Svalbard and Sápmi. Before this, she completed a master of architecture degree at the University of Waterloo. Her thesis, "Learning from Manoomin," focused on storying wild rice restoration efforts as a reconciliatory land practice in the Great Lakes region. She is currently working as a landscape designer in London (UK).

Olga Petri is a human geographer whose research examines the intersections of power, resistance, and marginalized identities in shaping urban spaces, particularly in non-Western authoritarian contexts. Her work spans queer life in late Imperial St. Petersburg, the politics of human-animal interactions in urban environments, and the environmental violence of the Anthropocene in Russia. Petri's first book, *Places of Tenderness and Heat: The Queer Milieu of Fin-de-Siècle St. Petersburg* (Cornell University Press, 2022), explores the lived experiences of male homosexuality in late Imperial St. Petersburg and was nominated for the Pushkin Prize in 2023. Her current research investigates the entanglement of human and animal lives in Imperial Russia, focusing on how nationalist ideologies and urban reforms shaped these interactions. Petri is developing a new project on the Violent Anthropocene, analyzing the environmental and geopolitical impacts of Russia's aggressive policies within global debates on climate change, biopolitics, and authoritarianism.

Andrey N. Petrov is a Professor of Geography and ARCTICenter Director at the University of Northern Iowa. Dr. Petrov is an economic and social geographer specializing in Arctic economy and sustainable development, emphasizing changing social-ecological systems and sustainability in the Arctic. His current research is focused on

(210) sustainable regional and community development, spatial organization, and restructuring of Arctic economies amid rapid environmental change. Dr. Petrov leads the Research Coordination Networks in Arctic Sustainability (Arctic-FROST) and Arctic Coastal Resilience (Arctic-COAST) as well as research projects in Alaska, Canada, and Northern Eurasia. He has extensively published on issues of socio-ecological change, human-environmental relations, economy, and demographic dynamics in the North. Dr. Petrov is a Past President of the International Arctic Social Sciences Association (IASSA) and Past Chair of the International Arctic Science Committee (IASC) Social and Human Working Group. He sits on the International Arctic Science Committee and the US Polar Research Board.

(60) *Lasse Rau* is an architectural and urban historian researching the global (275) circulation of models of environment, labor, and land in nineteenth- and twentieth-century planning. He is a PhD student in architectural history and theory at the Columbia University Graduate School of Architecture, Planning and Preservation (GSAPP). He has held teaching positions at the Rhode Island School of Design, Wentworth School of Architecture, and the Boston Architectural College. Lasse holds a master of science in architecture studies (SMArchS) from MIT and a bachelor in architecture from TU Berlin. His writing has been published in *Thresholds Journal* (MIT Press) and *Situation Magazine*.

(190) *Sophy Roberts* is a British author and journalist based in Dorset, England, whose work focuses on human stories that intersect with history, travel, and conservation. She is a graduate of Oxford University and the Columbia School of Journalism and began her career assisting the writer Jessica Mitford. She regularly contributes to the (106) *Financial Times*. Her critically acclaimed first book, *The Lost Pianos of Siberia*, was published in 2020. Her second book, *A Training School for Elephants*, tracing a forgotten colonial-era expedition in Africa's Great Lakes region, will be published in 2025.

Svetlana Romanova (Sakha/Even) is an artist and filmmaker born in Yakutsk, the capital city of the Sakha Republic, Russia, located south of the Arctic Circle. Her practice centers on the importance of Indigenous visual language, particularly in the Arctic regions, and gravitates towards critical self-historicization. She received a BFA from Otis College of Art and Design (2012) and an MFA from California Institute of the Arts (2014). Her films, including *Lena River* (2014), *Managa Bar/Rustam's Habitat* (2019), *Kyusyur/Stado* (2021), *Season of Dying Water* (2015/2022) and *Voyage of Jeanette* (2024), have been exhibited at venues around the world, including the National Art Museum of the Republic of Sakha, Walker Art Center, Flaherty NYC, e-flux Screening Room, Tampere Film Festival, Media City Film Festival, Images Film Festival, and the Academy Museum, among others.

Marya Rozanova-Smith (PhD) is a Research Professor at The George Washington University (GWU) and has taught Arctic Affairs at GWU's Elliott School of International Affairs since 2018. Rozanova-Smith is a Principal Investigator of the National Science Foundation-funded project "Understanding the Gendered Impacts of COVID-19 in the Arctic (COVID-GEA)." Her research interests include Arctic governance, urban sustainability, Indigenous urbanization, Indigenous Peoples empowerment, and gender equality in the Arctic regions. In addition to her academic work, Dr. Rozanova-Smith has been deeply involved in a range of social projects. She was the founder and chairperson of the Center for Civil, Social, Scientific, and Cultural Initiatives "STRATEGIA". She served as a Galina Starovoitova Fellow for Human Rights and Conflict Resolution at the Kennan Institute, part of the Woodrow Wilson International Center for Scholars.

Todd Saunders is a Norway-based Canadian architect known to infuse his contemporary buildings with an artistic sensibility that is deeply in tune with the uniqueness of northern terrains. His use of natural materials

(141) and simple yet striking geometries sets him apart as one of the most celebrated architects of his generation. He is recognized for constructing buildings that acknowledge and understand vernacular histories but create something entirely new. Born in Gander, Newfoundland, Todd Saunders studied at the Nova Scotia College of Arts & Design in Halifax and McGill University in Montreal before traveling extensively across Europe and beyond. He founded Saunders Architecture in his adopted city of Bergen, Norway, in 1998 and went on to develop a portfolio of commissions across Scandinavia, Canada, America, and other parts of the world. Todd Saunders lectures worldwide and has served as a visiting professor at Cornell University in Ithaca, New York, and Yale University in New Haven, Connecticut. In addition to his practice, he continues to pursue personal book projects such as *SHARE: Conversations about Contemporary Architecture — The Nordic Countries*, reflecting his commitment to the wider world of architectural design.

(342) *Anastasia Savinova* was born near the Ural Mountains in the former Soviet Union and is currently based in the North of Sweden. She holds a master of design degree from Samarskiy (384) Gosudarstvennyy Arkhitekturno-Stroitel'nyy Universitet (Samara State University of Architecture and Civil Engineering) and a master of fine arts degree from Konsthögskolan vid Umeå universitet (Umeå Academy of Fine Arts). Her artistic practice revolves around places, ecologies, and human relationships with the more-than-human world. She investigates how everything is intertwined and how we constantly emerge as part of something greater. She primarily works with sculptural installations that often include found objects and other elements, such as sound, video, drawing, and performance. *Genius Loci* is one of her early projects; it started when she was an architecture student and laid the foundation for her bricolage approach in later multidisciplinary projects.

Susan Schuppli is a researcher and artist based in the UK. Her fieldwork and documentary film practice is situated at the intersections between environmental struggles, climate science, and affected communities with a contemporary focus on the cryosphere and the politics of cold. Earlier projects examined material evidence from conflict zones to nuclear disasters. Her recent films include *Moving Ice, Signals from Svalbard, Listening to Ice, Gondwana, Arctic Archipelago* and *Ice Cores*. Investigations span legal analysis and public advocacy as well as theoretical reflection and creative exploration in order to understand how the transformations wrought by global burning are generating new forms of evidence. Granting agency to the more-than-human as a material witness informs her attempts at expanding the fields of action and justice. Schuppli's creative projects have been exhibited throughout Europe, Asia, Canada, and the US. She has published widely within the context of media and politics and is author of *Material Witness* (MIT Press, 2020). Schuppli is Professor and Director of the Centre for Research Architecture, Goldsmiths University of London where she is also a Research Fellow and Board Chair of Forensic Architecture.

Lola Sheppard is a registered Architect and founding partner at Lateral Office, a firm whose work and research focuses on powerful design relationships between the public realm, architecture, and environment in rural and remote communities, with a particular focus on the Canadian North. Lola received her bachelor of science in architecture and Bachelor of Architecture from McGill University and a master of architecture from Harvard Graduate School of Design. She is a professor at the School of Architecture, University of Waterloo. Lola is the recipient of two Holcim Awards for Sustainable Construction, the 2012 RAIC Young Architect Award, and the 2010 Prix de Rome. She is co-author of *Many Norths: Spatial Practice in a Polar Territory* (Actar, 2017). Lateral Office represented Canada at the 2014 Venice Biennale, with an exhibition entitled *Arctic Adaptations: Nunavut at 15*.

(404)

Sofia Singler is an assistant professor of architecture at the University of Cambridge and a fellow of St John's College, Cambridge. A native of Jyväskylä, Finland, Singler trained as an architect at the University of Cambridge and the Yale School of Architecture. She completed her PhD in architectural history at Cambridge as a Gates

(248)

Cambridge Scholar. Singler's primary research specialism is the critical analysis of the architecture, urbanism, design and thought of Finnish modernists Alvar, Aino and Elissa Aalto and their associates. Her other research interests lie in the histories and theories of modern architecture, Indigenous architectures in the Arctic—especially Sápmi—and architectural pedagogies for children.

(190)

(148)

Inuuteq Storch is a photographer who lives and works in Greenland. He is a graduate of the International Center of Photography in New York and of the Fatamorgana School of Photography in Copenhagen. Inuuteq's work is wide in genres (own photography and archive work and methods) but the content maintains a common thread in being about the identity of coming from Greenland. He has exhibited in Greenland,

(384)

Denmark, the United States, Norway, Sweden, Finland, Iceland, Canada, and Colombia. Inuuteq has published photobooks including *Porcelain Souls* (Konnotation, 2018), *Flesh* (Disko Bay, 2019) and *John Møller – Mirrored, Portraits of Good Hope* (Roulette Russe, 2021), and *Keepers of the Ocean* (Disko Bay, 2022).

(372)

Eimear Tynan is an associate professor of landscape architecture at UiT / The Arctic University of Norway. She teaches and supervises master's students, emphasizing fieldwork practices and contemporary landscape theory. In addition, she promotes critical thinking on how landscape architects are addressing and responding to current climate crises and environmental change, particularly in Arctic and sub-Arctic regions. Eimear is also a horticulturalist and chartered landscape architect with extensive experience in private and public practice in Ireland and Norway. Her practical experience has ranged from community consultation projects to detailed landscape construction works. She completed her PHD (2022) on the subject of time and material change along the coasts of three Norwegian high-Arctic islands. Her research interests include coastal change in urban and rural contexts, island studies, and the role of time in landscape architecture practice.

Bertine Tønseth is a human geographer and teacher from Bergen, Norway. Since 2019, Tønseth has been working full-time with landscape architect and anthropologist Brona Keenan to run Komafest, an arts organization based in Vardø that works with a variety of art and placemaking projects.

Michael Turek is a British-American photographer. His work focuses on documentary assignments for clients, including the *Financial Times*, *The Guardian*, *The New York Times*, and *The Paris Review*. His book, *CONTRAIL*, published by Roman Nvmerals, is included in the MoMA Archives and Library. His first photographic monograph, *SIBERIA*, was published by Damiani in 2020.

Mason White is a founding partner at Lateral Office, a firm dedicated to design as a research vehicle to pose and respond to complex, urgent questions in the built environment, engaging in the wider context and climate of a project—social, ecological, or political—with a particular focus on the role of architecture in far northern and remote communities. He is a fellow of the Royal Architectural Institute of Canada (RAIC). Mason received his bachelor of architecture from Virginia Tech and his master of architecture from Harvard Graduate School of Design. He is professor at the Daniels Faculty of Architecture, Landscape, and Design at the University of Toronto. He is the recipient numerous awards, including two Holcim Awards for Sustainable Construction, the 2010 Prix de Rome, among others. He is co-author of *Many Norths: Spatial Practice in a Polar Territory* (Actar, 2017) and *Pamphlet Architecture, Coupling: Strategies for Infrastructural Opportunism* (Princeton, 2010).

Bibliography

(20)
**Making and Remaking
the Capital of Greenland**
Peter Hemmersam

Andersen, Hugo Lund, Poul Lyager, Jens Boertmann, and Flemming Teisen. *Byplanforslag i Vestgrønland, Narssaq, Sukkertoppen, Egedesminde, Godthaab [Proposed Urban Plans in Western Greenland, Narssaq, Sukkertoppen, Egedesminde, Godthaab].* Grønlandsdepartementet, 1951.
Berman, Marshall. *All That Is Solid Melts into Air: The Experience of Modernity.* New York: Simon and Schuster, 1982.
Bruno, Andy Richard. "Making Nature Modern: Economic Transformation and the Environment in the Soviet North." PhD diss., University of Illinois at Urbana-Champaign, 2011.
Crinson, Mark. *Modern Architecture at the End of Empire.* Aldershot: Ashgate Publishing, 2003.
Gilmartin, Mary. "Colonialism/ Imperialism." In *Key Concepts in Political Geography*, edited by Carolyn Gallaher, Carl T. Dahlman, Mary Gilmartin, Alison Mountz, and Peter Shirlow, 115–23. London: Sage, 2009.
Grønlandskommisionen. *Grønlandskommissionens Betænkning [Report from the Greenland Commission].* Copenhagen: Grønlandskommisionen, 1950.
Healey, Patsy. "The Universal and the Contingent: Some Reflections on the Transnational Flow of Planning Ideas and Practices." *Planning Theory* 11, no. 2 (May 2012): 188–207.
Karakayali, Serhat. "Colonialism and the Critique of Modernity." In *Colonial Modern: Aesthetics of the Past – Rebellions for the Future*, edited by Tom Avermaete, Serhat Karakayali, and Marion von Osten, 39–47. London: Black Dog Publishing, 2010.
Kommuneqarfik Sermersooq. "Nuuk – Arktisk Hovedstad: Hovedstadsstrategi for Nuuk." Nuuk: Kommuneqarfik Sermersooq, 2016. ➡ sermersooq2028.gl/ download/hovedstadsstrategi/ hovedstadstrategi_dk.pdf.

Langkilde, Hans Erling. "Grønland under Forvandling [Changing Greenland]." *Arkitektur,* 1968.
Lefebvre, Henri. "The Urban Revolution [1968]." In *The Global Towns Reader,* edited by Neil Brenner and Roger Keil, 407–13. London: Routledge, 2005.
Madsen, Hans Helge. *Chicago – København, Alfred Råvads Univers.* Copenhagen: Gyldendal, 1990.
McCann, Eugene, and Kevin Ward. "Relationality/Territoriality: Toward a Conceptualization of Cities in the World." *Geoforum* 41 (March 2010): 175–84.
McFarlane, Colin. "Crossing Borders: Development, Learning and the North-South Divide." *Third World Quarterly* 27, no. 8 (2006): 1413–37.
Råvad, Alfred J. "Architekten som Sociolog: K. Store Bølger og Små [The Architect as Sociologist: K. Large Waves and Small]." *Architekten,* 1911.
———. "Grønlands Hovedstad: I. Indledning [The Capital of Greenland: I: Introduction]." *Architekten,* 1914.
———. "Grønlands Hovedstad: II. Beliggenheden [The Capital of Greenland: II: The Location]." *Architekten,* 1914.
———. "Grønlands Hovedstad: III. Stedet [The Capital of Greenland: III: The Place]." *Architekten,* 1914.
———. "Grønlands Hovedstad: IV. Den Æstetiske og Videnskabelige Side [The Capital of Greenland: IV: The Aesthetic and Scientific Aspect]." *Architekten,* 1914.
———. "Grønlands Hovedstad: V. 'All Sorts and Conditions of Men' [The Capital of Greenland: V: 'All Sorts and Conditions of Men']." *Architekten,* 1914.
———. "Grønlands Hovedstad: VI. Turist-Værdien [The Capital of Greenland: VI: The Tourist Value]." *Architekten,* 1914.
———. "Grønlands Hovedstad: VII. Eskimo Problemet [The Capital of Greenland: VII: The Eskimo Problem]." *Architekten,* 1914.
Robinson, Jennifer. *Ordinary Cities: Between Modernity and Development.* London: Routledge, 2006.

Scott, James C. *Seeing like a State: How Certain Schemes to Improve the Human Condition Have Failed.* New Haven: Yale University Press, 1998.
Sejersen, Frank. "Urbanization, Landscape Appropriation, and Climate Change in Greenland." *Acta Borealia* 27, no. 2 (2010): 167–88.

(31)
**Fabulous Urbanism:
Reading Soviet Arctic Cities
through Children's Literature**
Olga Petri

Atmodiwirjo, Paramita, Mikhael Johanes, and Yandi Andri Yatmo. "Mapping Stories: Representing Urban Everyday Narratives and Operations." *Urban Design International* 24 (2019): 225–40.
Bentham, Jeremy. *Panopticon; or, The Inspection-House.* Thomas Byrne, 1791.
Bruno, Andy. *The Nature of Soviet Power: An Arctic Environmental History.* Cambridge University Press, 2016.
Finnegan, Ruth. *Tales of the City: A Study of Narrative and Urban Life.* Cambridge University Press, 1998.
Gandy, Matthew. "Cyborg Urbanization: Complexity and Monstrosity in the Contemporary City." *International Journal of Urban and Regional Research* 29, no. 1 (2005): 26–49.
Haraway, Donna J. *When Species Meet.* University of Minnesota Press, 2008.
———. *Staying with the Trouble: Making Kin in the Chthulucene.* Duke University Press, 2016.
Hill, Fiona, and Clifford G. Gaddy. *The Siberian Curse: How Communist Planners Left Russia out in the Cold.* Brookings Institution Press, 2003.
Josephson, Paul R. *The Conquest of the Russian Arctic.* Harvard University Press, 2014.
Kaganovsky, Lilya. "The Negative Space in the National Imagination: Russia and the Arctic." In *Arctic Environmental Modernities: From the Age of Polar Exploration to the Era of the Anthropocene*, edited by Lill-Ann Körber, Scott MacKenzie, and Anna Westerståhl Stenport, 169–82. Palgrave Macmillan, 2017.

Kalemeneva, Ekaterina. "From New Socialist Cities to Thaw Experimentation in Arctic Townscapes: Leningrad Architects Attempt to Modernise the Soviet North." *Europe-Asia Studies* 71, no. 3 (2019): 426–49.

Kelly, Catriona. "Riding the Magic Carpet: Children and Leader Cult in the Stalin Era." *The Slavic and East European Journal* 49, no. 2 (2005): 199–224.

———. "'Thank-You for the Wonderful Book': Soviet Child Readers and the Management of Children's Reading, 1950-1975." *Kritika: Explorations in Russian and Eurasian History* 6, no. 4 (2005): 717–53.

Klapuri, Tintti. "Arctic Norway in the Russian Fin-de-siècle Imagination: Evgeni Lvov-Kochetov's Travelogue out in the Arctic Sea (1895)." *Nordiques* 37 (2019): 25–36.

Lajusia, Julia. "In Search for Instructive Models: The Russian State at a Crossroads to Conquering the North." In *Northscapes: History, Technology, and the Making of Northern Environments*, edited by Dolly Jørgensen and Sverker Sörlin, 110–36. UBC Press, 2013.

Lynch, Kevin. *The Image of the City*. MIT Press, 1964.

McCannon, John. *Red Arctic: Polar Exploration and the Myth of the North in the Soviet Union, 1932-1939*. Oxford University Press, 1998.

———. "To Storm the Arctic: Soviet Polar Exploration and Public Visions of Nature in the USSR, 1932-1939." *Ecumene* 2, no. 1 (1995): 15–31.

Olich, Jacqueline Marie. "Competing Ideologies and Children's Books: The Making of a Soviet Children's Literature, 1918-1935." PhD diss., University of North Carolina at Chapel Hill, 2000.

Penskaya, Elena. "Investigating the Laboratory of Popular Arctic Narrative in Russian Literature from the 1930s to the 1950s." In *Arctic Archives: Ice, Memory and Entropy*, edited by Susanne Frank and Kjetil A. Jakobsen, 253–68. Transcript Verlag, 2019.

Petrich, Shirley. "A Note on Three Contemporary Soviet Children's Stories." *Children's Literature* 2, no. 1 (1973): 221–23.

Semen, Danilov. *The Round House*. Translated by V. Berestov. Illustrated by Anatolyi Borodin. Izdetel'stvo Malysh, 1970.

Tuan, Yi-Fu. *Dominance and Affection: The Making of Pets*. Yale University Press, 1984.

(41)

"If You Do Not Say Anything, You Will Not Be Heard": The Mackenzie Research Institute and Anticolonial Environmental Activism in Inuvik
Caitlin Blanchfield

Aklavik Journal. Letter from R.G. Robertson, Deputy Minister, Department of Northern Affairs and Natural Resources to Major General H.A. Young, Deputy Minister, Department of Public Works, November 21, 1955. Gordon Robertson F "Description of 1956 Re-siting of Aklavik." Record Number R216, RG85-D-1-A, National Library and Archives Canada.

Andrews, Tom. Interview by author via Zoom. April 3, 2023.

Bell, Elizabeth, Doug Brown, Eric Gourdeau, and Addy Tobac. *The Man in the North Conference on Community Development Report*. Arctic Institute of North America, 1971.

Bennett, Mia M. "Gravel Grabs: The Rocky Foundations of Indigenous Geologic Power in the Arctic." *Ambio* 52, no. 7 (2023): 1184–97.

Bocking, Stephen, and Daniel Heidt, eds. *Cold Science: Environmental Knowledge in the North American Arctic during the Cold War*. Routledge, 2019.

Colin, Christopher. In *Repatriating Gwich'in Traditional Knowledge from the Dene Mapping Project*. Prepared by Randy Freeman. Down North Consulting for the Gwich'in Social and Cultural Institute, 2006.

Couthard, Glen. *Red Skins, White Masks: Rejecting the Colonial Politics of Recognition*. University of Minnesota Press, 2014.

De la Barre, Kenneth. "Memorandum of Record from Executive Director." December 2, 1970. Library and Archives Canada, MG28-I79, vol. 131.

Farish, Matthew, and P. Whitney Lackenbauer. "High Modernism in the Arctic: Planning Frobisher Bay and Inuvik." *Journal of Historical Geography* 35, no. 3 (2009): 517–44.

Fraser, Crystal Gail. "T'aih k'ïighe' tth'aih zhit dïidîch'üh (By Strength, We Are Still Here): Indigenous Northerners Confronting Hierarchies of Power at Day and Residential Schools in Nanhkak Thak (the Inuvik Region, Northwest Territories), 1959 to 1982." PhD diss., University of Alberta, 2019.

Gardner, Karen. "An Arctic Village Is Reclaiming Its Indigenous Architecture." *Sierra*, August 30, 2022. sierraclub.org/sierra/arctic-village-reclaiming-indigenous-architecture.

Gareis, Joy, and Ashely Mercer. "Celebrating the 50th Anniversary of Inuvik Research Laboratory." *InfoNorth* 58, no. 1 (2015): 132.

Graham, Amanda. "The University That Wasn't: University of Canada North, 1970-1985." Master's thesis, Lakehead University, 1994.

Gwich'in Traditional Knowledge: Rat River Dolly Varden Char. Gwich'in Renewable Resources Board, 2010. grrb.nt.ca/wp-content/uploads/2021/01/Gwichin-Knowledge-of-Rat-River-Char.pdf.

Hill, Dick. "Concepts Proposal for a Beaufort Institute." Unpublished manuscript, July 28, 1969. Personal collection of Dick Hill.

———. *Inuvik: A History*. Trafford, 2005.

Hill, Richard. "Inuvik: Canadian Development in Modern Arctic Living." NWT Archives/John H. Parker, Ephemera Collection/N-1988-509: 1–3, 1965.

Inuvialuit Regional Corporation. "COPE: An Original Voice for Inuvialuit Rights." irc.inuvialuit.com/sites/default/files/COPE-Original%20Voice%20for%20Inuvialuit%20Rights.pdf.

"Inuvik Research Laboratory." *Polar Record* 11, no. 73 (1967): 419.

445

MacDonald, Robert. "Challenges and Accomplishments: A Celebration of the Arctic Institute of North America." *Arctic* 58, no. 4 (2005): 443.

Meren, David. "'Commend me the Yak': The Colombo Plan, the Inuit of Ungava, and 'Developing' Canada's North." *Histoire Sociale* 50, no. 102 (2017): 343–70.

Nahanni, Phoebe. "The Mapping Project." In *Dene Nation: The Colony Within*, edited by Mel Watkins, 21–27. University of Toronto Press, 1977.

"The New Aklavik." *Aklavik Journal*, February 1956.

"Northern Affairs and National Resources (1953-12-16-196609-30)." *Parliament of Canada*. Accessed May 29, 2024. ⇒ lop.parl.ca/sites/ParlInfo/default/en_CA/Federal/areasResponsibility/profile?depId=6004.

Northwest Territories Archives. "Biographical History." Curtis Merrill Fonds. Accessed May 29, 2024. ⇒ gnwt.accesstomemory.org/174.

Ruiz, Rafico. *Slow Disturbance: Infrastructural Mediation on the Settler Colonial Resource Frontier*. Duke University Press, 2021.

"Scientists Coming to Aklavik." *Aklavik Journal*, June 1956. In *The Aklavik Journal: A Reprint of the Community Newspaper of Aklavik North West Territories, 1955-57*, edited by Bern Will Brown. Our Lady of the Snows Mission, 1996.

Scott, Felicity. *Outlaw Territories: Environments of Insecurity/Architectures of Counterinsurgency*. Zone Books, 2016.

Stoller, Mark P., and Thomas D. Andrews. "Mapping Denendeh: The Dene Mapping Project and the Enduring Legacy of Indigenous Cartographies." In *Just Relations: Anthropology and Law in Canada*, edited by Joshua Smith and Robert P. Wishart. University of Alberta Press, forthcoming.

Thrasher, Rose Mary. "Mackenzie Delta Environmental Project." *Delta Newsletter* no. 1, August 1970.

Town of Inuvik. "Community Profile." Accessed May 29, 2024. ⇒ inuvik.ca/en/doing-business/Community.

Tuck, Eve. "ANCSA as X-Mark." In *Transforming the University: Alaska Native Studies in the 21st Century*, edited by Beth Ginondidoy Leonard, Jeane Ta'aw xíwaa Breinig, Lenora Ac'aralek Carpluk, Sharon Chilux Lind, and Maria Shaa Tláa Williams, 252–64. Two Harbors Press, 2014.

van der Watt, Lize-Marié, Peder Roberts, and Julia Lajus. "Institutions and the Changing Nature of Arctic Research during the Early Cold War." In *Cold Science: Environmental Knowledge in the North American Arctic during the Cold War*, edited by Stephen Bocking and Daniel Heidt, 197–215. Routledge, 2019.

Wright, Tom. Interview by author. Inuvik, Northwest Territories. April 27, 2023.

Yip, Mike. *Inuvik*. Self-published, 1976.

(60)

Urbanisms of Refusal: Indigeneity and Land in Alaska
Lasse Rau

Arnold, Robert D. *Alaska Native Land Claims*. Alaska Native Foundation, 1978.

Bhandar, Brenna. *Colonial Lives of Property: Law, Land, and Racial Regimes of Ownership*. Duke University Press, 2018.

Burch, Ernest S. "Native Claims in Alaska: An Overview." *Études/Inuit/Studies* 3, no. 1 (1979): 7-30.

Case, David S., David Avraham Voluck, and David A. Voluck. *Alaska Natives and American Laws*. University of Alaska Press, 2012.

Champagne, Duane, Karen Jo Torjesen, and Susan Steiner, eds. *Indigenous Peoples and the Modern State*. AltaMira Press, 2005.

Chrisbens, Erin. "Indian Country after ANCSA: Divesting Tribal Sovereignty by Interpretation in Alaska v. Native Village of Venetie Tribal Government." *Denver Law Review* 76, no. 1 (1998): 307–43.

Clay Berry, Mary. *The Alaska Pipeline: The Politics of Oil and Native Land Claims*. Indiana University Press, 1975.

Cole, Terrence M. "Jim Crow in Alaska: The Passage of the Alaska Equal Rights Act of 1945." *Western Historical Quarterly* 23, no. 4 (1992): 429–49.

Coulthard, Glen Sean. *Red Skin, White Masks: Rejecting the Colonial Politics of Recognition*. University of Minnesota Press, 2014.

Ervin, Alexander M. "Styles and Strategies of Leadership during the Alaskan Native Land Claims Movement: 1959-71." *Anthropologica* 29, no. 1 (1987): 21–38.

Federal Bureau of Investigation. "Investigative Information on the Activities of the American Indian Movement (AIM), Formed in 1968 as a Civil Rights Organization, but Comprised of Many Militant Chapters with Extremist Beliefs." United States: Federal Bureau of Investigation, 1974.

Hopson, Eben. "Testimony before the Berger Inquiry on the Experience of the Arctic Slope Inupiat with Oil and Gas Development in the Arctic." Eben Hopson Archives, 1976.

Nichols, Robert. *Theft Is Property! Dispossession & Critical Theory*. Duke University Press, 2020.

Simpson, Audra. *Mohawk Interruptus: Political Life across the Borders of Settler States*. Duke University Press, 2014.

Stern, Charlene Barbara. "From Camps to Communities: Neets'aii Gwich'in Planning and Development in a Pre- and Post-Settlement Context." PhD diss., University of Alaska Fairbanks, 2018.

United States Senate. *Trans-Alaska Pipeline, Problems Posed by the Threat of Sabotage and the Impact on Internal Security: Hearing before the Committee on the Judiciary, Subcommittee to Investigate the Administration of the Internal Security Act and Other Internal Security Laws*. 94th Cong., 2nd sess., 1977.

Zahnd, Maximilien. "An Alaska Tax Story: Tribal Sovereignty, Settler Colonialism, and the Indigenous Tax Space." *Environment and Planning D: Society and Space* 41, no. 5 (2023): 784–804.

446

(68)
The Trail as Home: Claudio Aporta in Conversation with Bert De Jonghe and Elise Misao Hunchuck

ᐊᓂᔮᕐᓂᖅ (ANIJAARNIQ). Accessed May 29, 2024. anijaarniq.com.

Aporta, Claudio. "Markers in Space and Time: Reflections on the Nature of Place Names as Events in the Inuit Approach to the Territory." In *Marking the Land: Hunter-Gatherer Creation of Meaning within Their Surroundings*, edited by Robert Whallon and William Lovis, 67–83. Routledge, 2019.

———. "Routes, Trails and Tracks: Trail-Breaking among the Inuit of Igloolik." *Études Inuit Studies* 28, no. 2 (2004): 9–38.

———. "The Trail as Home: Inuit and Their Pan-Arctic Network of Routes." *Human Ecology* 37, no. 2 (2009): 131–46.

Canadian Press. "New Atlas Documents Traditional Inuit Trail Network." *CBC News*, June 12, 2014. cbc.ca/news/canada/north/new-atlas-documents-traditional-inuit-trail-network-1.2673559.

Lyon, G. F. *The Private Journal of Captain G.F. Lyon, of H.M.S. Hecla, during the Recent Voyage of Discovery under Captain Parry: With a Map and Plates*. John Murray, 1824.

Parry, William Edward. *Journal of a Second Voyage for the Discovery of a North-West Passage from the Atlantic to the Pacific: Performed in the Years 1821-22-23, in His Majesty's Ships Fury and Hecla, under the Orders of Captain William Edward Parry*. John Murray, 1824.

(81)
Drifting as Agency: Between Ice, Space, and Territory
Aniella Sophie Goldinger

Alfred Wegener Institute. "MOSAiC Expedition." Accessed June 7, 2024. mosaic-expedition.org.

Bennett, Jane. *Vibrant Matter: A Political Ecology of Things*. Duke University Press, 2010.

Bennett, Mia M., Scott R. Stephenson, Kang Yang, Michael T. Bravo, and Bert de Jonghe. "The Opening of the Transpolar Sea Route: Logistical, Geopolitical, Environmental, and Socioeconomic Impacts." *Marine Policy* 121 (2020): 104178.

Blanchfield, Caitlin. "Envirotechnical Lands: Science Reserves and Settler Astronomy." In *Technical Lands: A Critical Primer*, edited by Jeffrey S. Nesbit and Charles Waldheim, 188–203. Jovis Verlag, 2022.

Bode, Claudia, and Lizzie Yarina. "Thick Representations for Oceanic Space." In *The Urbanisation of the Sea: From Concepts and Analysis to Design*, edited by Nancy Couling and Carola Hein, 71–92. nai010 Publishers, 2020.

Brenner, Neil, and Nikos Katsikis. "Operational Landscapes: Hinterlands of the Capitalocene." *Architectural Design* 90, no. 1 (2020): 22–31.

Brenner, Neil, and Christian Schmid. "Planetary Urbanization." In *Urban Constellations*, edited by Matthew Gandy, 10–13. Jovis Verlag, 2012.

Bryant, Miranda. "Norway Votes for Deepsea Mining despite Environmental Concerns." *The Guardian*, January 9, 2024. theguardian.com/environment/2024/jan/09/norway-set-to-approve-deep-sea-mining-despite-environmental-concerns.

Bruun, Johanne, and Philip Steinberg. "Placing Territory on Ice: Militarisation, Measurement and Murder in the High Arctic." In *Territory beyond Terra*, edited by Kimberley Peters, Philip Steinberg, and Elaine Stratford. Rowman & Littlefield International, 2018.

Chierici, Melissa, Agneta Fransson, and Mats Granskog. "The Transpolar Drift Current — The Largest Arctic River — Transports Materials into the Central Arctic Ocean from Siberian Shelf across the North Pole." *The Nansen Legacy*, September 24, 2021. arvenetternansen.com/2021/09/24/the-transpolar-drift-current-the-largest-arctic-river-transports-materials-into-the-central-arctic-ocean-from-siberian-shelf-across-the-north-pole.

Couling, Nancy. "Imagining the Invisible: Spatial Design for the North Sea." *Planning Practice and Research* 37, no. 3 (2022): 276–98.

———. "Viscosity." In *The Urbanisation of the Sea: From Concepts and Analysis to Design*, edited by Nancy Couling and Carola Hein, 55–60. nai010 Publishers, 2020.

———. "Formats of Extended Urbanisation in Ocean Space." In *Emerging Urban Spaces: A Planetary Perspective*, edited by Philipp Horn, Paola Alfaro d'Alencon, and Ana Claudia Cardoso, 149–76. Springer, 2018.

Couling, Nancy, and Carola Hein, eds. *The Urbanisation of the Sea: From Concepts and Analysis to Design*. nai010 Publishers, 2020.

Dodds, Klaus. "A Polar Mediterranean? Accessibility, Resources and Sovereignty in the Arctic Ocean." *Global Policy* 1, no. 3 (2010): 303–11.

Easterling, Keller. *Extrastatecraft: The Power of Infrastructure Space*. Verso, 2014.

Edwards, Charity. "The Ocean in (Planetary) Excess." *Dialogues in Human Geography* 9, no. 3 (2019): 312–15.

Elden, Stuart. "The Instability of Terrain." In *A Moving Border: Alpine Cartographies of Climate Change*, edited by Marco Ferrari, Elisa Pasqual, and Andrea Bagnato, 51–61. Columbia Books on Architecture and the City/ZKM, 2019.

———. "Secure the Volume: Vertical Geopolitics and the Depth of Power." *Political Geography* 32, no. 2 (2013): 35–51.

Foscari, Giulia, and UNLESS, eds. *Antarctic Resolution*. Lars Müller Publishers, 2021.

Goldinger, Aniella Sophie. "Drifting Space and Unruly Velocities: More-than-Human Marine Spatial Planning in the Fram Strait." *Spool: Landscape Metropolis* 11 (2025).

The Indigenous Knowledge Social Network. "SIKU." ⇒ siku.org.

Jahn, Alexandra, Marika M. Holland, and Jennifer E. Kay. "Projections of an Ice-Free Arctic Ocean." *Nature Reviews Earth & Environment* 5 (2024): 164–76.

Kim, Yeon-Hee, Seung-Ki Min, Nathan P. Gillett, Dirk Notz, and Elizaveta Malinina. "Observationally-Constrained Projections of an Ice-Free Arctic Even under a Low Emission Scenario." *Nature Communications* 14 (2023): 3139.

Koenig, L. S., K. R. Greenaway, Moira Dunbar, and G. Hattersley-Smith. "Arctic Ice Islands." *Arctic* 5, no. 2 (1952): 66–103.

Krumpen, Thomas, H. Jakob Belter, Antje Boetius, Ellen Damm, Christian Haas, Stefan Hendricks, Marcel Nicolaus, et al. "Arctic Warming Interrupts the Transpolar Drift and Affects Long-Range Transport of Sea Ice and Ice-Rafted Matter." *Scientific Reports* 9 (2019): 1–9.

Nansen, Fridtjof. *Farthest North: Being the Record of Exploration of the Ship Fram, 1893-96, and of a Fifteen Months' Sleigh Journey.* Cambridge Library Collection, 2011.

Pan Inuit Trails. "Pan Inuit Trails." ⇒ paninuittrails.org/index.html.

PAME. "Arctic Shipping Status Report #1: The Increase in Arctic Shipping 2013-2019." 2019.

———. "Arctic Shipping Status Report #2: Heavy Fuel Oil (HFO) Use by Ships in the Arctic 2019." 2019.

Peters, Kimberley. "Drifting: Towards Mobilities at Sea." *Transactions of the Institute of British Geographers* 40, no. 2 (2015): 262–72.

Peters, Kimberley, and Philip Steinberg. "The Ocean in Excess: Towards a More-Than-Wet Ontology." *Dialogues in Human Geography* 9, no. 3 (2019): 293–307.

Peters, Kimberley, Philip Steinberg, and Elaine Stratford, eds. *Territory beyond Terra.* Rowman & Littlefield International, 2018.

Pharand, Donat. "The Legal Status of Ice Shelves and Ice Islands in the Arctic." *Les Cahiers de Droit* 10, no. 3 (1969): 461–75.

Ryan, Jonathan, Parnuna Dahl, and Brigt Dale. "Co-Production of Sea Ice Knowledge in Uummannaq Bay, Greenland." *Oceanography* 35, no. 3–4 (2022): 196–97.

Shake, Kristen L., Karen E. Frey, Deborah G. Martin, and Philip E. Steinberg. "(Un)frozen Spaces: Exploring the Role of Sea Ice in the Marine Socio-Legal Spaces of the Bering and Beaufort Seas." *Journal of Borderlands Studies* 33, no. 2 (2018): 239–53.

SmartICE. "SmartICE." ⇒ smartice.org/our-communities.

Steinberg, Philip, and Kate Coddington. "From Ice Law to ICE LAW: Constructing an Interdisciplinary Research Project on the Political-Legal Challenges of Polar Environments." Briefing note, 2014.

Steinberg, Philip, and Berit Kristoffersen. "'The Ice Edge Is Lost... Nature Moved It': Mapping Ice as State Practice in the Canadian and Norwegian North." *Transactions of the Institute of British Geographers* 42 (2017): 625–41.

Steinberg, Philip, and Kimberley Peters. "Wet Ontologies, Fluid Spaces: Giving Depth to Volume through Oceanic Thinking." *Environment and Planning D: Society and Space* 33 (2015): 247–64.

Steinberg, Philip, Greta Ferloni, Claudio Aporta, Gavin Bridge, Aldo Chircop, Kate Coddington, Stuart Elden, et al. "Navigating the Structural Coherence of Sea Ice." In *Laws of the Sea: Interdisciplinary Currents*, edited by Irus Braverman, 165–83. Routledge, 2022.

Strandsbjerg, Jeppe. "Cartopolitics, Geopolitics and Boundaries in the Arctic." *Geopolitics* 17, no. 4 (2012): 818–42.

United Nations. United Nations Convention on the Law of the Sea. 1986.

(100)

My Notes on Architecture in Inuit Nunangat
Nicole Luke

No notes.

(106)

A Most Curious Listener: Todd Saunders in Conversation with Bert De Jonghe and Elise Misao Hunchuck

Saunders, Todd, and Jonathan Bell. *Share: Conversations about Contemporary Architecture.* Artifice Press, 2022.

Saunders, Todd, Jonathan Bell, and Ellie Stathaki. *Architecture in Northern Landscapes.* Birkhäuser, 2016.

(116)

Kangiata Illorsua – Ilulissat Icefjord Centre
Dorte Mandrup

De Jonghe, Bert. *Inventing Greenland: Designing an Arctic Nation.* Actar Publishers, 2022.

(126)

The Case of Maniitsoq–Alcoa: The Re-emergence of a Conscious Subjectivity
Magdalena Haggärde
Gisle Løkken

Betasamosake Simpson, Leanne. *As We Have Always Done: Indigenous Freedom through Radical Resistance.* University of Minnesota Press, 2017.

Box, Jason E., Alun Hubbard, David B. Bahr, William T. Colgan, Xavier Fettweis, Kenneth D. Mankoff, and Michalea King. "Greenland Ice Sheet Climate Disequilibrium and Committed Sea-Level Rise." *Nature Climate Change*, August 29, 2022. ⇒ doi.org/10.1038/s41558-022-01441-2.

Coulthard, Glen Sean. *Red Skin, White Masks: Rejecting the Colonial Politics of Recognition.* University of Minnesota Press, 2014.

Deleuze, Gilles, and Félix Guattari. *A Thousand Plateaus: Capitalism and Schizophrenia.* Translated by Brian Massumi. University of Minnesota Press, 1987.

———. *What Is Philosophy?* Translated by Hugh Tomlinson and Graham Burchell. Columbia University Press, 1994.

448

Egede, Peter. "Erhvervsliv." In *Manîtsok' — Sukkertoppen 1782-1982*, edited by H. C. Petersen, 85–91. Manîtsup kommunia, 1982.

Gillman, Steve. "Most Ice on Earth Is Very Close to Melting Conditions." *Horizon: The EU Research Magazine*, January 6, 2020. ➡ ec.europa.eu/research-and-innovation/en/horizon-magazine/most-ice-earth-very-close-melting-conditions.

Greenland Development. Linkedin, accessed January 18, 2024. ➡ no.linkedin.com/company/greenland-development.

Hansen, Klaus Georg. "The Aluminium Smelter Project in Greenland: New Aspects of an Industrialization Process?" In *Urbanization and the Role of Housing in the Present Development Process in the Arctic*, edited by K. G. Hansen, S. Bitsch, and L. Zalkind, 85–101. Nordregio Report 2013:3.

Haraway, Donna. "Situated Knowledge: The Science Question in Feminism and the Privilege of Partial Perspective." *Feminist Studies* 14, no. 3 (1988): 575–99.

Kleemann, Naduk, ed. *Greenland in Figures 2022*. Statistics Greenland, 2022.

Lee, Matthew, and Jan M. Olsen. "US to Boost Aid to Greenland in Bid to Counter Russia, China." *Associated Press*, April 22, 2020.

Lyberth, Erik. "Tiden omkring anlæggelsen af 'Kolonien Manîtsok.'" In *Manîtsok' — Sukkertoppen 1782-1982*, edited by H. C. Petersen, 41–46. Manîtsup kommunia, 1982.

Naalakkersuisut. (Government of Greenland) "Greenland Hydropower Resources." Accessed April 2024. ➡ hydropower.gl/news.

NIRAS Greenland. *Økonomiske konsekvenser af etablering af aluminiumsindustri i Grønland: Analyse af kapasiteten*. Greenland Development A/S, 2007.

———. "Om NIRAS." Accessed April, 2024. ➡ nirasnorge.no/om-niras.

NIF, Norwegian Film Institute. "Winter's Yearning" [introduction]. Accessed January 18, 2024. ➡ nfi.no/eng/film?name=winters-yearning&id=1968.

Nuttall, Mark. "Living in a World of Movement: Human Resilience to Environmental Instability in Greenland." In *Anthropology and Climate Change: From Encounters to Actions*, edited by Susan A. Crate and Mark Nuttall, 292–310. Left Coast Press, 2009.

Nyseth, Torill. "Towards an Understanding of Place Reinvention." In *Place Reinvention in the North: Dynamics and Governance Perspectives*, edited by Torill Nyseth and Brynhild Granås, 149–64. Nordregio, 2007.

Pihl, Roger, Ulf Christensen, and Dag Thorkildsen. "Grønland." In *Store norske leksikon*. ➡ snl.no/Grønland.

Qeqqata kommunia. "Program for nasjonaldag 2022 — Maniitsoq og Sisimiut." Accessed March 13, 2024. ➡ qeqqata.gl/nyheder/2022/06/nationaldag?sc_lang=da

Sejersen, Frank. *Rethinking Greenland and the Arctic in the Era of Climate Change: New Northern Horizons*. Routledge, 2015.

Stryken, Arne Christian. *Grønland*. Topografisk forlag, 2005.

70°N arkitektur. *Takorluukkanut nalunaarusiaq // Visjonsrapport // Maniitsoq // 70°N arkitektur*. Report. 70°N arkitektur, 2010.

Torstholm Larsen, Sidse, and Sturla Pilskog. *Winter's Yearning*. Documentary film. Blåst Film AS, 2019.

(141)
Solar Sensing
Susan Schuppli

Daston, Lorraine, and Peter Galison. *Objectivity*. Zone Books, 2007.

Dixon, Guy. "New Documentary Recounts Bizarre Climate Changes Seen by Inuit Elders." *Globe and Mail*, October 19, 2010. ➡ theglobeandmail.com/arts/film/new-documentary-recounts-bizarre-climate-changes-seen-by-inuit-elders/article1215305.

Gates, Kelly. "The Cultural Labor of Surveillance: Video Forensics, Computational Objectivity, and the Production of Visual Evidence." *Social Semiotics* 23, no. 2 (2013): 242–60.

Hadley, Odelle L., and Thomas W. Kirchstetter. "Black-Carbon Reduction of Snow Albedo." *Nature Climate Change* 2, no. 6 (2012): 437–40.

Kirby, Vicki. "Matter out of Place: 'New Materialism' in Review." In *What if Culture Was Nature All Along?*, edited by Vicki Kirby, 15–32. Edinburgh University Press, 2017.

Kunuk, Zacharias, and Ian Mauro. *Inuit Knowledge and Climate Change*. Documentary film. Isuma TV, 2010. ➡ isuma.tv/inuit-knowledge-and-climate-change.

Pottage, Alain. "Law Machines: Scale Models, Forensic Materiality and the Making of Modern Patent Law." *Social Studies of Science* 41, no. 5 (2011): 621–43.

Thurston, Thomas. "Hearsay of the Sun: Photography, Identity, and the Law of Evidence." American Studies Crossroads Project at Georgetown University and the Center for History and New Media at George Mason University, 2009.

Warren, Stephen G. "Optical Properties of Snow." *Reviews of Geophysics and Space Physics* 20, no. 1 (1982): 67–89.

(148)
Keepers of the Ocean: At Home We Belong
Inuuteq Storch

Storch, Inuuteq. *At Home We Belong*. Photographic series, 2010–15.
———. *Keepers of the Ocean*. Disko Bay, 2022.

(160)
Place Bonding and Migration
Nadezhda Filimonova

Alrobaee, T. R., and A. S. Al-Kinani. "Place Dependence as the Physical Environment Role Function in the Place Attachment." *IOP Conference Series: Materials Science and Engineering* 698 (2019): 033014.

Anand, Rashmi Rani, and Poonam Sharma. "Assessing Inadequate Urban Infrastructure and Place Attachment

Perception among Residents of Gated Societies in Greater Faridabad, India." *International Journal of Social Science and Economic Research* 6, no. 2 (2021): 605–27.

Bobylev, Nikolai, Sebastien Gadal, Valery Konyshev, Maria Lagutina, and Alexander Sergunin. "Building Urban Climate Change Adaptation Strategies: The Case of Russian Arctic Cities." *Weather, Climate, and Society* 13, no. 4 (2021): 875–84.

Boccagni, Paolo, and Carlos Vargas-Silva. "Feeling at Home across Time and Place: A Study of Ecuadorians in Three European Cities." *Population, Space and Place* 27, no. 6 (2021): 1–13.

Bolotova, Alla, Anastasia Karaseva, and Valeria Vasilyeva. "Mobility and Sense of Place among Youth in the Russian Arctic." *Sibirica* 16, no. 3 (2017): 77–124.

Bolotova, Alla, and Florian Stammler. "How the North Became Home: Attachment to Place among Industrial Migrants in the Murmansk Region of Russia." In *Migration in the Circumpolar North: New Concepts and Patterns*, edited by Chris Southcott and Lee Huskey, 193–220. Canadian Circumpolar Institute Press, 2009.

Cygankova, Anna Aristokesovna, Ol'ga Viktorovna Romanchenko, and Ol'ga Leonidovna Shemetkova. "Infrastruktura Arkticheskoi Zony RF: Sostoianie, Ekonomicheskie Instrumenty Razvitiia i Prioritetnye Proekty" [The Infrastructure of the Arctic Zone of the Russian Federation: The State, the Economic Development of the Tools and Priority Projects]. *Regional Economy and Management: Electronic Scientific Journal* 4, no. 48 (2016): 1–14.

Fauzer, Viktor Vilgelmovich, Andrey Vladimirovich Smirnov, Tatyana Stepanovna Lytkina, and Galina Nikolaevna Fauzer. "Vyzovy i Protivorechiia v Razvitii Severa i Arktiki: Demograficheskoe Izmerenie" [Challenges and Contradictions in the Development of the North and the Arctic: Demographic Dimension].

Arktika: Ekologia I Ekonomika 12, no. 1 (2022): 111–22.

Filimonova, Nadezhda. "From Global to Local Climate Change Governance: Arctic Cities' Perceptions of the Uses of Expert Knowledge." In *Building Common Interests in the Arctic Ocean with Global Inclusion*, edited by Paul Arthur Berkman, Alexander N. Vylegzhanin, Oran R. Young, David A. Balton, and Ole Rasmus Øvretveit, 221–37. Vol. 2. Springer Nature, 2022.

Giuliani, Vittoria M., and Roberta Feldman. "Place Attachment in a Developmental and Cultural Context." *Journal of Environmental Psychology* 13, no. 3 (1993): 267–74.

Grey, Christopher, and Michelle O'Toole. "The Placing of Identity and the Identification of Place: 'Place-Identity' in Community Lifeboating." *Journal of Management Inquiry* 29, no. 2 (2020): 206–19.

Grønseth, Anne Sigfrid. "Migrating Rituals: Negotiations of Belonging and Otherness among Tamils in Norway." *Journal of Ethnic and Migration Studies* 44, no. 16 (2018): 2617–33.

Gunko, Maria, Elena Batunova, and Andrey Medvedev. "Rethinking Urban Form in a Shrinking Arctic City." *Espace-Populations-Societes*, nos. 2020/3-2021/1 (2021): 1–16.

Hauge, Åshild Lappegard. "Identity and Place: A Critical Comparison of Three Identity Theories." *Architectural Science Review* 50, no. 1 (2007): 44–51.

Hague, Cliff, and Paul Jenkins. *Place Identity, Planning and Participation*. Routledge, 2005.

Hazerova, Irina. "Bez Sveta Na Kraiu Sveta" [Without Lights at the Edge of the World]. *Krasnyi Tundrovik*, no. 92 (2015). nvinder.ru/article/vypusk-no-92-20294-ot-29-avgusta-2015-g/9299-bez-sveta-na-krayu-sveta.

Heleniak, Timothy. "Out-Migration and Depopulation of the Russian North during the 1990s." *Post-Soviet Geography and Economics* 40, no. 3 (1999): 155–205.

———. "The Role of Attachment to Place in Migration Decisions of the

Population of the Russian North." *Polar Geography* 32, nos. 1-2 (2009): 31–60.

Hemmersam, Peter. "Arcticness and the Urbanism of the North." *Arctic Yearbook* (2021): 1–15.

Hidalgo, M. Carmen, and Bernardo Hernández. "Place Attachment: Conceptual and Empirical Questions." *Journal of Environmental Psychology* 21, no. 3 (2001): 273–81.

Hudson, Christine, Torill Nyseth, and Paul Pedersen. "Dealing with Difference: Contested Place Identities in Two Northern Scandinavian Cities." *City* 23, nos. 4-5 (2019): 564–79.

Information and Analytical Center of the State Commission for Arctic Development Institute. *Opornye Naselennye Punkty Rossiiskoi Arktiki: Materialy Predvaritel'nogo Issledovaniia* [Support Settlements of the Russian Arctic: Preliminary Research Materials]. 2022. arctic-russia.ru/article/opornye-naselennye-punkty-novyy-subekt-prostranstvennogo-razvitiya-arktiki.

Istomin, K. V. "'Who Would Want to Lay down into the Permafrost?': An Attempt to Explain Differences in Migration Rates, Strategies and Attitudes in Two Russian Northern Cities." *Acta Borealia* 38, no. 2 (2021): 104–30.

Johansen, Harley, and Yelizaveta Skryzhevska. "Adaptation Priorities on Russia's Kola Peninsula: Climate Change vs. Post-Soviet Transition." *Polar Geography* 36, no. 4 (2013): 271–90.

Kalemeneva, Ekaterina. "From New Socialist Cities to Thaw Experimentation in Arctic Townscapes: Leningrad Architects Attempt to Modernise the Soviet North." *Europe-Asia Studies* 71, no. 3 (2019): 426–49.

Kuklina, Vera, Sargylana Ignatieva, and Uliana Vinokurova. "Educational Institutions as a Resource for the Urbanization of Indigenous People: The Case of Yakutsk." *Sibirica* 18, no. 3 (2019): 29–53.

Kyle, Gerard T., Andrew J. Mowen, and Michael Tarrant. "Linking Place

Preferences with Place Meaning: An Examination of the Relationship between Place Motivation and Place Attachment." *Journal of Environmental Psychology* 24, no. 4 (2004): 439–54.

Laruelle, Marlène. "Postcolonial Polar Cities? New Indigenous and Cosmopolitan Urbanness in the Arctic." *Acta Borealia* 36, no. 2 (2019): 149–65.

———. "The Three Waves of Arctic Urbanisation: Drivers, Evolutions, Prospects." *Polar Record* 55, no. 1 (2019): 1–12.

Laruelle, Marlène, and Sophie Hohmann. "Polar Islam: Muslim Communities in Russia's Arctic Cities." *Problems of Post-Communism* 67, nos. 4-5 (2020): 327–37.

Lestari, W. M., and J. Sumabrata. "The Influencing Factors on Place Attachment in Neighborhood of Kampung Melayu." *IOP Conference Series: Earth and Environmental Science* 126 (2018): 012190.

Lewicka, Maria. "On the Varieties of People's Relationships with Places: Hummon's Typology Revisited." *Environment and Behavior* 43, no. 5 (2011): 676–709.

———. "Place Attachment: How Far Have We Come in the Last 40 Years?" *Journal of Environmental Psychology* 31, no. 3 (2011): 207–30.

———. "Place Attachment, Place Identity, and Place Memory: Restoring the Forgotten City Past." *Journal of Environmental Psychology* 28, no. 3 (2008): 209–31.

Low, Setha M., and Irwin Altman. "Place Attachment: A Conceptual Inquiry." In *Place Attachment*, edited by Irwin Altman and Setha M. Low, 1–12. Plenum Press, 1992.

Lynnebakke, Brit, and Aadne Aasland. "Striking Roots: Place Attachment of International Migrants, Internal Migrants and Local Natives in Three Norwegian Rural Municipalities." *Journal of Rural Studies* 94 (2022): 488–98.

Nedoseka, Elena V., and G. V. Zhigunova. "Features of Local Identity of Single-Industry Town Residents (The Case of the Murmansk Oblast)." *Monitoring of Public Opinion* 52, no. 37 (2019): 98–111.

Nyseth, Torill, and Paul Pedersen. "Urban Sámi Identities in Scandinavia: Hybridities, Ambivalences, and Cultural Innovation." *Acta Borealia* 31 no. 2 (2014): 131 51.

Oktay, Derya. "The Quest for Urban Identity in the Changing Context of the City." *Cities* 19, no. 4 (2002): 261–71.

Orttung, Robert W., and Colin Reisser. "Urban Sustainability in Russia's Arctic: Lessons from a Recent Conference and Areas for Further Investigations." *Polar Geography* 37, no. 4 (2014): 37–41.

Paasi, Anssi. "The Institutionalization of Regions: A Theoretical Framework for Understanding the Emergence of Regions and the Constitution of Regional Identity." *Fennia* 164, no. 1 (1986): 105–46.

Parente, Genevieve, Nikolay Shiklomanov, and Dmitry Streletskiy. "Living in the New North: Migration to and from Russian Arctic Cities." *Focus on Geography* 55, no. 3 (2012): 77–89.

Parker, Gavin, and Joe Doak. "Place and Sense of Place." In *Key Concepts in Planning*, 156-70. SAGE Publications, 2014.

Paulgaard, Gry, and Marianne Neerland Soleim. "The Arctic Migration Route: Local Consequences of Global Crises." *Journal of Peace Education* (2023): 1–21.

Peng, Jianchao, Dirk Strijker, and Qun Wu. "Place Identity: How Far Have We Come in Exploring Its Meanings?" *Frontiers in Psychology* 11 (2020): 294.

Popov, Igor. "Prospects of Development for Urban Areas in the Russian Arctic." *Sibirica* 21, no. 1 (2022): 79–100.

Popova, O. N., and I. V. Vicentiy. "Migration Situation in the Russian Arctic (on the Example of the Murmansk Region)." *IOP Conference Series: Earth and Environmental Science* 302, no. 1 (2019): 012086.

Prokopova, Sofya, Svetlana Kravchuk, and Nikolai Garin. "Gorodskaia Sreda Arktiki: Optimizatsiia i Tsifrovizatsiia" [Arctic Urban Realm: Optimisation and Digitalisation]. *Akademicheskij Vestnik Uralniiproekt RAASN*, no. 3 (2021): 40–44.

Proshansky, Harold M. "The City and Self-Identity." *Environment and Behavior* 10, no. 2 (1978): 147–69.

Proshansky, Harold M., Abbe K. Fabian, and Robert Kaminoff. "Place-Identity: Physical World Socialization of the Self." *Journal of Environmental Psychology* 3, no. 1 (1983): 57–83.

Rozanova, Marya. "Indigenous Urbanization in Russia's Arctic: The Case of Nenets Autonomous Region." *Sibirica* 18, no. 3 (2019): 54–91.

Ryabova, L. A. "O Neotlozhnykh Merakh Po Povysheniiu Urovnia i Kachestva Zhizni Naseleniia Arkticheskoi Zony RF" [On Urgent Measures to Improve the Level and Quality of Life of the Population of the Arctic Zone of the Russian Federation]. *Sever i Rynok* 1, no. 29 (2012): 67–71.

Schweitzer, Peter. "Retrospektiva: Gorodskaia Antropologiia Na Severe i Iuge" [Indigenous Peoples and Urbanization in Alaska and the Canadian North]. *Etnograficheskoe Obozrenie*, no. 1 (2016): 10–22.

Searles, Edmund. "Placing Identity: Town, Land, and Authenticity in Nunavut, Canada." *Acta Borealia* 27, no. 2 (2010): 151–66.

Sergunin, Alexander. "Indexing Arctic Urban Sustainable Development Planning Strategies: The Case of Russia." In *Arctic Yearbook 2018*, edited by Lassi Heininen and Heather Exner-Pirot. Northern Research Forum, 2018.

Sieng, Vanessa, and Ágnes Szabó. "Exploring the Place Attachments of Older Migrants in Aotearoa: A Life Course History Approach." *Advances in Life Course Research* 57 (2023): 100560.

Toropushina, E. E. "Otsenka Urovnia Razvitiia Sotsial'noi Infrastruktury v Regionakh Severa i Arktiki Rossii" [Assessment of the Level of Development of Social Infrastructure in the Regions of the North and

Arctic of Russia]. *Eco*, no. 6 (2016): 99–108.

Zamyatina, Nadezhda. "Migration Destination Choice as a Criterion of Self-Identification: The Case of Young People Leaving Norilsk and Dudinka." *Sibirica* 16, no. 3 (2017): 57–76.

Zamyatina, Nadezhda, and Ruslan Goncharov. "'Agglomeration of Flows': Case of Migration Ties between the Arctic and the Southern Regions of Russia." *Regional Science Policy and Practice* 14, no. 1 (2022): 63–85.

———. "Population Mobility and the Contrasts between Cities in the Russian Arctic and Their Southern Russian Counterparts." *Area Development and Policy* 3, no. 3 (2018): 293–308.

(176)

Color and Comfort: A Tribute to the Children of Tasiilaq
Jakob Exner
Helena Lennert

No notes.

(179)

The Place on the Island by the Sea: Maaretta Jaukkuri and A K Dolven in Conversation with Elise Misao Hunchuck

Dillard, Annie. "Teaching a Stone to Talk: Expeditions and Encounters." *The Atlantic*, February 1981. ⇒ theatlantic.com/magazine/archive/1981/02/teaching-a-stone-to-talk/665214.

Jaukkuri, Maaretta. Email message to author. October 27, 2018.

Maaretta Jaukkuri Foundation. "The Foundation." ⇒ mjfoundation.no/the-foundation.

(190)

Travel Notes from Siberia
Sophy Roberts
Michael Turek

No notes.

(210)

Everything Is the Same
Svetlana Romanova

Bitsui, Sherwin. "The Sun Rises and I Think of Your Bruised Larynx." In *Shapeshift*, 15–16. University of Arizona Press, 2003.

Romanova, Svetlana. *Managa Bar*. Art installation, 2024.
———. *Rustam's Habitat*. Art installation, 2024.
———. *Voyage of Jeanette*. Art installation, 2024.

(224)

The Road of Life
Nicholas Gulick
Elena Krapivina

No notes.

(248)

Like a Phoenix: A New Chapter
Bertine Tønseth

No notes.

(260)

Landscape Architecture Education above the Arctic Circle
Thomas Juel Clemmensen

Barcelona International Landscape Biennal. "UiT Arctic University of Norway Wins Prestigious International Landscape Architecture School Prize 2023." ⇒ mailchi.mp/coac.net/2023_rosabarba_winners-6683687.

Harrison, Rodney. "Beyond 'Natural' and 'Cultural' Heritage: Toward an Ontological Politics of Heritage in the Age of Anthropocene." *Heritage & Society* 8, no. 1 (2015): 24–42.

MONEC. "Om Prosjektet: 'To Manage or Not: Assessing the Benefit of Managing Ecosystem Disservices.'" ⇒ monecorg.wordpress.com/om.

(268)

Snødepot
Akie Kono

No notes.

(274)

"We Need Our Own Places": Paths for Indigenization in the Russian Arctic City of Naryan-Mar
Marya Rozanova-Smith
Andrey N. Petrov

Administratsia NAO. "O korrektirovke Strategii sotsial'no-ekonomicheskogo razvitiia Nenetskogo avtonomnogo okruga na perspektivu do 2030 goda [On Adjusting the Strategy of Socio-Economic Development of the Nenets Autonomous Okrug until 2030]. ⇒ dfei.adm-nao.ru/media/uploads/userfiles/2016/06/03/0_корректировке_Стратегии_НАО_до_2030_года.pdf.

Anisimova, Alla, and Olga Echevskaya. "Siberian Regional Identity: Self-perception, Solidarity, or Political Claim?" In *Russia's Regional Identities*, edited by Edith W. Clowes, Gisela Erbslöh, and Ani Kokobobo, 120–35. Routledge, 2018.

Balzer, Marjorie. "Korennye Kosmopolity, Ekologicheskaia Zashchita i Aktivizm v Sibiri i na Dal'nem Vostoke" [Indigenous Cosmopolitans, Environmental Protection and Activism in Siberia and the Far East]. *Sibirskie Istoricheskie Issledovaniia* 2 (2014): 15–38.

Berg-Nordlie, Mikkel. "The Governance of Urban Indigenous Spaces: Norwegian Sámi Examples." *Acta Borealia* 35, no. 1 (2018): 49–72.
———. "No Past, No Name, No Place? Urban Sámi Invisibility and Visibility in the Past and Present." *Aboriginal Policy Studies* 9, no. 2 (2021).

Blackman, Margaret. "Anaktuvuk Pass Goes to Town." *Études Inuit Studies* 32, no. 1 (2008): 107–15.

Bruno, Andy, and Ekaterina Kalemeneva. "Creating the Soviet Arctic, 1917-1991." In *The Cambridge History of the Polar Regions*, edited by Adrian Howkins and Peder Roberts, 245–68. Cambridge University Press, 2023.

Coulthard, Glenn. *Red Skin, White Masks: Rejecting the Colonial Politics of Recognition*. University of Minnesota Press, 2014.

Coyle, J. "Where Are All the Koori Football Players? The AFL and the Invisible Presence of Indigenous Victorians." *Sport in Society* 18, no. 5 (2015): 604–13.

Dahl, Jens, Gail Fondahl, Andrey Petrov, and Rune Sverre Fjellheim. "Fate Control." In *Arctic Social Indicators: A Follow-up to the Arctic Human Development Report*, edited by Joan Nymand Larsen, Gail Fondahl, and Peter Schweitzer, 129–41. Nordic Council of Ministers, 2010.

De Jonghe, Bert. *Inventing Greenland: Designing an Arctic Nation*. Actar, 2022.

Degai, Tatiana S. "Places of Significance in Itelmen Country: Sacredness, Nostalgia and Identity in Kamchatka, Russia." PhD diss., University of Arizona, 2009.

Degai, Tatiana, Andrey N. Petrov, Renuka Badhe, Parnuna P. Egede Dahl, Nina Döring, Stephan Dudeck, and Thora M. Hermann. "Shaping Arctic's Tomorrow through Indigenous Knowledge Engagement and Knowledge Co-Production." *Sustainability* 14, no. 3 (2022): 1331-34.

Efimov, Valeriy, Alla Lapteva, and Ul'yana Borisova. "Problemy Vosproizvodstva Etnicheskoy Prinadlezhnosti Naroda Sakha" [Problems of Ethnic Belonging Reproduction of the Sakha People]. *Problemy istorii, filologii, kul'tury* 2, no. 44 (2014): 333–49.

Fogel-Chance, Nancy. "Living in Both Worlds: 'Modernity' and 'Tradition' among North Slope Inupiaq Women in Anchorage." *Arctic Anthropology* 30, no. 1 (1993): 94–108.

Furlan, L. M. *Indigenous Cities: Urban Indian Fiction and the Histories of Relocation*. University of Nebraska Press, 2017.

Gillis, Jacqueline. "'We Have a Very Colonial Way of Thinking...': Ontario Municipalities' Climate Collaborations with Indigenous Peoples." *Canadian Public Administration* 66 (2023): 496–513.

Hamilton, Lawrence C., and Rasmus Ole Rasmussen. "Population, Sex Ratios and Development in Greenland." *Arctic* 63, no. 1 (2010): 43–52.

Hansen, Klaus Georg, and Rasmus Ole Rasmussen. "New Economic Activities and Urbanisation: Individual Reasons for Moving and for Staying—Case Greenland." In *Proceedings from the First International Conference on Urbanisation in the Arctic*, 28–30. Nordic Council of Ministers, 2012.

Heleniak, Timothy. "Growth Poles and Ghost Towns in the Russian Far North." In *Russia and the North*, edited by Elana Wilson Rowe, 129–63. University of Ottawa Press, 2009.

———. "Migration and Population Change in the Russian Far North during the 1990s." In *Migration in the Circumpolar North: Issues and Contexts*, edited by Chris Southcott and Lee Huskey, 57–91. Canadian Circumpolar Institute Press, 2010.

Howard-Wagner, D. *Indigenous Invisibility in the City: Successful Resurgence and Community Development Hidden in Plain Sight*. Routledge, 2021.

Huskey, Lee, Matthew Berman, and Alexandra Hill. "Leaving Home, Returning Home: Migration as a Labor Market Choice for Alaska Natives." *The Annals of Regional Science* 38, no. 1 (2004): 75–92.

International Arctic Social Sciences Association. "IASSA Principles and Guidelines for Conducting Ethical Research in the Arctic." iassa.org/about-iassa/research-principles.

Jacobs, Curran Katsi'Sorókwas. "Two-Row Wampum Reimagined: Understanding the Hybrid Digital Lives of Contemporary Kanien'kehá:ka Youth." *Studies in Social Justice* 13, no. 1 (2019): 59–72.

Khakhovskaya, Liudmila. "Aborigeny v Gorode: Etnokul'turnyi Oblik Zhitelei Magadana" [Aboriginal People in the City: Ethnocultural Image of the Urbanites of Magadan]. *Sibirskie Istoricheskie Issledovaniia* 2 (2014): 39–59.

Kishigami, Nobuhiro, and Molly Lee. "Les Inuit Urbains." *Études Inuit Studies* 32, no. 1 (2008): 5–11.

Kuklina, Vera, Sargylana Ignatieva, and Uliana Vinokurova. "Educational Institutions as a Resource for the Urbanization of Indigenous People: The Case of Yakutsk." *Sibirica* 18, no. 3 (2019): 29–53.

Kuklina, Vera, and Natalia Krasnoshtanova. "The Urbanization of Indigenous Peoples of Northeastern Siberia." In *New Mobilities and Social Changes in Russia's Arctic Regions*, edited by Marlene Laruelle, 118–37. Routledge, 2016.

Kulchytskyi, Stanislav. "Building of the Soviet Titular Nations (1918-1938)." *Codrul Cosminului* 20, no. 1 (2014): 181–92.

Laakso, Johanna. "Contact and the Finno-Ugric Languages." In *The Handbook of Language Contact*, edited by Raymond Hickey, 519–35. John Wiley & Sons, 2020.

Laptander, R. "Processes of Remembering and Forgetting." *Sibirica* 13, no. 3 (2014): 22–44.

Laruelle, Marlene. "Postcolonial Polar Cities? New Indigenous and Cosmopolitan Urbanness in the Arctic." *Acta Borealia* 36, no. 2 (2019): 149–65.

———. "The Three Waves of Arctic Urbanisation: Drivers, Evolutions, Prospects." *Polar Record* 55, no. 1 (2019): 1–12.

Liber, George. "Korenizatsiia: Restructuring Soviet Nationality Policy in the 1920s." *Ethnic and Racial Studies* 14, no. 1 (1991): 15–23.

Lucero, N. "Being Indian in the City: Generational Differences in Negotiation of Native Identity among Urban Based American Indians." In *Indigenous in the City: Contemporary Identities and Cultural Innovation*, edited by C. Andersen and E. Peters, 193–213. UBC Press, 2013.

Lyarskaya, Elena. "'U Nikh Zhe Vse Ne Kak U Liudei...': Nekotorye Stereotipnye Predstavleniia Pedagogov Yamalo-Nenetskogo Okruga o Tundrovikakh" ["They Are

Not Like Other People...": Some Stereotypical Ideas of Educators of the Yamal-Nenets Okrug about People Living in Tundra]. *Antropologicheskii Forum* 5 (2006): 242–58.

Marceau, Stéphane Guimont, Jennifer Buckell, Marie-Ève Drouin Gagné, Naomie Léonard, and Raphaëlle Ainsley Vincent. "Settler Urbanization and Indigenous Resistance: Uncovering an Ongoing Palimpsest in Montreal's Cabot Square." *Urban History Review* 51, no. 2 (2023): 310–33.

Martin, Terry. *The Affirmative Action Empire: Nations and Nationalism in the Soviet Union, 1923-1939*. Cornell University Press, 2001.

Martynov, Viktor. "Urbanizatsiia Rossiiskoi Arktiki: Severnaia Gorodskaia Identichnost' kak Faktor Razvitiia" [Urbanization of the Russian Arctic: Northern Urban Identity as a Development Factor]. In *Rossiiskaia Arktika v Poiskakh Integral'noi Identichnosti: Kollektivnaia Monografiia*, edited by O. B. Podvintsev, 95–112. Novyi Khronograf, 2016.

McElroy, J. "Who Owns This City? Why Debates around Vancouver Place Names Are Divisive." *CBC News*, October 8, 2017. cbc.ca/news/canada/british-columbia/sign-name-changing-vancouver-oct-2017-1.4342822.

Müller-Wille, Ludger. "Precursors of Urban Processes in Finnish Sápmi in the 1960s." *Acta Borealia* 27, no. 2 (2010): 141–50.

Nejad, Sarem, Ryan Walker, Brenda Macdougall, Yale Belanger, and David Newhouse. "'This Is an Indigenous City; Why Don't We See It?' Indigenous Urbanism and Spatial Production in Winnipeg." *The Canadian Geographer* 63, no. 3 (2019): 413–24.

Norris, M., and S. Clatworthy. "Urbanization and Migration Patterns of Aboriginal Populations in Canada: A Half-Century in Review (1951-2006)." *Aboriginal Policy Studies* 1, no. 1 (2011): 13–77.

Nursey-Bray, M., M. Parsons, and A. Gienger. "Urban Nullius? Urban Indigenous People and Climate Change." *Sustainability* 14, no. 17 (2022): 10830.

Nyseth, Torill, and Paul Pedersen. "Urban Sámi Identities in Scandinavia: Hybridities, Ambivalences and Cultural Innovation." *Acta Borealia* 31, no. 2 (2014): 131–51.

Paasi, Anssi. "Territorial Identities as Social Constructs." *Hagar: International Social Science Review* 1, no. 2 (2000): 91–113.

Patrick, Donna, and Gabriele Budach. "'Urban-Rural' Dynamics and Indigenous Urbanization: The Case of Inuit Language Use in Ottawa." *Journal of Language, Identity, and Education* 13, no. 4 (2014): 236–53.

Patrick, Donna, and Julie-Ann Tomiak. "Language, Culture and Community among Urban Inuit in Ottawa." *Études Inuit Studies* 32, no. 1 (2008): 55–72.

Pedersen, Birgit Kleist. "Young Greenlanders in the Urban Space of Nuuk." *Études Inuit Studies* 32, no. 1 (2008): 91-105.

Petrov, Andrey, and Tatiana Vlasova. "Migration and Socio-Economic Well-Being in the Russian North: Interrelations, Regional Differentiation, Recent Trends and Emerging Issues." In *Migration in the Circumpolar North: New Concepts and Patterns*, edited by Lee Huskey and Chris Southcott, 163–92. CCI Press, 2010.

Petrov, A. A., and S. L. Chernyshova. "Cultural Heritage of the Indigenous Arctic Peoples of the Sakha Republic (Yakutia)." *IOP Conference Series: Earth and Environmental Science* 302, no. 1 (2019): 012035.

Petrov, Andrey N., Marya S. Rozanova Smith, Andrey K. Krivorotov, Elena M. Klyuchnikova, Valeriy L. Mikheev, Alexander N. Pelyasov, and Nadezhda Yu Zamyatina. "The Russian Arctic by 2050: Developing Integrated Scenarios." Faculty Publications 5192 (2021). scholarworks.uni.edu/facpub/5192.

———. "Indigenous Health-Care Sovereignty Defines Resilience to the COVID-19 Pandemic." *The Lancet* 401, no. 10387 (2023): 1478–80.

Podvintsev, O. B., ed. *Rossiiskaia Arktika v poiskakh integral'noi identichnosti: Kollektivnaia monografiia* [The Russian Arctic in Search of Integral Identity: A Collective Monograph]. Novyi khronograf, 2016.

Povoroznyuk, Olga. "Social Dynamics and Sustainability of BAM Communities: Migration, Competition for Resources, and Intergroup Relations." In *New Mobilities and Social Changes in Russia's Arctic Regions*, edited by Marlene Laruelle, 45–65. Routledge, 2016.

Pristupa, Alexey O., Machiel Lamers, Maria Tysiachniouk, and Bas Amelung. "Reindeer Herders without Reindeer: The Challenges of Joint Knowledge Production on Kolguev Island in the Russian Arctic." *Society & Natural Resources* 32, no. 3 (2019): 338–56.

Reisser, Colin. "Russia's Arctic Cities." In *Sustaining Russia's Arctic Cities: Resource Politics, Migration, and Climate Change*, edited by Robert W. Orttung, 15–34. Berghahn Books, 2017.

Rozanova-Smith, Marya. "Stay or Leave? Arctic Youth Prospects and Sustainable Futures of the Russian Arctic Communities." *Sustainability* 13, no. 21 (2021): 12058.

Rozanova, Marya. "Indigenous Urbanization in Russia's Arctic: The Case of Nenets Autonomous Region." *Sibirica* 18, no. 3 (2019): 54–91.

Rozanova-Smith, Marya, Stanislav Ksenofontov, and Andrey N. Petrov. "Indigenous Urbanization and Indigenous Urban Experiences in the Russian Arctic: The Cases of Yakutsk and Naryan-Mar." In *Urban Indigeneities*, edited by Dana Brablec and Andrew Canessa, 145–68. University of Arizona Press, 2023.

Rozanova, Marya S., and Valeriy L. Mikheev. "Rethinking Women's Empowerment: Insights from the Russian Arctic." *Social Sciences* 9, no. 2 (2020): 14.

Russian Federal State Statistics Service. "Russian Census 2002, 2010, 2020." rosstat.gov.ru/perepisi_naseleniya.

Rygaard, Jette. "The City Life of Youths in Greenland." *Études Inuit Studies* 32, no. 1 (2008): 33–54.

Schorkowitz, D. "Was Russia a Colonial Empire?" In *Shifting Forms of Continental Colonialism*, edited by D. Schorkowitz, J. R. Chávez, and I. W. Schröder, 117–47. Palgrave Macmillan, 2019.

Senese, Laura C., and Kathi Wilson. "Aboriginal Urbanization and Rights in Canada: Examining Implications for Health." *Social Science & Medicine* 91 (2013): 219–28.

Slavin, Samuil. *The Soviet North: Present Development and Prospects*. Translated by Don Danemanis. Progress Publishers, 1972.

Smith, Keri E. Iyall, and Patricia Leavy. *Hybrid Identities: Theoretical and Empirical Examinations*. Brill, 2008.

Sokolova, Flera, and Wooik Choi. "The Russian Arctic in the Post-Soviet Period: Dynamics of Migration Processes." *Region* 8, no. 2 (2019): 197–226.

Solovyeva, V., and V. Kuklina. "Resilience in a Changing World: Indigenous Sharing Networks in the Republic of Sakha (Yakutia)." *Polar Record* 56 (2020): e39.

Tomiak, Julie. "Contesting the Settler City: Indigenous Self-Determination, New Urban Reserves, and the Neoliberalization of Colonialism." *Antipode* 49, no. 4 (2017): 928–45.

Toulouze, Eva. "The Forest Nenets as a Double Language Minority." *Pro Ethnologia* 15 (2003): 95–108.

Vorobyova, O. I. "Sozdatel' Bukvarya i Nenetskoy Pis'mennosti Pervyy Nenetskiy Lingvist-Perevodchik Anton Petrovich Pyrerka" [The Creator of Orthography and Nenets Writing First Nenets Linguist-Translator Anton Petrovich Pyrerka]. *Vestnik Severnogo (Arkticheskogo) Federal'nogo Universiteta* 2 (2014): 56–60.

Vuolab, Siv Eli. "Negotiating an Urban Indigenous Identity: Expectations, Prejudices and Claims Faced by Urban Sámi in Two Contemporary Norwegian Cities." MPhil thesis, UiT Norges Arktiske Universitet, 2016.

Zamyatina, Nadezhda, Luis Suter, Dmitry Streletskiy, and Nikolay Shiklomanov. "Shrinking Cities, Growing Cities: A Comparative Analysis of Vorkuta and Salekhard." In *Urban Sustainability in the Arctic: Measuring Progress in Circumpolar Cities*, edited by Robert W. Orttung, 47–76. Berghahn Books, 2020.

(302)
 Nan Niwhazheh ti'goonch'uu
 (The land is our home)
 Arlyn Charlie

No notes.

(320)
 Qaammat Pavilion
 Konstantin Ikonomidis

Arke, Pia. *Etnoæstetik*. ARK, 1995.

(330)
 Time Line
 Jessica MacMillan

No notes.

(342)
 Genius Loci Norr
 Anastasia Savinova

No notes.

(352)
 Nakataq
 Maureen Gruben
 Kyra Kordoski

No notes.

(356)
 Envisioning Urban Futures
 in the Arctic Borderlands
 of Norway and Russia
 Morgan Ip

Anderson, Benedict. *Imagined Communities: Reflections on the Origin and Spread of Nationalism*. Verso Books, 1991.

Avermaete, Tom. "The Borders Within: Reflections upon Architecture's Engagement with Urban Limens." In *Border Conditions*, edited by Marc Schoonderbeek, 27–42. Architectura & Natura Press, 2009.

Awan, Nishat, Tatjana Schneider, and Jeremy Till. *Spatial Agency: Other Ways of Doing Architecture*. Routledge, 2011.

Dear, Michael. *Why Walls Won't Work: Repairing the US-Mexico Divide*. Oxford University Press, 2013.

Hemmersam, Peter. *Making the Arctic City: The History and Future of Urbanism in the Circumpolar North*. Bloomsbury Visual Arts, 2021.

Husbanken. "Gjenreist og Særpreget: En Planleggings- og Utbedringsveileder for Hus og Steder i Nord-Troms og Finnmark" [Rebuilt and Distinctive: A Planning and Improvement Guide for Houses and Places in North Troms and Finnmark]. November 2007.

Ip, Morgan. "Cultural Mapping and Digital Public Engagement in the Future North." *Nordisk Arkitekturforskning* 30, no. 3 (2018): 81–106.

———. "Urban Futures in the North: A Collective Imagination of an Arctic Borderland." PhD diss., Oslo School of Architecture and Design, 2022. ⇒ aho.brage.unit.no/aho-xmlui/handle/11250/3036740.

Isaachsen Willoch, Gunnar. *Vardøhus festning 650 år* [Vardøhus Fortress 650 Years]. Landstrykkeriet AS, 1960.

Jenkins, Paul. "Concepts of Social Participation in Architecture." In *Architecture, Participation and Society*, edited by Paul Jenkins and Leslie Forsyth, 9–22. Routledge, 2010.

Lund, Diderich H. "The Revival of Northern Norway." *The Geographical Journal* 109, nos. 4/6 (1947): 185–97.

Lynch, Kevin. *The Image of the City*. MIT Press, 1960.

Nasjonale turistveger. "Steilneset." ⇒ nasjonaleturistveger.no/no/turistvegene/varanger/steilneset.

Norsk Folkemuseum. "Arkitektkonkurranser og typetegninger" [Architectural Competitions and Type Drawings]. ⇒ norskfolkemuseum.no/arkitektkonkurranser-og-typetegninger.

Ødemark, John. "Cultural Difference and Development in the Mirror of Witchcraft: The Cultural Policy of Display at Steilneset Memorial." *Nordisk Kulturpolitisk Tidsskrift* 17, no. 2 (2014): 187–209.

Pavlides, Eleftherios, and Galen Cranz. "Ethnographic Methods in Support of Architectural Practice." *School of Architecture, Art, and Historic Preservation Faculty Publications*, January 1, 2011.

Turner, Victor W. *The Forest of Symbols: Aspects of Ndembu Ritual*. Cornell University Press, 1967.

Ventura, Jonathan, and Jo-Anne Bichard. "Design Anthropology or Anthropological Design? Towards 'Social Design.'" *International Journal of Design Creativity and Innovation* 5, nos. 3-4 (2016): 222–34.

Willumsen, Liv Helene. *The Witchcraft Trials in Finnmark, Northern Norway*. Skald, 2010.

(365)
Notes on an Arctic Landscape Architectural Practice
Mari A. Aston Bergset

Government of Norway. "Nature Diversity Act." Acts and Regulations. June 19, 2009. ⇒ regjeringen.no/en/dokumenter/nature-diversity-act/id570549.

Vereykina, Elizaveta. "Tourism Is Booming in Northern Norway." *The Barents Observer*, January 4, 2024. ⇒ thebarentsobserver.com/en/2024/01/tourism-booming-northern-norway-its-amazing-we-have-never-seen-so-many-guests-tour-operators.

Verte Landskap–Arkitektur & Lo:Le Landskap. *Bruk av Nordnorsk Vegetasjon i et næringsperspektiv* [Use of North Norwegian Vegetation in a Business Perspective]. Report. Troms og Finnmark Fylkeskommune, 2009.

(372)
Designing with Coastal Change in the High Arctic: Pedagogic Perspectives
Eimear Tynan
Bert De Jonghe

Hanssen-Bauer, I., E. Førland, H. Hisdal, S. Mayer, A. Sandø, and S. Sorteberg, eds. *Climate in Svalbard 2100: A Knowledge Base for Climate Adaptation*. Report no. 1/2019. Norwegian Centre for Climate Services, 2019. ⇒ miljodirektoratet.no/globalassets/publikasjoner/m1242/m1242.pdf.

Heatherington, Catherine. "Revealing Change." In *Revealing Change in Cultural Landscapes: Material, Spatial and Ecological Considerations*, edited by Catherine Heatherington, 1–18. Routledge, 2021.

Mathur, Anuradha. "Terrains of Wetness." In *Delta Dialogues*, edited by Christophe Girot, 45–62. gta Verlag, ETH Zurich, 2017.

Nordli, Øyvind, Przemysław Wyszyński, Herdis M. Gjelten, Ketil Isaksen, Ewa Łupikasza, Tadeusz Niedźwiedź, and Rajmund Przybylak. "Revisiting the Extended Svalbard Airport Monthly Temperature Series, and the Compiled Corresponding Daily Series 1898-2018." *Polar Research* 39 (2020): 3614.

Peters, Kimberley, Philip Steinberg, and Elaine Stratford, eds. *Territory beyond Terra*. Rowman & Littlefield, 2018.

Phelan, Joseph. "Svalbard: The Arctic Islands Where We Can See the Future of Global Heating." *The Guardian*, May 13, 2023. ⇒ theguardian.com/environment/2023/may/13/svalbard-the-arctic-islands-where-we-can-see-the-future-of-global-heating.

Ryan, V. "How Iterative Designing Works." Technology Student. ⇒ technologystudent.com/despro_flsh/iterative1.html.

(384)
Entangled Arctic: Home/Land in the House/Territory
Lola Sheppard
Mason White

Appadurai, Arjun. "Introduction: Commodities and the Politics of Value." In *The Social Life of Things: Commodities in Cultural Context*, edited by Arjun Appadurai, 3–63. Cambridge University Press, 1986.

Bäckström, Elin. "Transforming Space and Society in Kiruna." *Uppsala University News*, March 24, 2022. ⇒ uu.se/en/news/archive/2022-03-24-transforming-space-and-society-in-kiruna.

Brenner, Neil, ed. *Implosions/Explosions: Towards a Study of Planetary Urbanization*. Jovis, 2014.

CBC News. "Indigenous Groups Paying the Price for Russia's Massive Arctic Fuel Spill." July 13, 2020. ⇒ cbc.ca/news/canada/north/norilsk-nickel-russian-fuel-spill-consequences-1.5645408.

Dingman, Erica M. "Greenlandic Independence: The Dilemma of Natural Resource Extraction." *Arctic Yearbook 2014* (2014): 228–43.

Duhaime, Gérard, and Andrée Caron. "The Economy of the Circumpolar Arctic." In *The Economy of the North: ECONOR 2020*, edited by Solveig Glomsrød, Gérard Duhaime, and Iulie Aslaksen, 28–77. Arctic Council Secretariat, 2021.

Elden, Stuart. *The Birth of Territory*. University of Chicago Press, 2013.

Garland, Anne, Anamaria Bukvic, and Anuszka Maton-Mosurska. "Capturing Complexity: Environmental Change and Relocation in the North Slope Borough, Alaska." *Climate Risk Management* 38 (2022): 100452.

Government of Canada. "Nunavut Lands and Resources Devolution Agreement." January 18, 2024. ⇒ rcaanc-cirnac.gc.ca/eng/1702495657169/1702495761711.

Harris, Dianne. *Little White Houses*. University of Minnesota Press, 2012.

Hayden, Dolores. *The Grand Domestic Revolution*. MIT Press, 1982.

Jóhannesson, Hjalti. "Lessons from Alcoa in East Iceland." *Nordregio* 2 (2007). ⇒ archive.nordregio.se/en/Metameny/About-Nordregio/Journal-of-Nordregio/Journal-of-Nordregio-no-2-2011/Lessons-from-Alcoa-in-East-Iceland.

Latour, Bruno. "On Actor-Network Theory: A Few Clarifications Plus More than a Few Complications." *Soziale Welt* 47 (1996): 369–81.

456

Lowenhaupt Tsing, Anna. "On Nonscalability: The Living World Is Not Amenable to Precision-Nested Scales." *Common Knowledge* 18, no. 3 (2012): 505–24.

Mikhayluk, Vitaly. "The Condemned: Living in a Khrushchyovka." In *Russia beyond the Headlines*, edited by P. Kortin, M. Korshunoc, and L. Bellinello. 2017. rbth.com/longreads/khrushchyovki.

Quinn, Eilís. "The Arctic Railway." *Eye on the Arctic*, September 22, 2019. newsinteractives.cbc.ca/longform/the-arctic-railway.

Rose, Miriam. "A Nice Place to Work In? Experiences of Icelandic Smelter Employees." *Saving Iceland*, February 20, 2017. savingiceland.org/2017/02/a-nice-place-to-work-in-experiences-of-icelandic-aluminium-smelter-employees.

Swyngedouw, Erik. "Globalisation or 'Glocalisation'? Networks, Territories and Rescaling." *Cambridge Review of International Affairs* 17, no. 1 (2004): 25–48.

———. "Place, Nature and the Question of Scale: Interrogating the Production of Nature." *Diskussionspapier* 5 (2010): 1–19.

Tester, Frank. "Iglutaasaavut (Our New Homes): Neither 'New' nor 'Ours': Housing Challenges of the Nunavut Territorial Government." *Journal of Canadian Studies* 43, no. 2 (2009): 137–58.

———. "IGLUTAQ (in my room): The Implications of Homelessness for Inuit: A Case Study of Housing and Homelessness in Kinngait, Nunavut Territory." Report prepared for the Harvest Society, Kinngait, Nunavut Territory, April 2006.

Thompson, John. "Greenland Capital Boasts Deep-Water Port, Hydro-Electric Dam and Much More." *Nunatsiaq News*, July 19, 2007. nunatsiaq.com/stories/article/Greenland_capital_boasts_deep-water_port_hydro-electric_dam_and_much_more.

(397)

A Palliative Design for a High Arctic Landscape
Caitlin Jakusz Paridy

Brode-Roger, Dina. "Mining, Materiality and Memory: Lingering Legacies in Longyearbyen." *Journal of Contemporary Architecture* 9, no. 1 (2022): 213–36.

Cheung, Wayne. "Surface and Bed Topography Mapping of Foxfonna & Rieperbreen Glacier, Svalbard, 1936–2020." Master's thesis, Saint Petersburg State University and Hamburg University, 2020.

DeSilvey, Caitlin. *Curated Decay: Heritage Beyond Saving*. University of Minnesota Press, 2017.

———. "Palliative Curation and Future Persistence: Life after Death." In *Cultural Heritages*, edited by Cornelius Holtorf and Anders Hogberg, 122–38. Routledge, 2020.

Haseen-Bauer, Ingrid, E. J. Førland, H. Hisdal, S. Mayer, A. B. Sandø, and A. Sorteberg. *Climate in Svalbard 2100*. Norwegian Environmental Agency, 2019. miljodirektoratet.no/globalassets/publikasjoner/M1242/M1242.pdf.

Nagell Ylvisaker, Line. "Gruve 7 har kull til sommeren 2025 – så er det tomt" [Mine 7 Has Coal until Summer 2025 – Then It's Empty]. *Svalbardposten*, September 27, 2023. svalbardposten.no/gruve-7-har-kull-til-sommeren-2025-sa-er-det-tomt/516544.

(404)

When Is Now? The Case for Temporal Ambiguity in Critiques of Sámi Architecture
Sofia Singler

Äikäs, Tiina, and Anna-Kaisa Salmi. "North/South Encounters at Sámi Sacred Sites in Northern Finland." *Historical Archaeology* 49, no. 3 (2015): 90–109.

Anderson, Stanford. "Memory without Monuments: Vernacular Architecture." *Traditional Dwellings and Settlements Review* 11, no. 1 (1999): 13–22.

Berg-Nordlie, Mikkel. "The Governance of Urban Indigenous Spaces: Norwegian Sámi Examples." *Acta Borealia* 35, no. 1 (2018): 49–72.

Bjørklund, Ivar. "Domestication, Reindeer Husbandry and the Development of Sámi Pastoralism." *Acta Borealia* 30, no. 2 (2013): 174–89.

———. "The Mobile Sámi Dwelling: From Pastoral Necessity to Ethno-political Master Paradigm." In *About the Hearth: Perspectives on the Home, Hearth, and Household in the Circumpolar North*, edited by David Anderson, Rob Wishart, and Virginie Vaté, 75–92. Berghahn Books, 2013.

Boym, Svetlana. *The Off-Modern*. Bloomsbury Academic, 2017.

Brablec, Dana, and Andrew Canessa, eds. *Urban Indigeneities: Being Indigenous in the Twenty-First Century*. University of Arizona Press, 2023.

Bushart, Magdalena. "Am Anfang ein Missverständnis: Feiningers Kathedrale und das Bauhaus-Manifest." In *Modell Bauhaus*, edited by Bauhaus-Archiv, 25–31. Museum für Gestaltung, Stiftung Bauhaus Dessau und Klassik Stiftung Weimar, 2009.

Carpo, Mario. "Architecture: Theory, Interdisciplinarity, and Methodological Eclecticism." *Journal of the Society of Architectural Historians* 64, no. 4 (2005): 425–27.

Curtis, William J. R. *Modern Architecture since 1900*. Phaidon, 1996.

Frampton, Kenneth. *The Other Modern Movement: Architecture, 1920–1970*. Yale University Press, 2021.

Hakovirta, Jenni. "Building a Case for Indigenous Architecture with Mixed-use Anarâškielâ Language Nest and Home for Elderly." Master's thesis, University of Oulu, 2021.

Haugdal, Elin. "'It's Meant to Decay': Contemporary Sámi Architecture and the Rhetoric of Material." In *The Handbook of Contemporary Indigenous Architecture*, edited by Elizabeth Grant, Kelly Greenop,

Albert L. Refiti, and Daniel J. Glenn, 201–24. Springer, 2018.

Heynen, Hilde. *Architecture and Modernity: A Critique*. MIT Press, 1999.

Hinkson, Lauren, ed. *Josef Albers in Mexico*. Guggenheim Museum Publications, 2017.

Lehtiranta, Reetta. "Kotiin? Paikallisten suhde arkkitehtuuriin Inarissa" [Home? Local Relationship to Architecture in Inari]. Master's thesis, University of Oulu, 2022.

Louekari, Lauri. "Sámi Cultural Centre Sajos, Inari." *Arkkitehti*, no. 5 (2012): 28–37.

Mallie, Tara, and Michael J. Ostwald. "Aboriginal Architecture: Merging Concepts from Architecture and Aboriginal Studies." In *Cumulus 38° South: Proceedings of the Cumulus Conference*, edited by Liam Fennessy, Russell Kerr, Gavin Melles, Christine Thong, and Emily Wright, 483–96. Swinburne University of Technology and RMIT University, 2009.

Matunga, Hirini. "A Discourse on the Nature of Indigenous Architecture." In *The Handbook of Contemporary Indigenous Architecture*, edited by Elizabeth Grant, Kelly Greenop, Albert L. Refiti, and Daniel J. Glenn, 303–30. Springer, 2018.

Nango, Joar. "In Practice: Joar Nango on Building a Library of Sámi Architecture." *Architectural Review*, 2022.

Nango, Joar, and Silje Figenschou Thoresen, eds. *The Indigenuity Project*. Motto Books, 2013.

Pelkonen, Eeva-Liisa. *Untimely Moderns: How Twentieth-Century Architecture Reimagined the Past*. Yale University Press, 2023.

Raynsford, Anthony. "Provoking the 'Thingness' of History: The Anti-Teleological Hermeneutics of Steen Eiler Rasmussen." In *104th ACSA Annual Meeting Proceedings: Shaping New Knowledges*, edited by Robert Corser and Sharon Haar, 543–48. ACSA Press, 2016.

Singler, Sofia. "Contradictory Contemporaneity? Sámi Building in Nordic Architectural Discourse." In *Joar Nango*, edited by Axel Wieder. Sternberg Press, forthcoming.

St John Wilson, Colin. "The Other Tradition." *AA Files*, no. 24 (1992): 3–6.

Upton, Dell. "Starting from Baalbek: Noah, Solomon, Saladin, and the Fluidity of Architectural History." *Journal of the Society of Architectural Historians* 68, no. 4 (2009): 457–81.

van Doesburg, Theo, et al. "Manifest I of 'The Style', 1918." *De Stijl* 2, no. 1 (1918): 2–5.

Vellinga, Marcel. "The Inventiveness of Tradition: Vernacular Architecture and the Future." *Perspectives in Vernacular Architecture* 13, no. 2 (2006/2007): 115–28.

Williams Goldhagen, Sarah. "Something to Talk About: Modernism, Discourse, Style." *Journal of the Society of Architectural Historians* 64, no. 2 (2005): 144–67.

(417)

Ultima Thule Museum of Natural History: Containing the Full Reconstructions of the Landscapes of Svalbard, of Instruments of Prophecy, and of Accidental Monuments with an Account of Its Architectural Oddities: With a Repository Containing Some Important Historical Artifacts Salvaged prior to the Disappearance of the Arctic
Brandon Bergem
Jeffrey Garcia

Main Text

DenHoed, Andrea. "The Making of the American Museum of Natural History's Wildlife Dioramas." *The New Yorker*, February 15, 2016. ➡ newyorker.com/culture/photo-booth/the-making-of-the-american-museum-of-natural-historys-wildlife-dioramas.

Harvard Canvas. "Hockney-Falco Thesis." ➡ canvas.harvard.edu/files/4653874/download?download_frd=1.

Manaugh, Geoff. *The BLDG BLOG Book*. Chronicle Books, 2009.

Marjanović, Igor, and Jan Howard. *Drawing Ambience: Alvin Boyarsky and the Architectural Association*. Mildred Lane Kemper Art Museum and Museum of Art, Rhode Island School of Design, 2014.

Morrill, Ruth. "A Dual-Grid System for Diorama Layout." *Curator: The Museum Journal* 39, no. 4 (1996): 248–57.

Niesner, Lisi, and Gloria Dickie. "The Wider Image: Climate Change Thaws World's Northernmost Research Station." *Reuters*, April 19, 2023. ➡ reuters.com/investigates/special-report/climate-change-svalbard-ice.

Rogers, Elizabeth Barlow. "Representing Nature: The Dioramas of the American Museum of Natural History." *SiteLINES: A Journal of Place* 8, no. 2 (2013): 3–7.

Rossby, H. Thomas, and Peter Miller. "Ocean Eddies in the 1539 Carta Marina by Olaus Magnus." *Oceanography* 16, no. 4 (2003): 77–88.

Salazar, F. "Claiming Ultima Thule." *Hakai Magazine*, September 8, 2020. ➡ hakaimagazine.com/features/claiming-ultima-thule.

SIOS. "Svalbard Integrated Arctic Earth Observing System: The Current State." February 20, 2024. ➡ sios-svalbard.org/system/files/common/Documents/SIOS_CurrentState.pdf.

Spitsbergen Svalbard. "The Spitsbergen Treaty." ➡ spitsbergen-svalbard.com/spitsbergen-information/history/the-spitsbergentreaty.html.

Steve, Lacking. "Durer, Drawing, and Digital Thinking." In *Leonardo's Legacy: International Conference on Computer Graphics and Interactive Techniques*, 145–52. Savannah, 2023.

Szalczer, Eszter. "Nature's Dream Play: Modes of Vision and August Strindberg's Re-Definition of the Theatre." *Theatre Journal* 53, no. 1 (2001): 33–52.

Wallace-Wells, David. *The Uninhabitable Earth: Life after Warming*. Tim Duggan Books, 2019.

458   Wecker, Menachem. "The History and Future of the Once-Revolutionary Taxidermy Diorama." *Smithsonian Magazine*, October 11, 2016. ➡ smithsonianmag.com/science-nature/ode-once-revolutionary-taxidermy-display-180960707.

Whitaker, Ian. "The Problem of Pytheas' Thule." *Classical Journal* 77, no. 2 (1981): 148–64.

Diorama Narratives

Andreassen, Elin, Hein B. Bjerck, and Bjørnar Olsen. *Persistent Memories: Pyramiden – A Soviet Mining Town in the High Arctic*. Tapir Academic Press, 2010.

Breili, K., M. J. R. Simpson, E. Klokkervold, and O. Roaldsdotter Ravndal. "High-Accuracy Coastal Flood Mapping for Norway Using Lidar Data." *Natural Hazards and Earth System Sciences* 20, no. 2 (2020): 673–94.

Brunvand, Jan. "Norway's Askeladden, the Unpromising Hero, and Junior-Right." *Journal of American Folklore* 72, no. 283 (1959): 14–23.

Norwegian Government Security and Service Organization. "Svalbard Environmental Protection Act." April 12, 2012. ➡ regjeringen.no/en/dokumenter/svalbard-environmental-protection-act/id173945.

Rawlence, Ben. "'The Treeline Is out of Control': How the Climate Crisis Is Turning the Arctic Green." *The Guardian*, January 20, 2022. ➡ theguardian.com/news/2022/jan/20/norway-arctic-circle-trees-sami-reindeer-global-heating.

Schlaghamerský, Jiří, Martina Bílkoba, Andrea Špalek Tóthová, and Miloslav Devetter. "Enchytraeids in Imported Soil and Organic Deposits in Pyramiden, an Abandoned Mining Town on Spitsbergen in the High Arctic." *Elsevier Science BV* 192 (2023): 108–27.

Wallace-Wells, David. *The Uninhabitable Earth: Life after Warming*. Tim Duggan Books, 2019.

Image Credits

Cover

Graphic elaboration of photographic image by Marc Ihle of Ramfjordmoen, Norway (2021) by Studio Folder (2024).

(18)

Index of Places

Index of Places [map]. Designed by Studio Folder (Milan, 2024) for *Arctic Practices: Design for a Changing World* (2025). Data: Natural Earth / GLIMS Consortium, 2005. *GLIMS Glacier Database*, Version 1. Boulder, Colorado, USA: NASA / National Snow and Ice Data Center, *Sea Ice Index*, Version 3.0. Boulder, Colorado, USA: National Snow and Ice Data Center / ESA. *Land Cover CCI Product, Version 2*. Arctic Biodiversity Data Service (ABDS).

(20)

Making and Remaking the Capital of Greenland
Peter Hemmersam

1. From Alfred J. Råvad's "Grønlands Hovedstad: III. Stedet (The Capital of Greenland: III: The Place)," *Architekten* 16(23), (1914) 239.
2. From Alfred J. Råvad, "Architecten som Sociolog. Store Bølger og Små (The Architect as Sociologist. Large Waves and Small)," *Architekten* 14(6), (1911) 56.
3. Photograph by Connie Eriksen.
4. Photograph by *Grønlandsposten*.
5. Photograph by Vincent van Zeijst (Wikimedia Commons, CC BY-SA 3.0).

(31)

Fabulous Urbanism: Reading Soviet Arctic Cities through Children's Literature
Olga Petri

1. Drawn by A. Borodin in *The Round House* by Semen Danilov (1970), cover.
2. Drawn by A. Borodin in *The Round House* by Semen Danilov (1970), 12.
3. Drawn by A. Borodin in *The Round House* by Semen Danilov (1970), 10.
4. Drawn by A. Borodin in *The Round House* by Semen Danilov (1970), 2.
5. Drawn by A. Borodin in *The Round House* by Semen Danilov (1970), 3.
6. Courtesy of TsGANTD Sankt-Peterburga (f. 17, op. 2-2, d. 467, l. 35).
7. Courtesy of TsGANTD Sankt-Peterburga (f. 17, op. 2-2, d. 467, l. 96).

(41)

"If You Do Not Say Anything, You Will Not Be Heard": The Mackenzie Research Institute and Anticolonial Environmental Activism in Inuvik
Caitlin Blanchfield

1. *Mackenzie Delta* [map]. Designed by Studio Folder (Milan, 2024) for *Arctic Practices: Design for a Changing World* (2025). Data: Natural Earth / OpenStreetMap / *Conservation of Arctic Flora and Fauna (CAFF) working group of the Arctic Council*. Arctic Biodiversity Data Service (ABDS) / *Global Self-consistent, Hierarchical, High-resolution Geography Database (GSHHG)*, Version 2.3.7. Paul Wessel, SOEST, University of Hawai'i, Honolulu, HI and Walter H. F. Smith, NOAA Geosciences Lab, National Ocean Service, Silver Spring, MD / *2020 Land Cover of North America at 30 m*. Canada Centre for Remote Sensing (CCRS) / Canada Centre for Mapping and Earth Observation (CCMEO), Natural Resources Canada (NRCan).
2. Photographer unknown (1968). Courtesy Aurora College.
3. Photographer unknown. Courtesy of the Northwest Territory Archives (Bern Will Brown fonds, N-2001-002: 04759).
4. From the personal collection of Dick Hill.

(60)

Urbanisms of Refusal: Indigeneity and Land in Alaska
Lasse Rau

1. Courtesy of the Department of the Interior, Bureau of Land Management, March 1974.
2. Color photograph by Ruth Ann Marie Schmidt, June 17, 1972.

(68)

The Trail as Home: Claudio Aporta in Conversation With Bert De Jonghe and Elise Misao Hunchuck

All photographs are by the author, Claudio Aporta.

(81)

Drifting as Agency: Between Ice, Space, and Territory
Aniella Sophie Goldinger

All visuals are by the author, Aniella Goldinger.

(100)

My Notes on Architecture in Inuit Nunangat
Nicole Luke

All images are by the author, Nicole Luke.

(106)

A Most Curious Listener: Todd Saunders in Conversation with Bert De Jonghe and Elise Misao Hunchuck

1–4. Courtesy of Todd Saunders.
5. Photograph by Alex Fradkin (2013), courtesy of Todd Saunders.
6. Photograph by Nils Vik (2006), courtesy of Todd Saunders.

(116)

Kangiata Illorsua – Ilulissat Icefjord Centre
Dorte Mandrup

Photographs are by Adam Mørk. Drawings are by Dorte Mandrup.

(126)

The Case of Maniitsoq–Alcoa: The Re-emergence of a Conscious Subjectivity
Magdalena Haggärde
Gisle Løkken

1–2. All photographs are by and courtesy of the authors, Magdalena Haggärde and Gisle Løkken, 70°N arkitektur.
3. Whale watching platform visual by and courtesy of the authors,

Magdalena Haggärde and Gisle Løkken, 70°N arkitektur.
4–9. All film stills are from Sidse Torstholm Larsen and Sturla Pilskog's documentary film *Winter's Yearning* (Blåst Film AS, 2019).

(141)
Solar Sensing
Susan Schuppli

1–3. Courtesy of the author, Susan Schuppli.
4. Film still from Zacharias Kunuk and Ian Mauro's *Inuit Knowledge and Climate Change* (Isuma TV, 2010).

(148)
Keepers of Ocean:
At Home We Belong
Inuuteq Storch

All photographs by the author, Inuuteq Storch.

(160)
Place Bonding and Migration
Nadezhda Filimonova

No images.

(176)
Color and Comfort:
A Tribute to the Children
of Tasiilaq
Jakob Exner
Helena Lennert

All photographs are by Nukaaraq Isbosethsen (2016).

(179)
The Place on the Island by the Sea: Maaretta Jaukkuri and A K Dolven in Conversation with Elise Misao Hunchuck

1 and 2. Photographs by and courtesy of Elise Misao Hunchuck (2019 and 2020, respectively).

(190)
Travel Notes from Siberia
Sophy Roberts
Michael Turek

All photographs are by Michael Turek.

(210)
Everything Is the Same
Svetlana Romanova

All film stills provided by the author, Svetlana Romanova.

(224)
The Road of Life
Nicholas Gulick
Elena Krapivina

All photographs are by the author, Nicholas Gulick.

(248)
Like a Phoenix: A New Chapter
Bertine Tønseth

1. *Closed Chapter* (2017) courtesy of Pøbel.
2–8. Photographs by and courtesy of Bertine Tønseth (2017).

(260)
Landscape Architecture
Education above the Arctic Circle
Thomas Juel Clemmensen

1 and 4. Photographs by and courtesy of Thomas Juel Clemmensen (2019 and 2023, respectively).
2 and 3. Photographs by and courtesy of Marc Ihle (2021).

(268)
Snødepot
Akie Kono

All photographs are by the author, Akie Kono (Lo:Le Landskap AS).

(274)
"We Need Our Own Places":
Paths for Indigenization in
the Russian Arctic City of
Naryan-Mar
Marya Rozanova-Smith
Andrey N. Petrov

1. Diagram by the authors, drawn by Studio Folder (2024).
2. *Nenets Autonomous Region* [map]. Designed by Studio Folder (Milan, 2024) for *Arctic Practices: Design for a Changing World* (2025). Data: Natural Earth / OpenStreetMap /

Global Self-consistent, Hierarchical, High-resolution Geography Database (GSHHG), Version 2.3.7. Paul Wessel, SOEST, University of Hawai'i, Honolulu, HI, and Walter H. F. Smith, NOAA Geosciences Lab, National Ocean Service, Silver Spring, MD / ESA. *Land Cover CCI Product*, Version 2 (2017).
3. Photograph by and courtesy of Professor Andrey Gretsov (2009).
4. Photograph by Kirill Skorobogatko (2014). Shutterstock image license.

(302)
Nan Niwhazheh ti'goonch'uu
(The land is our home)
Arlyn Charlie

All photographs are by and courtesy of the author, Arlyn Charlie.

(320)
Qaammat Pavilion
Konstantin Ikonomidis

1. Photograph by Konstantin Ikonomidis (2023).
2–3. Photographs by Jens Fog Jensen (2021), courtesy of Konstantin Ikonomidis.
4–5. Photographs by Konstantin Ikonomidis (2021).
6. Photograph by Julien Lanoo (2021), courtesy of Konstantin Ikonomidis.

(330)
Time Line
Jessica MacMillan

1–6, 11. Photographs by Preben Irgens.
7. Still from video Interview with Artica resident Jessica MacMillan by Tom Warner.
8-9. Photographs by Jessica MacMillan.
9. Photograph by Kanerva Karpo.
10. Jessica MacMillan.
All courtesy of the author, Jessica MacMillan.

(342)
Genius Loci Norr
Anastasia Savinova

All visuals are by the author, Anastasia Savinova.

463

(352)

Nakataq
Maureen Gruben
Kyra Kordoski

Installation documentation by
Argenis Apolinario (2022), courtesy
of the artist, Maureen Gruben.

(356)

Envisioning Urban Futures
in the Arctic Borderlands
of Norway and Russia
Morgan Ip

1. *Norwegian–Russian Borderlands*
[map]. Designed by Studio Folder
(Milan, 2024) for *Arctic Practices:
Design for a Changing World*
(2025). Data: Natural Earth /
OpenStreetMap / *Conservation
of Arctic Flora and Fauna (CAFF)
working group of the Arctic Council*.
Arctic Biodiversity Data Service
(ABDS) / *Global Self-consistent,
Hierarchical, High-resolution
Geography Database (GSHHG)*,
Version 2.3.7. Paul Wessel, SOEST,
University of Hawai'i, Honolulu, HI, and
Walter H. F. Smith, NOAA Geosciences
Lab, National Ocean Service, Silver
Spring, MD / *EU-Hydro River
Network Database 2006-2012,
Europe*, Version 1.3, Nov. 2020 /
*GHS-POP R2023A - GHS population
grid multitemporal (1975-2030)*.
European Commission, Joint
Research Centre (JRC) / Flanders
Marine Institute (2023). Maritime
Boundaries Geodatabase, version 12.
2–6. Photographs by and courtesy
of the author, Morgan Ip (2016).
7. Photographs by and courtesy of
the author, Morgan Ip (2015).

(365)

Notes on an Arctic Landscape
Architectural Practice
Mari A. Aston Bergset

1. Photograph courtesy of Aspen
Bergersen. Alamy Photo Stock image
license, November 2024.
2. Image courtesy of HOLAR / Ola
Roald Arkitekter AS.
3. Photograph by and courtesy
of Michály Stefanovicz.

(372)

Designing with Coastal Change
in the High Arctic: Pedagogic
Perspectives
Eimear Tynan
Bert De Jonghe

1. Photograph by Arne Torbjørn
Pedersen (1950-60). Courtesy of
The Svalbard Museum.
2. Aerial photograph by unknown
photographer (1936). Courtesy
of the Norsk Polarinstitutt /
Norwegian Polar Institute.
3. Aerial photograph by Marthe
Ottem (2021). Courtesy of the
University Centre of Svalbard (UNIS)
and the Norwegian University of
Science and Technology (NTNU).
4. Photograph by and courtesy of
Eimear Tynan (2023).
5. Drawing by and courtesy of
Julie Hjelt Wold (2023).
6. Drawing by and courtesy of
Sofie Randall King (2023).
7. Drawing by and courtesy of
Tomine H. Furelid (2023).

(384)

Entangled Arctic: Home / Land
in the House / Territory
Lola Sheppard
Mason White

1. *Nuuk, House, Territory* by CCDT
(2020—21).
2. Resolute, House, Territory by
CCDT (2020—21).
3. Inari by CCDT (2020—21),
photography by Giorgio Lazzaro and
courtesy of Lateral Office.
4. CCDT, 17th Mostra di
Architettura di Venezia (Venice
Biennale of Architecture), entitled
How Will We Live Together?, Venezia,
IT. Installation view (2020—21),
photography by Giorgio Lazzaro and
courtesy of Lateral Office.

(397)

A Palliative Design for
a High Arctic Landscape
Caitlin Jakusz Paridy

All visuals are by Caitlin Jakusz Paridy.

(404)

When Is Now?
The Case for Temporal Ambiguity
in Critiques of Sámi Architecture
Sofia Singler

1. Courtesy of the Aalto University
Archives.
2, 4. Courtesy of the Finnish
Heritage Agency.
3. Courtesy of Statsbygg.

(417)

Ultima Thule Museum of
Natural History: Containing
the Full Reconstructions of
the Landscapes of Svalbard, of
Instruments of Prophecy, and
of Accidental Monuments with
an Account of Its Architectural
Oddities: With a Repository
Containing Some Important
Historical Artifacts Salvaged
prior to the Disappearance of
the Arctic
Brandon Bergem
Jeffrey Garcia

All visuals are by and courtesy of
Brandon Bergem and Jeffrey Garcia.

Arctic Practices
Design for a Changing World

Edited by
Bert De Jonghe
Elise Misao Hunchuck

Graphic design & cartography
Studio Folder

Research support
Transpolar Studio

Copy editing
Elise Misao Hunchuck

Proofreading
Elizabeth Kugler

Printing and binding
Gráfiques Jou, Barcelona

Paper
Coral Book 120 g/m²
Fedrigoni Woodstock Grey 170 g/m²

Typography
Gaisyr by Dinamo
Tor Grotesk by Threedotstype

Published by
Actar Publishers,
New York, Barcelona
actar.com

Printed in Europe
in March 2025

Distribution
Actar D, Inc.
New York, Barcelona

New York
440 Park Avenue South,
17th Floor
New York, NY 10016, USA
T +1 212 966 2207
salesnewyork@actar-d.com

Barcelona
Roca i Batlle 2-4
08023 Barcelona, ES
T +34 933 282 183
eurosales@actar-d.com

ISBN: 978-1-638-40133-9
LCCN: 2025931667